Planets in Houses

Other Para Research Publications:

Astrology, Nutrition and Health
by Robert C. Jansky

Huna: A Beginner's Guide
by Enid Hoffman

Planets in Aspect: Understanding Your Inner Dynamics
by Robert Pelletier

Planets in Composite: Analyzing Human Relationships
by Robert Hand

Planets in Love: Exploring Your Emotional and Sexual Needs
by John Townley

Planets in Transit: Life Cycles for Living
by Robert Hand

Planets in Youth: Patterns of Early Development
by Robert Hand

Robert Pelletier

Planets in Houses

*Experiencing Your
Environment*

Para Research
Rockport
Massachusetts

International Standard Book Number: 0-914918-07-9

Edited by Margaret E. Anderson
Type set in 9 pt. Paladium by Elizabeth Bauman
Printed by Nimrod Press
Bound by Stanhope Bindery

Published by Para Research, Inc.
Whistlestop Mall
Rockport, Massachusetts 01966

Manufactured in the United States of America

First Printing, May 1978, 6,000 copies

*For my godson Kevin
and Sandra, Gary, Daryl,
George, Raelene and Patricia*

Contents

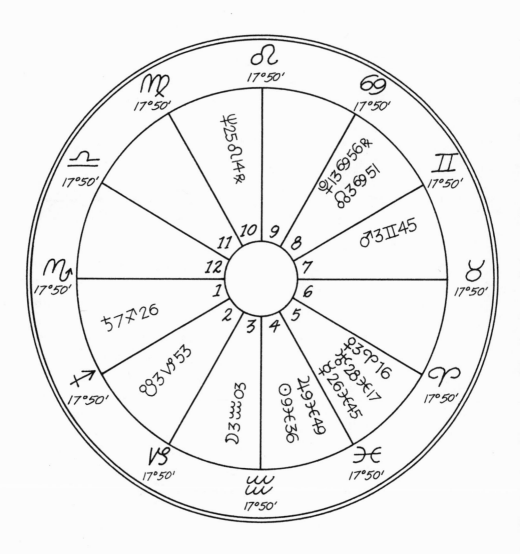

Natal chart of Robert Pelletier

Birthdate: Birthplace:
February 28, 1927   Dover, New Hampshire
                     Longitude 070W53
Birthtime: Latitude 43N12
11:20 P.M. Standard Time
3:20 Greenwich Mean Time   Ascendant calculated for
10:08:25 Sidereal Time   Geocentric Latitude

Calculations by Para Research

Foreword

As used in astrology today, houses are designed to give us a proportional representation of the space surrounding the birth or other event on earth that we are symbolically depicting. If we were doing a painting, the houses would symbolize not only the framework but also the proportion and size of the canvas. Thus the houses are an integral and important part of the total picture of personality as presented through the horoscope as used in astrology.

Robert Pelletier's new book offers more practical advice on planets in houses than any other book that I am familiar with. He introduces the powerful derivative house method and at the same time offers delineations to live and work with. This book is both a reference work and a teaching guide.

The derivative house system shows how each house in turn is related to each of the other houses in the chart. The delineations here enrich this concept by showing how the derivative house system appies to every planet in every house. As a result, we see the effect of Uranus in the second house, and then we see how that position colors and is colored by each of the other houses in the chart. This approach provides some very valid and valuable insights, which are quite often overlooked by the astrologer who notes only the more obvious relationships among factors in the chart.

The use of the derivative house system is not new to astrology. What is new in Pelletier's presentation is the detailed and systematic treatment of the method, applied across all the houses and all the planets. In this truly monumental modern work, the author provides a serious topic for everyone who is interested in astrology, from the student to the professional. For the student there are direct and powerful delineations. For the professional there is additional insight into how the chart works as a whole as well as a related entity.

The book goes even beyond the basic concept of house interrelatedness; there is an exposition of all 144 Sun–Moon house polarities as well as a general discussion of the interpretation of houses. In addition, there are numerous diagrams throughout the book to visually aid the reader.

Pelletier is well known for his preference for and staunch defense of the equal house system, but that does not mean that the derivative house method can be used only with the equal house system. It can be used with any house system that the astrologer works diligently and assiduously with. Like a pencil, it is a tool that can make a mark on many different substances. The derivative house method works for many types of house or chart structuring. There is no one correct system to use, just as there is no one correct or ultimate use of astrology. They are all simply our tools, as are the houses, the final framework of the horoscope.

Michael P. Munkasey

Introduction

Of the many chart factors that the astrologer must examine in order to delineate a horoscope effectively, the house positions of the planets are among the first to gain attention. Houses, also called sectors, departments or fields, always refer to life's circumstances; it is the conditioning of circumstances that offers resistance to the irresistible energies of the planets. The influence of the houses can be compared to the force of evolution, for which we must make adjustments or modifications in our personal desires and behavior so that we can function within the master plan. Survival often depends on successfully making necessary concessions to conditions over which there is no control within the environment, which consists of everything and everyone. While much of our experience is benign, to be sure, problems do occur when we either cannot adapt or refuse to adapt.

The circumstances of life can bring conflict and frustration to the individual, often coinciding with temporary defeat and unhappiness. These difficulties, however, are necessary for character growth and development and eventual fulfillment of one's creative potential. While there is an endless variety of material conditions to deal with in the world, we can choose, by our attitudes and behavior, the effect of those conditions on us. By focusing on our inner forces as well as on the outer, visible effects, we can create purpose in life.

Before going further in introducing the purpose of this text, it is appropriate here to clarify the influence of the other major chart factors: the planets, signs and aspects. In astrology, the signs of the zodiac establish a psychological frame of reference through which the various dynamics of personality, as represented by the planets, operate. Thus the individual's basic temperament is inclined to function according to the energy of the signs that the planets occupy; the planets themselves indicate patterns of growth and behavior. The planetary aspects add charge to the potential shown by the planets, signs and houses, producing the active life force that we observe and know as behavior. The houses, representing fields of activity in the chart, introduce the limits within which planetary behavior occurs.

In beginning a chart analysis, it is common practice to note the overall hemispheric and quadrant emphasis to establish a general pattern of planetary distribution. This is significant in that the quadrants and hemispheres establish how a person is focused, whether subjectively (lower hemisphere) or objectively (upper hemisphere), toward self-awareness (left hemisphere) or awareness of others (right hemisphere). Therefore, the first quadrant, from the Ascendant to the Nadir, is subjective self-awareness; the second quadrant, from the Nadir to the Descendant, is subjective awareness of others; the third quadrant, from the Descendant to the Midheaven, is objective awareness of others; and the fourth quadrant, from the Midheaven to the Ascendant, is objective self-awareness. This kind of analysis is particularly meaningful when there are concentrations of planets in any of these areas of the chart. This overview of the houses provides the basis for further exploration of the chart. Also, it is rare for the particulars to violate or contradict the overall direction of the chart as determined in this way.

The ruler of a house—the planet ruling the sign on the house cusp—has authority over the affairs of that house, whether the house is empty or occupied, and is an active extension of those affairs. Since each planet rules one or two houses, the affairs of the ruled houses are necessarily implicated in the affairs of the house occupied by the planets. If a planet is not in the house it rules, it must adapt to the circumstances of the house it is in, which modifies what it can do. For example, if the Sun is in the twelfth house, the solar energy is modified, and the individual must make certain adjustments in his or her self-expression. If the Sun is the ruler of the seventh house, then that person's self-expression relates to the welfare of others.

The more planets that there are in one house, the more complex are the circumstances. On the other hand, when there are no planets in a house, the circumstances represented by that house require less direct attention than the areas of activity indicated by the houses that do contain planets. The affairs of the unoccupied houses are woven into those of the occupied houses through the planets ruling the empty houses. Any activity that relates to an unoccupied house is integrated into the activity of the house in which the ruler is located.

Another consideration about planets in houses is whether they are direct or retrograde. Retrograde planets seem to have a lower visibility in the houses, although low visibility is not the same as insufficiency. While there is usually some delay in utilizing the skills shown by retrograde planets in the "observable" sense, there is certainly no negation of those skills.

It has been my experience that when astrologers have difficulty understanding the meanings of the planets in the houses, it is because they are confused as to which house the planet is operative in. We assume that a planet occupying the space between the cusps is therefore in that house, yet the planet may actually be operative in another house. The sign on the cusp of a house imposes its mode or character on the affairs of that house, and any planet in that sign is intimately connected with the affairs of that house as well. Conversely, if a planet in a house is not in the sign that is on the cusp, it probably has less influence in that house. That planet has a closer affinity with the house that has on its cusp the sign that the planet is in. Thus, in some instances a planet should be read as being operative in a house other than the one it actually occupies, simply because it is in the sign that appears at the cusp of another house.

To give an example, suppose a person has the Sun at 18° Aries and physically in the second house, with the third cusp at 28° Aries. With the 5° orb method, the Sun would be associated with the second house because it is 10° from the cusp and physically in the second house space. The interpretation would be that this person would find it especially painful to be criticized because he is insecure, and thus he would refrain from stating his opinions for fear of being regarded as unstable. I consider this analysis to be incorrect because it does not associate the Sun with the third house, which has Aries on the cusp, and a planet in a sign has a familiarity with the affairs of the house that has that sign on its cusp. My interpretation is that this person's mind is constantly searching for answers to his many questions. He will make an issue of being allowed to pursue that search and will not tolerate anyone who tries to restrain him. He will be eager to express his views at every opportunity. Of course you will have to examine many charts before you can see this matter clearly. I do not make this statement on the basis of a theoretical assumption but from the evidence of years of practical application.

Another important issue is to determine exactly where a house really is. I maintain that the house is, in fact, *the line of the cusp*, and that planets operate differently in a house depending on their position relative to the cusp. Figure 1 shows different positions for Mars relative to the first house cusp: A, just before the cusp; B, on the cusp; C, deep into the house; and D, in Libra, close to the cusp of the second house. The closer a planet is to the degree on the cusp (A and B), the more powerful and precise is its involvement with the affairs of that house. Astrologers often say that a planet that makes an exact trine to the Ascendant is very strong. This implies that the energy of that 120° aspect is strongest when it is exact, and that when it deviates and forms an orb of

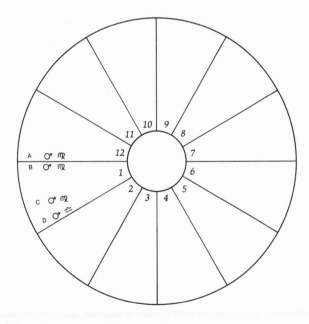

Figure 1. Planetary Positions in a House

influence, its strength is diminished to some extent. This acknowledges that there is a greater source of energy, relative to the affairs of that house, at the cusp and that the strongest placement for a planet in a house is close to the cusp.

When a planet is well into a house (C), as it is usually understood, its influence diminishes rather than increases. As it approaches the "hidden" or dark side of the house (D), there is "spillage" into the next house, because of the natural sequential order of experience from one house to the next. Figure 1 also illustrates the fact that Mars in this chart has an affinity for the eighth house and the third house, because Mars rules Aries and Scorpio, which are on the cusps of those houses.

Derivative Houses

The purpose of this book is to show how we tend to behave when dealing with the pressure of circumstances, as described by the houses of the horoscope and the planets that are in them, and to understand how circumstantial pressures induce certain developmental patterns and attitudes. This information is largely the result of my extensive work with the derivative house technique, which is based on the fact that each of the twelve houses, representing the circumstances of life, is related to every other house. This frame of reference is consistent with most, if not all, of life's activities when you consider that people, their situations and circumstances are inextricably combined.

Whether we use the term derivative houses, counting houses or renumbering houses, this valuable technique is used by astrologers more extensively than is recognized, but in most cases it is not applied as fully as possible. It is used most commonly in horary chart analysis, but it can be applied in delineating natal charts with excellent results; in fact, I have found it to be the best way to extract very comprehensive information from a chart. While some of the inferences are subtle, they are also very revealing. In this section I will explain how to apply the derivative house method in delineation and show how it reveals incredible details about a person's life.

The derivative house method consists simply of regarding a house as the first house of the particular circumstance in question. One way to visualize this concept is to turn the horoscope wheel clockwise one house so that the second house is at the Ascendant (Figure 2). What was previously the third house is now located in the space that is usually labeled the second house. As another example, turn the horoscope wheel clockwise eleven houses so that the twelfth house is at the Ascendant (Figure 3); in this position, the third house occupies the space we normally assign to the fourth house. Using this method, each house has twelve different meanings as a result of the twelve interhouse relationships, including its relationship to itself. At the same time, of course, each house retains its own traditional, essential meaning. The derivative house method can reveal a twelve-sided series of meanings about the matters of the house that is under scrutiny. For instance, when you delineate the first house, you draw on the resources or influences of the other eleven houses to determine how you exercise your desires to express yourself and what problems you face in doing so. You also determine in what ways you can enhance your position by drawing on the opportunities shown by the other houses, yet they all relate to the focus you establish of the first house.

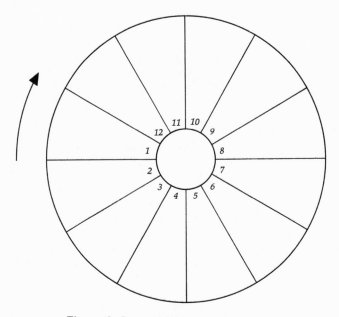

Figure 2. Second House at the Ascendant

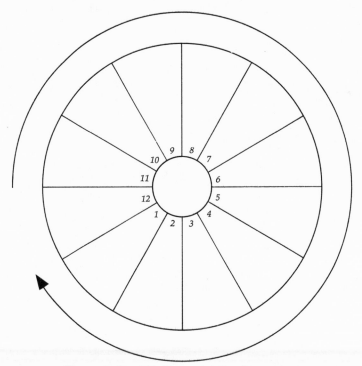

Figure 3. Twelfth House at the Ascendant

Let's take a simple example to illustrate more clearly how the derivative house method reveals details about a person that cannot be found in any other way. Suppose a person has the Sun in the third house, squaring Saturn in the sixth (Figure 4). Before considering any of the other houses that are involved through the rulerships of the Sun and Saturn, we can draw several conclusions. Because of the square between the Sun and Saturn, we know that this person has endured personal conflicts and frustrations and must learn to face responsibility. If this is a married woman with one child, the Sun in the third house may mean that she has strict obligations to take care of her mother, since the third house represents the twelfth house (obligations) to the fourth house (mother). The Saturn square may indicate that she has feelings of guilt associated with these obligations. Saturn in the sixth house may burden her with the full responsibility of caring for her child, since the sixth house is the second house to the fifth house and thus shows her child's (fifth house) needs (second house). Her husband, who is currently in a hospital and unable to earn a living, may be the cause of this burden (Saturn) of lack of support. Again, the woman's sixth house is the twelfth house (confinement) to the seventh house (her husband). We can suggest from this that her mental state might be near the breaking point as a result of her constant worries about whether she can hold on to the job (Sun square Saturn from the third to the sixth). If Saturn happens to be the ruler of her twelfth house, there is a high probability that she will eventually join her husband as a patient in the hospital. It is also possible, with Saturn in the sixth house, that the woman's mother told her it was her duty to work, because the sixth house is the third house (communication) to the fourth house (her mother).

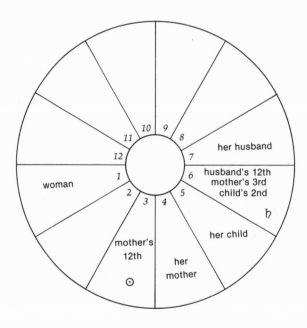

Figure 4. Derivative House Relationships

It is very important to understand one point about this method, because it is true for every chart. The houses of a person's chart do not describe other people in reality; they describe only how the person experiences others. This fact is illustrated dramatically when you describe three different "parents" through the charts of three siblings, even though the parent is the same person! And you would be correct as far as each of those children is concerned. What you are really delineating is the individual's view of his or her interaction with someone else.

When I first started to present this system in my classes, some students found it difficult to grasp how I could regard the third house as the second from the second, the third from the first, the fourth from the twelfth and so on. They thought that I was going around the chart in reverse order. In fact, I refer to the houses in reverse order, but simply because I retain the house under consideration in its normal house sequence. The students' problem was that they assumed that the third house was "frozen," that the second house was the third's twelfth, that the first was its eleventh, and the twelfth was its tenth. This is true, but it does not show how the third house reacts to the circumstances of those houses; it shows only how those houses react to the third. My concern, and this is the point of view expressed in this book, is how the third house reacts to the circumstances of the other houses. This point of view necessitates renumbering the house by referring to the houses preceding it in reverse order. Students are accustomed to discussing the eleventh house as their son-in-law (their daughter's husband's seventh) or their father's bank account (second from the tenth) or their brother's recognition in his career (the tenth from the third). But the novelty of renumbering the same house when referring to each of the other houses is startling at first, although that is just what you do when you delineate a chart.

How to Use This Book

Each of the twelve chapters in this book presents several kinds of information. The first two pages of each chapter present the traditional meaning of the house and briefly summarize the meanings of its relationship to each of the other houses. The position of the other houses in relation to this house is shown graphically by the wheel at the beginning of the chapter. For example, the third house chapter shows the third house in the usual first house position, with the other eleven houses in their correct relative positions, as well as their house relationship to the third.

Then, on the next twenty-four pages of each chapter, the meaning of each planet in that house is discussed in two ways. If you have the Sun in the third house, you would look up that placement on pages 76 and 77. The left-hand page presents the Sun in the third as it reacts to the other houses, which is, of course, the derivative house system that I have just explained. On the left side of this page is a column of twelve wheels corresponding to the twelve separate house relationships. The house of the chapter is shown in black, and the house it is related to in each paragraph is shown in gray. Notice the clockwise movement of the gray segments as you look down the page.

The right-hand page presents the same information in a somewhat different form, describing the relationship between the house under consideration and certain groupings of the other houses. This synthesis, which I explain in detail in the next section, is based on an aspect frame of reference for the houses of the horoscope. The wheels in the right margin depict in black the house of the chapter, with the aspectually related houses in gray.

After the section on planets in the house, each chapter contains summaries of the meanings of the Sun in that house in relationship to the Moon in each of the twelve houses. This is explained in more detail in the section, *Sun-Moon House Polarities.*

The Houses in Aspect

In the section of each chapter that deals with the planets in that house, the right-hand pages present the house relationships from an aspectual point of view. The first of the five paragraphs on the page deals with the two houses that form a trine, or fifth-and-ninth-house relationship to the house under consideration. You may wish to refer to the corresponding left-hand page to see the connections more clearly. For example, for the Sun in the sixth house (page 160), we see that the trine comes from two different relationships: the "5th to the 2nd" and the "9th to the 10th," as decribed on the facing page. When you combine these with the "1st to the 6th" delineation, you have the synthesis of their influences, which is presented in the trine summary paragraph. In this

| 1st to the 6th | 5th to the 2nd | 9th to the 10th | Trine: 2, 10 |

example it must be understood that the sixth house bears a fifth house relationship to the second house, because it is five houses from the second house. Using the second house as the frame of reference, the sixth house represents the effort you extend in performing certain tasks because you want to enjoy (fifth) the rewards you earn (second). Again, because the sixth is the ninth when you use the tenth as a frame of reference, you apply yourself with the highest degree of integrity as well as skill (sixth house), because you know that only by ethical practices (ninth house) can you earn true respect and honor (tenth house). We have taken the affairs of the second and tenth houses and applied the traditional connotations of the fifth and ninth houses to them, because of the trine relationship among them, which involves any planet in those houses. The first paragraph, therefore, combines the affairs of the houses that are involved in a ninth-and-fifth-house trine relationship to the house under consideration—in our example, the sixth house.

The second summary paragraph deals with two houses that are in sextile, third-and-eleventh-house, relationship to the house being considered. The sextile relationship represents the *attitude* (third house connotation) that most frequently leads to successfully realizing one's goals (eleventh house connotation). In our example of the

Sun in the sixth house, the sixth house is in a sextile relationship to the fourth house and to the eighth house. This means that you realize the importance of learning to take care of yourself and stand on your own (fourth house) which happens as you apply your skills (sixth house). You reach your goals by being willing to make the commitment to provide the services (sixth house) that people require (eighth house).

| 1st to the 6th | 3rd to the 4th | 11th to the 8th | Sextile: 4, 8 |

The third summary paragraph deals with the houses that cross, or are in square and opposition aspects, to the house being considered. This is represented in the natural wheel by the cross that is formed among the first, fourth, seventh and tenth houses. Here we encounter the circumstances that offer frustration or resistance, yet ultimately provide us with the opportunity to grow through learning to cope with stress. In our example, the sixth house is in a fourth house relationship relative to the third house and in a tenth house relationship to the ninth house. Obviously, the sixth house is in a seventh house relationship with the twelfth house. These combined three frames of

| 1st to the 6th | 4th to the 3rd | 7th to the 12th | 10th to the 9th | Cross: 3, 9, 12 |

reference indicate the intimidating circumstances with which the sixth house Sun must function. With the Sun in the sixth, you need to find a suitable medium in which to apply your acquired skills (sixth house) through formal training so as to distinguish yourself through career (ninth house square). You can establish security by cultivating your ideas into skills and by being responsible for building a solid foundation for your life's efforts (third house square). The twelfth house opposition offers you a challenge and a choice; either you react responsibly to the pressures brought by the houses that form fourth and tenth house relationships to the sixth, or you resign yourself to a life of relative obscurity for failing to respond to the demanding social problems that await your attention.

The fourth summary paragraph synthesizes the meanings of the houses that are in inconjunct aspect (sixth-and-eighth-house relationships) to the house being considered. A discomforting predicament usually prevails through the activities shown by the houses that form this relationship, associated mainly with feelings of inadequacy or insufficiency. With the Sun in the sixth, the sixth house forms a sixth house inconjunct with the first house and represents your struggle to find the right means to express yourself so that what you accomplish adequately defines you. The sixth house also forms an eighth house inconjunct with the eleventh and shows that your overindulgence of others is motivated by the expectation that they will give you the help you need for your own success.

| 1st to the 6th | 6th to the 1st | 8th to the 11th | Inconjunct: 1, 11 |

The fifth summary paragraph concerns the houses that are adjacent or semisextile to the house being considered: in the natural horoscope wheel, the second and twelfth house relationships to the first house. The semisextile relationship relates to the resources gained by the activities of the house and the unconscious issues that may frustrate the affairs of that house. Using our example of the Sun in the sixth house, moving

| 1st to the 6th | 2nd to the 5th | 12th to the 7th | Semisextile: 5, 7 |

clockwise, the fifth house immediately precedes the sixth house, and thus the sixth house is in a second house relationship to the fifth house. Finally, the sixth house is in a twelfth house relationship to the seventh house. This means that you gain resources from successfully applying your creativity and talents (fifth) which are so valuable to your work (sixth), and that you feel anxious that you may be less competent than your competitors (seventh) in your ability to perform (sixth).

The actual summaries in the text offer a much broader presentation than I have given in the foregoing examples. My purpose in this introductory section is to share with you how these summaries are formulated and synthesized.

Sun-Moon House Polarities

In each chapter, following the description of the ten planets in that house, there is a discussion of the Sun in that house in relationship to the Moon through all twelve houses. For example, the chapter on the sixth house presents the meaning of the Sun in the sixth house in combination with the Moon in the first house, second house and so on. The Sun and Moon play vital roles in personal development and fulfillment, and the significance of their 144 possible combinations throughout the houses deserves special attention. I refer the reader to the introductory material on the first house, where I discuss the roles of the Sun and Moon in addition to that of the Ascendant. The houses are the environmental conditions through which the vital and plastic energies of the Sun and Moon adapt and develop.

The Sun is the directive force that propels us to seek fulfillment in our identities by using our creative potential in its highest possible development. The struggle to achieve this objective is, to me, the essential purpose of life. Love is at the beginning and end of this process. The middle? That too is love and is the center around which the beginning and end are focused, without which neither have any meaning at all.

In essence, the Moon is the accumulated experiences of the past and shows how we function as a result of those experiences. Much of this residual effect becomes instinctual, and a large portion of it is absorbed and categorized in the survival mechanism. The subconscious, however, remains pliant and open to input from the conscious self. Though the Moon represents the mechanics of survival, it only serves the purpose of the Sun, which is love.

Calculating Houses

The issue of how to divide the horoscope to determine the sign and degree that will occupy the various house cusps is indeed a controversial and complex one. Few astrologers agree on the correct method, and even fewer understand the subject well enough to speak about it with any degree of authority. (Michael Munkasey shares his background and insights on this matter in the appendix of this book, entitled *Thoughts on the Use of House Systems,* where he discusses the theoretical rationale of the different house systems.) Here, I wish to present my own reasons for adopting the equal house method, which consists simply of using the Ascending sign and degree, calculated in the customary manner, and using the same degree of the remaining signs in sequential, counterclockwise order on the other eleven house cusps. For example, if you have 14° Leo rising, then 14° Virgo is on the second house cusp and 14° Libra is on the third cusp, and so on around the chart. With this technique, there are no intercepted signs. Because the Midheaven has special significance, I always include its position in the chart, entering it on the outer rim of the wheel of the chart in the ninth or tenth house, as indicated. With other house systems, when the equinoctial signs Aries or Libra rise in the Ascendant, the Midheaven is 90° away from the Ascendant, which gives an identical MC as with the equal house method. The greatest difference in the angle between the Ascendant and the Midheaven of different house systems occurs when the solstice signs, Cancer and Capricorn, rise.

The tropical zodiac begins at 0° Aries, an imaginary point, the moment at which the Sun's path intersects the celestial equator. This usually occurs on or about March 21 every year. From this starting position, thirty-degree divisions of space are allocated to each of the remaining signs of the zodiac. It is my belief that the horoscope wheel should be divided according to the same frame of reference, as it is with the equal house method. It seems superfluous to demand mathematical or astronomical precision of a frame of reference for houses that is purely symbolic. While different purposes are served by using the nearly twenty-five different methods of slicing the sky to obtain the signs and degrees belonging to each slice, my own purposes have been consistently well served by using the equal house division. Up to now, because of lack of accurate birthtime data, it has been difficult for astrologers to make an objective choice by testing one set of house cusps against another.

But, regardless of your choice of house division system or method, I wish to emphasize that *the interpretive material of this text is applicable.* Furthermore, it is highly possible that the delineations may help you decide which house a planet in your chart is most closely related to.

Chapter One

First House

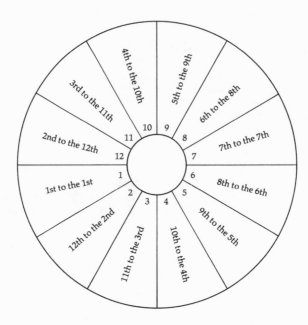

The first house begins at the Ascendant and is the base from which the remaining houses derive significance. This house, along with the sign on its cusp, infuses you with the energy to cope with situations you face as you fulfill your destiny; the rising sign represents how you project yourself into your environment. The first house is basically primitive, in that it requires you to assert yourself in dealing with life situations that may threaten your survival. This house represents your self-awareness, temperament and disposition.

It is necesary to relate the first house to two other important factors in the horoscope, the Sun and Moon. The Moon encapsulates all the reactions you've had in previous life experiences. Although some people may reject the validity of reincarnation, I believe that the position and aspects of the Moon in the horoscope indicate how the individual responds to stimuli without previous causative input from learning experiences in this life. The Moon is the line of least resistance. It is easiest to describe a child by focusing on the Moon, but by age twelve, a person's development is better described by other chart factors, especially the Sun. The Moon is the nourishment on which the Sun depends for its development, yet what the Moon offers must be filtered through the Ascendant. In other words, everything previously learned, which is now part of your subconscious, must be adapted to the present circumstances, as shown by the houses. The Moon is the past, with all your previous programming and memories. In the process of evolution, those individuals and species that could not adapt became extinct, and those that could adapt survived. The Moon represents the repetitive learning process in the face of constant hazardous conditions, which became known as instinct.

The Sun is the future and the fulfillment of your potential, which is a lifelong process. Between the future, the Sun, and the past, the Moon, is the now, the current thrust into the environment, which offers opportunities for growth. The houses represent the varied areas of life and pressures you must deal with. With your previously learned skills, now called instincts, you react according to the design of the chart, testing its potentials again and again, always striving to achieve perfection. The first house is where you first encounter the circumstances of the outside world. In the twelve-act drama of life, the first house introduces you, the star.

Derivative House Meanings

1st to the 1st   This represents the concept of self and the visible essence of your projection to others. It is the urge to assert and promote yourself.

2nd to the 12th   Your fears and anxieties limit your ability to use your hidden resources and make a contribution to your social responsibilities.

3rd to the 11th   Understanding yourself enables you to define the goals you hope to achieve, so that you do not extend yourself beyond your potentials.

4th to the 10th   The position you want in life forces certain restrictions on you and determines the responsibilities that you must accept.

5th to the 9th   Getting an education will allow you to promote yourself better in working toward your goals by giving you the self-confidence you need.

6th to the 8th   Once you are motivated by concern for others' needs, you will endure whatever sacrifice is required to learn the skills.

7th to the 7th   Every challenge is an opportunity to learn about the areas in which you lack development and experience. Deficiencies in others mirror your own.

8th to the 6th   Knowing that others have needs is the stimulus that urges you to extend yourself in their behalf, even though that means sacrificing personal desires.

9th to the 5th   You know that you alone must develop your potentials into skills so that they will be useful. You express yourself this way because you care.

10th to the 4th   Your success or failure is determined by how well you can establish a foundation for your life that is exclusively your own, not your parents'.

11th to the 3rd   You must resolve the answer to every question you have, for the future as you conceive it is within your own consciousness.

12th to the 2nd   Any self-doubts can be eliminated if you stabilize yourself in a focused life endeavor, knowing you have important values to share.

1st to the 1st You see opportunities for development in all the circumstances of your life. Gaining recognition for your achievements is important, so you use your creative gifts to that end. Your enthusiasm allows you to persist in reaching your goals.

 2nd to the 12th You work hard to promote your talents because you are anxious to impress people. Your temperament is suited to serving the public, and your creative imagination would be an asset in public institutions.

 3rd to the 11th You know how to win friends and influence people with your charming manner and winning ways, and you can depend on support from others when you need it. You plan carefully, because you know that is the best way to achieve your goals.

 4th to the 10th Your career must provide self-determination and freedom to perform your duties in your own way. This facet of your personality could be a response to early parental intimidation that threatened your self-image.

 5th to the 9th You know that travel is broadening, so you mix business with pleasure in your travels whenever you can. You try to stay well informed about your competitors as well as about your associates.

 6th to the 8th You handle other people's resources better than they do and better than you handle your own assets. You know how to motivate others to extend themselves for your benefit.

 7th to the 7th Your outgoing nature conceals the fact that you are rather easily intimated by competitors. You keep to yourself any doubts about your ability to cope with challenging situations, because you would be ashamed to have people know your weaknesses.

 8th to the 6th There may be some sacrifice involved, but you must make an effort to help those who can't help themselves. This could be your opportunity to prove your worth to others and to improve your own self-image.

 9th to the 5th You are willing to invest in training to develop your creative potentials, because you know it will help you achieve your goals. Also, being well trained impresses others. You want to be the best in whatever you do.

 10th to the 4th Your parents stimulated you to improve on your early circumstances, and you are grateful for the lessons they taught you. The frustrations you experienced instilled a desire to succeed on your own and choose your own course in life.

 11th to the 3rd You know that you will reach your goals and objectives by putting your ideas to work. With your creativity, you can build your future without relying on others too much. You will probably always have good relations with your brothers and sisters.

 12th to the 2nd You find it depressing to be without funds, but remember that it is more urgent to acquire substantial values. To neglect personal development in the pursuit of material wealth would be a waste of your talents.

Trine: 5, 9   You are optimistic and have faith in your ability to succeed. People easily let you exert your influence, so you have little difficulty in promoting your plans. You are aggressive, outgoing and personable. If you persist, your talents will be recognized, which is very important to you. Getting some formal training will help you achieve your ambitious objectives and refine your creative talents. Even your competitors will admire you, for you try to be the best in whatever you undertake. It is heartwarming to know that the public appreciates you, as do those close to you. You enjoy traveling, and when possible you try to mix business and pleasure. You learn all you can about your competitors' strengths and weaknesses, but you also try to stay on good terms with them.

Sextile: 3, 11   You want a lot out of life, so you use your creative ideas to reach your future goals. A self-made person, you would rather not depend on others for assistance, but you will help anyone who deserves it. You enjoy a broad social circle and are quite influential with friends and close associates, so there is always someone who will do favors for you. You plan for long-range goals rather than immediate results. You've learned much from your parents' failures and successes, and this knowledge guides you as you pursue your goals.

Cross: 4, 7, 10   Though you appear to be in complete command of every situation, you are more easily intimidated than you would care to admit. You feel most threatened by people who are your equal in creative talent, because you hate to admit that you can't always compete successfully. By improving your skills, you can avoid this problem in the future. It isn't easy for you to distinguish between people who are just trying to win over you and those, actually your staunchest allies, who offer constructive criticism. Your childhood has left scars, and you tend to look for conflicts where none exist. But you are determined to improve on your early circumstances. The frustrations of that time produced some anxiety about your ability to rise above the conflicts that come up in interhuman relationships. You want to live up to your parents' expectations, but you also want to pursue your own destiny without guilt. You are basically loyal, but you know that you must rise to your fullest potential.

Inconjunct: 6, 8   Your dilemma is to choose between indulging yourself and making some meaningful contribution to improve other people's lives. This is a powerful problem, because you are not inclined to make concessions to others. If you give the matter more thought, however, you will understand that your public stature will increase only if you contribute your vast creative talent where it will be appreciated. Also, this will improve your self-image. You can motivate people and teach them to use their own resources.

Semisextile: 2, 12   You work hard to promote your talents because you are afraid that otherwise you won't be recognized. Your temperament is suited to serving the public and to handling demanding responsibilities. Your self-esteem is tied to the value that the public places on you for your services. You don't like to be without funds, but human values are more important than acquiring great material wealth. To neglect character development is to waste your potential and place a low value on your worth.

1st to the 1st Your personality is changeable, alternating between periods of deep response to your environment and periods when you project yourself outwardly. You are so emotionally sensitive to every experience that you often lose your composure. Sometimes you act aggressive in order to protect your feelings.

 2nd to the 12th Being insecure, you realize you must be firm and refuse to be controlled by strong personalities. People seek your company because you are naturally protective and have a calming effect on them. Don't underestimate the value of your creative imagination.

 3rd to the 11th You tend to be suspicious of your friends, assuming they want your friendship only because you are willing to do favors for them. You need people who can share your emotional highs and lows. You dwell on the future and worry about whether you will be financially and emotionally secure in your later years.

 4th to the 10th It isn't easy for you to gain the career position you want, because you aren't really sure you can achieve it on your own. Breaking ties with the past is difficult but necessary if you are to become self-sufficient. You should learn to like yourself for your achievements.

 5th to the 9th Even though you know the importance of education for your career, you may not be willing to make the investment. You expect others to open doors for you, but with proper training you could open them yourself.

 6th to the 8th You are willing to work to help those in need, but be careful not to deplete your own resources. Sacrifice is not difficult for you if you know that it is appreciated.

 7th to the 7th It always seems that you have to make concessions to others, which makes you feel inferior to them. You aren't easily convinced that people really like you, so you keep them at a distance. When you do allow others into your life, you tend to dominate them to compensate for your insecurity.

 8th to the 6th You owe it to yourself to invest in your own development. Be wary of people who suggest that you are destined to serve the needs of others, thereby neglecting your own top-priority needs.

 9th to the 5th Developing your creative potential will help raise your credibility. With training you will learn to appreciate your enormous creative gifts, which will allow you to succeed in professional and personal relationships.

 10th to the 4th Your family ties may be so strong that they deprive you of a life of your own. Don't deny yourself something because others make you feel obligated to them. That's slavery, not loyalty.

 11th to the 3rd You should start thinking about becoming independent, so that you can sustain yourself in your later years and reach the goals you choose.

 12th to the 2nd Try to accept reality and learn to use your creative imagination to build tangible assets for your later years. Instead of feeling sorry for yourself, uncover your hidden talents and put them to use.

Trine: 5, 9 Your mood depends on your feelings at the moment. When you are emotionally high you are outgoing, but you are shaken by any unsettling experience. Because of your emotional nature, you tend to lose your composure under stress. You become aggressive only when you have to protect yourself from abuse. It is essential that you improve your self-image, which you do by getting a formal education. This will allow you to compete successfully and will help you cope with your personal relationships. You must be able to deal objectively with the problems of the real world and not allow abrasive situations to disturb you emotionally. You need to develop your creative imagination in order to be productive. You must raise your credibility by capitalizing on your gifts. Education will help you find a way to express your understanding, compassion and concern for less fortunate people.

Sextile: 3, 11 You want friends who understand your moods and feelings of inadequacy, but you often assume that people want your friendship only because you are so willing to help them. You are deeply concerned about your future and whether you will have sufficient resources to sustain yourself in later years. You are anxious to translate your ideas into tangible rewards so that you needn't depend on others. Although you should set up a plan to achieve your goals, you tend to dawdle. You may feel that you are always making concessions to others, but you aren't really sure that you can do without them. Making concessions is a way to maintain contact with people, but it does make you feel inferior, which may cause some discomfort.

Cross: 4, 7, 10 Your family ties may be so strong that you don't have a life of your own. Breaking with the past will be difficult, but it must be done if you hope to become self-sufficient. Your goal should be to pursue your own destiny and to like yourself for what you can accomplish. It isn't easy for you to secure a position in your career, because you aren't sure you can succeed on your own. But remember, you cannot afford to deny yourself the benefits of using your talents imaginatively and purposefully. Loyalty to family is admirable, but not when it interferes with your destiny. When it does, it becomes slavery. No one has the right to expect you to put your own destiny aside in order to help realize theirs. Coping with these deep frustrations will not be easy, because their roots are buried in your early conditioning.

Inconjunct: 6, 8 You willingly help people who need your tender loving care, but you should understand when to conserve your energy in order to avoid exhaustion. You are too eager to be available when someone says they need you, perhaps because you want human companionship at any cost. Direct some of your energy to developing your own creative potential. Sacrifice some of your time for others if you want to, but remember to put yourself at the top of your list of priorities.

Semisextile: 2, 12 Don't underestimate the value of your creative imagination, which can help you solve your own and other people's problems. You have a calming effect on people in their time of need; they feel protected in your presence. Since you are insecure, however, you must be firm and refuse to allow others to dominate you. Learn to accept reality and use your talents to build tangible assets that will sustain you in later years. Don't feel sorry for yourself, and don't bury your talents.

1st to the 1st   You are insatiably curious and eager to be involved in a variety of situations. You know how to use your experiences to benefit your continuing development. Your self-expression is often inspired and imaginative.

 2nd to the 12th   Security is more important to you than it seems, but you often fail to plan ahead for security because you are so fascinated with the present.

 3rd to the 11th   Living for the moment as you do, it is imperative to concentrate more on your goals and objectives. You have many ideas for gaining a good position, with all its benefits. Your many friends are very important to you.

 4th to the 10th   Your lack of concentration makes it difficult to focus on an objective. You hate the confinement of a daily routine because it limits your freedom, but you won't be really free until you apply yourself and earn it.

 5th to the 9th   Education is essential, for it gives you the ability to understand the people with whom you are involved. You enjoy traveling because it broadens the mind and is relaxing.

 6th to the 8th   You must learn to work to serve the needs of others. That is how you will make your best contribution and gain financial security in your later years.

 7th to the 7th   You have fairly good judgment in handling relationships, but you hate to make decisions hastily. Your greatest opportunities will probably come through appreciating and learning from other people's opinions.

 8th to the 6th   You have considerable insight into the problems of the people you deal with, and you can motivate them to take advantage of their natural talents. This gives you an advantage over your competitors, because you perceive their weaknesses.

 9th to the 5th   Your creative potential could fail you unless you realize how important it is to develop your talents. Your love of people and your high ideals give you a responsibility to use your creative talents for the benefit of others.

 10th to the 4th   Your early environment has enabled you to establish your own roots. Even if you sever ties with the past, you won't forget its lessons.

 11th to the 3rd   You know that your future is in your own hands. Your ideas attract attention and give you what you need to realize your goals. You are preoccupied with gaining freedom from want, which is precious to you.

 12th to the 2nd   Your greatest fear should be of failing to live up to your potential. Focus on serving others in the best way you can, for that will give you great returns. If your energies are self-seeking, the stability of your affairs will be undermined.

Trine: 5, 9 You express your opinions so precisely that no one questions your meaning, and you eagerly accept a challenge from anyone who disagrees with you. Your respect for education and your insatiable curiosity give you an advantage over less-informed competitors. When you take time to examine all the details, you solve problems quickly and accurately. You try to understand others' motivations, and you learn a great deal from them. You learn from your experiences, and you enjoy traveling to promote your ambitions. Getting away from the daily routine renews your mental and physical energy. Your great creative potential only needs to be developed so that you can establish your credentials in your field. You know what you can and cannot do, and you strive to maintain the highest ideals.You put a lot of thought into your endeavors, and you have faith that you will succeed. You may seem lucky, but actually you are inspired and imaginative in using your creative gifts. Your partner should understand how important it is that you achieve your goals. You feel that your mutual interests will be better served if each of you compromises to some extent.

Sextile: 3, 11 You try to live each day as fully as possible, for you know that your future security and independence depend on it. You know how to put your ideas to work for your later years, when you want to be free from obligation. You take advantage of opportunities provided by your friends, and you don't forget favors you have received in the past. You realize that your future is in your own hands, and you won't really feel fulfilled until you see tangible evidence of your success.

Cross: 4, 7, 10 It is important that the public consider your ideas substantial. You depend on associates and competitors to show you where your skills need refining. Although it isn't easy for you to admit you are wrong, you concede when your career goals are at stake. You are willing to learn, which will help you grow. You show good judgment in relationships, and you don't make binding commitments lightly. You learn something from everyone you contact. Your early environment taught you the importance of establishing roots. Having to stand on your own in spite of frustrating early conflicts stimulated your creative potential. Because of this conditioning, you find it painful to be confined by a daily routine that restricts your freedom. But you are willing to work to gain the professional status that will give you that freedom.

Inconjunct: 6, 8 You may not realize that your greatest liability is neglecting the people on whom you depend for success. When you understand what the public expects, you will accept the responsibility of serving them. This will be your greatest contribution to your own future. You have much insight into what's wrong with people, and they look to you for understanding. This insight is useful in your career because you understand your competitors' weaknesses.

Semisextile: 2, 12 Failing to implement your creative talent and exploit your ideas would put you at a disadvantage. You must put your facility for communication to work if you want to benefit from it. Underestimating your worth would be a tragic waste of inspired imagination. You can accomplish much if you respond to the needs of the society and let your creative talent become its asset.

1st to the 1st   You are genial, warm and affectionate. You always try to be pleasant because you truly enjoy people. You win the approval of those around you by conceding to their desires if you can.

 2nd to the 12th   Secretly fearing that you will be rejected by the people you deal with, you are hospitable and generous toward those who need help. You are spiritually uplifted when you help relieve other people's burdens.

 3rd to the 11th   You are quite preoccupied with acquiring the material resources that will sustain you in later years. You cultivate good relations with your friends because you are genuinely concerned about them, and you hope the concern is mutual.

 4th to the 10th   You will have to extend yourself to achieve recognition in your career. You won't feel fulfilled until you can overcome your fear and hesitation and assert yourself to get what you want in life.

 5th to the 9th   Even though it takes a lot of hard work to succeed, it will be easier if you are well informed and trained. You enjoy getting an education. You also know how to keep the lines of communication open to associates and competitors alike, which gives you an advantage over them.

 6th to the 8th   You admire people who can apply themselves to get what they want. You help others when they need it, but you expect them to appreciate your efforts.

 7th to the 7th   You attract people and encourage them to be open and frank with you. Your winning ways bring you support and enthusiasm for your proposals. However, you are cautious about revealing all your plans for fear of losing your advantage over others.

 8th to the 6th   You understand your adversaries' limitations and weaknesses. Your greatest contribution to them and to yourself is to help them in their moment of need, which will earn you their gratitude.

 9th to the 5th   You want the best for your children, and you encourage them to develop their own creative potentials. But you may neglect to take advantage of your own potentials by overindulging in pleasurable activities.

 10th to the 4th   You will have to learn to stand on your own before you can hope to achieve any accomplishments. If you wait for your parents' approval, you will never establish your own goals.

 11th to the 3rd   Being insecure about financial affairs, you dwell on finding the best way to free yourself from material anxiety during your later years.

 12th to the 2nd   Your preoccupation with material matters can be a liability if it interferes with acquiring more enduring human values. Your preoccupation with security can make you hard and spoil an otherwise charming public image.

Trine: 5, 9 Your affectionate nature and willingness to compromise endear you to everyone. You cleverly allow others to think they can win over you, but really you are biding your time until you are more sure of your position. Hating disharmony, you concede to others' demands unless they are completely unfair. You know that the best way to handle people is to understand their motivations. You eagerly seek an education to improve your chances for success. You choose your associates for their intellectual accomplishments and savoir-faire, which can be assets in your profession. You keep the lines of communication open to associates and competitors alike, so you are always abreast of what's happening. Wanting the very best for your children, you encourage them to take advantage of opportunities to develop their creative potentials. But do not neglect your own creative talents in favor of self-indulgent pleasures.

Sextile: 3, 11 You know that the best way to satisfy your need for material security is to put your ideas to work. If you implement your plans successfully, you won't need to worry about financial security. You know how to win the support of close friends in reaching your objectives, and you make a sincere attempt to show concern for theirs. These warm ties will be rewarding to you in the future, when you may need friends more than you do now. You get your superiors to approve your ideas, especially when you show them how your ideas will benefit them.

Cross: 4, 7, 10 You will benefit from being more aggressive when you are challenged. You cannot be the peacemaker all the time, and making concessions to those who are wrong will establish your weakness and limit your success. Luckily, you attract people who are open and frank. Be cautious about revealing all your plans so that you can maintain some advantage over others. You should accept responsibility for extending yourself in your career and learn to overcome the fear of competition as you strive to reach your objectives. You may worry that you will never live up to your parents' expectations, but your only obligation is to live up to your own potentials. You must define your goals and decide how you will reach them, according to your own capabilities. You must be self-sustaining as soon as possible, so you can make your own mistakes and benefit from your own successes. If you settle for less, you will get less.

Inconjunct: 6, 8 You can relieve your guilt about not living up to your potentials by making some important contribution toward meeting the needs of other people, including your associates, your partner and those who cannot help themselves. You will earn their gratitude forever if you make some sacrifices to help them in their moments of need. You are usually willing to do this but you want your efforts to be appreciated. Knowing the weaknesses of your competitors gives you a distinct advantage over them.

Semisextile: 2, 12 You feel uplifted when you help people who are burdened with problems, but also you are afraid of being rejected. You try to be generous toward those who need attention and care, but be wary of people who make excessive demands. You only need to prove to yourself that you have warm, human qualities and enduring values and that your preoccupation with financial security has not made you insensitive. Your public image is charming.

1st to the 1st   You are restless and eager and when stimulated, your aggressive nature springs into action. It is the thrill of competition that makes you accept challenges. You thrive on sensationalism and conflict.

 2nd to the 12th   Your greatest problem is that you tend to reject responsibility for your actions. People resent you for this, but they will admire you if you help them convert their liabilities to assets, so that they can succeed by their own efforts.

 3rd to the 11th   You live for the moment and often neglect to plan for the future, which you consider too abstract. You feel that you will always have the privilege of indulging yourself as you choose, and you expect to be well paid for your professional skills.

 4th to the 10th   How independent you become depends on how far you are able to accept another person's authority over you. Resisting authority only impedes your progress and demonstrates your incompetence.

 5th to the 9th   You have the energy, now you only need training and education. You will be able to sell yourself more effectively when you know what people expect of you. Learn how to open the doors of opportunity yourself without waiting for others.

 6th to the 8th   You are willing to try anything once, and you are often careless about taking chances. You go beyond prudent levels to win people's approval because you believe that they expect you to prove yourself to them.

 7th to the 7th   Your direct and sometimes blunt approach alienates people, and you incur their displeasure because you are unable to compromise or meet them halfway.

 8th to the 6th   Some people avoid dealing with you directly, because you give the impression that you will try to take advantage of them. You capitalize on your ability to detect other people's weaknesses.

 9th to the 5th   You will never need anyone else to advertise your talents, because you promote them so well yourself. You have high expectations for your children, and you urge them to achieve even if they lack your enthusiasm.

 10th to the 4th   You have a feeling of satisfaction when people realize that you achieved your goals on your own, in spite of early environmental frustrations.

 11th to the 3rd   You know you should plan ahead, but you are easily distracted by current interests that seem more important. But you are aware that you can get anything you want out of life if you put your mind and energy into it.

 12th to the 2nd   Don't assume that you can assert yourself in any way you want. You must build substantial character values that will help you gain the security you need. Otherwise your efforts will barely be remembered. It is essential to make a self-inventory to see whether you are wasting a lot of energy.

Trine: 5, 9   You have a driving ambition to make an impression on the world. When stimulated, you energetically accept any challenge that will demonstrate your courage and ability. You thoroughly enjoy competition and the thrill of meeting problems head on, and when you succeed, you literally glow. But don't neglect the formal training you need for greater polish and savoir-faire. You can accomplish far more by finesse than by brute force. If you can learn the art of friendly persuasion, you will achieve the same results without wasting energy in unnecessary conflicts. Education will teach you how to deal with people and win their cooperation. You have high hopes that your children will reach out to their destiny with the same enthusiasm you show. You have little difficulty attracting lovers, but your attention tends to wander once you've achieved victory. You need a partner with wisdom and patience to cope with your competitiveness and to help you to be more objective and realistic in your goals.

Sextile: 3, 11   You know you should plan ahead, but you are too busy worrying about your current interests to take the time. You have no doubt that you will succeed. With your active mind and physical daring, you can implement your ideas and get whatever you want. Living for the moment, however, only satisfies the moment. You consider the future too abstract to focus on, but if you don't plan for your future security, you can't expect to get it. Your friends might have some helpful suggestions. Although you are well paid for your professional skills, you will not be financially independent in your later years unless you start saving.

Cross: 4, 7, 10   You will achieve greater harmony in your dealings when you learn to concede to authority and face reality. You must restrain yourself to avoid displeasing those in authority over you. True, you must take the initiative in order to accomplish anything worthwhile, but be very sure that the situation warrants your response. You cannot afford to antagonize people in important positions by being impertinent or insensitive to their feelings. If you do, you will meet adversaries at every turn. Try to compromise and listen to good advice, especially from those who really care for you. It will cost you very little and may pay handsome dividends.

Inconjunct: 6, 8   Because you can provide services that people need and will pay for, you will always have opportunities for employment. Refusing to help will undermine your chances for success and earn you contempt. Probably you will use the opportunity to show what you can do. Be careful not to overreact to what you think is expected of you. You are eager to win public approval in order to prove yourself. Some people may avoid you, thinking that you will try to take advantage of them. Your ability to detect human weaknesses gives you an advantage over your competitors.

Semisextile: 2, 12   When you intimidate people in order to get what you want, you are the eventual loser. If you fail to build solid human values that people can relate to, they will lose respect for you and quickly forget your accomplishments, no matter how spectacular. On the other hand, if you accept responsibility for your actions, you will be rewarded by the everlasting appreciation of those whom you have helped. You can help people become more self-reliant by teaching them to take advantage of their own resources and to capitalize on their natural talents.

1st to the 1st   You are optimistic about your ability to succeed, but you tend to take on more than you can handle. You are generous to a fault, so you don't always get the full benefit of your efforts.

 2nd to the 12th   You feel guilty about the social injustices that you observe, and you consider yourself morally obligated to serve those who are less capable. But don't neglect your own interests, or you will find your generosity abused.

 3rd to the 11th   You know how to relate to everyone, no matter what their social or professional position. You don't classify people according to their social, religious or political affiliation, but regard them simply as people.

 4th to the 10th   You are easily annoyed if your parents try to interfere with your goals. You want to feel that you've achieved on your own merits. You seek a profession that offers opportunities for continued growth.

 5th to the 9th   You feel that education is very important. You enjoy learning about everything that will give you greater confidence in your career. People seek you out because they know you are well informed and can help them.

 6th to the 8th   You feel spiritually obligated to serve those who cannot help themselves. You are eager to show people how they can work out their own problems.

 7th to the 7th   You can take your place among large groups as easily as among individuals. You attract people who are important and influential. People usually feel comfortable with you because you make them feel important.

 8th to the 6th   You are overly sacrificial in offering to help those who may be able to help themselves. Be wary of the temptation to take advantage of people who are unable to defend themselves.

 9th to the 5th   You have strong religious beliefs, which is the reason for your deep, spiritual need to help people with your creative talents. You will offer your children the opportunity to grow and reach their fullest potentials.

 10th to the 4th   You know you must continue to grow and develop in order to live up to your potentials. Family responsibilities may interfere with your freedom to choose a life of your own.

 11th to the 3rd   You dream that in your later years you will be free to indulge in all the activities you've postponed. You are gifted with ideas that you can cultivate for future enrichment. Planning is a high priority for you.

 12th to the 2nd   You are probably a big spender, paying little attention to all the tomorrows you must face. On the other hand, you needn't become morbidly preoccupied with money. Better to "render unto Caesar."

Trine: 5, 9   You are the supreme optimist, long on enthusiasm but a bit short on applying yourself to your goals. You are overly generous and thus lose out on many benefits you've earned. Everything you do is in a broad perspective, and you are often embarrassed because you cannot live up to your own expectations. You tend to overextend yourself in grandiose schemes, but you believe in yourself and refuse to accept defeat. You sometimes find it difficult to focus on a subject because your interest wanders. You eagerly absorb every bit of information, for you know your career will benefit if you are well informed. You will also derive greater self-confidence, for you know you can accept increased responsibility. People look to you for help with their major problems. You feel a strong spiritual responsibility to help others, and you derive much inner satisfaction from exploiting your creative talents in this way. You hope your children will also learn generosity and find enrichment in giving of themselves.

Sextile: 3, 11   Your understanding goes beyond your immediate circle of friends. You relate easily to everyone, regardless of their special characteristics. You don't classify people according to their social, religious or political affiliations, but regard them simply as people whose company you enjoy. You dream of being able to do all the things you have had to postpone for reasons of expediency in your career. But your dreams may not come to pass if you don't plan for them well enough. It is absolutely essential to save during your productive employment years, leaving nothing to chance.

Cross:4, 7, 10   You are at ease with groups of people, and you enjoy having them seek your advice. You pride yourself on your good judgment, but you should be ready to compromise when others present arguments that contradict your position. You can make the best of any situation, because you know how to make people feel important. Your parents may have conditioned you to seek their approval before making your own plans for a career. Though you are naturally dutiful and loyal to your parents, their suggestions or interference in your affairs will annoy you. You want to live up to your own potentials rather than their expectations, unless they happen to be the same. For best results, establish your own priorities and stick to them. You can easily be distracted from your objectives by allowing others to make unfair demands on you. They will try to make you feel guilty for neglecting your obligations to them.

Inconjunct: 6, 8   You trust people even when you know little or nothing about them. But sometimes you know more than you admit, and you may try to use your knowledge to gain an unfair advantage. In such instances, let your moral judgment guide you to do what is right. You are able to help others in their moment of greatest need, and if you can afford it, you might offer your services without charge. You are eager to show people how to be more self-sufficient.

Semisextile: 2, 12   Be aware of your careless disregard for money; you need to be more conservative! You tend to spend beyond your limit, so keep a watchful eye on your bank balance and pay some attention to your future needs. You put others' needs above your own, and you feel guilty about unjust conditions in society. Your compassion and understanding of other people's problems will enrich you even more than they benefit those who receive your unselfish generosity.

1st to the 1st You are serious, cautious and responsible in your undertakings. You underestimate your own worth and are therefore apprehensive about meeting competition. But your fear of challenge is groundless.

2nd to the 12th Easily embarrassed by failure, you avoid taking on burdens unless you are absolutely sure you will succeed. Still, a deep spiritual commitment urges you to help others with their problems.

3rd to the 11th Selective about making friends, you are drawn to persons who are mature enough to stand on their own. You know that your future financial security must come from effectively using your own resources.

4th to the 10th You consider yourself less important than your colleagues and, fearing ridicule, you assert yourself defensively even when you know you are right. Your superiors are aware of your competence, however.

5th to the 9th Learning comes easily to you, and you rarely forget what you have learned. You value education as the first essential step toward achievement. You know it is the only way to exploit your creativity wisely.

6th to the 8th You are suspicious of those who seek your talents and fearful that they will exploit you for their benefit. If you can accept the responsibility of working to serve others' needs, you will gain their admiration and respect.

7th to the 7th You are stimulated to match the good judgment you observe in others. It is important to become more self-disciplined in developing your talents to improve your competitive position.

8th to the 6th You assume that other people are more competent than you. The reverse is more likely, but until you know this you will serve others, if only to win their approval. Don't sacrifice your own goals in helping others achieve theirs.

9th to the 5th You are quite talented, but you have difficulty in demonstrating it. Your natural gifts can probably be developed without extensive formal training, if you learn to use them efficiently.

10th to the 4th The frustrating austerity of your early years may have restricted your development. Your diligence and willingness to work, however, should enable you to gain your objectives in spite of these limitations.

11th to the 3rd You have many ideas to promote, though you may have to defer them because of more pressing priorities. You apply yourself with purpose and dedication. Having to postpone working toward your objectives earlier in life may have angered you, but it was worthwhile if you resolved that problem.

12th to the 2nd Money for its own sake doesn't really impress you. You realize that there are more important values that can sustain you in pursuing your destiny. You don't want to be identified with your possessions.

Trine: 5, 9 Though you are serious and responsible, your low estimate of your own worth makes you apprehensive about meeting competition successfully. You are more talented than you know, and the only way to realize this is to look upon challenges as opportunities to establish your credentials. Experience is your best teacher, and you rarely forget what you've learned this way. Getting an education will improve your ability to compete successfully. In time you will learn to use your skills and talents efficiently for everyone's betterment. You need this feedback to reassure you that you've done a good job. Eventually you will learn how to organize your creative resources so that they are always productive. Don't take yourself so seriously; it makes it difficult for you to display any human weaknesses.

Sextile: 3, 11 Your fear of making a poor showing among opponents causes you to choose your few friends carefully. Because you aren't sure that you can stand securely on your own, you associate with people who are mature and don't make demands. You find it so difficult to take care of your own affairs that you won't volunteer to assist others. By developing your many good ideas you can achieve financial independence for your later years. With persistence, dedication and planning, you can certainly capitalize on your mental assets and achieve your objectives. You must have a plan that is geared for success, even if you don't feel ready for the position you want. Probably you are better prepared to take action than the average person.

Cross: 4, 7, 10 You want to be accepted as an equal by the people you deal with. You admire their good judgment and compare your efforts with theirs. When you become less defensive and more self-disciplined, you will discover how much you can accomplish. But before this can happen, you have to approve of your skills and efforts. You proceed too cautiously, fearing ridicule and assuming that you are less important than others. There's no shame in failing if you learn from the experience. Your superiors consider you very competent. You secretly want to earn your parents' respect for successfully fulfilling your potentials. If your early home life was austere, you should be pleased that you have risen above those limiting circumstances.

Inconjunct: 6, 8 Your natural reticence comes from suspecting that others may try to exploit your talents. This will diminish when you realize that they naturally seek your services to fulfill their needs. When you accept the responsibility for working with and for others, you will be well paid for your efforts. Also you will gain the respect that you need so desperately. Serving the needs of the public often involves sacrifice, but what better way to demonstrate your credentials and win approval for your efforts. Be careful, however, not to sacrifice your own goals so that others may gain theirs.

Semisextile: 2, 12 You have a deep spiritual commitment to serving the needs of those who are unable to help themselves. Easily embarrassed by failure, you may avoid this responsibility for fear of letting down the people who depend on you. You probably don't realize how much you can help others become self-sufficient. Then they will no longer require your assistance. If you are as unconcerned with material matters as you say, you will gain enormous personal satisfaction from applying your skills dutifully and establishing the kind of human values that will surely improve your self-image.

1st to the 1st   A rebel at heart, you insist on being allowed to develop in your own way. Your irresponsibility may irritate people who accept their responsibilities, and your disregard for rules makes you seem somewhat unstable.

 2nd to the 12th   You would like everyone to enjoy the freedom you have, and you could dedicate your life to serving the needy and disadvantaged. But don't become affiliated with projects whose purposes are obscure. If you do, you'll regret it.

 3rd to the 11th   Your friends include people who are highly evolved as well as those who are indifferent to development. You don't interfere in their affairs, and you demand the same courtesy from them. You don't make plans, assuming that everything will work out for the best.

 4th to the 10th   You prefer a career that allows you self-determination. You don't take discipline well, so your development and growth in your chosen field may be slow and unpredictable.

 5th to the 9th   You enjoy people who aren't afraid to speak their minds, provided they have something worthwhile to say. Your keen perception tells you what's right or wrong with current politics, so you could become involved in this field.

 6th to the 8th   You are generally permissive in your attitudes about sex, and you don't get upset when individuals decide on a moral code that differs from society's.

 7th to the 7th   You want a strong-minded mate who will permit you to be yourself. You would never allow your partner to dominate you. You might be interested in a trial marriage before making a binding contractual agreement.

 8th to the 6th   You should avoid acting hastily or on impulse. Otherwise you run the risk of unnecessary physical exhaustion. You tend to function largely on nervous energy, and you want to do everything right away, because you never know what will happen tomorrow.

 9th to the 5th   You know that you cannot be free unless you develop your creative potentials. You reach out to people, eager to understand them. Your children may resent your permissiveness. Although they may admire your exciting lifestyle, they may not want it for themselves.

 10th to the 4th   If you don't establish a firm base, it may be difficult to achieve your goals. Your argument is that you don't want to get "locked into" a situation that would inhibit you. You probably resent the frustration you felt in your early years.

 11th to the 3rd   Your future is in your hands to shape as you wish. With your many ideas, you can achieve the security and independence that you need. Any kind of limitation is intolerable. You think free, so you are free.

 12th to the 2nd   You alternate between being preoccupied with money and considering it a cross to bear. Because of that attitude, you may be on the fringes of poverty.

Trine: 5, 9   Basically a rebel, you demand the right to grow and develop in your own way. More inhibited people consider you unstable because of your revolutionary behavior and your ability to detach yourself from responsibility. You aren't afraid of responsibility, but you want to know whether your freedom will be curtailed if you accept it. You don't generally make rules for others, and you wish people would remember this before they ask you to obey theirs. You really enjoy people who think for themselves. You have a great regard for education because it helps people to think more clearly and to live with greater self-determination. You also realize that formal education is the best way to develop your creative potentials so that you can use them more productively. Your children may resent you for being permissive, assuming that you don't really care what happens to them.

Sextile: 3, 11   You have an exciting array of friends, ranging from genteel to coarse. You have a unique ability to remain relatively unaffected by the lifestyles of those around you. Your cool detachment may cause you some anxiety later on because you don't plan ahead, assuming that everything will turn out well. With your abundance of ideas, you can do so much more to shape your future. With a little foresight, your financial security and independence can be assured.

Cross: 4, 7, 10   Your emotional indifference and disregard for the facts of life may delay your rise to a position of prominence. You expect others to let you do everything in your own way, and you resent their authority over you. This resentment may be left over from the frustrations of dealing with your parents early in life. Learn to compromise so you can gain the support you need for your endeavors. Your partner must be willing to let you be yourself, and never try to dominate you in any way.

Inconjunct: 6, 8   On a personal level, you are quite uninhibited in seeking to satisfy your physical needs and sexual appetite. You feel that everyone has to live according to their own code of behavior. On a more impersonal level, you can accomplish a great deal when you use your innovative ability to serve the needs of the people you deal with. If you want your ideas and suggestions to win greater approval, you may have to make some sacrifices to show that you understand other people's problems. Plan your actions more carefully so you won't be in danger of nervous exhaustion from pushing yourself to meet deadlines.

Semisextile: 2, 12   With your belief that everyone should have the freedom you enjoy, you may dedicate yourself to help people who are in need or disadvantaged. While it isn't easy for you to put others before yourself, you would derive much satisfaction and spiritual uplift if you did. Money alone cannot tell you whether your efforts are truly productive, although you may sometimes be preoccupied with financial matters. You must apply yourself to some significant human need. In that case, you might even think of money as a major burden, because you dislike the obligations that come with large amounts of it. On the whole, you are not overly concerned with money as an end in itself, but as a means to achieve more rewarding objectives.

1st to the 1st You are extremely sensitive and inclined to create illusions rather than accept reality. You may find it difficult to express yourself, and you often withdraw to avoid unpleasantness. An idealist, you abhor the injustice that prevails in society.

 2nd to the 12th You need to become involved in social activity to help relieve human need, but it would be easy for you to turn your back on this problem. Don't let others take advantage of your generosity to satisfy their own selfish desires.

 3rd to the 11th Evaluate your goals carefully and make plans for achieving them. It would be a good idea to meditate on your objectives, which may be buried deep in your subconscious. Be wary of friends who give you advice, for they may not understand you at all.

 4th to the 10th Your development and success in your career may be limited by the feeling that you don't deserve to succeed. Stop making comparisons with competitors. Establish realistic goals and don't make excuses to others, who may be too preoccupied with their affairs to really care.

 5th to the 9th Because of your affinity for philosophical and spiritual matters, you need a formal education in order to develop your higher mental faculties. Even though you usually perceive what people really mean, you can be misled by deliberate untruths.

 6th to the 8th Your highest ideals can be eroded if you become fascinated by purely physical modes of self-expression. There is no dishonor in temptation unless it diverts you from your primary goals. You can nourish the needs of society with your compassion and love.

 7th to the 7th Your greatest danger is being deceived by others. Check everyone's credentials and believe only the facts you can check. You should get legal advice even for insignificant contracts.

 8th to the 6th Serving others is what you do best, but you shouldn't neglect yourself. Try to determine how you can make your best contribution without asking for suggestions. Relax and be sure to get sufficient rest.

 9th to the 5th You have amazing sources of inspiration, but you need training to exploit your creative talents for optimum results. You could leave a lasting impression on others by your sacrifices.

 10th to the 4th Your early years made a deep impression and forced you to rely on your own resources. You were probably disoriented when you first made the transition from dependence to security and independence.

 11th to the 3rd Only you will know if you are using your ideas constructively to serve your future goals. It is important for you to know that your efforts are fulfilling a social obligation.

 12th to the 2nd Plan all your financial moves so that you don't have to be unduly preoccupied with money. You can't afford to be distracted from your more urgent goals.

Trine: 5, 9 You are very sensitive and easily influenced to submit to people and situations. Your unsureness makes others apprehensive about dealing with you. To avoid unpleasantness, you often withdraw when you should be more aggressive. You are upset by people in important positions who have distorted social values. An idealist with a deep appreciation of philosophical and spiritual matters, you are pained to see how little is done to improve the quality of life for many people in society. Your compassion goes out to those who are sociologically and economically locked into unfortunate situations. By getting a formal education, you can give professional attention to these social conditions. You need to be as well informed as possible so you aren't deceived or misled. With your creative imagination, you can establish a secure place for yourself in your career and in society.

Sextile: 3, 11 Carefully evaluate your goals and adhere to a program for reaching them. Be wary of friends who tell you what to do, for they probably don't understand you at all. Meditating may help you find answers that would be difficult to find in any other way. Occasionally you should withdraw from harsh reality to contemplate your ambitions and goals. Only you will know if your goals are realistic and effective when you work at them. You must see some social benefit from your efforts in order to get fulfillment and peace of mind.

Cross: 4, 7, 10 Your early environment made an indelible impression on you. You had to rely on your own resources as you grew to maturity, and the painful transition from dependence to independence may have caused you to feel persecuted and temporarily disoriented. You wanted to be your own person, not an extension of your parents' expectations. You are easily deceived, and you should seek legal counsel even for insignificant deals. Don't believe anything unless you can confirm it with unassailable sources. By assuming that people will try to take advantage of you, you will free yourself from unnecessary anxiety. Realizing your ambitions depends on whether you feel that you deserve to succeed. You may feel that others must always come first, but that is persecution. Don't compare your achievements with other people's—you owe it to yourself to succeed at your own pace, no matter what that is.

Inconjunct: 6, 8 You want to serve others, but you must not do yourself a disservice in the process. Don't let other people tell you what you should do for them. You could undermine your health by doing too much and getting too little rest. You can play an important role by nourishing those who need your spiritual fortitude and compassion. But you could be swept along by the pressure of decaying elements if you are distracted by purely physical modes of self-expression. There is no dishonor in temptation unless it diverts you from your more noble objectives.

Semisextile: 2, 12⁻ You need to be involved in some social activity in which you can make an important contribution. But make sure the project isn't serving the selfish interests of parasites. You need to be realistic about your finances, so that you aren't distracted from your primary goals. You tend to spend carelessly without a thought for tomorrow. Plan your affairs so you can be free to work with and for the people who need your understanding and compassion.

1st to the 1st You know that you can control the general direction of your destiny. Though you may go to extremes, you have the sense of purpose to change conditions in your environment, which will improve your chances for success.

 2nd to the 12th You are defensive in protecting your weaknesses. You don't want anyone to take advantage of you, but you will let them if it will help correct intolerable social conditions.

 3rd to the 11th You can turn to powerful friends for support, some of whom fear you while others simply respect you. When your trust is violated, you are extremely annoyed. You will scheme, if necessary, to achieve your goals.

 4th to the 10th Your psychic ability gives you an advantage over your competitors, for you can detect deception and take steps to protect yourself. You rarely get into a compromising situation. It isn't easy for you to submit to authority, which can result in trouble.

 5th to the 9th You speak out against offensive sociopolitical conditions. In your personal and business dealings, you insist on fair play and justice. An education will give you enormous leverage to promote better government and a better society.

 6th to the 8th After much soul-searching, you may decide to live up to people's trust in you. You will win high praise from the public for your willingess to serve its interests.

 7th to the 7th Your privacy is very important to you, and few people who know you violate it, for you can be vindictive. Preferring to be left alone, you will nevertheless fight for your rights if anyone tries to obstruct them.

 8th to the 6th When someone appreciates a service you have done, your vitality is regenerated. Be careful not to distort your objectives by a lust for personal gain, for that power can become destructive.

 9th to the 5th When you help others with your creative resources, your accomplishments are unlimited. Once you are trained to use your talents wisely, the lives of everyone you contact will be immeasurably improved.

 10th to the 4th The frustration you experienced with your parents should have given you the ambition to succeed on your own merits. You may have to break with the past to improve on your early circumstances, but your future requires it.

 11th to the 3rd You've always known you could do more with your potentials than others seem to do with theirs. You need to harness your ideas to an objective, and then you will be enthusiastically dedicated to your goals.

 12th to the 2nd An extreme desire for power can undermine your plans for gaining what you want. If you are obsessed with greed, you may become its final victim. Better to use your energy to improve social conditions.

Trine: 5, 9 You can choose how to achieve your ambitions. Although you go to extremes in asserting your will, you have a strong sense of purpose, and you will reshape your environment in order to achieve your goals. Perhaps the frustration of your early years made you decide to let nothing stand in your way again. Your destiny may require you to make an important contribution to society, for you are concerned about political conditions at all levels. You aren't afraid to speak out when elected officials fail to carry out their promises. You respect education because you know the public must be informed in order to be effective. You know how to gain public support in protesting the misuse of power by elected officials. In your personal and business affairs you insist on fair play. You sincerely hope that your children will also stand up for their rights. You want them to take advantage of the opportunities you provide to take their place in the world. You want to know that society can use your resources to improve human conditions.

Sextile: 3, 11 You can turn to powerful friends for support. You know how to scheme when necessary to achieve your objectives, and you don't tolerate anyone who violates your trust. Most of your friends respect you for this, but few genuinely like you. You know what you want out of life, and you know you can do more with your ideas than others can with theirs. Having an objective helps you focus your ideas effectively. Your current situation may not be challenging, but it may be the catalyst you need to get started. It is important to be involved in some significant social activity that requires your talent. Otherwise you will never feel that your life has been meaningful.

Cross: 4, 7, 10 You must learn to modify your extremism and take advantage of opportunities. Rather than try to control your competitors, wouldn't it be more profitable to gain their support? Why not assume that they would welcome you? You can convert fear into dedication if you present a worthwhile purpose that will benefit others as well as yourself. Don't worry about being undermined; you can "smell" deception when it first appears. You are in control of most situations, so you have nothing to lose and everything to gain through cooperative effort. You may have to break with the past before you can make a commitment to your goals. Your personal relationships will be enhanced if you are free to indulge in them with no strings attached. Your success in marriage will indicate how well you've handled the frustrations of your childhood.

Inconjunct: 6, 8 After much soul-searching, you may decide to do what you can to justify people's trust in you. If you are willing to serve the interests of others, you may earn gratitude and sincere appreciation for your efforts. In this way you can also motivate others to follow your example. Make sure that you aren't motivated solely by desire for personal gain, or the process may disintegrate and fail.

Semisextile: 2, 12 You may undo all your accomplishments if you assume that you can get away with anything. Try to be more moderate and compromise when it seems appropriate. You can undermine your position by being too self-indulgent, neglecting other people's needs. If you are responsive to your social obligations, you will gain many benefits. After all, much of your success comes from the public sector.

Sun in First, Moon in First

You are self-centered and self-motivating in your endeavors and ambitious to establish your position before the world to realize your objectives. In asserting yourself, you often alienate those with whom you might want a relationship. Basically you are a self-sustaining person who gives the impression that you don't need others, even though you know that isn't true. You really do need others to help you realize your goals, because being apart from the mainstream of social involvement creates loneliness. You may choose to maintain the contacts made in your early life through your education or training. You want to prove yourself on your own merits, independent of family ties. You are clever in gaining the lead in your relationships without seeming too demanding. As the saying goes, you allow others to pursue you until they are caught.

Professionally, you handle power effectively, probably because you learned to deal with it as a youth in your own family. You may not be rebellious by nature but you resent people who try to force you to relinquish control over your destiny. While people respect you because you seem to have it all together and admire the way you attack problems head on, they may also resent having to make concessions to you. Very likely you will achieve your goals and attain the position you want because you have faith in your ability to succeed.

Sun in First, Moon in Second

In your desire to have everything that will make life more comfortable, you sometimes take chances that you later regret. Your behavior is contradictory in that you assert yourself, displaying complete command of the situation, but at the same time you experience much inner emotional turmoil because you are apprehensive about maintaining the position you have taken. In other words, your willfulness disrupts your need for stability in your affairs. At times you show great interest in accomplishing some important social task, and you arouse people to support you in your ideas. Yet, when the time comes to get involved, especially if it means making a financial contribution, you are probably the last to come forth.

Your superiors may have difficulty getting you to do things their way. But because you can usually justify your position and because you are able to stay with a problem until you solve it, you quickly earn their respect.

Your magnetism is unmistakable in your relationships, so much so that others rarely see how your indulgences toward them weaken their defenses and allow you to gain control over them. There is nothing you won't do for your partner so long as your integrity and self-determination are not questioned.

Sun in First, Moon in Third

You are eager to assert yourself and always have whatever information you need. As a result, there are few who can match you in a direct confrontation. You have the presence of a performer, which is simply your way of getting the attention you want as well as good public relations. You might have trouble convincing your superiors that your high visibility is enough to satisfy their expectations for more action and less promise. In a sense, you aspire to being the "wheel" among those in your immediate surroundings, and you have a gift for handling others so that they don't resent your aggressiveness.

Children positively adore you and consider you the image they want to emulate. Your mate is as defenseless to your charm as others you face in your daily activities. Everyone admires and respects your strength, and your readiness to be involved with people and situations adds diversity to your life. You may be impatient, but you are never bored. Your education gives you the polish you need to ease into a position of prominence.

Powerful parental overlay may have diluted your own sense of identity. Possibly only through a break with your family, or at least having a separate residence, will you have the chance to be yourself.

Sun in First, Moon in Fourth

Two forces within you are locked in a struggle in your striving for significance and identity. Your emotional, feeling self binds you to family in debt and gratitude for their efforts in your behalf during the developing years. As you mature and realize that you have a life of your own, some resentment will develop. You must integrate these factors without guilt to insure your personal fulfillment, rendering unto others what is theirs and unto yourself what is rightfully yours.

You probably want a career that gives you the opportunity to manage others with sensitivity and understanding. It might be to your advantage to be self-employed if at all possible. Although you have the drive and ambition to rise in importance, you would actually be more comfortable with less visibility.

Even though you seem career oriented and have the temperament that often indicates success, you rely heavily on those you love for support, because you are emotionally vulnerable to the abrasive conditions that a career often brings. Appreciation by those you love will enable you to handle any problem. Your children depend upon you and trust that you are deeply concerned for their best interests.

Sun in First, Moon in Fifth

Your desire to achieve something worthwhile in your endeavors is enhanced by your ability to take advantage of the benefits your parents provided. You make the most of opportunities to demonstrate your creative talents without alienating competitors. However, you assert yourself positively when you encounter resistance to your plans. Because you can also demonstrate sensitivity for others, you usually gain their support in reaching your goals.

Romantic involvements that distract your attention may delay you in realizing your ambitions. You may need to sacrifice some personal pleasures to provide the energy you need for the demands of a career. Once established in your profession, you will want to spend more time with loved ones and indulge your family with all the advantages you can provide.

Your eagerness to enjoy yourself may prove costly unless you exercise restraint in spending and stay aware of how far you are extending your credit. This is somewhat embarrassing and uncomfortable for you since you like to give the impression that nothing is ever really beyond your control. You probably enjoy a wide circle of friends, and you hate to let people down in their expectations of you. Plan ahead cautiously so that you are never expected to perform beyond your ability.

Sun in First, Moon in Sixth

You are assertive enough to gain all that you desire, yet you are emotionally at odds with others, who seem unable to accomplish anything without your help. While you may resent this apparent intrusion on your time and energy, the truth is that you are psychologically dependent on the people you meet in your professional affairs who give you the opportunity to demonstrate how competent you really are. If you are really sure of yourself, you need not defend yourself by stating that you are or by complaining that everyone else is unqualified or untrained. Prove yourself by being sati. Your upbringing gave you an understanding of human frailty, and serving others can only enhance you in your career. Stimulate people to become independent enough to eventually succeed without you. Because you burn up energy so rapidly, take time to recuperate after any arduous task.

You want a partner who needs you and who is also supportive to your goals, someone to whom you can turn when you face reversals, yet allows you to stand on your own when conditions improve. You want your children to enjoy the best and to be self-reliant as well in pursuing their own destinies.

Sun in First, Moon in Seventh

It is in response to the challenges and competition presented by others that you eventually prove yourself. Challenge is the most stimulating condition for you, and you literally glow as you rise to the occasion. When situations bog down and you get bored and lose interest, you thrive on the many confrontations you face. It disturbs you to be ignored, as you are much more sensitive than others realize. You are completely involved with the world around you, your ultimate ambition being to gain full control over your circumstances. You make certain concessions in order to win others' support in your climb to prominence.

The most suitable career for you is one in which you have both self-determination and the leverage of power. Get an education that supports your purposes, which probably involve working with large numbers of people from a position of authority.

While you may have some difficulty gaining the independence you need from family obligations, you can use your charm to avoid alienation. You need to be involved in a partnership, so marriage can be an asset to you in your plans for the future. Your mate must be willing to share your enthusiasm for what you hope to accomplish, which will improve the quality of life for the family.

Sun in First, Moon in Eighth

As you assert yourself in your drive for achievement, there are times when you have to make sacrifices. Some of these may require you to indulge others in their needs, which you could regard as an investment in your own plans to reach your goals. You are sensitive to an appeal for help, especially when it is a sincere request for assistance. Because you are responsive to people's needs, you are in a desirable position to win recognition for your efforts, and you might choose a career in public service. You can earn a comfortable income from the products, services or professional expertise that you offer. You owe the public the benefit of your developing talents and skills, and once you are established, your growth is assured.

At some time in your life, you have to make the commitment of utilizing your gifts to enhance the quality of life for others, including your partner and your children. Your driving desire to see your children rise to prominence can blind you in your ability to accept what they may choose to do with their lives if it differs from your expectations. You pride yourself on how well you can satisfy your partner's needs, and in return you demand the privilege of mobility for yourself.

Be guarded about revealing your ideas until they are sufficiently developed so you can apply them. You run the risk of sharing too easily and having others appropriate your ideas for their benefit, excluding you from the rewards they bring.

Sun in First, Moon in Ninth

The basic factors of integration are so well established in your consciousness that you have a notable advantage over others. You have the talent to get what you want out of life and the basic resources that will allow you to succeed. While this might seem like an ideal situation, you may not take full advantage of it. Having the potential does not guarantee success; it still requires development so you can translate potential into effective skills. You are knowledgeable in a wide variety of subjects and can easily hold your own among the most learned people. What you probably lack is the assertiveness to pursue your luck to the ultimate benefit it can provide.

You bring much understanding and spiritual insight into the affairs of those you must deal with in your daily routine. You are growth oriented and are worthy of a position of trust and authority. You handle your assigned duties with responsibility.

You may meet your partner in the course of developments relative to your career, perhaps at a learning institution. You are more comfortable with someone similarly engaged in his or her own career so that you are on a mutually developing wave length. Your children doubtless adore you, for you always manage to have time for them.

Sun in First, Moon in Tenth

Your basic survival instincts and the foundation of experiences early in your development are at odds with your drive to achieve in life. There is an inner frustration between your inclination to follow the line of least resistance and your conscious awareness that you must assert yourself in exploiting your creative potential. This results in difficulty dealing with persons in authority, as you mistakenly assume that they are somehow determined to obstruct you. Perhaps parental conditioning has led you to believe that you are not qualified to make your own way in life. Once you understand this, you needn't feel that you have to prove yourself to their satisfaction, only to your own. Acquiring the appropriate skills to establish your authority in your chosen field is an absolute must for your own sense of worthwhileness.

Your rise to success may follow severe limitations early in life. You derive many benefits from your ability to cope with frustration. Your success is then all the more precious to you.

Deliberate long and hard before you commit yourself to a permanent marital relationship. Be sensitive to any residual resentment you hold from your early years that can disturb the harmony of your personal relationship. You work diligently for those you love, especially your children, to give them every advantage you didn't have. As they succeed in their own way, you feel grateful for having had the opportunity to support them.

Sun in First, Moon in Eleventh

Your self-confidence indicates your comfortable outlook on life. You are high spirited and know that the future is yours to shape. You realize that everything you want comes from planning and from utilizing your talents. You may also have the advantage of assistance from others when you need it, and your appreciation shows in your willingness to return the favor. You treasure the many lessons of past experiences that benefit you today, yet you have a progressive outlook, facing every day eagerly for what it brings. You view a career as a means toward fulfilling yourself, and you are likely to choose an environment in which you can master handling a large number of people. You make others feel important, especially young people, who you can stimulate to excel according to their own needs.

You have a permissive and tolerant nature that rarely condemns others for their failings. People enjoy your company, for your positive attitude is most uplifting. You seek a partner who shares your positive outlook on life and who will work with you to reach mutual goals. You want to share a full life with the one you love, and you aren't content with having only a part-time relationship. You enjoy sharing with your children, who will have a deep love for you.

Sun in First, Moon in Twelfth

Unresolved emotional anxieties distract you from asserting yourself as aggressively as you could in pursuing your ambitions. You have a subtle feeling that perhaps you offend people when you come on strong, yet you persist in this behavior. You must learn more about yourself and how your feelings of guilt affect your ability to take action for fear of arousing resentment in others. Your sensitivity is not so much a sign of weakness as it is just your being human. Your gifted imagination can be a great benefit to you in your search for fulfillment.

Your temperament is well suited to institutional work, as in a service organization where you can serve others and give them the strength they need to become more self-sufficient. You are a champion for persons who are treated unjustly or are socially, economically or politically disadvantaged.

You seek a partner with whom you can be dependent on an equal basis, offering each other both support and strength.

You may spoil your children by overindulging them, making sacrifices for them that put a strain on you. Don't feel that you are not doing enough; they are probably quite satisfied with your efforts. Only your own guilt feelings are causing you anxiety.

Chapter Two
Second House

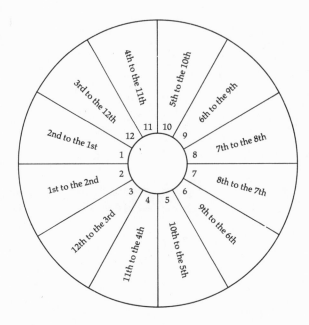

The second house represents your need to sustain yourself by acquiring the necessities of life, such as nourishment, clothing, protection from the elements, a place to live and so on. When life was more simple, the earth usually provided these resources. As life became more complex, a system of bartering was instituted so that the resources missing from one's environment could be obtained through exchange with others. Eventually, a monetary system was developed to replace the arduous and time-consuming task of making direct contact with those who may have lived at some distance. This evolved into today's highly mechanized system of monetary exchange. But the basic principle remains of exchanging money for goods received, with each person deriving what they need from the other.

The same principle holds for your job; you receive money from those who have it for your services, which they need. Another, less visible process that begins in this house is the feeling of self-worth; as your skills improve you can demand more in return for your efforts. Your value judgment results from the interchange with others.

The second house is also the immediate future and everything that relates to subsistence and survival. These urgent matters are why earning a living and having enough to eat are so important, for without them life cannot continue. By focusing properly on these vital issues, you achieve a feeling of personal security and contentment in gaining the comforts of life. But you can easily undermine your potential by refusing to take whatever action is required to implement your plans so that your needs can be satisfied. This is because the first house, with its drive, is the twelfth house from the second, and failing to exercise your options defeats you in satisfying your needs.

The second house also represents the basic resources that you were born with. This means that even without further training, you have the basic knowledge to function with sufficient skill so you can survive. These are primitive features, of course, and further growth and development will enhance your ability to utilize these basic skills so that you can enjoy a more abundant life. As your performance and credibility improve, so does your feeling of self-worth, with a resultant increase in earning ability. Your reaction to the pressure of circumstances described by the second house determines your value judgment about yourself and others.

Derivative House Meanings

1st to the 2nd   This represents the means through which you can gain a feeling of self-worth and the basic resources that sustain you in all your endeavors.

2nd to the 1st   You need to feel secure in your projections and be able to assert yourself to become truly self-sustaining.

3rd to the 12th   Understanding your personal weaknesses allows you to make adjustments in planning for your eventual retirement.

4th to the 11th   You want to be free from insecurity in the future, so you are careful to establish a proper foundation for your enterprises.

5th to the 10th   Success in your career reassures you of your worth and allows you to seek even more substantial objectives.

6th to the 9th   Devotion to your craft rewards you with opportunities to prove yourself in an ever-expanding field of activity.

7th to the 8th   You are intimidated by other people's assets, which remind you of your own inadequacies, but they also motivate you to match their performance.

8th to the 7th   You realize that you can attract support from others if you show a willingness to make sacrifices for them, although that is very painful.

9th to the 6th   You learn more by doing than by discussing theory, and once you know you are helpful to others, no one is more devoted in their craft.

10th to the 5th   Your love for your career may reflect your deep concern for your children and your desire to give them the opportunities you lacked.

11th to the 4th   Because of your early environment, you have developed a strong desire to achieve freedom from want in your life.

12th to the 3rd   Although you are not gifted in communication, your later years will be enhanced if you broaden your social contacts. You know more than you admit.

1st to the 2nd   Security is your most important consideration, and you put a lot of energy into acquiring the necessities of life, to have an advantage over those who lack them. You judge people by their physical assets, paying little attention to their human qualities.

 2nd to the 1st   You can profit by developing your talents to gain your objectives. You must broaden your perspective and learn that there are other facets to life besides money and material assets. Be appreciative when others help you reach your goals.

 3rd to the 12th   You probably want to retire from your profession as early as possible. With your inspiration, you can develop your ideas to get the results you want and retire early. You hate to depend on others.

 4th to the 11th   You cultivate friendships with people who are in a position to help you achieve the security you want. You want to be independent so that you can enjoy your later years without being obligated to anyone.

 5th to the 10th   Your superiors are usually impressed with the way you use your abilities to achieve their objectives. They know they can depend on you to give everything to your job, because in general you like your work.

 6th to the 9th   You are basically an honest person who doesn't dare to break the law for fear of jeopardizing your security if you were found out. Although you understand the importance of education, financial limitations may frustrate your desire for learning. But you might decide to go to school, even if you have to work part time.

 7th to the 8th   You envy people who are successful, and you find it profitable to form alliances with others in money-making schemes. When you compare your accomplishments with other people's, you are stimulated to match or exceed them.

 8th to the 7th   People trust you with their possessions, and you might follow a career as a financial advisor. You are keen in capitalizing on financially promising suggestions. But you are equally eager to demonstrate your affection for someone who is stable, trusting and fascinating.

 9th to the 6th   You can succeed in business because you are well informed about all the details, and you handle them with complete control. You may have to travel in your business, which you are willing to do if success and future growth of the business depend on it.

 10th to the 5th   You enjoy what yo do because it gives you the opportunity to exploit your creative talents. You also need a vehicle for realizing your future goals and independence. You want your children to assert themselves as you have, but don't be too demanding of them. Let them live too.

 11th to the 4th   You want to show your appreciation for your parents' assistance in your formative years. Perhaps you are simply paying off a debt that you incurred from them earlier.

 12th to the 3rd   In conversation with others, avoid the subject of money, for it can be boring. Listen to other people's advice, for their ideas could prove beneficial to you in the long run.

Trine: 6, 10 You are preoccupied with material matters because you judge your success in monetary terms. You want every comfort, and you use all your resources to gain them. But your single-minded focus may divert you from developing qualities of true worth. You must have other interests, so that you will be a well-rounded person with a variety of perspectives. You should succeed quite easily, because of your ability to help your superiors achieve their objectives. You probably like your work, and you bring much creative talent to it. You are well informed and in control of your responsibilities. You will accept the necessity of travel as part of your job, especially if it will help your chances for growth with the company.

Sextile: 4, 12 You have much inspiration and can develop your ideas in order to achieve your goal of early retirement. Not wanting to depend on others for anything, you apply yourself to gain the security that will make dependence unnecessary. You appreciate the assistance you received from your parents in your formative years, and you want to be sure that their needs are provided for. It is a credit to you that you don't forget anyone who has been partly responsible for your success.

Cross: 5, 8, 11 You cultivate friendships with influential people, and you use the opportunies they provide to get what you want. You hope that someday you won't have to depend on anyone. You fear financial embarrassment, so you plan to achieve your goals and succeed by exploiting your creative resources. The success of others spurs you to match their accomplishments. The only alliances you are interested in are those that show financial promise. You are particularly effective in devising schemes to make a lot of money. The demands of your family stimulate you to put your talent to work. You want to give your children what they need to make their own way in life. This is an important goal for you, and you will discipline yourself to the task. If you are too demanding of your children, they may be unable to develop according to their own needs, through their own experiences. Your romantic interests are directed to finding a stable, honest, warm and loyal partner to share your life with. You will not settle for less even if it means delaying marriage until you are older.

Inconjunct: 7, 9 A person of integrity, you usually stay within the law in your dealings, knowing too well that otherwise your gains may be lost. Getting an education could be a problem because of finances, but you are willing to work to pay for it. You know that your future goals will be easier to reach if you are formally trained and well informed. You could succeed as an advisor or manager of other people's financial affairs, because people feel that they can trust you in these matters, and they can.

Semisextile: 1, 3 Don't be afraid to assert yourself when you have the opportunity. Your timidity at such times could cause you to lose. There is some risk in most endeavors involving money, but you won't gain anything if you don't take some chances. On the other hand, you limit your risks by your painstaking evaluation of the facts. A bit of friendly advice: try to avoid talking only about money, for it tends to bore people. Cultivate an interest in other areas and show that you are familiar with topics that other people are concerned with.

1st to the 2nd Because you are apprehensive about the stability of your material resources, you never refuse gifts from others, and you don't necessarily reciprocate. You try to compensate for your emotional insecurity by accumulating material possessions.

 2nd to the 1st Fearing the loss of your resources, you assert yourself cautiously toward others. You prefer not to be involved in other people's affairs, so you avoid any group functions that require donations of time or money.

 3rd to the 12th Your first priority is fulfilling your own needs, but when that is accomplished you might enjoy helping others who genuinely need assistance. You want to be free of anxiety about economic problems.

 4th to the 11th You are worried about having to face difficult economic conditions in the future, so you use every resource to improve your financial circumstances and increase your material holdings. You prefer friends who don't make demands on you.

 5th to the 10th Your objectives are well defined, and you easily win the approval of your superiors for the effort you put into your tasks. Your work should bring you before the public, because you identify with the public, and you can win their appreciation.

 6th to the 9th Having a high regard for education, you constantly strive to increase your knowledge. You know you can improve your earning ability by being well informed, so you are willing to invest in getting an education.

 7th to the 8th There is no point in comparing your resources to other people's, unless doing so urges you on to succeed in your endeavors. You are attracted to successful people, and you admire them for gaining freedom from economic worries.

 8th to the 7th You are suspicious of people who make demands, so you question their motives and try to pin down what your efforts will cost. You don't generally discuss your financial affairs openly, and you talk about them privately only with those you trust.

 9th to the 6th You adapt to job assignments fairly well and learn new skills easily. You want people to consider you responsible and trustworthy, and you take every opportunity to improve your skills when special training is available.

 10th to the 5th You underestimate your abilities and thus fail to capitalize on them. Your fear of risks makes it difficult to fully exploit your creative potentials. If you truly care about the people you love, you will try to live up to your potentials.

 11th to the 4th Don't forget the people who helped you in the past, especially your parents. It's not likely that you would forget, for you feel a close tie with them. Their contentment gives you much happiness, but be careful not to shortchange yourself in helping them.

 12th to the 3rd You have an obligation to yourself to take advantage of your creative ideas. Don't let your preoccupation with security interfere with your social life. If you cut the lines of communication with the people who can enrich your life, you will be lonely.

Trine: 6, 10 Your worries about security are unnecessary, for you can convert your creative talents into tangible assets. You never refuse any unsolicited gifts, though you may not reciprocate. It isn't that you aren't generous, but that you are anxious to have the necessities of life. You are preoccupied with having what you want always at hand. You enjoy life's comforts and feel that if you don't take care of yourself, who will? Because you are a deep-feeling person with unusual sensitivity to the pain of unsatisfied desires, you seek a career that will provide security and fulfillment. In your career you do whatever is necessary to achieve stability and security and get everything you want. You easily win the approval of your superiors for your efforts, and you know they consider you an asset. You would work well before the public because you can identify with people's problems, and you earn appreciation for your accomplishments. You learn new skills easily and adapt yourself to the requirements of any situation. Basically honest and sincere, you win the respect and admiration of your fellow workers as you handle your responsibilities with patience and dedication.

Sextile: 4, 12 You are compassionate to the needs of less fortunate people, and although you do not give material gifts, you give of yourself to help those who truly need you, and that is a far greater gift. You realize your social obligations, and you do extend yourself when others won't. But it is just as important to develop your creative ideas for your own sake and to indulge yourself in them. Don't let your preoccupation with security interefere with your social life, however. You may be lonely if you sever the lines of communication with people who can make your days happy with the joy of sincere companionship.

Cross: 5, 8, 11 Avoid making comparisons with other people's success and what they have gained thereby. This will result only in much inner tension as you try to match their accomplishments. You have to live up to your own potentials and capitalize on your resources to achieve financial security. You are attracted to people who seem in complete control of their destinies, but you can do just as well if you focus on exploiting your own talents. Don't be afraid to take measured risks on occasion, if only to reassure yourself that sometimes that pays dividends. Although you prefer friends who don't make demands, by being an isolationist you are likely to miss many opportunities.

Inconjunct: 7, 9 You know your earnings will increase if you are well informed, and you are willing to work if necessary to pay for your eduation. But you are a realist and will probably select a course of study that can easily be translated into increased security and even provide tenure in your occupation. You are not the most adaptable person, but you can adjust to learning new skills when necessary. You are responsible and trustworthy, but you are suspicious when people make demands, and you are curious about their motives.

Semisextile: 1, 3 Your fear of asserting yourself may allow people to try to take advantage of you. Learn to be more aggressive in promoting your ideas and programs and don't be afraid to let others know that you won't allow them to use you. It isn't wrong to concentrate on accumulating material resources, but this should not take all your time.

1st to the 2nd   You understand money and how to manipulate your affairs to get the most financial benefits. Your mind figures the true value of any item before you buy it. You are interested only in people who have substantial human values.

 2nd to the 1st   Basically unyielding in your opinions, you aren't easily convinced to change your mind when you are wrong. You are reasonably conservative about your resources and prefer not to discuss your income and how you earn it.

 3rd to the 12th   You are drawn to stable enterprises that serve the public, and you have a wealth of ideas for promoting your objectives. People in high places are impressed with your mental ability, and they realize that your proposals merit serious attention.

 4th to the 11th   Friends who make demands can cause mental strain, especially when they try to capitalize on your talents for their own selfish reasons. You try not to alienate them, because you might need them in the future, but you'd rather go about your business without interference.

 5th to the 10th   Your ability to solve problems easily is one of your best assets and attracts favorable attention from your superiors and fellow workers. Your goals are well defined, and you seek only those career opportunities that will add to your worth, materially and as a person.

 6th to the 9th   No matter what your formal training has been, you always continue to educate yourself. You know how to apply your knowledge and skills in the real world to solve problems and earn a decent income.

 7th to the 8th   Competing with others for financial advantage provides a real challenge, and you enjoy proving that you are more ingenious than your competitors in winning patrons for your services. People trust you to handle their financial affairs well.

 8th to the 7th   You are immediately aware when anyone tries to undermine you or resorts to unfair practices. You are willing to make sacrifices for the "right" person who you hope will share your life, and no gift is too costly when you want to impress that person.

 9th to the 6th   Knowing that the public wants the best service it can buy, you work to provide that service. You want to be the best in whatever you do, and you strive to improve by learning new skills.

 10th to the 5th   Success will come through exploiting your creative talents and making them available to the public. You should try to engage in pleasurable activities more often to relieve inner tensions. Try not to get so caught up in living up to your family's expectations.

 11th to the 4th   Your experience with your parents has given you a firm base on which to build your future. You are responsible and determined to achieve the independence of a stable income, with a program for security in your later years.

 12th to the 3rd   Loosen up a bit and develop an interest in a variety of subjects that have absolutely nothing to do with your career. Cultivate people who can help you forget your daily routine occasionally.

Trine: 6, 10   The emphasis you place on both human and material values enables you to derive much satisfaction from your endeavors. You understand the necessity of using your deductive ability to get the most from your resources, and you are never at a loss to apply your talents gainfully. Eager to demonstrate your creative talent, you attract the attention of your superiors, who will give you opportunities to establish a place for yourself in your career. You also attract favorable notice from the public, for you serve their interests well. Your concern for security leads you to improve your skills to augment your earning ability. Your goals are reasonably well defined, and you waste little time getting your career plans under way to achieve your aims as soon as possible. You are willing to invest time and energy in getting the education you need.

Sextile: 4, 12   Appreciative of the good influence of your parents in your early years, you try to live up to their expectations and be a credit to them. You were taught to build a solid foundation for your life in order to be independent in your later years and gain the security you feel you need. You have a wealth of ideas that you can promote in order to achieve that objective. You would find it painful to depend on others for anything. Occasionally you should break out of your job routine and cultivate an interest in activities that are totally removed from it. Focus more attention on developing your creative imagination, and indulge yourself in purely enjoyable activities. Let your hair down now and then and learn to relax.

Cross: 5, 8, 11   Competing with others stimulates you to use all your resources. You rarely come out on the short end of a challenging situation, because you use a "nuts and bolts" logic to disarm your opponent. Thus you win people's trust and patronage, and they allow you to handle their affairs. You know how to exploit your creative abilities to win public confidence. Because you work so diligently in using your skills, you do ask that your efforts be appreciated. You want your partner's admiration for your achievements, and you hope your children will live up to your expectations for them. You want them to take advantage of the opportunities you've given them to make a life for themselves, and you would be disappointed if they let you down.

Inconjunct: 7, 9   Not only do you want to achieve financial independence, you also want the public to think of you as a person with solid human values. You strive to provide services that will satisfy the most demanding individual, and you expect to be well paid for your efforts. You continue to improve your skills, knowing that this will assure you of a steady income. Though you may think twice before spending money for schooling, you realize that you must stay informed to meet the challenge of your competitors, so you continue to educate yourself at all times, regardless of your formal training. You accept the daily trials of the real world, knowing that you can solve any problems that come your way and earn a decent income at the same time.

Semisextile: 1, 3   You are unyielding in your views and tend to turn a deaf ear to others' suggestions, especially when they criticize your activities. You should broaden your interests by taking up subjects that are totally removed from your profession or daily routine. The worst thing you can do is to remain ignorant of other people's ideas or to become detached from them by refusing to communicate.

1st to the 2nd You find the comforts of the good life particularly attractive, and you enjoy the material and physical pleasures of comfortable circumstances. Status is also important to you, and surrounding yourself with beautiful possessions helps you achieve it.

2nd to the 1st "To have and to hold" is your motto, and heaven help the person who tries to take away your possessions. Your feeling of self-satisfaction is based on what you have and what you hope to acquire. You judge other people by their possessions.

3rd to the 12th You try to hold on to what you now own to provide security for your later years. You would find it shattering to be without any means of support, so you make sure that you can always convert some of your assets to cash if necessary.

4th to the 11th Not wanting to feel obligated to anyone, you maintain a certain distance from even your closest friends. You are sociable and charming, but you won't tolerate anyone who makes demands on you. Apprehensive about the future, you are usually prepared for anything.

5th to the 10th You cultivate relationships with socially prominent people, and you impress them with your charming manner and stable temperament. You will not be satisfied until you achieve a position of status with its increased benefits.

6th to the 9th While you respect education and those who are informed, you tend to avoid further education yourself, because you have an aversion to purely mental pursuits. You keep your affairs in order because you deplore untidiness.

7th to the 8th You envy people who seem to have the Midas touch. It fascinates you to form alliances with them and watch your financial holdings grow. You might benefit from an investment club in which members pool their resources to buy and sell securities.

8th to the 7th You are willing to compromise if benefits will follow. You don't make generous gestures except to gain something. You endear yourself to important people to win their trust, and you accept help from others so you can manipulate them.

9th to the 6th You dream of having enough money to travel to all the romantic places, in style, of course. You are willing to earn your way, but you prefer jobs that aren't too routine and give you the opportunity to prove how capable you are.

10th to the 5th A romantic at heart, you bring much pleasure to those you love. You want the best for your family, and you have high hopes that your children will rise to important and secure positions.

11th to the 4th The security you achieve through your efforts is the result of your parents' early training. They considered it important that your future be free from anxiety about material needs, and they hoped you would appreciate their efforts. You are grateful for their influence, and you know that your goal-seeking will fulfill their dreams.

12th to the 3rd Your preoccupation with your physical needs might distract you from developing your other talents fully. Round out your development by becoming interested in subjects that other people know about. This will broaden your enjoyment of life.

Trine: 6, 10   You are concerned with security, and you will apply yourself to earn the many comforts you want. A stable and responsible person, you know how to gain important positions by impressing the right people with your fine qualities. Once established in your profession, you slowly increase your effectiveness by taking on additional duties that will result in the tenure you want. Your professional contacts give you opportunities to gain the comforts that make your life pleasurable and mean so much to you. You consider yourself competent to take your place beside the people you admire, and you know how to conduct yourself to win their respect in return. You like living "in style," and the pleasure you get from social activities allows you to be quite content with your general circumstances.

Sextile: 4, 12   You want to be free from material dependence on others, and you don't want anyone to depend on you. Your parental conditioning made you determined to pay your own way and become independent. You appreciate what you learned early in life, and you know your parents are happy that you benefited from their influence. An opportunist, you maintain a safe distance from friends who might make demands. Because you are apprehensive about achieving your goal of complete security, you always make certain that you have assets that can be converted to cash if circumstances require it.

Cross: 5, 8, 11   You are easily intimidated by people who make a showy display of their assets, but you envy their Midas touch. You will form ties with persons who may prove beneficial to you in the long run. In making investments, you proceed cautiously, hoping to avoid unnecessary losses. You like to devise schemes that will improve your financial picture and allow you to give your family extra advantages. You have high expectations that your children will take advantage of your expertise and make the best use of their available resources. You tend to limit your romantic attentions to persons who have a talent for earning a comfortable living.

Inconjunct: 7, 9   Your ability to compromise emerges when you want to cultivate partnership interests, and in such instances you make greater sacrifices than usual. You are willing to help your mate achieve greater financial leverage in his or her endeavors, but you don't want to help on a permanent basis. Even so, you consider the time you contribute a wise investment. It might prove beneficial to invest time and money in further education to improve yourself. This will augment your ability to meet social obligations and enhance your status. You have an aversion to purely mental pursuits, but you should make the effort just the same.

Semisextile: 1, 3   Avoid the inclination to be self-centered in your interests. Other people want life's comforts nearly as much as you do, but you make an issue of it. Don't neglect your human and social values, for they may enhance your position with others far more than a display of possessions. Being is as important as having. In this regard, pay attention to how others round out their lives with varied interests. Be sociable even when you know you won't gain materially from it. By associating with people who have broad interests, you will become better informed and learn of many new ways to enjoy yourself.

1st to the 2nd You generally know what you want, and you use all your talents to get it, especially if it will increase your income. You need a lot of money because you spend freely. Acting on the spur of the moment can cause you financial embarrassment, but you recover quickly.

 2nd to the 1st When you indulge yourself, you don't answer to anyone, but your easy-come, easy-go attitude makes it difficult to accumulate any reserves.

 3rd to the 12th You know how to capitalize on other people's needs. You work hard to provide services that people need, and you expect to be well paid. You consider it a weakness of character to be obligated to others, for it gives them an advantage over you.

 4th to the 11th The need for security for your later years bothers you more than you admit, and you strive to earn as much as possible from your efforts. You may have to mobilize all your resources in a conservative plan of action to reach your goal of freedom from want.

 5th to the 10th You get along with your superiors because you don't threaten them, and you do help them achieve their objectives. You are ambitious, and you know how to cultivate friendly relations with important people to win promotions and increased earnings.

 6th to the 9th You know that further education will improve your competitive position and enable you to convert your knowledge to tangible assets. You hate asking questions, but you value a good suggestion if you can benefit from it.

 7th to the 8th When you observe others achieving financial security from their endeavors, you are stimulated to match or surpass their performances.

 8th to the 7th You find it exciting to have an opportunity to handle other people's assets. Financial counseling might be an attractive field for you.

 9th to the 6th You are wary about forming close ties with associates or with people who show a romantic interest in you. You study these contacts carefully to learn people's motivations for wanting to become aligned with you.

 10th to the 5th Realizing that your rise to prominence will require a great deal of creative effort, you try to utilize all your talents to achieve it. You also hope to encourage your children to take advantage of the opportunities you provide so that they too will reach their goals.

 11th to the 4th The legacy of influence from your parents is a firm base from which to achieve independence and security by your own efforts. You appreciate the advice you received in your early years, for you know that your future security will be derived from it.

 12th to the 3rd Take advantage of your creative ideas and don't underestimate their value. If you make certain of your information before expressing yourself, you will win the trust and assistance you need to fulfill your desires and goals.

Trine: 6, 10 You capitalize on all your resources to get what you want when you want it. A free spender, you will always need a good income to maintain stability, but sometimes you are careless in handling money. You are wary about forming close ties until you know the other person's motives, and you are cautious about contacts that might prove costly in the long run. You should be equally cautious in the way you handle your assets. You are quite clever in cultivating good relationships with your superiors, who are impressed with your ability to help them achieve their job objectives. Your skill in winning support in your profession will pay dividends when you are considered for promotion. In addition to knowing how to put your best foot forward, you also have some insight into your competitors' weaknesses, which gives you an advantage over them. Because you are reasonably ambitious, you could use this information to make substantial gains in your career.

Sextile: 4, 12 In general you understand your failings, but you also are aware of other people's failings. You know how to be helpful to those who genuinely need assistance, but when you provide professional services, you expect to be well paid. You don't want to be obligated to others for fear that this will indicate weakness on your part. You consider yourself quite self-sufficient. Your early environment gave you ample opportunities to learn to make your own way and earn security and independence. You are grateful for your parents' foresight in stimulating you to be self-reliant, and you know that they wanted you to realize your goals.

Cross: 5, 8, 11 You are intimidated when you observe others, especially competitors, making gains from endeavors that you could have been involved in. You judge others by their professional accomplishments and resultant assets. It might be better to develop your own attributes. Others will admire you for your accomplishments if you put forth the energy to exploit your creative talents and if you are willing to forego some of life's pleasures while you pursue that goal. This is the only way you can achieve the stability in your affairs that will give you greater financial independence in your later years. Perhaps your children will provide the stimulus you need to succeed for yourself and to give them opportunities you might have missed.

Inconjunct: 7, 9 In your search for ways to increase your earnings, you might overlook getting an education, which could simplify your problems. You must be willing to extend yourself, no matter how difficult it seems, to improve your skills through suitable training, either in formal, academic schooling or as an apprentice. It will be exciting when people seek your services because they trust your ability to handle their affairs as though they were your own. This course will involve sacrifices, but the eventual dividends will make the sacrifices seem unimportant.

Semisextile: 1, 3 If you take enough time to plan your moves carefully, you will be abundantly rewarded for your efforts. Learn all you can about a situation before expressing your opinion. This will win people's respect and admiration for your rational attitude and incline them to request your services. Your drive and ambition attract notice, but you will have to control your easy-come, easy-go temperament, which might make some people apprehensive about putting their trust in you.

1st to the 2nd   You have a strong desire to grow as a person as well as to increase your tangible assets by capitalizing on your available resources. You are generous to a fault and should learn to be more conservative.

 2nd to the 1st   One of your best attributes is your willingness to assert yourself in hopes that your efforts will be rewarded. You show admirable daring in taking chances, but try to be somewhat cautious so you don't overextend yourself.

 3rd to the 12th   Avoid becoming involved in situations that you are not completely familiar with and those that seem risky. If other people's plans or ideas sound too good to be true, they probably are, so be careful, for you tend to be an easy mark.

 4th to the 11th   Although you may receive some help from your friends, you would rather achieve your goals on your own, because you don't want to be obligated to others. The best base to work from is your personal assets.

 5th to the 10th   You are quick to respond to opportunities in your chosen career. Your skill and talent are probably sought after by your superiors, who know that you will live up to their expectations and even do more than is expected.

 6th to the 9th   You have a reputation for being intelligent and easy to get along with. You are knowledgeable in many subjects, and people enjoy having you around because you help them solve their problems. Because you are trustworthy, people reveal their private lives to you.

 7th to the 8th   You are eager to satisfy other people's needs, no matter whether those needs are physical desires or professional services. There is some envy in you, however, which stimulates you to want as much as others have, if not more.

 8th to the 7th   You intuitively sense what others want, and you are willing to provide those services, as long as they pay you for it. Although you know your true worth, you may overstate it, which will make some people feel intimidated. Don't borrow unnecessarily, for you tend to take on more than you can handle.

 9th to the 6th   You understand that in order to succeed, you must be able to provide services for people who cannot help themselves. You also realize that your ability in your work can be improved by getting further education and training.

 10th to the 5th   Whatever field you choose for a career, you know that you must take advantage of all your creative potentials and make them work for you. You have high expectations for your children and high hopes for your romantic relationships.

 11th to the 4th   Depending on how firmly you establish your roots, you will be able to gain the security you want to indulge yourself in your later years. Your parents provided reasonably good training so that you will be able to achieve your objectives without too much strain.

 12th to the 3rd   If you do everything you say, you should come out well in the end, but often your claims of achievement are little more than plans. Keep your ideas and plans within realizable limits.

Trine: 6, 10 In your desire to develop, you must take advantage of your basic resources. You are generous, but you should exercise greater self-control just for self-preservation until you are more firmly established in your career. You know how to take advantage of opportunities, and you have no difficulty winning support from your superiors, because you always do more than is expected. You also know that to succeed you must get some formal education or special training, and it would be good to take care of this as soon as possible. Education will improve your ability to serve other people who cannot help themselves, thus assuring your own feeling of fulfillment.

Sextile: 4, 12 You are aware of your own limits, and you understand why you must never get involved in a situation without being thoroughly informed about it. You realize that you should avoid schemes that seem too good to be true. Still, you want so much to make some contribution to the world that you might become careless and give the people you deal with too much benefit of the doubt. You want to establish your own roots, and the early conditioning and wise counsel of your parents or guardians should help you achieve this objective without difficulty. You know that your future security depends on how well you build the foundation for your life now.

Cross: 5, 8, 11 You have little excuse for not achieving substantial growth in your personal and professional affairs. Your envy of others' success is sufficient to stir you to action to acquire as much as they have. You also want to influence important people who can provide opportunities for you. But you prefer not to rely too much on friends, because you don't want to be obligated to them. You would rather make full use of your assets and resources to win a place for yourself in your chosen field. This means that you must develop and use all of your creative talents as the key to opportunity. It would be a serious mistake to overindulge in pleasurable activities that take time and energy away from your career. In your love relationships, your high expectations could strain your finances because you like to indulge yourself and your partner. It would be better to apply your energy and resources for your children, so that they may benefit from your experience when they go their own way.

Inconjunct: 7, 9 You easily convince people that they need your services. Because you are so knowledgeable, people enjoy your company, and they know you can help them solve their problems. Your intuition tells you the right thing to say, which will enhance your reputation. You would probably succeed as a counselor or financial adviser, because people freely share their secrets with you. Some may be intimidated by your expertise in many subjects, but that's their problem. Learn to control your spending, for you tend to go beyond your means, and don't borrow unless you cannot avoid it. Be ready to make concessions to others if you want their support when an opportunity comes up. The sacrifices you make will be a wise investment in your future.

Semisextile: 1, 3 Be as eager to fulfill your promises as you are to take advantage of your natural talents and resources. Unless you are prepared to carry out your plans, stifle the inclination to tell everyone about them. You can certainly come out well in any endeavor you attempt because you have faith in your ability to succeed. Try to consolidate your efforts so as to derive the best results from any activity.

1st to the 2nd You value your assets and resources and use them conservatively, but you tend to underestimate your competence. You are cautious about mobilizing your talents for fear of being ridiculed if the results are not what you expected.

 2nd to the 1st You make only those promises that you can fulfill, and you expect others to honor their contracts as well. While you may not be especially aggressive in your dealings, everything you have has been earned.

 3rd to the 12th Other people do not share your low opinion of yourself, for you are stable, self-disciplined and dependable in your financial dealings. Most people respect you for this and admire your sense of ethics.

 4th to the 11th You choose as friends only those who will respect your privacy and won't interfere in your affairs. Fear of being dependent on anyone makes you plan for your future security. You judge people by the criteria of acquisitions and accomplishments.

 5th to the 10th In your professional endeavors you try to satisfy your responsibilities, but you don't usually volunteer extra services unless you will be paid for your efforts. You easily win the confidence of your superiors for your professionalism and creativity.

 6th to the 9th You are probably well-trained and do your job well, and it is unlikely that you will lose it to a more capable person. You value the training and education you have gone through, knowing how much hard work it required.

 7th to the 8th You are intimidated when challenged by someone who is less capable, but you eagerly accept competition when your opponent has skills that you admire. Your mate must have qualities that you respect, such as honesty, determination, self-reliance and responsibility.

 8th to the 7th Others must show interest in you before you are willing to make an emotional commitment to them. But you will extend yourself and make substantial sacrifices for the person who shows definite signs of affection for you.

 9th to the 6th Long ago you learned that the only way to succeed is to be the best in your field. So you make a heavy investment to develop your talents. Your fellow workers might consider you a bit detached, but they cannot fail to recognize your skill.

 10th to the 5th You are annoyed when people use their position to win your submission, but this will change as you become more proficient. You know how to get the best results with the least effort by using your talents efficiently.

 11th to the 4th Your home is probably your castle, and you remember your parents' advice fondly. Real estate could be important to you and provide the future security you want.

 12th to the 3rd You don't indulge in idle conversation unless you have something important to say. Contemplative by nature, you spend a lot of time trying to find the best use for your creative talents. Your silence may annoy those who want to share their thoughts with you.

Trine: 6, 10 You concentrate on utilizing your material resources productively to earn a comfortable income. However, you underestimate your competence, assuming that someone else with your talents would do more. This makes you constantly strive to excel in your field of endeavor, which is how you will achieve recognition. With your low self-image, it is important to be the best in order to improve your chances for success. You must make a heavy investment in developing your creative potentials so that you will be qualified to take on increasing responsibilities. Your attention to your duties endears you to your superiors, who admire your resourcefulness and imagination. This is the only way you can truly enjoy what you do. You are determined to learn as much as possible in your field in order to have security and independence.

Sextile: 4, 12 You are better informed than you realize and more qualified to achieve your goals. People respect your determination and self-discipline, and they know they can depend on you to help them solve their problems. You are concerned about social problems at all levels of society—local, national and international. You are grateful for your parents' influence in helping you shape your own life, and you want to win their respect and admiration for your accomplishments. A home of your own gives you a sense of "belonging" and the comfort of having roots. You are willing to work for life's necessities, and because you are basically honest in financial dealings, you have no uncomfortable moments when you reflect on your achievements.

Cross: 5, 8, 11 The best way to improve your self-image and understand your abilities is to accept challenges from qualified competitors. You must realize that you have much to offer and can compete successfully. When you know your capabilities as well as your limitations, you will no longer fear people who try to intimidate you and win your submission. You owe it to yourself to translate your creative potentials into useful skills that will eventually bring you the security you want. This will also eliminate your apprehension about having to depend on others later in life. This could be a problem, because you don't have a wide circle of friends who could help you.

Inconjunct: 7, 9 You try very hard to understand people, and you probably had to apply yourself diligently to get an education. By being a good listener, you learn a lot about people. People tell you their secrets because they sense that they can trust you with privileged information. If someone needs help, you extend yourself freely, even making some sacrifices. This is also true for those to whom you are emotionally drawn, but you rarely make a commitment until you are sure that the feeling is mutual.

Semisextile: 1, 3 Your cautious nature protects you from losses, but it also denies you many benefits that you could enjoy by being more aggressive. Your mind works overtime trying to solve problems that haven't even cropped up. You are eager to acquire as much information as possible, and you spend a lot of time thinking deeply about ways to apply the knowledge you have. You strain at the bit in anticipation of the chance to use what you know to improve your earning ability. Learn to share whatever information you have, and don't be afraid to admit that you don't know something. No one can know everything, so why should you be any different?

1st to the 2nd   Although you are generally indifferent about money, you show remarkable ingenuity in getting it when you need it. You are more interested in the freedom that money can provide than in the money itself. You never want to become a slave to material concerns.

 2nd to the 1st   You reserve the privilege of seeking your fortune in any way you see fit. You want to find a way to earn what you need without sacrificing the freedom you value so highly. You also try to avoid any occupation that would force you into a boring and dull routine.

 3rd to the 12th   You probably have hidden talents that you want to exploit, but you might experience some problems in trying to translate them into cash. With your concern for the problems of society, you could apply your skills to help find solutions.

 4th to the 11th   You look to the future with great anticipation of realizing all of your goals. In order to enjoy that kind of success and the independence it brings, you must plan now and apply yourself. Be wary of friends who just want to ride on the crest of your success.

 5th to the 10th   Your indifference about achieving goals is not encouraging. You aren't too impressed with acquiring status because of the restrictions that go with it. Unless you enjoy your career, everything you derive from it will mean little. You bring much creative intuition to your professional activities.

 6th to the 9th   You place a high value on honesty. Through some ingenious method you will acquire the education you need to achieve your goals.

 7th to the 8th   People who show off their assets really annoy you. You are much more fascinated if they can demonstrate superior skills and explain how they used them for a productive and useful purpose.

 8th to the 7th   Though you are willing to make sacrifices to help others, you won't make concessions just to smooth the way in dealing with people. You are curious about the motives of people who strive to acquire material possessions.

 9th to the 6th   You usually see through people who distort the truth or whose ethical standards seem questionable. But you permit them to do what they want, as long as they don't try to interfere with you.

 10th to the 5th   You are sufficiently satisfied with your frame of reference, and you know that to succeed you must depend on your own creative potentials. You want a lover who will sustain you in your defeats as well as share in your successes.

 11th to the 4th   You stay on good terms with your parents, even though they may not understand your occasional detachment. Because they respect your need to develop your own identity, they are willing to give you sufficient room to grow.

 12th to the 3rd   You remind people that you will pursue your own course in life no matter what they say. You don't mind reversals because you know they are to be expected. But you wish people would stop implying that you are unstable and undependable.

Trine: 6, 10 You are more concerned about human values than about money, although you know that money can bring you greater freedom from the tedious, routine ways of earning a living. You prefer to devise innovative methods to satisfy your needs, so that earning a living becomes interesting and challenging. You have only a modest desire for material possessions, because you don't want to be a victim of your possessions. Likewise you are uninterested in status because of the restrictions it imposes. You do impress your superiors, and if you are motivated, you could easily win public recognition for your accomplishments. You accomplish a great deal in your career because you make the most of your opportunities. You quickly detect insincerity and dishonesty in people, but you don't usually interfere as long as they don't try to involve you. You can succeed without resorting to underhanded methods and always have freedom to come and go as you want.

Sextile: 4, 12 You have talents that you haven't yet uncovered, but you must accept responsibility for developing them. This untapped potential can increase your earnings and give you greater freedom. You are concerned about social conditions that demand improvement, but you doubt that you could do anything to help. The favorable conditioning of your early years has allowed you to make your own way with few restrictions. You hope to retire early enough to enjoy the benefits of your productive years and indulge yourself without worrying about money.

Cross: 5, 8, 11 You don't respond when people try to impress you by displaying their possessions, but you are favorably impressed when they demonstrate how they have used their skills for meaningful accomplishments. You are moved by the positive qualities that have enabled them to use their time and energy productively. You hope to do the same, and you look to the future with high expectations of achieving your goals. But success requires planning; very little happens by chance alone. Choose your friends carefully and be wary of those who just want to ride along on your success. Your ability to separate personal from professional affairs is admirable, but you may not form any permanent ties until your career is well established. You want your children to have the same self-determination that you had, and you hope that they will demonstrate their strength as individuals.

Inconjunct: 7, 9 You have a natural ability to get the training you need to succeed. You might consider the long process of formal education too painful to endure, but think of what you will gain from your efforts over a lifetime. There are few easy roads to success, and avoiding responsibility isn't one of them. You must make sacrifices in order to earn a better position. When you realize how highly motivated your competitors are, you might apply yourself more energetically.

Semisextile: 1, 3 Don't put such a high value on your personal freedom that it prevents you from accepting responsibility, for that is an opportunity to establish your credentials and prove your worth. You are gifted with ideas and the ability to solve problems, but those are assets only if you use them. Your annoyance with people who insist that you could do more is an admission that you doubt your abilities, and it proves that you do lack stability and dependability to some extent.

1st to the 2nd Your earnings fluctuate with the times, so that you seem to be in a constant state of instability. You tend to get less for your efforts than others do, or so you think. Be realistic about your earning ability and be disciplined in spending money.

 2nd to the 1st Feeling that your efforts don't produce the results you want, you assume that you have overestimated your abilities. But don't criticize yourself too severely when your earnings decrease; the fault may be in the general economy and not in your own ability.

 3rd to the 12th Apprehensive about future security, you borrow now and then to tide you over until conditions improve. But it is a mistake to do so unless you are absolutely sure that your low economic situation is only temporary.

 4th to the 11th Your security must come from your own efforts. This is the only way to avoid asking your friends for help, which sometimes causes friendships to erode. Learn how to make careful plans, or have someone help you plan.

 5th to the 10th By paying close attention to reality, you can rise to considerable prominence. You may feel you aren't being paid as well as you deserve in your career, but the best way to correct this is by doing the very best job you can.

 6th to the 9th Don't fail to get an education, for that will enable you to demand as much for your efforts as the market will tolerate. If you don't know exactly what kind of training you need, consult a vocational counselor to determine what field your skills are best fitted for.

 7th to the 8th Avoid comparing your accomplishments and earnings with other people's. Instead, compare the talent and energy you put forth. Remember that it is unwise to lend money, because your chances of recovering it are not great.

 8th to the 7th If you must invest, seek the services of an advisor. Never form an alliance without getting legal advice to make sure your interests are protected. Also you should investigate what motivates your associates in their dealings with you. Don't assume that your mate wants more than you can give.

 9th to the 6th Stay informed about current business trends and get whatever training is necessary to fill the demand. If you diversify your skills, you will always have a job, and nothing will be left to chance.

 10th to the 5th If you believe in yourself, you can achieve almost anything. Capitalize on your creative imagination, but be realistic about your abilities, or you will suffer disappointments. Satisfying the needs of the people you love may give you enough reason to achieve.

 11th to the 4th You must be willing to pursue your objectives alone. If you want to be free from obligation to others, you must make a plan for your own future.

 12th to the 3rd You have enormous creative resources that you can effectively harness for your benefit. Don't listen to people who say "You can't do this," or "You can't do that." You should conserve your tangible assets and establish a retirement program that you can adhere to without difficulty.

Trine: 6, 10 You seem uncertain about your career, as though you weren't sure of yourself or your abilities. You may feel that you aren't adequately rewarded or that you are often overlooked when a promotion is in order. You tend to be pessimistic, and you seem to have difficulty in holding on to your assets. But it is futile to assume anything about other people's finances and savings. The issue is whether you can evaluate your own assets and resources fairly. Your earnings tend to reflect the current economic picture, so it is essential to save regularly as a cushion against adverse conditions. Use your imagination to seek a career that will give you the greatest yield. You cannot afford to do anything less than your very best in your field. Don't accept a low profile in your job; if you do, you will find yourself permanently assigned to it. Stay informed about business trends and retrain yourself if necessary to stay employed. Instead of feeling sorry for yourself, use that energy to develop more diversified skills.

Sextile: 4, 12 You can easily identify with other's needs if they parallel your own. You may want to consider a career that serves broad social needs, for your sympathetic nature could be effective in that area. By observing others' insecurity in this kind of endeavor, you can increase your own feeling of security. Also you would derive much contentment from doing something worthwhile while earning a good living. Learn to stand alone and devise a program that will provide for your future independence and security. You need to be free from feelings of obligation to others.

Cross: 5, 8, 11 Comparing your accomplishments with other people's will just wear you down. There is much you can do to prove that you have skills and talents; it's a matter of finding how you can help fulfill people's needs. You have some psychic ability, which could be advantageous in professions such as medicine, research, working with animals or psychology. Psychic investigation could give you the opportunity to demonstrate your skills. Avoid lending money unless it is absolutely necessary, for your future security may be threatened by such practices. Believe in yourself and trust that you *will* succeed when you learn self-discipline. Serving the people you love may stimulate you to achieve when you would not do it for yourself.

Inconjunct: 7, 9 Getting an education should have a high priority in your life, because being well informed reduces the factor of chance in your accomplishments. There is no excuse today for not getting some formal training for a meaningful career. With education or training you are in a position to demand as much for your talents as the market will tolerate. Never form an alliance without legal advice to protect your interests. You want a lot for the partner you choose, perhaps much more than he or she wants for himself. You don't have to prove your love by how much you can provide—the sacrifices you make certainly attest to that fact.

Semisextile: 1, 3 Your many ideas only need to be implemented to prove that you are able to stand your ground and earn a comfortable income. The worst way to handle this would be to spend valuable energy complaining about a problem when you could use your creative imagination to solve it. Learn to turn a deaf ear to people who say, "You can't do this," or "You can't do that." What do they know?

1st to the 2nd   You tend to overestimate your power, based on your accumulated assets. If you are motivated by the desire to do whatever you want with your power, people are likely to resent you.

 2nd to the 1st   If you go to extremes in pressuring people to submit to your desires, you might lose much more than you gain. When you realize that generosity is its own reward, you can be enormously helpful to those who need help, and they will appreciate it.

 3rd to the 12th   You understand your obligations to society, and with a little effort you can help solve many of its problems. It's simply a matter of giving society what it requires, while still satisfying your own needs.

 4th to the 11th   You can enjoy a comfortable life if you plan ahead for your future financial independence. You must know that you can't indulge yourself during your productive years and then expect others to sustain you later.

 5th to the 10th   Few people will resist your demands as you strive for an important position. Your superiors are impressed with your abilities, and you should have little difficulty in getting what you want in your career.

 6th to the 9th   A professional or political career might seem attractive because you could have the authority to accomplish your desires. There is a spiritual factor underlying your eagerness to handle this kind of social responsibility.

 7th to the 8th   Your values will be challenged by people with different opinions, and those who envy your accomplishments may harass you. But because you are secure in the righteousness of your own motivations, you fear no adversaries.

 8th to the 7th   You could succeed in finance and investment because you understand money and have a flair for making it serve those who have it. Your intuition is helpful in making investments. You know what people expect of you, and you capitalize on this.

 9th to the 6th   Whether or not you can reach your objectives depends on getting the right training and education. You need polished skills and total awareness of your abilities in order to reach the limits of your potentials.

 10th to the 5th   You know your abilities as well as your limits. Love is an important force in your life and may be the catalyst for your success. Providing for your children's needs stimulates you to extend yourself.

 11th to the 4th   You should have everything you need for your later years. You hope to have enough time and money to help solve the problems of society. You will probably get involved in social programs and make a fine contribution to society.

 12th to the 3rd   Don't be so preoccupied with acquisitions that you communicate with the world around you only on your own terms. If you adopt a more spiritual attitude, you will be ready when someone needs help. More than other people, you can alter the destinies of those who are unable to help themselves.

Trine: 6, 10 You place much emphasis on accumulating possessions because they give you an artificial sense of power. Regardless of your motives for acquiring these resources, you risk incurring other people's resentment if you use your assets to enforce your will. It is natural for people to fear and resent someone who uses this kind of advantage. You generally get what you want by impressing people in important positions that you can accomplish almost anything if given the opportunity. You should have little difficulty with superiors, for they will delegate to you the necessary authority to satisfy their objectives. You have the savoir-faire to use your skills effectively and attain the limits of your potentials. You will probably succeed because you are not afraid to take chances in demonstrating your abilities, which you do with dramatic flair.

Sextile: 4, 12 You realize the importance of making some contribution to fulfill your social obligations. Perhaps you are motivated by a feeling of guilt for having prospered at the expense of the public, or perhaps you understand and want to help solve the awesome problems of society. You doubtless will have everything you need to enjoy a fairly early retirement, and your free time will allow you to become involved in the needs of the public.

Cross: 5, 8, 11 You have a powerful urge to be secure and totally independent of others. You will probably make investments or invest in a retirement plan that will assure you of this goal. But you will attract hangers-on who will try to talk you into sharing your bounty with them. The only way this could be a problem is if you've accepted favors in the past that you must repay. You know your abilities and your limits. However, the important factor is love, which may have inspired you to succeed. The need to serve your children's best interests will certainly be a major consideration as you exploit your creative talents to the fullest.

Inconjunct: 7, 9 It will take a lot of moral fortitude to resist the temptation to get what you want through collusion or by issuing ultimatums. But with some religious training or spiritual awareness, you can easily achieve your goals without resorting to those methods. You've probably had to work hard to learn as much as you have, and you pride yourself on being a self-made person. You understand the power associated with money, and you also recognize the social responsiblity this entails. Your intuition will help you make wise investments, both for yourself and in counseling others. You put a high premium on your services because you know you can get the results people want. When the price is right, you don't deny yourself whatever you can get, either in acquiring worldly goods or satisfying physical desires.

Semisextile: 1, 3 Try to communicate with people in terms that they can understand. Learn to relate to others and encourage them to trust you. You can be a positive force, helping people gain confidence to seek their own destinies. A little sharing can pay big dividends when you observe the fruits of your efforts to help people who need your stimulating encouragement. You cannot fail to win their appreciation. Don't be afraid to ask how you can help, for the chances are you can do much more than you realize.

Sun in Second, Moon in First

This combination makes it difficult for you to get started, so there may be considerable delay before you can realize your ambitions and gain the security and stability you want. The basic problem is that your emotional nature frequently distracts you; you assume that others are more qualified than you, which is not true at all. You are too preoccupied with yourself. You should direct some of your energy toward others, with whom you must work to establish a place for yourself in society. Try to play down your emotions and rely more on the evidence before you act.

You should become established in your career before you think about forming a permanent relationship. You cannot afford to deal with emotional distress while trying to stay focused in the demands of your career. Your need to share your life with someone makes you vulnerable to anyone who gives you attention. Learn to stand on your own with the positive affirmation that you can and will succeed.

You will be happier if you are self-employed, so that the pressure of competition can be deferred until you gain more self-confidence. Then you will thrive on proving that you offer a better product or service than your competitors. Try to get away from your daily routine now and then to replenish your energy and enthusiasm.

Sun in Second, Moon in Second

Your drive to gain security and stability can carry you away to the point of paranoia. If you are driven in this way, it is a sign of your deep insecurity about your own self-worth. By accepting your responsibility for developing your creative potentials and by learning to apply them gainfully, insecurity need not be such an important issue. You are impressed with matters that are visible and tangible, and you use that medium to determine your success, often making nonproductive comparisons between what you have versus what others have. This is a waste of valuable time.

You could find satisfaction in such fields as financial management, land development, or investments involving natural resources. You have a sixth sense that only needs cultivating to reap the benefits. You probably have a feel about situations that alerts you to examine them more carefully before making a commitment. As time passes, you can rely more on this faculty to "tune you in" to what's happening.

You have a highly developed libido, and you need a partner who is equal to it to keep you satisfied. It may be a good idea to postpone marriage until you are sure you have found a suitable partner for a long-term contractual relationship. You are not overly indulgent with your children, a quality that will make them respect you.

Sun in Second, Moon in Third

You desire a comfortable lifestyle that will allow you to develop your many interests. You enjoy social gatherings and pleasurable activities with close friends. Your ample curiosity makes you a good conversationalist, though you may get ponderous when making a point. You generally speak out only when you are well informed about the subject. You need to overcome your fear of making mistakes, for only by taking chances can you realize success.

You work well with people in such fields as communications, investigative journalism or education. You have the persistence to derive the most minutely detailed information with all the supportive evidence to justify your position.

You are probably more generous with strangers than with those who are closest to you. You are a disciplinarian to your children, because of your concern for their growth and maturation. Though you are extremely inquisitive about others, you rarely share your innermost thoughts with anyone except perhaps your partner. You feel most secure in the relationship when the lines of communication are open, and any tension that exists can be discussed and cleared to your satisfaction.

Sun in Second, Moon in Fourth

You have a highly sensitive nature with a strong need for material security. The sooner you become self-sufficient, the sooner you can feel comfortable in a family life of your own where others depend on you. Emotionally vulnerable as you are, you want the stability of a comfortable income before starting a family of your own. Before you can offer assistance to others, you need to establish yourself.

You are temperamentally suited for a career dealing with the everyday problems people have to cope with, for you can offer them useful guidelines. A career in business is fine if it brings you into close contact with the public; home management, real estate, property investment or vocational guidance for young persons would also be suitable. You have a keen imagination and the ability to appraise situations accurately through an active sixth sense. You do well in enterprises that involve contact with the public.

Your partner must be someone who is devoted to you and who appreciates what you do for the family. Your children know that you usually give in to their demands when they turn on the charm.

Sun in Second, Moon in Fifth

You appreciate the pleasures of the good life, which you can easily gain by taking advantage of your gifted imagination to promote and utilize your talents. Self-discipline is essential to derive all the benefits from your potentials; once developed, they will yield constant gains. The principal deterrent you may face is being distracted by romantic alliances or by other personal pleasures that drain your financial resources.

Fulfillment in your career comes through making a determined effort and mobilizing your resources efficiently. This may include making a sacrifice to get whatever training you need. You might find a career in education, vocational training, recreational enterprises or investment appealing. They certainly are compatible with your nature and with your ability to deal with pressures.

You probably have a rare closeness with those you love in that you participate with them in their interests. This is sure to produce a tightly knit family group that appeals to you in every way.

Sun in Second, Moon in Sixth

You feel secure and are well organized for achieving your goals. You know that you have the necessary resources with which to succeed, and you have a talent for making the most of them. You have well-developed values and can derive satisfactory results with even the most modest resources. You expect a lot out of life and are resourceful and enterprising enough to reach your objectives.

You probably do best if you are self-employed so that you can pace your own growth. You would feel restricted in organizations that limited your progress or didn't recognize your capabilities. Your greatest asset is your skill in solving problems, which can be applied in many different situations. A career in masonry, carpentry, heating and refrigeration or general construction might be rewarding. In any case you would rise to a level of responsibility in managing operations. You are a "can do" individual who is sometimes impatient with theory when practical sense is required.

Though devoted to your family, you may experience some difficulty with your partner if furthering your goals requires you to be increasingly absent from the domestic scene. You justify your dedication to the demands of your career with your children's needs, and this is difficult to challenge.

Sun in Second, Moon in Seventh

You do not function at your best unless you are involved in some kind of relationship. You will seek a career that provides a substantial income to satisfy the obligations of a relationship, to lessen the pain of being away from the person you love. You feel that you must make special efforts to prove yourself to the one you love, as though your personality were not attractive enough for a romantic alliance, which is not the case, of course. Perhaps the environment in which you grew up conditioned you to expect failure in romance, or you may still have strong ties to your family, making it difficult to get involved in a personal relationship. Time will alleviate this problem. Once involved in a permanent relationship, you will be able to make worthwhile strides in your career and your other interests. Selling would be a suitable career and would show you how well you perform in dealing with people. You can win the public's sympathy with your warmth and sincerity.

The contacts you make through your partner could give you the opportunity to rise to prominence in your career, thus allowing you and your family to have everything that makes for a satisfying relationship.

Sun in Second, Moon in Eighth

The uncomfortable contrast between your active desire nature and your passive emotional nature is often projected as confusion about who and what you are. You want to find the answer reflected in those around you, especially the people whom you are close to. You want so much for others to need you that you sometimes pursue them in hopes of making them dependent on you. Through them you want to learn more about how you function, and eventually, you hope to gain a truer perspective of yourself and a more serene outlook on life.

You attract only people who can give you a glimpse of yourself as you are reflected in them. As a rather harsh example, you might attract cantankerous or argumentative people because you haven't dealt with that inclination in yourself and you need to see it dramatized in others. It might be advantageous to select a career in which you help people with their problems, such as medicine, research or counseling.

Your children may feel that you are unable or unwilling to understand them, because you seem preoccupied with your partner and with deriving contentment for yourself. Your partner may expect so much from you that it is difficult to cope with the tension. If you persist, you will be able to deal with this.

Sun in Second, Moon in Ninth

You are geared for success in your accomplishments, provided you get the necessary training to excel in your creative development. Your psychological makeup is indicative of a true professional who is eager to improve the quality of life for the people whom you contact, both professionally and socially. There is a contradiction in this placement, for which you must be accountable. The Sun's position shows that you expect to be paid well for your services, but the Moon's position requires you to provide help even when it seems clear that you won't be paid. This does not mean that you must become a victim; your emotional nature impels you to extend yourself to those who need help, but you are realistic enough to know your limitations. Eventually you will learn where to draw the line.

Many fields are suitable for your temperament, including politics, education, writing, journalism, law and medicine. You would do well in industry, but that would not allow you to use your skills to best advantage.

Your partner should be as informed and growth-oriented as you are. You need someone who understands you and who is willing to grow with you in your relationship. You expect your children to abide by the rules, but you give them all the love they need.

Sun in Second, Moon in Tenth

You will very likely achieve success in your endeavors because your need to assert yourself is well integrated with your emotional stability. You can function smoothly with few distressing situations, which you handle adequately when they do occur. You have a natural talent for doing the right thing at the right time to gain what you want. However, that does not mean you will necessarily utilize your potentials fully, since this blend often produces considerable apathy.

A public career would be ideal for you and would allow you to enjoy a better than average income. You have the ability to elicit the best response from your superiors, colleagues and the public you serve. This combination does indicate problems involving your partner. Your devotion to duty and career security may interfere with the time you spend with your mate, so problems could develop. Your high earnings may temporarily keep your partner from taking action, but resentment seems certain to grow if the condition persists.

Sun in Second, Moon in Eleventh

Your desire for security is frustrated because you find it difficult to make the necessary investment of time and energy. This becomes a self-defeating situation, in that your unwillingness to let go of the past increases your anxieties about the future. Make a determined effort to use your resources more efficiently in a program to realize your plans for the future. Once you get over your initial fear of reversals, you will be able to face the days ahead more effectively. Close friends may try to use you to benefit themselves, so be wary of forming ties. Lack of self-discipline is the greatest deterrent to your success in a responsible position. Learn to accept people in positions of authority, and be willing to learn new skills so you are ready when an opportunity is presented.

Your partner is more supportive of your needs than you realize and is a true friend as well. Pay attention to your mate's suggestions, which certainly deserve consideration. You have enough talent to enjoy a comfortable life that fulfills your children's needs.

Sun in Second, Moon in Twelfth

Your desire for security and stability in your daily life does not interfere with your ability to render worthwhile services to those who need assistance. Your compassion goes out to people who must live in uncomfortable circumstances through no fault of their own. Probably you do extend yourself to fulfill your social obligations. Though a second-house Sun does not generally indicate a giver, you are sentimental enough to feel uneasy when you don't. Your willingness to listen to people who come to you with problems is often helpful to them. Your inner and outer worlds are reasonably harmonious and you telegraph this orderliness to those around you.

Your creative ideas are substantial, and they work because you embroider them with imagination before they are implemented. You could derive much satisfaction in a career of service to the public, especially in major programs to improve the quality of people's lives, perhaps in a retirement or convalescent home, medical or rehabilitative therapy facility. You should also enjoy happiness with your partner, although your devotion to duty can cause some strain unless you both are involved in the enterprise.

Chapter Three

Third House

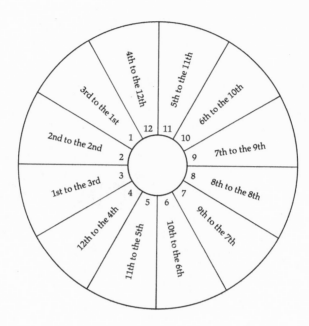

Your earliest attempts to participate in the affairs of the world around you occur through the circumstances of the third house. This house is subtly associated with Gemini, and through it you can enlarge your field of activity in the world. You ask questions to satisfy your increasing curiosity about your immediate surroundings. You developed the ability to communicate with others, which will eventually allow you to establish yourself in a broader social environment. Through the circumstances of this house, you developed ideas and opinions; ultimately, the most refined answers are derived through the influence of the ninth house, which is opposite the third. Your opinions and attitudes result from the desires and ambitions expressed in the first house, which develop substance and purpose in the third house. In this process you have to find ways to solve any prolems that come up, which is how you learn to give meaning to your life and your endeavors.

Through this house you learn how to share your thoughts and ideas with those closest to you, such as your brothers and sisters at first and the people you encounter daily later on. The seeds of cooperation are sown in this house; you learn how to make concessions to others whose opinions and attitudes differ from yours. An incredible amount of learning takes place in the early years, and an important part of that is learning to live in harmony with others.

Derivative House Meanings

1st to the 3rd   Through the circumstances of this house, you become involved with the world around you. Your mental faculties are enhanced by social contact.

2nd to the 2nd   Your ideas improve your potential for increased earnings if you apply them toward that objective. You generally know what you are worth.

3rd to the 1st   Ambition and desire must be blended with intellectual skill so that you can devise a plan that will allow you to gain your objectives.

4th to the 12th   Any feeling of frustration about reaching your goals probably results from overemphasizing your inadequacies. Study yourself and be free.

5th to the 11th   Once you define your goals, the feeling of elation will enable you to better utilize your ideas with endless plans for achieving them.

6th to the 10th   Your ideas and your energetic efforts will allow you to realize your ambitions. Worry in your job can cause some physical discomfort.

7th to the 9th   Your greatest test is trying to live up to your claims. A good education will relieve this anxiety. Others respect your knowledge.

8th to the 8th   You get your best stimulation from knowing that others depend on you in their moment of need. With this motivation, you make sacrifices for them.

9th to the 7th   The public expects a lot from you and often seeks your help with their problems. You have the understanding they require.

10th to the 6th   Your mental tension is relieved when you work diligently to gain the skills that are necessary to achieve the position you want.

11th to the 5th   Concerned for your children's future, you try to make the most of your creative potential, which benefits both them and you.

12th to the 4th   Because you are overly focused on intellectual matters, you may fail to develop the sensitivity that will endear you to your closest friends.

1st to the 3rd You satisfy your urge for creative expression by using your skills in effective communication. You are eager to know as much as possible about a variety of subjects, but you are easily distracted, and your attention tends to wander.

 2nd to the 2nd You earn a substantial income by taking advantage of your creative assets and capitalizing on your wealth of ideas. Once your mind is made up, you make every possible contact to put your plan into action.

 3rd to the 1st No one else could promote you as well as you can. You realize that a valuable idea is useless unless you spread it around. Open and free with your opinions, you let everyone know where you stand.

 4th to the 12th Learn to guard against making careless remarks that could undermine people's trust in you. Be informed before saying anything and resist the temptation to circulate rumors. You could be sorry when they finally get back to you.

 5th to the 11th You have excellent prospects for getting everything you want out of life, because you don't live in the past. You know how to use your talents and resources to plan for your future. Help your friends when they need it, for they probably helped you earlier.

 6th to the 10th Knowing that success requires determination and hard work, you tend to overextend yourself physically. Your superiors admire you for doing more than your share of tasks. By being more moderate you can avoid exhaustion and anxiety from overwork.

 7th to the 9th To successfully meet the challenge of competition, you must get an education. Don't allow others to intimidate you because of your lack of training. You cannot afford to turn down chances for advancement.

 8th to the 8th You have a gift for anticipating other people's moves in their dealings with you. You can improve your public image by making occasional sacrifices to help others who are truly in need. You probably indulge in private sexual fantasies.

 9th to the 7th Your flair for saying the right thing at the right time endears you to others. You might apply this talent in public relations, teaching or a similar field. There is a better than average chance that you will meet your mate while you are in school.

 10th to the 6th Your wealth of ideas is not enough to guarantee success; you must also be willing to work to promote them. Be alert to the possibility of professional envy from your fellow workers and be discriminating about the people with whom you share information.

 11th to the 5th With your skill in effective communication and your seemingly inexhaustible creative ability, your future looks bright. You need a family or close friends who can share your good fortune and make the effort seem worthwhile and satisfying.

 12th to the 4th Develop your talents as soon as you can, for you will work better if you become independently secure. You must seek your own goals rather than those suggested by your parents, and you must be flexible enough to take advantage of opportunities.

Trine: 7, 11 Your affable disposition is the result of having so many interests and wanting to stay in the mainstream of social activity. Your ability to express yourself dramatically attracts people's attention. Your views are reasonably well informed, but you are willing to change them as you gain new information. You are eager to get on with achieving your goals, and your optimism about the future helps you get through difficult situations. You do learn from past mistakes, which helps you plan more carefully for the goals you aspire to reach. If you put your ideas into action you are very likely to get what you want out of life. Luckily, your easy way with words convinces people to give you the necessary cooperation for success in your endeavors. A formal education will enhance your natural talents and give you greater finesse and polish. Public relations, education, writing or a related profession would give you the stage you need to express your creative potentials.

Sextile: 1, 5 Because you express yourself freely, everyone knows exactly where you stand. Your self-promotion yields significant results, for you realize that your innovative mind is useful only when you apply it and spread your ideas around. You are optimistic that your children will fare as well, and you hope their success will justify the energy and effort you've expended on them. You are a friend to your children and should enjoy good relations with them throughout your life.

Cross: 6, 9, 12 It is urgent that you acquire as much training as possible in order to deal successfully with competitors. With education, your ability to meet challenges will improve so much that no one will be able to intimidate you with claims of great competence. You must be as determined to find answers as you are to ask questions, or you will be poorly equipped for open competition. Be sure that you don't overstate your abilities, because making claims about your qualifications that you cannot possibly live up to will certainly ruin your image. You might be tempted to do this because you are repelled by the idea of being forced into an obscure position. But this need never happen if you use your natural talent for learning. If you develop great expertise in your career, your credentials will certainly be recognized.

Inconjunct: 8, 10 More important than merely talking about what you hope to achieve is the need to physically apply yourself to that objective. It will mean hard work, but few alternatives will give you the same yield. You will have no difficulty convincing superiors of your capabilities, and your chances for improving your position on the job are better than most people's. You may have to make some sacrifices on your way up the ladder, but such an investment will pay handsome dividends. Don't be afraid to help someone who is in a similar position, for that can be an investment also. Those you help will reciprocate with favors when you need help in the future.

Semisextile: 2, 4 If you want to derive the utmost benefit from your natural talents, you must establish your independence as early in life as possible. The longer you delay making your own decisions, the more opportunities you will miss. It is especially important that your decisions be based strictly on your own beliefs rather than on your parents' ideas. Thinking for yourself is the first step toward building an identity that is exclusively your own.

1st to the 3rd   You are naturally inquisitive, especially about your immediate environment and family. Your mind is quite retentive, and you rarely forget anything you learn. But your emotional bias makes it difficult to separate fact from fiction sometimes.

 2nd to the 2nd   Security is very important to you, and being well informed helps you find ways to be secure. With your imaginative personality, you can choose among many careers. Dealing with the public would be one way to use your talent effectively.

 3rd to the 1st   You are afraid that people may reject you, so you spend much time in self-analysis in order to learn how to win their approval. You underestimate your talents and assume that others are more capable, but people are impressed with how well informed you are.

 4th to the 12th   You want to be loved and appreciated and may choose to remain obscure until you are sure you won't be rejected. You focus too much on your failings and assume that others are trying to take advantage of you.

 5th to the 11th   Your friends probably like you more than you like yourself. You like doing things for them to show you care, and they reciprocate. Putting your creative imagination to work will help alleviate your insecurity about your future.

 6th to the 10th   Because of your feelings of insecurity, you extend yourself more than necessary in your career. You feel you have to do more in order to get the results you want. Limit the amount of your time that you volunteer.

 7th to the 9th   With your easy-going personality, you must be more aggressive in making beneficial personal contacts, especially with people who are well informed. Encourage contacts with people whom you admire, for they may also stimulate your development.

 8th to the 8th   You are somewhat defensive when others show an interest in you, because you question their motives. Give people a chance to show their intentions before you jump to conclusions. You are unsure whether their interest is physical or intellectual.

 9th to the 7th   You are impressed with those who have strong religious convictions and whose ethical standards aren't easily swayed. You learn from every person you meet, and you impress them as well.

 10th to the 6th   You must not allow your emotions to interfere with your progress toward your goals. Indecision may be a problem at times, but you can solve your career problems better if you avoid intimate contact with fellow workers or discussion of your private life.

 11th to the 5th   Your creative ideas need to be developed continually. Your ingenuity in finding new uses for your talents can help make your future secure. Capitalize on friends who will sincerely support you in your goals.

 12th to the 4th   While it isn't easy to break strong family ties, you shouldn't allow any obligations to your parents to get in the way of important personal interests. You can build a life for yourself only if you have the courage to insist on making progress through self-determination and independence.

Trine: 7, 11 Because of your natural curiosity, you accumulate considerable knowledge about many subjects. While your ability to retain information is notable, you sometimes have difficulty discriminating between fact and fiction. This is mainly because you allow your feelings to interfere with logic, which results in an emotional bias even in important matters. In your eagerness to communicate what you know you often take liberties with the facts, especially when you want to impress people. At times you truly believe that events occurred as you have related them. Your gift of creative imagination only needs development to help you realize your goals and give you financial security for your later years. Pay more attention to your friends' suggestions for achieving your goals. You are on good terms with most or all of your friends, and you are happy to do favors for them, knowing that they will reciprocate.

Sextile: 1, 5 Because you like people and have a talent for dealing with them, you might seek a career in communications. You indulge in much self-analysis, which has made you reasonably familiar with people's motivations. You could capitalize on this knowledge in a career that uses social contact as a tool for communication, such as writing or journalism. You easily show people that you are well informed, and you stimulate them to enter freely into conversation with you. You should direct your attention to those who need your understanding and compassion.

Cross: 6, 9, 12 Your fear of rejection and not being loved causes you to remain in an obscure position until you gain greater self-confidence. In this area your imagination works against you. Pay more attention to others; they have their hangups and fears too. Then apply yourself to becoming proficient in your career to take advantage of every opportunity. Your most urgent priority is to get a formal education, so you can learn to use logic rather than emotion when you are faced with problems involving people. You must know as much as you can about human behavior in order to make accurate judgments. Don't take the chance that your feelings will give you the necessary information for making proper decisions.

Inconjunct: 8, 10 You should not have any serious problem in winning approval from your superiors, because you are usually available for extra duty. You assume that it is your obligation to volunteer, because you feel you must do more than others to get the results you want. In spite of this, you become defensive when superiors show an interest in you, for you suspect them of insincerity. Personal involvement with people is part of your destiny, and it is the best investment you can make to win deserved appreciation for your efforts in behalf of others. You may experience some uncertainty and anxiety about the best way to satisfy your partner's desires.

Semisextile: 2, 4 Take advantage of your natural talents to gain the security you need to feel truly comfortable with your accomplishments. This might cause some discomfort and strained relations with your parents, if they disagree with your plans. The worst thing you can do is to yield to the pressure of family ties and deny yourself the privilege and opportunity to prove that you are capable of succeeding without interference from them. Your progress and success depend largely on establishing your independence and self-determination.

1st to the 3rd   Basically, you are a person of ideas, which you express fluently and effortlessly. Your skill in communication is second to none. Although you are acquainted with many subjects, you waste precious time on trivia.

 2nd to the 2nd   You appear detached from material concerns, but this is far from the truth. You plan your moves artfully to take full advantage of your abilities. Although you know how to make money, you need help in organizing your ideas to make them work.

 3rd to the 1st   You usually have the last word in a conversation, but you probably initiated it also. Your talent for dialogue is one of your best assets. You are sensitive, curious and ingenious at promoting yourself, which makes you quite popular.

 4th to the 12th   Not knowing something really bothers you. You tend to assume that you are the subject of any conversation that doesn't include you. You must learn to withdraw occasionally for a quiet moment to allow your imagination and inspiration to flow more freely.

 5th to the 11th   You are well liked by your friends because you don't threaten their egos. There is never a dull moment when you are around, for you lend sparkle and wit to any gathering. You give and accept help from close friends.

 6th to the 10th   Your supervisor and your colleagues think well of you and depend on you to help solve their problems. Your career takes a lot out of you, physically and mentally, so learn to stay within your limits.

 7th to the 9th   Although you are well read and learn easily, a formal education is essential to your success. Don't be embarrassed because your competitors are better informed. It's fun to ask questions, but it's the answers that count.

 8th to the 8th   You have a talent for making successful, sound investments, so don't be intimidated by people who make a show of their abilities. Convert your sexual fantasies into a powerful desire to provide professional services that people will pay for.

 9th to the 7th   Your competitors are fascinated by your talent for having the right answers at the right time. You can win patronage for your skills because you impress people with how well you understand their problems.

 10th to the 6th   Look for an occupation that requires your particular mental abilities. Your career should make continual demands on you to grow and develop, but don't be concerned if you don't succeed at first. With persistence and application, you will achieve your goals.

 11th to the 5th   You want the best for your children, and you hope that they agree with your ambitions for them, but be ready to concede if they don't. You may enjoy many love affairs, and you don't look forward to settling down.

 12th to the 4th   Unless you can break the ties with your parents, it will be rather difficult to implement your ideas. If your opinions differ from those of your family, that's good. It indicates that you are getting ready to think for yourself and build toward your goals independently, which is the only way that will give you complete satisfaction.

Trine: 7, 11 You are basically a person of ideas, which you express fluently and effortlessly. Life is fascinating to you, and you never tire of pursuing knowledge about every possible subject. Your friends support you in your endeavors, knowing that you will not give up. They like you because you never threaten them with your superior knowledge, allowing their egos to remain intact. You bring sparkle and wit to any gathering, though you are serious when necessary. You aren't unduly preoccupied with the future, for you never doubt that you will achieve your goals. You may accept help on occasion and you are eager to reciprocate when someone needs assistance. You have no trouble in dealing with the public, and you always seem to have the appropriate answers to people's problems. You will find it easy to attract a suitable mate to share your life, insisting only that your partner be as eager as you are to grow and develop. Combining your talents will benefit both of you. Your greatest assets are your insatiable thirst for knowledge and your ability to dramatize your ideas.

Sextile: 1, 5 You usually set the stage for an encounter by first organizing your ideas. People have no difficulty following your train of thought, for you make proposals with ingenious sensitivity. Your logic almost always impresses your listeners. In your personal life, you enjoy a variety of loves, but the idea of settling down with one individual is at first discomforting. Your creative ideas may be your "children." If you have a real family, however, you hope that they agree with your ambitions for them, but if they don't, be prepared to concede to their desires.

Cross: 6, 9, 12 It is especially important to get a formal education; the people whom you contact professionally will respect the polish that an education provides. You can't afford the embarrassment of losing to a competitor simply because you are uninformed. While it is fun to ask questions, it's the answers that count; besides, it bothers you not to know something. You might benefit by withdrawing from society now and then, to allow your imagination and inspiration to work. Seek a career that will continually make demands on you, and avoid routine endeavors that will crush your creative spirit. With persistent effort, you will realize your ambitions.

Inconjunct: 8, 10 You might be distracted by indulging in sexual fantasies or dreams of a great career. When the time comes to demonstrate your skills and act out your role in the marketplace, your strong passionate nature will help you succeed. Your passion will be translated into a strong desire to win the coveted prize, whether it's a contract, a sale or a person that arouses you. Stay within safe limits on the job. Extending yourself can take a lot out of you, mentally and physically.

Semisextile: 2, 4 You know how to make the best of a situation and how to capitalize on all your resources in order to increase your earnings. You should seek advice to help you get your resources organized, or you will waste precious time in disorder. This could be a residual effect of your early conditioning when you were expected to share your parents' views and opinions. If your views are different, you may not be able to make the right decisions for yourself except by trial and error. This is why you should have help until you learn to fully understand and appreciate the value of your own ideas. Eventually you can establish an orderly pattern in your thinking.

1st to the 3rd You have a charming manner, and you are able to compromise and make people feel comfortable. You express yourself easily and effectively to individuals or groups. Usually you are on your best behavior, hoping to win approval.

 2nd to the 2nd Your affable manner enables you to get what you want out of life. Your judicious use of language helps you meet the right people to serve your objectives, and you handle them with finesse.

 3rd to the 1st Congenial with those in your immediate invironment, you are considered an easy person to get along with. You cultivate good relations with everyone and always try to avoid conflict in order to better fulfill your objectives.

 4th to the 12th You are not usually assertive enough to protect yourself from those who try to take advantage of you. Your gentle temperament gives the impression that anyone can make demands on you without resistance.

 5th to the 11th You aren't too preoccupied with future security, because you've made the necessary plans to solve that problem. You enjoy good times with sincere friends in comfortable circumstances, and you will always be blessed with these conditions.

 6th to the 10th You prefer to avoid great physical exertion, so you may seek a career that involves you socially with the public. Others may not consider you a hard worker, but your supervisor knows you are thorough and responsible. Don't give in when superiors ask you to do more than your share.

 7th to the 9th Basically ethical in your dealings, you cringe when asked to take liberties with the law or your own standards. You are always a good listener, but you appreciate it when others give you an opportunity to express your views.

 8th to the 8th Realizing that most people are motivated by self-interest, you make concessions in order to please them. You know that by so doing you'll gain immeasurably in the long run, so it is a wise investment on your part.

 9th to the 7th You are attracted to people of polish and refinement, and in seeking a partner you are especially drawn to someone who shows respect for you. You are willing to grow and want a mate who will share in that with you.

 10th to the 6th You are annoyed by people who constantly complain, especially those who never have a kind word about anyone. You know you must work to earn a living, but unless you can improve your skills and become more competent in your career, you will be unhappy.

 11th to the 5th Children respond to your affection for them. You probably want a family, and you will be attracted to someone with similar desires. You want to be included in your partner's future plans, so that you both can enjoy the results of your efforts.

 12th to the 4th You might encounter problems if your parents disapprove of your goals. If they don't approve of the partner you have chosen, you may have to make a painful choice. You could experience deep anxiety about this, but making a life of your own depends on it.

Trine: 7, 11   Most people are comfortable with you because of your charming manner and your willingness to compromise. You enjoy the company of refined persons like yourself who can express themselves easily with groups and individuals. You bring out the best in people, which helps in realizing your objectives. You make many concessions to others, especially your partner, in order to win approval. You want to always have the respect of your mate because you feel that is important in making your relationship endure. You aren't too worried about your future security because you have planned for any conditions that may arise. You are more concerned about keeping compatible ties with your close friends who share your desire for the comfortable circumstances that you so thoroughly enjoy. The chances are that you can always count on the favors that life seems to bestow on you.

Sextile: 1, 5   Generally easy to get along with, you try to cultivate the most favorable relations with everyone in your immediate environment. You feel that it is especially important to avoid conflict at all costs because you are so disoriented by lack of harmony. You usually include your children in your plans, and as they grow up they will have fond memories of their formative years. You keep the lines of communication open so that they will always share with you their fortunate experiences as well as their problems. They know you will help them with their burdens, just as you naturally apply psychology in relating to your partner.

Cross: 6, 9, 12   You always endeavor to improve yourself, thereby adding to the essential values that you bring to the people with whom you are personally or socially involved. Basically an ethical person, you cringe when others expect you to take liberties with your high standards. In such instances you must assert yourself as protection from those who would take advantage of you. Your gentleness gives the impression that you would not resist. It is painful for you to listen to people who constantly berate others and never have a kind word to say about anyone. You may encounter this among the people you work with. But they will serve as a stimulus to improve your skills so that you may choose a better work environment.

Inconjunct: 8, 10   Your aversion to manual labor leads you to seek an occupation that deals largely with the public in a social environment. You handle your responsibilities thoroughly, as your supervisors know, but it is essential to determine just what your duties are. Otherwise you will find yourself taking on more than you should. You work best in personal contact with your patrons, because your willingness to make concessions in serving their needs endears you to them.

Semisextile: 2, 4   You will get the greatest yield from your creative resources by putting your best foot forward. You generally display your most advantageous qualities so that people will approve of you and of what you are trying to accomplish with your skills. Your admirable values help you win the cooperation you need in order to earn a comfortable living. It wasn't always this way, however, for you remember that your parents or guardians did not always approve of your decisions. They probably disagreed with your chosen partner as well as your other friends. But it was up to you to decide on your most important priority.

1st to the 3rd When provoked, you express yourself in an undisciplined way. Although you may not be a physically violent person, the results are violent when you unleash your verbal attacks. It is not that you are dishonest, but you do lack tact.

 2nd to the 2nd You promote your ideas eagerly in order to improve your material circumstances. Generally you strike while the iron is hot in the belief that he who hesitates is lost. You aren't easily put off when someone suggests that your plans won't work.

 3rd to the 1st Your lack of self-control can get you into a lot of hot water, especially with people close to you in your immediate environment. But they may thank you for rousing them to action if they would otherwise have missed an opportunity.

 4th to the 12th Not knowing when to be silent is your greatest liability. You appear arrogantly self-confident, but in fact, you can't stand to be upstaged by anyone. Your lack of self-assurance makes you put others on the defensive to distract them from your weaknesses.

 5th to the 11th Getting your ideas and plans into shape will help you achieve your goals, but you need more self-discipline to mobilize your efforts. You have the support of your friends, who admire your courage and aggressiveness.

 6th to the 10th Your driving ambition to gain recognition may cause some problems with colleagues or superiors by reminding them that they aren't doing all they could. You may be envied because you are able to accomplish so much work.

 7th to the 9th You are constantly searching for ways to improve your skills, and getting additional training on the job might be a good way. Consider the expense of education as an investment in your future, for it will enhance your ability to meet competition successfully.

 8th to the 8th Expressing your physical desires occupies much of your attention. You can sense when others are similarly motivated, and you have little difficulty making the necessary contact. You could succeed as an investment counselor, for people trust you.

 9th to the 7th Your ability to get what you want impresses your competitors and stimulates the opposite sex, who find you exciting. You will easily find a mate because you express your affections openly. Your gift for conversation fascinates people and encourages them to respond.

 10th to the 6th Knowing that your future is bright if you capitalize on your talents, you work diligently at putting your ideas to work. You realize that others will do the job if you don't, so you constantly strive to improve your skills and proficiency.

 11th to the 5th A smooth talker, you won't accept a no answer from anyone to whom you are romantically attracted. You have a large retinue to choose from at all times. In speculative enterprises you take measured risks, believing implicitly that you will succeed.

 12th to the 4th Your self-driving ambition to succeed and your desire for complete independence may possibly upset your parents, who consider you reckless and immature. To act otherwise, however, would threaten your ability to succeed.

Trine: 7, 11   You are a master at debate, and no one who has provoked you will ever forget the verbal attack you unleashed. While you may not be physically violent, you lack tact and self-discipline when challenged. This same lack of control also causes some problems in getting your ideas into shape so you can more effectively achieve your ambitions. No one questions your honesty (they wouldn't dare), but your methods leave much to be desired. Still, your friends usually support you in your endeavors, for which you should be grateful. Your competitors are impressed by your exciting display of aggression and fascinated by how successful your suggestions are in stimulating an active response from others. You apply the same leverage in your more personal and intimate relationships, and few people can resist you when you dramatize your feelings about them.

Sextile: 1, 5   In your eagerness to be in on the activity around you, you skillfully maneuver yourself into positions where others must turn to you for stimulus. Though your antics often get you into hot water, some people may thank you for urging them to seize an opportunity that they might otherwise have missed. In your romantic escapades you rarely accept no for an answer, and you usually have a sizable list of partners to choose from to satisfy your needs. You are something of a gambler at heart, but you take risks only when there is a high probability of success.

Cross: 6, 9, 12   Even when gainfully employed, you constantly seek to improve your position through additional training and education. You want to be ready when a challenging opportunity comes along for which you must compete. Your greatest liability is not knowing when to be silent. Your arrogant self-confidence masks the fact that you can't stand to be upstaged, but becoming better informed will make this dodge completely unnecessary. You can then put all your energy into finding the best way to apply your talents.

Inconjunct: 8, 10   Most people are envious of how much work you accomplish, and of course your superiors are delighted. Your driving ambition to succeed and gain the recognition you deserve may bring on some problems with the people you work for, if your efforts remind them of their inadequate performance. You have the necessary drive to succeed in advising others about their financial affairs. Not only do you appear concerned about their best interests, you truly are. You know how people are motivated by their desires and you have little difficulty making the right contacts, whether in your work or to satisfy your own physical needs.

Semisextile: 2, 4   Your aggressive nature might have caused you some anxious moments while you were growing up, when you had to confine yourself to the limits imposed by your parents. They may have considered you too big for your britches then or simply reckless and immature. Your need to demonstrate your independence might have alienated you from them. Your subsequent development made you realize that you had to act when you felt that it was appropriate, knowing that "he who hesitates is lost." Even now, you aren't easily dissuaded by people who say that your plans won't work, and you always manage to prove them wrong.

1st to the 3rd You have excellent mental abilities, but you sometimes neglect following through on your ideas to take full advantage of them. With your comprehensive understanding of a great many subjects, you can choose from a wide range of careers.

 2nd to the 2nd Capitalizing on your natural talents will allow you to expand your fields of endeavor. Your gift for converting talent into earnings is notable, but you must learn to consolidate your resources.

 3rd to the 1st A freedom-loving person, you function best when you can say and do what you want without having to ask permission. You are not restricted by narrow perspectives nor distracted by trivia.

 4th to the 12th Avoid taking unnecessary risks that will put a strain on your abilities. Not wanting to be obligated to others, you sometimes take on too much. Get your head out of the clouds and put your feet firmly on the ground to avoid disappointment.

 5th to the 11th Your wheeling and dealing never cease to amaze your friends, who are fascinated by your wealth of ideas. They admire your courage in taking on heavy burdens without great strain. They know, as you do, that your enthusiasm will see you through to your goals.

 6th to the 10th You work hard at your job and accept the long hours as part of your struggle to achieve the position and status you want. But you should get some rest, or you risk physical exhaustion. You are trying too hard to live up to your parents' expectations.

 7th to the 9th A self-made person, you understand the areas where you are strong and where you still need answers. You can cite the names of people who succeeded without a formal education who made a deliberate effort to acquire knowledge in other ways. You learn from those who have failed and never forget the reasons for their failure.

 8th to the 8th Though you could succeed in the communications field, your prospects are even better as an investment counselor. People trust in your talent and your professional competence. Your strong physical desires may be chilled by people who seem coarse or vulgar.

 9th to the 7th You seek a mate who shares your desire for mutual growth and development. In times of stress, your partner may lean heavily on you for understanding and compassion, which you will be eager to offer.

 10th to the 6th Never content with your level of achievement, you constantly strive to get more from your efforts by improving your skills. With a certain amount of inspiration and vision, you can be the best in your field.

 11th to the 5th You want the very best for your children, and you hope they will respond to the advantages you give them and will rise to their own potentials. In your romantic affairs, you always look ahead to see how well your current partner will fit into your future plans. You don't make commitments casually, no matter how in love you are.

 12th to the 4th Your early training may not have given you many opportunities, but you had the foresight to make plans for success. Don't let your parents make demands that interfere with your goals. On the other hand, you shouldn't neglect your parents.

Trine: 7, 11   You are well informed on many subjects, but you sometimes neglect to follow through on a project to derive the most benefit from your knowledge. You are easily distracted by any new interest, so you must learn to focus your attention. You are an eager conversationalist, but you lack the organizing ability to make this talent serve a useful purpose. You are the eternal student, perhaps because you are still searching for a career that will make enough demands on your intellectual abilities. You could do a satisfactory job in many fields, including education, law, politics, medicine or the social sciences. You always meet the requirements of any task because you are totally enthusiastic while that problem occupies your attention. Your compassion and understanding will be appreciated by your mate. You find it gratifying to know that your mate shares your desire for growth and development.

Sextile: 1, 5   Because you suffer from mental growing pains, you need to be free to expand as you want. You know that without this freedom, you would be unable to ventilate your mind and keep it active. You have great hopes that your children will respond to the advantages you have given them and will rise to their fullest potentials. In choosing a partner, you look ahead to see if that person will be able to fit your plans and grow with you.

Cross: 6, 9, 12   You admire people who have distinguished themselves through their achievements, and you hope to emulate them. You may not choose a professional career, but you will conduct yourself professionally in your work. You know the limits of your training and education, but you also know that you can make a place for yourself in the world and win recognition as well. You learn from those who fail as well as from those who succeed, and because you are never satisfied with your level of accomplishment, you continue to pursue greater conquests. With some inspiration and imagination, you can be the best in your field. But don't take on tasks that strain your abilities, because of course you have your limits. Having your feet on the ground will help you keep your goals within sight.

Inconjunct: 8, 10   The best investment you can make in your own future is being willing to use your talents to help people solve their problems. People usually trust implicitly in your ability to understand them and guide them in the best direction. You should set aside periods for pleasant rest and relaxation to help you unwind from the hazards encountered in your struggle to achieve the status you want. You've set your course, but you can always alter it. You have strong physical desires, but they are easily chilled by coarseness and vulgarity.

Semisextile: 2, 4   Stay clear of people who try to divert you from your objectives by preying on your feelings. Your greatest obligation is to fulfill your own potentials. You are vulnerable to such diversions because of the conditioning of your early years, when your efforts were curtailed by your parents. It's not that your loyalties are divided but that you must learn how they can coexist. You owe it to yourself and to those you serve to make your rich creative talents available to the world. It will be easier to convert your talents into cash if you learn how to consolidate your resources.

1st to the 3rd   The restrictions of your early conditioning may have prevented you from being even mildly optimistic about the future. Withdrawn and contemplative, you are a good student of human behavior. You aren't a fast learner, but what you learn leaves a deep impression on you.

 2nd to the 2nd   Although apprehensive about your ability to earn a living, you manage to get the best possible results from the available resources. Learning to handle your affairs efficiently will reduce the possibility of losses.

 3rd to the 1st   You take yourself seriously and are overly preoccupied with your negative qualities. Because you never forget your past failures, you find it difficult to be optimistic about the future. But remembering your mistakes can help you avoid repeating them.

 4th to the 12th   Subconsciously, you don't really like yourself enough, so when you suffer a reversal it is "just what I expected." Your determination and persistence make up for your lack of aggressiveness.

 5th to the 11th   Your circle of friends may not be wide, but those you have are dependable and can be relied upon when you need them. You know you will achieve your goals eventually, but you often wonder if it is worth the effort to do so.

 6th to the 10th   You more than satisfy your superiors' demands, but you still get depressed when you don't come up to the level of work they require. Perhaps you subconsciously feel that you must live up to goals chosen by your parents, which you resent.

 7th to the 9th   As painful as it seems, you absolutely must get some formal education, or your future is indeed limited. You need to define what you hope to gain in life and determine the best way to succeed. You should realize that getting an education is a good start.

 8th to the 8th   You are temperamentally qualified for a professional field, such as economics, education, finance or law. Sex isn't the most important concern in your life; if it is available, that's fine, but if not you don't get too uptight.

 9th to the 7th   You are attracted to people who are serious, conservative and responsible. You need to respect your partner and be respected in return. It is important to know deep inside that your efforts are very important to the one you love.

 10th to the 6th   You don't expect to receive gifts, and you probably don't give any, either. You work hard for what you get, and you hope that in time you will receive sufficient reward for your labors.

 11th to the 5th   You expect your children to take advantage of the opportunities you've given them. A true disciplinarian, you treat your children fairly. Although friendly with them, you aren't usually affectionate, any more than you are with a romantic partner. When you say you care, you really mean it.

 12th to the 4th   You may harbor resentment for the lack of opportunity or the discipline you endured while growing up. If you are alienated from your parents, consider it a catalyst that has forced you to rely on your own resources.

Trine: 7, 11   Your serious nature is largely the result of restrictive early conditioning, but your introspectiveness has probably made you a fairly good judge of character. A withdrawn individual, you learn as much as possible about your immediate environment. Although you do not learn quickly, you have become a good student, because of your ability to retain information. Those friends you have are mostly dependable, no-nonsense people. Your goals in life are defined, and although your dreams for the future are cautious, you know that you will realize them if you have enough time. Your associates admire your mental abilities and turn to you for answers to their problems. You apply yourself painstakingly to any subject that interests you, and your mind works efficiently to understand every detail. You respect those you love, and you expect respect from them, especially your partner. Being appreciated by your mate helps secure your relationship.

Sextile: 1, 5   Not being well informed bothers you, and you make it a point to find out what you want to know. Your views about your capabilities tend to be negative, and you never forget the reasons for any mistakes you've made. You discuss a subject only when you are thoroughly informed about it, so people often consider you an authority. You hope to make the best of your creative potentials so that your future will be free from anxiety. You expect your children to take advantage of the opportunities you have given them. A true disciplinarian, you treat your children fairly, but they may not realize that you love them, because you don't display your affection. This is also the case with a romantic partner, but when you say you care, you really mean it.

Cross: 6, 9, 12   Your most pressing priority should be to get a good education. You respect people who demonstrate their competence, and you should realize that they could not do this without being well informed. An education will help you develop your mental abilities and derive the most benefit from your ideas. You will understand what is expected of you in your career, so that you can serve others as well as yourself. Being educated will reduce your negative attitude about your chances for success. You can fulfill your creative potentials only if you accept the necessity of painstaking, hard work. The return depends completely on the investment that you make.

Inconjunct: 8, 10   Don't try to live up to your parents' expectations and ignore your own dreams for the future. Although you may not complete your tasks very quickly, your superiors will recognize that you are very thorough. Self-employment may be a way to achieve greater personal satisfaction. Your interest might be in economics, education, financial counseling or law: these will allow you self-determination and enough time to do the best possible job. You are probably not too distracted by physical or emotional needs, so you can devote sufficient energy to your career.

Semisextile: 2, 4   Your early conditioning may have restricted you or inhibited you from becoming more independent. And yet those frustrations may have been the stimulus you needed to force you to rely on your own resources. Your sense of caution and reserve will help reduce the possibility of financial losses. Your ability to plan will net you optimum results with even the most meager assets.

1st to the 3rd You were born with a rebellious attitude, which has continued, perhaps without cause. Your mind devises ingenious ways to avoid being obligated to others, and any attempt to restrict you or alter your opinions is futile.

 2nd to the 2nd You always have clever schemes for increasing your resources, so you are never far from what you need. Only the most progressive people show an interest in your ideas and are daring enough to take a chance on them.

 3rd to the 1st You never fail to state your position to anyone who will listen. You take liberties in giving your opinion even when no one asks for it. People are fascinated by your gregarious nature and your ability to share your ideas.

 4th to the 12th You probably don't know how clever you really are, but others do. If you aren't careful, they will take advantage of you. You are only acting naturally, but others see how they might use your wildly creative talent for their own benefit.

 5th to the 11th Friends enjoy your company because your whirlwind of ideas never fails to produce some excitement in a crowd. You are not as concerned as you should be about the future, with a "here today, gone tomorrow" attitude that puts off all thought of future problems.

 6th to the 10th You put so much nervous energy into your career that you may become rather irritable. You overreact to your superiors' expectations and do more than is required. Complaining about the way things are run may be risky, if your superiors are easily offended.

 7th from 9th Your insatiable curiosity provokes you to learn as much as possible about everything, and your knowledge amazes listeners. In conversation you shock people in order to drive home a point. You aren't afraid to speak your mind, but you should listen too.

 8th to the 8th You feel that you understand why people behave as they do. You are fascinated that sex motivates people to do things having nothing to do with sex and that people lose their ethical perspective over money. Your views on sex are permissive.

 9th to the 7th You believe that you can learn more about social relationships by dealing with people than by studying a textbook. You enjoy the drama of human contact. You regard marriage more as a relationship of mutual consent than as a formal contract.

 10th to the 6th You will have to contain your impatience to have everything *now* and plan a program that will assure you enduring future benefits. You abhor routines, and you try to get what you want without that pain.

 11th to the 5th Your latent creative potential is worth nothing unless you develop it. You want your children to enjoy the privileges of the freedom you have enjoyed, and you will literally glow as you see them succeed according to their own identities and without your help.

 12th to the 4th Your greatest test is to decide which destiny is more important, yours or the one your parents have chosen for you. With your usual skill, you will have little trouble convincing them that you will succeed with or without their approval.

Trine: 7, 11   Although you may not behave like a rebel, you think like one, and you contain yourself only because you lack a cause. You expect people to indulge you when you feel like expressing yourself; in fact, you demand their indulgence. Freedom means more to you than to most people, and you go to great lengths to guarantee your right to express your opinion freely. You have a distinct abhorrence of being obligated to others except when you've chosen to serve them. Even when first meeting you, people get the impression that it would be difficult indeed to exercise any control over you. They see that you won't climb on a popular bandwagon simply because it is fashionable. You learn something from almost every person you meet, and you learn more about social relationships through direct contact than any textbook could teach you. You move with agility among the variety of people who are your friends. They are fascinated by your whirlwind mind that finds life and relationships exciting and stimulating. Perhaps you are a bit too detached in your lack of concern for the future, which may bother people who don't have your "here today, gone tomorrow" attitude.

Sextile: 1, 5   You hope to give your children a legacy of self-determination so that they will be able to successfully exploit their talents and grow according to their individual identities. No one can ever say that you aren't willing to share what you have gained from your experience, and on some occasions you will listen to other people's ideas.

Cross: 6, 9, 12   You are even more clever than you think, but you need formal training to direct your mental faculties properly and better utilize your ingenuity. Without such training, your contemporaries might steal your ideas and capitalize on them. Get advice from sincere and trusted friends, for they are probably more aware of your potential than you are. Though you consider routine painful and unnecessarily time-consuming, your impatience for instant results could be disappointing. If you want enduring benefits, you should prepare an orderly plan for achieving your goals and adhere to it.

Inconjunct: 8, 10   With reasonable self-control, you can avoid the nervous irritability that often results from the pressure of career demands. You doubtless do more than is required by your superiors because you overreact to their expectations. It is more than likely that you are easely annoyed by traditional procedures in your work environment. Unless your superiors are unusually progressive, voicing your objections will probably alienate them. You are sensitive to peoples' general motivations, and feel that you should do what you can to serve their desires. You are intrigued by the fact that sex often motivates people to take actions having no direct connection with sex. And you are equally fascinated to observe how the desire for material things causes so many people to lower their usual ethical standards, if only temporarily.

Semisextile: 2, 4   It goes without saying that your destiny, as you define it, is far more important than any goals suggested by your parents, which probably served their interests rather than yours. You are so resourceful in finding ways to capitalize on your assets that it should be unnecessary to submit to anyone, except to ask for advice occasionally.

1st to the 3rd   You have an exceptional intellect, and at times you are struck by inspired ideas for ways to solve your own problems and those relating to your immediate environment. Examine all your ideas very carefully to determine their objective value.

 2nd to the 2nd   Use your natural resources and imagination to find ways to earn a living. Your tendency to be careless about money matters causes your assets to erode seriously without your realizing it. Indifference to money may be a virtue, but still the rent must be paid.

 3rd to the 1st   You only think that you know yourself. You've created an acceptable image, and you believe what you see reflected by others because it is comfortable. You make an impression on the people with whom you talk, but they are not always sure you are telling the truth.

 4th to the 12th   You operate largely on a subconscious level and try to avoid any unpleasant truths about yourself. With a little honesty you can be free from fears about your hangups. Everyone has some of these unacknowledged hangups, but you must learn to take advantage of your hidden talents and better utilize your creativity.

 5th to the 11th   A trusted friend can help you plan for your future goals. Your plans might include helping others develop their creative abilities. Certainly, without a goal, little can come from even the most talented gift of creative inspiration.

 6th in the 10th   You will have to apply yourself diligently to secure your rightful place in the world. Avoid people who expect you to do more than your share.

 7th to the 9th   To better fulfill your obligations to yourself and society, you must get some formal training. Through education you can replace the vague impressions you receive in personal dealings with an objective understanding of how the mind works under all conditions.

 8th to the 8th   Enjoy your sexual fantasies as a safety valve, because your libidinous energy will find other outlets if not released. Fear of this energy makes you apprehensive about getting too close to people except in social application of your duties.

 9th to the 7th   The public will seek your expertise when they need someone who truly understands people with the sincere compassion that you display. Try not to moralize when their behavior offends you—they would not need your help if they didn't have problems.

 10th to the 6th   You need organization and planning in order to use your talents and get the most benefit from them. It's not your ideas that get results, but your ability to use your creative abilities with skill and competence.

 11th to the 5th   Your inspired imaginings have great possibilities, but you have to believe this to make it a fact. You might choose to sublimate your dreams to those of your children so that they will have a chance to succeed when you either couldn't or wouldn't.

 12th to the 4th   It is highly probable that your parents' enormous influence during your early years was the deciding factor in whether you would rise to fulfill your creative potential. You alone had to make the choice.

Trine: 7, 11   Your concept of reality is quite different from other people's, you have either a highly idealized view of life or a morbidly negative outlook. Your extrasensory apparatus is finely tuned to mental faculties that most people are unaware of, which allows you to solve problems with relative ease. Helping to solve social problems is part of your responsibility. However, you must always submit your ideas to a more discriminating person to ascertain whether they truly serve an important need. You will need guidance from someone who understands you and in whom you have complete trust. You need to define your goals and then devise a program for realizing them. Without a goal, you will derive little benefit from your gifted creative imagination. Once you are established, the public will certainly seek your talent and compassion. Don't moralize about their behavior; they wouldn't seek your help if they didn't have problems.

Sextile: 1, 5   You tend to interpret your experiences in such a way that you feel comfortable in self-analysis. This is because you are really quite uncertain about yourself. Most people are impressed with you, but they are never sure that you are just what you seem from your conversation. You have the ability to effectively dramatize your creative talents so well that they are obviously inspired. But you must remain in contact with the real world, where your talents can be the major tools for reaching your goals. You have admirable dreams for your children, but you may have to put aside your own dreams in order to help achieve theirs. But that seems unwise; you should find an alternative solution so that your aspirations can coexist with your children's.

Cross: 6, 9, 12   You have a subconscious aversion to facing yourself honestly and admitting your failings. When you realize that everyone has personal hangups, you may be less disturbed by it. Also locked up in your mind are enormous creative resources and the inspiration to make them come alive in the world. You are bothered by social injustices, and your compassion for persons who are limited by socieconomic conditions causes you to feel guilty. A formal education will give you the means to do something about your social obligations. Applying yourself to society's problems could be the direction of your career interests. Just remember that feeling depressed about life's problems doesn't solve them, but active commitment can help. Perhaps your partner, who sympathizes with your ideas, will support you in your endeavors.

Inconjunct: 8, 10   Stay clear of a career in which martyrdom is the expected consequence of your efforts. Do only what you know will get results and be wary of a superior who tries to make you feel guilty for not wanting more. You don't generally get too close to your associates except professionally, which is fine. Enjoy your sexual fantasies and regard them as a suitable safety valve for releasing much of your libidinous energy. Releasing this energy more directly could cause problems.

Semisextile: 2, 4   Although your parents had a strong influence on you while you were growing up, you must choose your own direction in life even if it offends them. Your careless disregard for material matters can prove a liability in the hostile world of challenge and competition. With your imagination, there are literally endless ways to capitalize on your talents and derive a comfortable living from them.

1st to the 3rd   You are fascinated by mysteries and want to solve them. Large environmental changes have a deep effect on you, because you are easily disturbed when familiar conditions are altered.

 2nd to the 2nd   You know how to benefit from even the most ordinary assets, like taking old shellac 78 records and creating a demand for them as "collector's items." You have a gift for creating value in something that is, for all practical purposes, valueless.

 3rd to the 1st   The unknown and the occult excite you, as does anything that may contain hidden danger. This is why you want a career that incorporates some of the skills required in dealing with secrets.

 4th to the 12th   You have a secret fear of the unknown, but this is exactly what entices you to seek the answers to occult problems. Be careful, for you may be tampering with dangerous subjects that you know very little about.

 5th to the 11th   You are in full command of the future you want to build for yourself. You have the ability to alter current attitudes and promote ideas that may someday become commonplace. Your friends find you exciting even if your ideas are unusual.

 6th to the 10th   You want to make a contribution to society, and you could stimulate new industrial procedures or political ideologies. You also want personal achievements, and personnel changes in your job could give you that opportunity. But take care that you aren't the victim of such changes.

 7th to the 9th   You feel challenged by political, legal and religious philosophies and deeply aroused when tradition or custom dictates that you must abide by them. You are especially angered when the reasons for these beliefs are no longer valid, and you refuse to concede.

 8th to the 8th   You are concerned about the fact that people in powerful government positions can apply financial leverage that alters the destinies of many people. In your personal affairs, however, you apply similar pressures to win compliance with your desires.

 9th to the 7th   You admire people who refuse to stand idle while a powerful personality gains control of the masses. This is the sort of person you would like to share your life with. You inspire the people with whom you deal closely.

 10th to the 6th   You must develop all your creative potentials in order to be prepared for any eventuality. Realizing your objectives depends on this, and of course you are far more effective when you are well trained.

 11th to the 5th   You are impatient with people who just talk about the future. You instill self-reliance in your children so they won't have to depend on you. You are deeply concerned about their future, and you would feel guilty if you did not tell them of the hazards ahead.

 12th to the 4th   Your parents might not agree with your dedication to working to improve the quality of life for yourself and others. They may consider you an extremist, and you are, but you also have the ability to accomplish great things that will endure as long as necessary.

Trine: 7, 11   You have a distinct gift for solving problems, especially when the problem has already defied other attempts. The more mysterious the circumstances, the better, for it gives you an opportunity to search deeply and test your abilities. You are concerned about social and political conditions in your environment, because they usually have a direct effect on your life circumstances. Your preoccupation with the future stimulates you to do what you can to bring about conditions that you can live with. This is why you admire other people with backbone who have a feeling of social responsibility and who challenge demagogues who would gain control of the masses. Such an individual would earn your respect and attract your attention as a possible marriage partner.

Sextile: 1, 5   You are impatient with people who do little more than talk about the future. You cultivate self-reliance in your own children, so that they can choose their own life directions independently. Because of your concern for them, you also make them aware of the hazards that lie ahead. Your perceptive ability has far more depth than your contemporaries realize, and they may be surprised when you show a decided interest in the unknown and the occult.

Cross: 6, 9, 12   You should become thoroughly informed about any subject that deeply interests you. You must know as much as possible about the political, social and religious philosophies that often serve as catalysts for important social changes. You resent the fact that people continue to adhere to old attitudes when the reasons for them are no longer valid. Be prepared for every eventuality by developing all your creative potentials. You protect your future interests when you can accept the opportunities that are offered to you.

Inconjunct: 8, 10   If you develop your skills adequately, you won't have to accept the bottom line offered in your career. You will serve yourself best if your profession requires you to apply your skills in serving the best interests of society at large. If you work diligently to give your best, you are less likely to be harassed by the people who are affected by your decisions. Your awareness of public and individual needs will arouse you to make your skills available, especially if you know that your efforts will work and be appreciated. You are concerned about the financial leverage that people in important positions use to alter the destinies of the masses. But you apply similar pressure to gratify your personal desires.

Semisextile: 2, 4   Though your parents might not agree with your goals and objectives and your driving commitment to them, they must admit that you have a talent for making the most out of even ordinary assets. You consider every challenge as an ultimatum, forcing you to go to extremes to win, if necessary. You can usually make a seemingly worthless situation appear to have great value. You are most attracted to programs that aim to provide lasting results for everyone who is affected by them.

Sun in Third, Moon in First

You are intensely curious about everything, and you try to be well informed on many subjects. But you worry about not knowing enough to qualify when an opportunity is presented. You needn't worry so much about this matter, because you are personable, and you quickly gain a working knowledge of a situation, even if it is completely foreign to you. With your progressive attitude, you will achieve your goals with relative ease. Generally you will have the support you need from others until you feel able to handle your problems on your own. You make your way in any kind of social situation because of your winning personality, which makes everyone feel comfortable with you. You keep your feelings to yourself, and only your closest friends know how much you want a truly affectionate relationship of your own.

Your active imagination and creative intellect suggest journalism, reporting, writing, education or marital counseling as suitable mediums of expression. You would derive much pleasure in such enterprises, because they allow you freedom to set your own pace. Your partner must understand how important it is that you grow together.

Sun in Third, Moon in Second

Your conditioning has allowed some misgivings to develop about your ability to gain the security you want. In part, this is because your parents did not give you permission to assert yourself unless it met with their approval. Consequently, you grew up not knowing if you could succeed on your own. Your parents doubtless wanted the best for you, but they may have denied you the opportunity to learn from experience. You should become self-sufficient as soon as possible and have a place of your own.

You may work at many different occupations before finding the one that is best for you. As your experience grows, so will your ability to be discriminating, and finally you will select a pleasant and fulfilling career. Banking or investment would allow you to grow steadily with some assurance of security later on. Artistic pursuits also seem consistent with your temperament and would give you some flexibility in using your talents.

You are a good candidate for marriage, and you would work to make it stable. You are a warm, loving person who clearly enjoys doing things that please your partner. You want to share as much with your mate as you can so that boredom won't arise.

Sun in Third, Moon in Third

You may have been conditioned to feel frustrated about your identity, but your thirst for knowledge will reveal that you have the potential to succeed. A higher education will show you how capable you are and will free you from the programming that denied you access to yourself. You function best when you aren't restricted as to how you accomplish your objectives. Having someone breathe down your neck distracts you from giving your best efforts. You should have self-determination in your career, because routine tasks would stifle and bore you. Education, travel, writing, communications or the aerospace industry would be ideal for you. In these fields, new developments occur continuously to keep your enthusiasm high.

Your partner should be as desirous for growth as you are. If you are both career people, you can coordinate your efforts in planning for the future. You probably operate at a high pitch most of the time, so you need periods during which you can relax.

Sun in Third, Moon in Fourth

You tend to confuse your emotions with your rational thinking. Though generally optimistic about your ability to succeed, you sometimes experience deep anxiety because of early family conditioning that made you feel insufficient without their approval. Being responsible for your decisions is a necessary part of maturing. When you learn to do this successfully, you can grow increasingly confident and better able to handle future problems, which is urgent if you are to establish yourself in the world. Being self-sufficient will provide pressure to take advantage of your creative ideas and use them more resourcefully.

You must face the challenge of competition, which will give you the opportunity to taste success and feel the glow of accomplishment. After you experience success, you will become addicted to it, and you will have overcome a major hurdle in your life. A career involving contact with the public is recommended, for you have a talent for mixing with people and a sensitivity that endears you to others. Your sense of humor may save the day when you would otherwise be emotionally crushed.

Sun in Third, Moon in Fifth

You have a substantial creative imagination, which will bring you many long-range benefits if you apply yourself to the task. The problem is that if your parents, especially your mother, overindulge you during your developing years, it may never seem important enough to make the effort. Then you will waste precious time. With your dramatic ability, you easily can get attention and the support you need. Favorable reaction from others inspires you to continue.

A career in communications or working with young people would be suitable for your temperament and would give you the feedback you need to know you are utilizing your rich imagination effectively.

Your partner should be as romantic as you are and eager to share your goals. Your outlook on life is genuinely youthful. You should enjoy a truly satisfying relationship with your children, although you may try to hold onto them too long.

Sun in Third, Moon in Sixth

You are engaged in an inner struggle to carry out your ideas in the real world in an orderly way. You are filled with plans for the future, but you have difficulty translating them into practical efforts that yield tangible results. There is nothing you can't accomplish with self-discipline, but you have to get over your feeling of inadequacy. You let others get an edge on you in competition by giving them the impression that you don't mind doing favors for them, but that only enhances their position. You don't have to indulge others simply because they ask you to. The best way to handle your resentment of authority is to become an expert in some field yourself.

A career of service to the public would be desirable for you, because you seem to have the answers to their problems. Your sensitive nature and capacity for reasoning will allow you to achieve the goals you want and win public approval as well.

Your partner will probably lean heavily on you for support, and the interchange that results can enrich the relationship. You will find it difficult to understand your partner's feeling of emotional frustration that you are not completely devoted.

Sun in Third, Moon in Seventh

Your circumstances allow you to express yourself and become involved in the world around you, an ideal situation for continuing development and success. You have a deep need to relate to others, professionally and socially, and you utilize your creative ideas better through the people you are involved with. However, lingering ties to your family make you inwardly apprehensive that you will not be accepted.

But the public will accept you, which should simplify taking your place before the world. You could excel in any career that brings you into close contact with the public, such as education, counseling, selling or social services. You could work most effectively with children who have learning disabilities and who require sympathetic understanding. You can show them how to be self-sufficient.

Having a permanent partner will give you emotional comfort so that you can direct your efforts to your career. You derive much satisfaction from indulging your mate.

Sun in Third, Moon in Eighth

You want very much to be in the mainstream of social activity, but you feel you must earn that privilege by doing favors for people, whether they deserve them or not. You are projecting your own feeling of inadequacy onto others to justify that they need your help. This will only delay getting started in your career. Also, making unnecessary sacrifices for others denies them the opportunity to use their own resources. All you really owe others is to develop your skills so you can make a worthwhile contribution to society.

You could succeed in such fields as medicine, education, counseling, therapy or financial advice. These fields will allow you to use your ability for appraising people's problems and offering suggestions for handling them successfully. Knowing you have been helpful relieves your anxiety about contributing to society.

You try to be generous to your family, although you may feel that your partner's needs are never satisfied. This may be only your subjective negativity and not be consistent with your partner's opinion.

Sun in Third, Moon in Ninth

You are attracted to situations in which you must extend yourself before the public, but your early conditioning makes you have misgivings about doing this. You have the mistaken idea that others know more than you do, so you are overly cautious in asserting yourself in challenging situations. You might be surprised to learn that others consider you a walking encyclopedia who is qualified to discuss any topic.

Through a career in communications you could effectively apply your ideas and gain greater self-confidence in your abilities. Although change is important to allow you to grow to your potential, you tend to resist it, fearing that you aren't ready for it. Success will come more readily if your effort is shared with a sympathetic partner, someone who understands your shortcomings and anxieties and can support you in making the most of your creative potential. If your careers are parallel, this will stimulate you to grow together. Your development has come largely from people who believe in you, and before long, you will believe in yourself. Your partner and children mean everything to you, and you will more than satisfy their expectations.

Sun in Third, Moon in Tenth

Although you prefer activity that brings you before the public, you are not sure you can withstand the abuses that you may encounter in dealing with those in authority. You are easily unsettled by disharmony, and you feel that this is a heavy price to pay. Your parents conditioned you to question your qualifications for success unless your plans had their approval. You probably identify with your father in seeking the kind of success that fulfills his expectations.

You should seek a career before the public, so that the reaction you get is honest and objective. Public relations, education, hotel management or a similar field will allow you to utilize your talents in ways that will give you the success you want. You may have to extend yourself in the beginning, but if you persist, it will become almost effortless and very enjoyable.

Unless your partner is completely sympathetic with your career aims, it would be better to delay marriage until you are established professionally. Probably you will select someone who is career-minded or at least professionally trained in some field. Your mate should understand that your career will make many demands on your time.

Sun in Third, Moon in Eleventh

You have a wide range of interests, and you understand the need to plan for your goals to achieve success. The Sun in the third indicates strong parental influence during your formative years, but you are content with your own identity, and eventually you can resolve any family conflicts that have developed. You communicate well and socialize easily, which ensures that you will always have friends.

You could enjoy success in law, politics, education, social activities or even in the performing arts, perhaps as a broadcaster in radio or television. Each of these jobs requires close contact with the public, which you excel in.

Your marriage should prove quite satisfactory, and you should enjoy a pleasant relationship with all members of your family. You prefer an uncomplicated lifestyle in which everyone participates actively.

Sun in Third, Moon in Twelfth

You are insatiably curious and have developed a large fund of ideas, but you imagine that you may never get the chance to use them. Your desire to be fulfilled is hampered by the necessity to make some adjustments in your habits. You do not realize that anything you want to achieve carries the responsibility of learning new skills. Although you seem eager for changes, you are upset when they actually happen.

You are qualified for a career that requires you to help others solve their problems, perhaps in social work or medicine. Or you might prefer writing, illustration or design. You have the capacity to enjoy life in all its dimensions and to grow in your ability to handle its many problems. Your life will never be uninteresting.

An early marriage may be unrealistic until you can gain greater perspective about what you want to accomplish in life. It would be ideal if you and your partner had similar objectives. Having children too soon will be burdensome if you haven't clearly defined your goals.

Chapter Four

Fourth House

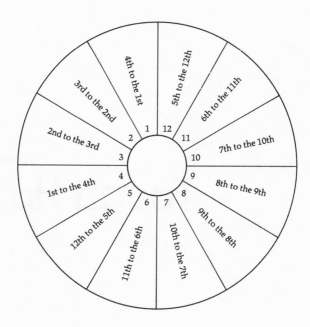

Although older astrology texts, as well as many new ones, regard the fourth house as representing the father, I have not found this to be true except in very rare instances. On the contrary, I have found that the fourth house is most closely associated symbolically with Cancer, the fourth sign of the zodiac, and the mother. It can be thought of as the roots from which you spring and the roots you must eventually establish for yourself. The most intimate relation we know is that which binds a mother and child, and, in fact, many people, even as adults, fail to truly sever that tie. The fourth house and Cancer represent the last stages of the previous life experience, and unless you can detach yourself satisfactorily from your mother, you haven't really let go of the past. The sign and house that follow are Leo and the fifth house, and you cannot expect to function with true vitality in your own being if you remain attached to the entity that spawned you. If you do, the resulting situation is parasitic, and when the parent dies, the parasite must also die.

Some of the most painful life situations are caused by lingering ties to a parent, but these are extreme cases of dependency or insufficiency that make it nearly impossible for the person to establish individual roots. The fourth house is highly emotional and requires the most painstaking examination and compassionate understanding. Two forces at work here are your unwillingness to detach yourself and your parent's unwillingness to let you go. In most instances, the parent concurs that you should be allowed to make your own way and learn through your mistakes, but there is still some resistance to letting it happen just yet. Extending yourself in pursuit of your own destiny requires the most laborious effort, and often, when you finally break the ties and decide to make your own way, there are some guilt feelings. This rarely happens if the parent is sufficiently aware of her role and if there has been some meaningful communication between you about your respective positions and needs. Through this house you gain some perspective on what you must do in order to become self-sufficient and secure. The key to your destiny is in this house, and with a solid foundation here, you can reach for the fulfillment shown by the tenth house, its opposite.

Derivative House Meanings

1st to the 4th   This represents your mother and the circumstances of your early years, but you must build new roots that are consistent with your needs as you pursue your destiny.

2nd to the 3rd   Emotional ties may deter you as you try to realize the full value of your own mental ability. Your ideas can sustain you in your own roots.

3rd to the 2nd   Your preoccupation with security shows that you must find a way to compensate for having struggled to find and fulfill your own destiny.

4th to the 1st   Becoming independent immediately brings urgent responsibilities in which you must excel so you can realize your ambitions.

5th to the 12th   You secretly indulge in dreams in which you rarely fail in your endeavors. If you develop your creative imagination, those dreams can become reality.

6th to the 11th   Although your future may seem distant, if you establish a firm foundation and apply yourself, it will be closer than you could imagine.

7th to the 10th   It is necessary to fully utilize your early beginnings as the motivation for your success. Your emotional fragility is the main deterrent.

8th to the 9th   Once you are educated, you will have the urge to truly extend yourself in the world. You hope to bring understanding to those you deal with.

9th to the 8th   Those who truly need your services inspire you to accept them as your responsibility, and you perform your service with devotion.

10th to the 7th   You are easily intimidated by competition, but nevertheless you must answer the call and accept the responsibility.

11th to the 6th   You always want to be of service to those who need you, and you find it hard to believe that you will ever be free of this kind of burden.

12th to the 5th   You are easily won over by your children, and you may neglect your own needs and development for them. You question it when others say they love you.

1st to the 4th   You have strong family ties, and even if you move away from your birthplace, you will return often to renew old ties. You would feel most secure and comfortable working at home or at least in familiar surroundings.

 2nd to the 3rd   Because you identify closely with your parents and siblings, it might be difficult for you to act independently without asking for their approval. You should live apart from your parents to learn how resourceful you can be.

 3rd to the 2nd   Your parents may have chosen a career for you, but you should think for yourself and find a profession based on your own beliefs and needs. You have a mind of your own, which will allow you to gain plenty of security.

 4th to the 1st   You can become independent and secure only by accepting your responsibilities. When you are on your own, you will learn to assert yourself, accept occasional setbacks and take on the challenge of competition.

 5th to the 12th   You tend to fantasize about victories before you have proven that you can win. Don't be content with only moderate gains, for apathy and indolence are signs of failure. Use your creative imagination to cope effectively with the demands of the real world.

 6th to the 11th   Your childhood may have been comfortable, but you will have to work to make the future equally secure. Stop relying on memories of your childhood; instead, learn from friends who have built their own lives.

 7th to the 10th   Heavy career demands may make you doubt that you can succeed, but your competitors have the same anxieties. Resolve your doubts by establishing goals and seeking them aggressively. Important people will recognize your abilities, even if you can't.

 8th to the 9th   You need to get an education to help you grow and to reveal your talents. Self-doubt and procrastination are your greatest liabilities. When you discover what you can do, you will be motivated to reach your goals successfully.

 9th to the 8th   Find out what career will allow you to fulfill the most important human needs and thereby earn public approval and respect. Get the right training so you can provide that service and earn a comfortable living.

 10th to the 7th   Don't be overly impressed by your competitors, for with training you can easily surpass them. Learn from others' successes and failures, and cultivate contacts with people who can help you. Your partner will stimulate you to exploit your talents and give you good reason to succeed.

 11th to the 6th   You look forward to the time when you can be free of the daily harassment and effort of earning a living. If you use all your resources and talents, you can certainly reach that goal.

 12th to the 5th   Don't underestimate your creative abilities, and don't let any member of your family convince you that you can't do something.

Trine: 8, 12   You have strong family ties, and you need to have the security of familiar surroundings in order to feel at ease. Because of this need, you would be more comfortable working in an environment where you know most of the people you deal with. To win approval for your accomplishments, you must first understand what people need and then get the right kind of training to satisfy that need. Indulging in daydreams about your future accomplishments is futile unless you accept the responsibilities that go along with success. If you are somewhat apathetic and content with only a modest level of achievement, it is highly unlikely that you will ever gain public recognition for your efforts. With proper motivation, however, and by using the resources of your creative imagination, you could make a substantial contribution to fulfill your social obligations.

Sextile: 2, 6   You are afraid that you cannot earn enough to feel secure, but this anxiety will diminish as you start putting your ideas to work and more confidently assert your right to think for yourself. The value of your ability to solve problems can be determined only when you apply what you know. You will become independent and free from obligation to others according to the amount of effort you put into developing your creative talents and resources.

Cross: 1, 7, 10   The public at large will provide every opportunity you need to achieve distinction in your career. When you live up to society's expectations, you also live up to your potential. Fearing failure, however, you tend to withdraw from a challenging opportunity when you feel intimidated by competitors. If you can resolve your self-doubt and fear, you will soon have proof of your capabilities. You will become more aggressive and determined to reach your goals as soon as you realize that setbacks and reversals are normal for most people who are pursuing an objective. Someone you love, perhaps your partner, will give you the stimulus you need to exploit your talents. This will win that person's respect and also improve your own self-image and feeling of self-respect.

Inconjunct: 9, 11   The future is yours to shape and mold. You can make it comfortable and secure or dreary and dull, depending on how ambitious you are. You must slowly pull away from depending on others or allowing them to depend on you. Then you can begin to lay the foundation on which to build your future. The best motivation for this is education and training. Start by turning a deaf ear to people who try to make you feel guilty for refusing to help them when you know they can help themselves.

Semisextile: 3, 5   You will progress more rapidly and become more self-reliant if you live apart from your family. You must learn the joy of being truly independent and realize that you are competent to make the most of your mental assets and resources. Only then can you be sure enough of your talents to dismiss anyone, including a member of your family, who says you can't do this or that.

1st to the 4th   You react to the world much as your parents did. Your strong family ties have made you very dependent on others for security, but you can develop self-confidence by learning to use your talents to benefit yourself. You don't need anyone else's approval.

 2nd to the 3rd   Learn to convert your ideas into tangible assets and use them to build a life of your own without being dependent on others. Try not to contaminate your ideas with irrelevant emotions.

 3rd to the 2nd   It isn't easy for you to be realistic about making your own life. If you can accept responsibility for finding a way to earn a good living, the financial rewards will give you security and compensate for any emotional anxiety.

 4th to the 1st   Loyalty to your loved ones is admirable, but too much nostalgic lingering in the past can be a liability. You must accept the past, present and future in their proper perspective, or your individual development will be severely limited.

 5th to the 12th   Your keen imagination can help you become independent. If you reach out to help less fortunate people, you will learn how competent you are in coping with the world. With your sympathetic understanding, you can do a great deal for others.

 6th to the 11th   You are cautious about extending yourself to strangers, for you feel most secure with the circle of friends who understand your emotional frailties. But you must make an effort to gain financial security for your later years, when the friends you have depended on may be gone.

 7th to the 10th   Your sensitivity will slow your progress unless you learn to assert yourself. Be gregarious and demanding, if necessary, to achieve the goals you have set up. Others will not feel threatened, because you are always considerate of their feelings.

 8th to the 9th   A formal education will reveal the realities of life and prepare you for occasional setbacks. You must develop your intellectual skills so that you don't have to rely on feelings and hunches.

 9th to the 8th   With an education, you will be ready to make a contribution that will establish your value to the world and satisfy an important social need. Others will be attracted to your resourcefulness and dedication.

 10th to the 7th   Having a partner will allow you to function at your best, for you need a mate to give you support and the confidence to fulfill your goals. You must accept competition if you want to know the sweet taste of success.

 11th to the 6th   Let your preoccupation with the past yield to a program for improving the future. You can realize your goals if you apply yourself diligently, with all your imagination. There is no substitute for hard work.

 12th to the 5th   Don't delay developing your talents, for you will become apathetic. Your anxieties will vanish as you learn to exploit your creative potentials. It may be hard for you to enjoy friendship and romantic love, because you are vulnerable to displays of affection. Don't make a commitment until you know your partner cares for you.

Trine: 8, 12 Your early family conditioning caused you to develop strong parental ties. This is fine in itself, but it may deny you the opportunity to grow to maturity with enough self-confidence to become secure in your individual achievements. You tend to submit your plans to members of your family, hoping to win their approval and support. You must acknowledge the importance of becoming self-supporting and on your own as soon as possible. You will learn the value of your natural talents when you are forced to use them imaginatively to solve your daily problems. Once you stop feeling sorry for yourself, you will be able to extend yourself to people who are less fortunate or capable and learn how competent you are in dealing with such situations. Your natural compassion for those in need can be used best by getting an education so that you can make a worthwhile contribution to help others. When people need help, they naturally turn to someone like you.

Sextile: 2, 6 Your emotional dependence on others makes you greatly preoccupied with financial security. You assume that if your material needs are satisfied, you will be more stable, but unless you truly believe that you can form personal relationships without family interference, that stability is only an illusion. Develop goals that are within your reach and work diligently toward them. You can achieve the long-lasting security you want if you plan realistically and work for it.

Cross: 1, 7, 10 The first major crisis you must deal with is learning to live with yourself and, if possible, on your own, especially if you always ask for your parents' approval or if they insist that you should not do this or that. Once you decide that you will make your own way, it will be easier to choose your career direction. You will never be indifferent to those you love, but it is essential to put past, present and future in proper perspective. A partner will give you the initiative to accomplish more than you might otherwise. Knowing that your partner appreciates you will provide sufficient reason to extend yourself in your career. If you accept competition as an opportunity to demonstrate your capabilities, your victories will be even sweeter.

Inconjunct: 9, 11 Getting an education to reveal your talents is the best investment you will ever make. Your compassion for others means little unless you are trained to help them deal with their problems. When you can confidently help those who need your skills and understanding, you will also have the comfort of knowing that you can make your future as secure as you want it to be.

Semisextile: 3, 5 You have many intangible assets that you can draw on when you need to. Once you learn to convert them from ideas to definitive action, you should succeed in your chosen career. But be careful that you don't indulge in daydreams or wishful thinking. Put your anxieties on the shelf and stop delaying your progress by being apathetic and indolent. You should feel guilty only if you refuse to develop your creative potentials or if you underestimate your talents. This same negative attitude can make you assume that you aren't loved because you do not deserve it. It might be easier to wait for others to demonstrate their feelings before you make any commitment, thus reducing the possibility of romantic disappointment.

1st to the 4th   You know the importance of thinking for yourself, even though you've been strongly conditioned to pattern your thinking after your parents' beliefs. You may resent their intrusion.

 2nd to the 3rd   You know that in order to develop and achieve your goals, you must be allowed to think for yourself, uninfluenced by anyone else, although you may keep close ties with your parents. Your good memory and your store of knowledge should serve you well.

 3rd to the 2nd   You are clever in devising money-making schemes, for you understand how money talks, and you use this knowledge to further your ambition. Your need to be free and secure inspires you to capitalize on your ideas.

 4th to the 1st   At first it wasn't easy for you to express yourself except in ways that would offend your parents. Later you realized that unless you resist your family, you will never get an opportunity to make a life of your own.

 5th to the 12th   You are not fully aware of all your talents, because you have allowed others to tell you what to do. In spite of this, you know that one day you must make a dramatic break and exploit your imagination in your own way.

 6th to the 11th   You can realize your fondest dreams only by making a deliberate effort to do so. It is worth using all that energy, if only for your own peace of mind. You will have to work to gain a place in society if you want security in your later years.

 7th to the 10th   It may seem impossible to attain a prominent position because of your dependence on your family, but you would like to prove that you can do it anyway. When you resolve your fear of competition, you could do well in a career in which you work from your home, such as real estate, insurance or accounting.

 8th to the 9th   A financial career would be a suitable way to express yourself and also satisfy your emotional anxieties. As a financial counselor, you could win the approval of others for your services and at the same time make an investment in your future.

 9th to the 8th   An education will give you the self-confidence you need. But the suggestions made here are meaningless unless you are truly motivated to improve your circumstances.

 10th to the 7th   Get help from your associates and learn from competitors, for they can be a catalyst to your success. Listen to your mate's suggestions; you probably chose your life partner because of his or her versatile mind. Your partner should share your dreams.

 11th to the 6th   Only determination and persistence will bring you security in your later years. You will probably change direction often in your life, which is fine, as long as you keep to a plan that will eventually bring you security.

 12th to the 5th   Unless you believe in yourself, you can't realize your dreams. Don't underestimate what your talent can accomplish when used imaginatively. Learn to get the attention of people who can open doors. You don't make exaggerated claims about yourself.

Trine: 8, 12 Being so close to the other members of your family makes it difficult for you to think for yourself. You are inclined to pattern your habits and attitudes on your parents' line of reasoning. Because of this emotional conditioning, you tend to keep your opinions to yourself unless they concur with your parents' ideas, for you feel obligated to them. Eventually you will have to take responsibility for using your mental abilities for your own interests, even if it causes you some temporary anxiety. Your keen imagination will serve you well if you are daring enough to exploit it openly. A formal education will help you understand how capable you can be, and from this will come the self-confidence you need for success. Along with your intellectual abilities, you have great sensitivity to other people's feelings, and you try to do what is best for them.

Sextile: 2, 6 You may often change your course of action in working toward your goals, which is all right if you keep your primary objective in focus. The need to establish security for your later years will help you maintain a plan of action and see it realized. It would be ideal if the same force would stimulate you to stand on your own. Money is very important to you, and few people can match your talent for acquiring it. You know that money is necessary to achieving your goals. You hate to depend on anyone for support, so you try to capitalize on your own ideas to make that unnecessary.

Cross: 1, 7, 10 Your highest priority should be to accept the challenges of competition. There is no easy way to gain public recognition for your accomplishments except through self-discipline and determination to succeed. That will improve your self-image and assure your growth in your position. Your partner may be more helpful than you realize, and you should pay attention to any suggestions he or she offers because you will probably benefit from them. Even your competitors can serve your purposes if you learn how they succeed. But your mate is your best source of inspiration, and you both will be rewarded by living up to each other's expectations. You need a partner who understands you and who will support you when your self-confidence sags.

Inconjunct: 9, 11 Your best motivation comes from people who need your expertise to solve their problems. You owe them your continued understanding and professional skill as long as they need it, for it is through this kind of interchange that you will attain your future goals. Be wary of friends who make excessive demands unless they give you some consideration for your efforts. At the same time, you must know that only hard work will bring you the security you need and are so preoccupied with.

Semisextile: 3, 5 Take advantage of your excellent mind and develop it into your greatest asset. You are enormously resourceful in capitalizing on your ideas, but you must avoid people who try to distract you from your plans. The knowledge you've gained will help you secure a career position. The worst trap you could fall into is to allow family considerations to inhibit your development. With a little imagination you can accomplish a great deal by exploiting your creative potentials. You will have to sell yourself and your ideas, but don't underestimate their quality. It is unlikely that you would exaggerate your abilities, anyway.

1st to the 4th   You are very fond of the people who loved and helped you as a child. You appreciate any kindness and try to reciprocate. A tranquil home is soothing to you, and you hope your own home will have that quality.

2nd to the 3rd   Because you dislike conflict, you don't argue when other people disagree with your views. You will become less hesitant and more self-reliant when you have to make your own decisions. Don't let others dominate you and interfere with developing your talents.

3rd to the 2nd   You long for a comfortable life surrounded by beautiful objects, and to attain that end, you will resist those who oppose you. You must put your ideas to work if you want any rewards. Remember, others are free with advice when their own security is not at stake.

4th to the 1st   You know you must resist those who try to control you, but you don't want to hurt your loved ones. Decide how much you owe others and how much you owe yourself. Don't compromise unless there is no alternative.

5th to the 12th   You may never go far from home, but you love to fantasize and dream. Use your fine imagination to beautify your home and surround yourself with fine music, art and good friends. A secret romantic, you enjoy many imaginary love affairs.

6th to the 11th   You could use your creative talents and build security for the future in a field such as decorating, designing or renovating. You don't like to make demands on your friends, but if asked, they would help you get started.

7th to the 10th   A peaceful person by nature, you would find it difficult to accept the tension that goes with success. You may prefer moderate goals with lesser risks and greater harmony.

8th to the 9th   You offer kindness and even gifts to those who show an interest in you, especially when you are attracted to a particular person. You will do anything to win the love of someone who seems sincerely interested, and you are able to keep your partner's attention.

9th to the 8th   You are an understanding listener and know just what to say to please others. But you hesitate to commit yourself until you are sure of the other person's motives. You want to be considered refined and polished, so you always act with propriety.

10th to the 7th   You are attracted to those who are as polished and charming as you are. You want your partner to hold you in high esteem, so that you are a credit to him or her as you pursue your career.

11th to the 6th   You want your later years to be free from financial worries, and you believe they will be. To gain that end, you are willing to work hard and give up some immediate pleasures. You will take advantage of any opportunity that will allow you to retire early.

12th to the 5th   You generally maintain a low profile, because you assume that your creative potential is not very special. Don't neglect to exploit your talents. You are reasonably fond of children, but they might interfere with your personal objectives.

Trine: 8, 12   Your fond memories of the early years at home have made you appreciate those who indulged you. Because of this conditioning, you are conciliatory and you often display your thanks for the benefits you received. You enjoy the finer things in life, and you want a good home embellished with every refinement. You feel a spiritual obligation to help those in need, and even if you are unable to provide material assistance, you find ways to show that you are sincerely concerned. You usually say the right thing at the right time to encourage others to think well of you, and people are impressed with your willingness to lend a hand. You are guarded, though, about making a commitment until you are sure that the other person isn't trying to take advantage of you.

Sextile: 2, 6   You are preoccupied with having every possible comfort, and you try to devise ways to get them without having to invest more than is absolutely necessary. Security is very important to you, but you should not have too much difficulty in fulfilling your needs if you use your ideas imaginatively to that end. If forced by conditions beyond your control, you will compromise your immediate desire to implement your long-range plans for future security.

Cross: 1, 7, 10   You should look for a career that will allow you to fulfill your creative potential and to learn whether you can accept competition. You may choose a career in which the risks are minimal and the gains equally modest, because you abhor tension and the disharmony of competition. Unless you stand firm in your goals, others may try to gain control over you. It would be a great help if someone dear to you would give you the stimulus you need to succeed. Not wanting to alienate the people you deal with in your daily affairs, you are inclined to make unnecessary concessions. Your mate could give you the support you need, and his or her advice could be most helpful when you feel overwhelmed by increasing tension.

Inconjunct: 9, 11   Though you don't make demands on your friends, they will very likely help you plan your future if you ask. You must accept the fact that any security you hope to gain will have to come from your own efforts. Getting an education will allow you to reach your goals. In fact, your goals can't be realized unless you invest in an education, which is the bottom rung of your ladder of achievement. People like you because you are never too busy to listen to their problems, and they feel you understand them better than anyone else. You have a talent for showing people how they can make the best of their own skills and become self-reliant.

Semisextile: 3, 5   Learn to rely on your ability to solve problems, for your solutions are as valid as other people's. It's all right to disagree with those who have different opinions, for dissension is healthy. Your creative talents deserve to be fully exploited; failing to develop them is only shortchanging yourself. If you assume that you are not desirable to the opposite sex, you will delay the time when you can have a warm, affectionate relationship with someone whom you find attractive. The chances are good that you will eventually marry someone you have known a long time who has only recently emerged as a potential partner.

1st to the 4th   You are restless and uneasy when forced to submit to others' demands. You have a strong desire to be independently secure and free of obligation to others. Your parents may resist your efforts to make a life of your own, which could strain your relationship.

 2nd to the 3rd   You feel that when your talents and ideas are developed, they will adequately satisfy your needs. You hate to be told that it's risky to leave home, for you want to make up your own mind, even if you have to learn the hard way.

 3rd to the 2nd   You will develop the skills required to earn a good living because you have a great need for security. You want to accumulate enough money to make investments and assure your future financial independence.

 4th to the 1st   You must establish your own roots so you can build your future through your own efforts. Don't be indifferent to your family, for you may need their help some day. Get all the facts before you act, and take suggestions from those with experience.

 5th to the 12th   You can avoid unnecessary risks by being well informed. You still have to account for your actions. Your contribution to society might be through helping those who have been treated unjustly. Don't associate with any shady individuals.

 6th to the 11th   It will take great effort and self-reliance to gain independence for your later years. Develop your creative talents to assure your future security. People may try to use you for your skills, but you will learn to help only those who deserve it.

 7th to the 10th   Be prepared for rejection as you rise in your career. You will learn who to serve and who should serve you. Your parents may pressure you to live up to their goals, but as you become more self-reliant, you won't need their approval.

 8th to the 9th   The behavior code set up by your parents will help you establish your own rules of right and wrong. Getting an education will give you further advantages so you won't have to resort to illegal or dishonorable practices.

 9th to the 8th   Your preoccupation with financial security gives people confidence that you can help them in their business affairs. They believe that you will serve their interests well because you have a great deal of self-confidence.

 10th to the 7th   You may prefer to work independently, but take advantage of opportunities presented by competitors or friends. Learn from others' failures and listen to your partner's suggestions. You need assurance that your mate admires and needs you.

 11th to the 6th   You will acquire many friends through your work, and you will use them to gain your objectives. Don't expect others to yield every time, for their desires and future security are as important to them as yours are to you.

 12th to the 5th   Fulfilling your own needs is far more important than sacrificing yourself to your family. You may postpone marrying to avoid responsibilities. Marrying hastily may curtail your ambitions. If you wait, it will be easier to fulfill your family duties.

Trine: 8, 12 You are annoyed when conditions force you to submit to other people's demands. As you grew up, you felt resentful when you had to fulfill family obligations or take on other people's responsibilities. You wanted to be independent as soon as possible, even though it caused some bitterness at home. You especially want to make your own way and make your own mistakes, which is part of the maturing process. There will be hazards to face, and you must accept full responsibility for your actions. Your best path for development would be through some broad social program where your efforts can have the best results. You will have to be discriminating in choosing who to associate with in your endeavors. Because you encourage people to trust you and believe that you understand their problems, it is important not to violate their confidence.

Sextile: 2, 6 You believe that actions speak louder than words as you strive to acquire the necessary financial resources to fulfill your ambitions. You find it especially upsetting to be without funds, and you make a point of knowing as much as possible about money and devising schemes to earn it. You equate freedom with financial independence, but you should develop human qualities to offset any lean periods. People tend to help those who demonstrate admirable qualities and shun those who are totally preoccupied with money. You must work hard to develop friendships that will benefit you when you are in need and learn to make concessions to others, for their priorities are as important to them as yours are to you.

Cross: 1, 7, 10 Your greatest difficulties will come when you face reversals or rejection in your career. Establishing goals within reasonably safe limits will allow you to gain experience and proficiency in your field. Don't try to fulfill your parents' expectations, for the only potentials you must live up to are your own. Once you are independent, you are accountable only to yourself. Take advantage of opportunities offered by your associates and learn why your competitors sometimes fail. Your partner could be a valuable source of creative imagination if you listen to his or her ideas. You are stimulated when your mate admires your successes and comforted by support when things go wrong.

Inconjunct: 9, 11 Be very careful of friends who are always asking favors. See to it that you help only those who deserve it. Work out a program of action designed to give you the security you need for your later years. You will be guided by the sound ethical standards you learned in your formative years. Getting an education will extend the limits of your goals and give you the necessary leverage to successfully meet any challenge without having to resort to questionable practices.

Semisextile: 3, 5 You have to learn the hard way, but you never forget what you learn. Your greatest asset is your ability to put your ideas into action, if you can learn not to act until you have fully explored the consequences. Probably you want to make substantial gains in your career before considering marriage, and that is the course you should take. You cannot afford the responsibilities and limitations of a family while you are trying to establish a place in your career. You need as much mobility as possible during this period of your life.

1st to the 4th   Your childhood circumstances were comfortable, and your parents provided you with warmth, affection and material security. Because of your fond memories of those years, you would like to help your parents in their twilight years.

 2nd to the 3rd   Your parents allowed you to develop freely according to your own abilities and encouraged you to cultivate your own ideas, talents and dreams. Your siblings felt that they could turn to you for help with their problems.

 3rd to the 2nd   You have innumerable ideas for earning a comfortable living, but you aren't decisive enough to act on them. You must take the responsibility for carrying out your plans. You are more concerned with having moral substance than with making money.

 4th to the 1st   Use the advantages of your upbringing to become self-sufficient on your own merits. Don't avoid the responsibility for making your own life. You can achieve any goal you set your sights on if you spurn apathy and indolence.

 5th to the 12th   You have a vast storehouse of creative resources that are available when you need them. Find out what social conditions your talents can serve; you will feel good about yourself if you respond to a genuine need.

 6th to the 11th   If you hope to achieve security in your later years, you must plan your future goals carefully now. Don't give in to friends' demands, for they may deter you from your goals. A soft touch, you may neglect your own needs to help others.

 7th to the 10th   You are not very impressed with status and position, and the effort of reaching the top may be too great to make up for the loss of freedom. You must develop strength and courage to persist in competition. A docile person, you may prefer not to try rather than to try and fail.

 8th to the 9th   An education is the best investment you can make for security in your later years, for it will help you develop self-awareness and self-sufficiency. You will learn to be philosophic about your highs and lows and you will understand people's problems better.

 9th to the 8th   People will seek your professional services because they are impressed by your knowledge and believe that you can help them. And you can, even if you don't know you have such a talent. Self-analysis will give you spiritual strength.

 10th to the 7th   You may avoid competition for fear of failing, but as you mature, you will learn that competition is the key to your greatest accomplishments. You don't need anyone's approval to rise to prominence if you are willing to use your talents to benefit the public.

 11th to the 6th   If you are willing to work to serve others' needs, every year will bring increased fulfillment. Don't dwell on your health, but keep working to gain financial independence so you can express your creative imagination where it is needed.

 12th to the 5th   Your greatest mistake would be failing to cultivate your creative talents. Use your assets imaginatively and demonstrate your unconditional spiritual concern for others.

Trine: 8, 12   Your early environment gave you the opportunity to develop and express your creative talents. Your great imagination is an asset that enables you to devise ways to utilize your resources. This will benefit the general public in more ways than you realize. Your depth of understanding and your compassion for less fortunate individuals can be the foundation on which to build enriching life experiences. You don't really fear occasional reversals and setbacks, because you believe in yourself. Your attitude encourages others to seek your assistance in developing the same positive outlook in their lives.

Sextile: 2, 6   Knowing that your future security depends on your willingness to work, you are able to mobilize all of your assets and resources to achieve the greatest yield and assure the security you need. Even though you know quite a lot, you need constant reminders that you are doing the right thing with your knowledge. You have the creative imagination to meet crises and to adapt whatever resources you have to succeed in spite of obstacles. You can reach any goal you set for yourself if you continually add to the vast amount of information you already have. Don't be afraid to extend yourself in unfamiliar situations that show some promise of greater security, for it is unlikely that you will overreach yourself to the point of diminishing returns. You should cultivate a more optimistic attitude in order to enhance the likelihood of succeeding more often than not.

Cross: 1, 7, 10   Overprotection in your early years could make you feel inclined to avoid the responsibility for making a life of your own. When you are away from the familiar comforts of home, you are not sufficiently impressed with your ability to succeed. To earn your place in society and become increasingly independent of your family, you will have to accept the awesome challenges that will come when you begin to assert yourself in competition. It is senseless to wait until you have perfected all your skills or gained the approval of your contemporaries before asserting yourself. You are probably better equipped and prepared than you know to meet challenging situations, as your success in competition will reveal.

Inconjunct: 9, 11   Before you can hope to distinguish yourself in your career or field of interest, you must deal with your fear of competition. Learn to blend imagination with creativity and use this talent to establish your position. An education will enhance your worth and enable you to derive the greatest benefits from your creative talents. Learn to put a value on your services and demand a proper return for them.

Semisextile: 3, 5   You should play down your own negative appraisal of your worth and capitalize on your assets. Don't assume that people don't appreciate you and that you have to make special compromises so that they will like you. Be yourself, and you will earn respect for your accomplishments. You are better liked than you realize, and your close romantic attachments attest to this.

1st to the 4th Your childhood was characterized by austerity and discipline, which you learned to accept or take the consequences. You may have decided that your parents didn't love you. Perhaps you resented their authority and their seemingly unfair rules.

2nd to the 3rd You learned very early to speak up only if you had something important to say. Your good mind will develop if given the opportunity, and you will skillfully capitalize on your ideas to obtain financial rewards. Explore different ways to apply your talents.

3rd to the 2nd You know the value of your talents, and you can learn how to handle your financial affairs to enhance your worth. Basically conservative, you discuss only matters that you understand, and you think through all your plans before making a commitment.

4th to the 1st An unaggressive person, you maintain a low profile because you aren't sure you can function independently. You enjoy your parents' protection and find it difficult to act without having their approval.

5th to the 12th You feel that you can manage very well by yourself without other people. You deliberately isolate yourself from society and quietly plan the best use of your talents. You look forward to the time when you will be independently secure.

6th to the 11th You carefully choose friends who will make few demands; it is not that you are unwilling to help others, but you want to offer your services on your own terms. Future security is your most important priority.

7th to the 10th You are impressed by people who reach the top, but you know that to do so yourself, you must develop your talents and learn to make your own life. It will be a struggle to master your frailties, but you have enough self-discipline to succeed.

8th to the 9th An education will improve your ability to understand people's motivations. You intuitively understand the meanings underlying people's words. Others know that you are someone to reckon with on serious matters, and they won't brush you aside.

9th to the 8th The people you deal with are impressed by your professionalism and believe you can handle their affairs competently. Knowing you are well thought of will help you think well of yourself. You might enjoy the field of finance.

10th to the 7th You know that you can achieve only if you respond to competition. When you are stabilized in your profession, you should look for a partner who will respect your accomplishments, support you in your low moments and share your successes.

11th to the 6th You make a continuing effort to develop and grow, for you know that your eventual independent security will be worth the effort. It is likely that you will become so infatuated with success that you will keep postponing retirement.

12th to the 5th You may avoid romantic alliances because of the responsibility involved, and you may postpone having children because you fear they will delay your independence. When you do have children, you will be a disciplinarian like your parents.

Trine: 8, 12 Because of the austerity and discipline of your early years, you now have a great respect for law and order. However, when you were growing up you probably resented authority, and you have painful memories of having to submit without question. In order to succeed, you realize that you must establish certain priorities. You know that you have a talent for serving others' needs, and you also know that if the public appreciates your skills, they will be willing to pay dearly for them. You don't mind satisfying their needs, but you demand a strict accounting for any services rendered. Perhaps you are a "loner," carefully planning how to take advantage of your talents in ways that will have the most constructive and productive results.

Sextile: 2, 6 You have the mistaken idea that individuals or groups expect you to always perform at peak capacity. Probably you are afraid that you will let them down, which would be very painful to deal with. It might help if you realized that attaining excellence always involves occasional setbacks and reversals. Through these experiences you will learn how to improve your craft, and no one can expect more from you than that. You know that to become independent you must detach yourself from the hidden feelings of obligation to those who were dear to you in your early years. You must establish your priorities so that you can use your creative potential smoothly and purposefully. As soon as you derive a reasonable financial return for your efforts and can visualize a time when you will have earned the freedom you desire, you will feel secure on your own merits. Then you will not have to answer to anyone for your actions.

Cross: 1, 7, 10 Although you are accustomed to discipline, your attempts to meet the challenge of competition have been half-hearted because you are afraid of being hurt by failure. To avoid failing, you plan to develop your natural resources of talent. Your growth may be painfully slow and unrewarding at first, but once you know that you will succeed, you will persist until you reach your goals.

Inconjunct: 9, 11 The prospect of rising to the heights of achievement is especially awesome, considering the parental restraint that you had to endure. Your education should have given you a glimpse of the success that would be yours if you could rise above your feeling of obligation to those who were unwilling to help you in your early years. Focus on the position you want and be comforted by the thought of the financial security and freedom that success will bring you.

Semisextile: 3, 5 Never doubt for a moment that your ideas are a significant factor in helping you prove your worth to yourself, above all, and to others who will serve as the platform for your eventual success. Don't let anyone imply that you cannot do this or that. Your most serious liability is that you doubt your own creative potential and the enormous gains you can make when you begin to utilize it. You must start by liking yourself enough that you know you deserve to succeed. It isn't necessary to win the world's approval before acting. You will be the greater loser if you wait.

1st to the 4th   Your need to function in your own way is frustrated by obligations to your family. Conditions in your environment make you want to become independent of responsibilities that you feel are not truly yours to fulfill.

 2nd to the 3rd   You have the ingenuity to capitalize on your ideas, and capital provided by your parents could be instrumental in getting you started. If you expect them to make a contribution, however, you will have to make concessions and fulfill your obligations to them.

 3rd to the 2nd   You are preoccupied with becoming financially independent. This indicates that you need to stand on your own in order to realize your goals and objectives.

 4th to the 1st   Because you disdain discipline, you are forced to demonstrate your ability to express yourself without the support of either of your parents.

 5th to the 12th   Your fear of being dependent on others makes you eager to take advantage of your gifted imagination. You feel a strong obligation to the public, and you know that you can make a substantial contribution to improve social circumstances.

 6th to the 11th   You are willing to work hard and apply yourself in any capacity that will guarantee you the greatest eventual financial independence. You are impatient with friends who often make demands on you.

 7th to the 10th   Reaching an important position may be demanding, and you are aware that the competition will be keen. But you know you can rise to any challenge, although you might have some difficulty becoming stabilized in your position.

 8th to the 9th   You understand the importance of higher education and you realize that you must invest in getting some training in order to succeed in your career .

 9th to the 8th   In your profession you understand how to fulfill the needs of others. You will look for a partner who has strong intellectual interests, someone with whom you can enjoy a good physical relationship.

 10th to the 7th   Your destiny is closely tied to public affairs. Your opportunities for success in your career will come from serving the needs of the public.

 11th to the 6th   You know that the financial security of your later years depends on using your resources and making them as productive as possible.

 12th to the 5th   You fear romantic attachments because of the responsibility involved. You devote considerable effort to finding ways to use your creative talents imaginatively, and you are often inspired in the way you apply them.

Trine: 8, 12   You had to subdue your desire for independence until you had matured sufficiently to take advantage of your gifted imagination. Your early home life may have caused you to rebel against the tedious and confining duties your parents required you to carry out. However, you were generally willing to make sacrifices, because you knew that one day you would be able to invest the necessary time and effort to serve the public interests in your own unique way. You feel a strong kinship with your fellow man and want to show that you care by helping to relieve the burdens of some and correcting injustices toward others. You are truly a caring person with strong enough convictions that you can speak up for those who are unable to defend themselves.

Sextile: 2, 6   You are reasonably well focused to derive the greatest yield from your creative insight. You are not particularly disturbed at the prospect of financial difficulties, and you are prepared to use other means if necessary to gain the freedom to come and go at will. You will align yourself with people whose purposes are in harmony with your own until you achieve the personal and financial integrity to stand alone. You understand the value of your natural talents, for they will provide you with a substantial income and give you the opportunity to prove what you can do. You are clever in devising ways to utilize your talents effectively, and you are determined that your efforts will provide the desired results.

Cross: 1, 7, 10   You know that to attain an important position that will give you the leverage to accomplish your goals, you must be willing to accept challenge and competition. It will be necessary to control your urge to assert yourself impulsively. You will have to make some concessions to others if you want to win their cooperation and help in achieving your objectives. You must give others the chance to offer suggestions, for you will find that many opportunities will come from totally unexpected sources. You will gain much support from a mate or partner who has the perception and foresight to help you realize your fondest dreams and aspirations.

Inconjunct: 9, 11   Good intentions are not enough, and you know that to do your best work you must be fully informed. When others speak, you listen carefully and pick up many ideas. You will even go without some of your favorite comforts and spend time and energy to work toward gaining your goals successfully. This involves some sacrifice, but you know that it serves your future security and independence from want.

Semisextile: 3, 5   All your life you may have to define and redefine your motivations. In your need to achieve material comforts and be free from conditions that seem to threaten or limit you in any way, you may make too many concessions and lose sight of your more enduring accomplishments on behalf of society. You must be careful not to become obsessed with achieving financial success at the risk of losing sight of your most important objectives. You belong to the society you live in, and you must respond to the most pressing human needs by using your creative talent and inspiration to serve them. It would be too bad to review your past and see that you indulged yourself to the exclusion of helping those with whom you shared a social and spiritual destiny.

1st to the 4th You were conditioned by your early environmental circumstances to feel obligated to the people who provided you with the necessities of life.

 2nd to the 3rd Learning to capitalize on your own ideas will prove very advantageous in your efforts to establish your independence from your family.

 3rd to the 2nd You will gain significant benefits by using your creative imagination to satisfy your material needs, and you will also learn how worthwhile your talents can be when they are applied thoughtfully.

 4th to the 1st Your feeling of inadequacy contributes to your insecurity. This makes it even more urgent to assert yourself, even at the risk of having occasional setbacks or reversals. In this way you will strengthen your integrity.

 5th to the 12th Your condescending manner may interfere with the enormous contribution you can make to society when you apply your creative gifts. Don't relegate yourself to obscurity.

 6th to the 11th You will realize your future goals and objectives when you apply more energy to making careful plans. You must be wary of taking on any obligations to your friends unless you know they are willing to pay for your services.

 7th to the 10th Either you feel that your parents' relationship is uncomfortable, or there is some distrust between you and one or both of them. As a result, you may find it nearly impossible to live up to their expectations, which you may feel guilty about. You could lose interest in achieving goals that are within your capabilities.

 8th to the 9th You may feel that the time and preparation required to reach your goals entails making too many sacrifices. However, you should realize that getting an education is the best investment you can make in your future.

 9th to the 8th Your greatest development will come as you reach out beyond the narrow confines of your early environment. Self-analysis is required for this process.

 10th to the 7th Your success in dealing with competitors is the catalyst you need. Through the opportunities provided by your dealings with the general public, you will learn that you can succeed.

 11th to the 6th You should look for a career with a future, so that your efforts will earn you the position and financial security you want for your later years.

 12th to the 5th Your greatest liability is that you don't believe in yourself. You have the feeling that no one appreciates you or could possibly love you. You are extremely sensitive emotionally and feel crushed if your attentions are rejected. The worst thing you can do is fail to take advantage of your creative potentials. Your warmth and tenderness are the ingredients for an ideal relationship.

Trine: 8, 12   You feel obligated to those who helped you, but subconsciously you know you have an obligation to yourself too. Your own fulfillment depends on making sacrifices to learn how to function independently. Education will teach you to make decisions on your own. Your early environment was too limited to allow you to explore the opportunities that lay beyond your parents' perception. You have a broad view of the world, and there is no limit to what you can do for society, but you must be available. Getting an education will sharpen your vision and make you more aware of your creative gifts. If you accept obscurity, you will persecute yourself later for not using your talents. Instead, establish your position in the public spotlight.

Sextile: 2, 6   You know you have talent, but it isn't easy to apply it to derive the material benefits you need. It may be difficult to get support from those who were close to you in your early years. Find out how to use your skills and get the feedback you need to prove that you are on the right track. You don't want to waste time, so you may try your hand at whatever comes along, just to get started in your career. A job with a good future will provide financial security in your later years. If your work doesn't make sufficient demands on your talents, examine your motives. You could become locked into a job that gives few rewards in accomplishment and satisfaction. In other words, don't accept a job simply because it gives you security and satisfies your material needs.

Cross: 1, 7, 10   Your greatest hurdle is to get over the notion that you cannot succeed in competition. You must be willing to risk occasional setbacks if only to prove that you can succeed in spite of them. You need an opportunity to show what you can do with your creative imagination, especially in dealing with the public. For confirmation, look to your achievements, not to your parents' approval. Your responsibility is to make an important social contribution by using your sympathetic understanding to help people with problems. The admiration, appreciation and support you win will improve your self-esteem.

Inconjunct: 9, 11   Apathy is your greatest problem, for your attempts to rise to your fullest potential may be half-hearted. You will have to make sacrifices to get the training you need, but you cannot afford to deny yourself this advantage. Your anxieties about future financial security may be relieved if you plan your career very carefully, first getting the education you need to be effective. Decide what you want and prepare a program for getting it. You don't have to listen to friends who make suggestions about what you should do with your life. Learn to say no when they request your assistance if it diverts you unnecessarily from your objectives.

Semisextile: 3, 5   Don't neglect your personal affairs by devoting too much time to your professional goals. Once you learn to believe in yourself, you will attract satisfying relationships. Avoid being so obligated to your family that you neglect relationships that make you feel loved. A romantic at heart, you idealize the person you respond to. While it is desirable to have high ideals in searching for a lover, it is more realistic to expect some imperfection. Your lover will serve as a stimulus as you pursue your objectives and will make the sacrifices seem worthwhile.

1st to the 4th There was much tension in your early environment because of the demands of authority. This circumstance has induced you to become master of your own fate.

 2nd to the 3rd The sometimes subtle pressure of developing ideas stimulates you to take the necessary chances to become financially independent of those close to you.

 3rd to the 2nd You understand that you may have to be forceful in getting people to pay attention to your creative ideas in order to get the resources you need for developing them. Having sufficient money stabilizes your anxieties.

 4th to the 1st Alienating circumstances in your home will force you to assert yourself and feel confident so that you are able to succeed on your own.

 5th to the 12th Although you may prefer to bide your time until you feel sure that you can succeed in your endeavors, you *know* that some day you will make an important impact on society. You are willing to cultivate your talents quietly until you arrive at the right moment for using them.

 6th to the 11th Though at present you may consider yourself obliged to help your friends when they expect favors, you also know that when you realize your goals you will have the financial security to indulge only those who merit your attention.

 7th to the 10th Career demands may seem oppressive at first, but you have the enormous advantage of being able to withstand competition to reach the position you want. You may also want to prove to those closest to you that you can achieve without their assistance.

 8th to the 9th Because you are afraid of remaining in obscurity, you will do anything to get an education. You know that by making the necessary sacrifices you will reap enormous dividends.

 9th to the 8th You feel a strong spiritual dedication to serving the needs of your fellow man, and you demand to be given the opportunity to prove yourself.

 10th to the 7th You attract people who are hypnotized by your compelling desire to rise above your early circumstances. Your partner must support you in this; he or she must be as eager as you are for your success.

 11th to the 6th No stranger to hard work, you are willing to work hard and apply yourself to demonstrate how competent you are. The long-term yields will be substantial, and your eventual financial independence is assured.

 12th to the 5th You make subtle demands on your romantic partners, and you don't take rejection gracefully. Take special care that your family obligations don't interfere with developing your creative potentials, thus further delaying your independence.

Trine: 8, 12 Your early circumstances conditioned you to feel strongly obligated to your family. Pressures from those in authority over you produced deep-seated tensions that will be relieved only when you can stand on your own. You know that one day you will have to do this, but you are inclined to let the situation ride until a crisis forces your hand. You have a strong desire to be useful to others, but you aren't sure you can express yourself within the narrow confines of family life. You would like to prove your effectiveness in dealing with the problems of the larger society. You know you have the creative imagination to improve social conditions, so you apply yourself in developing your talents on your own. Subconsciously you know that when the time is right you will move to fulfill your destiny. The delays you encounter until then only deepen your commitment and give you the courage to withstand the demands of those who are close to you. You know that eventually your contribution will be appreciated.

Sextile: 2, 6 Knowing that you need to be financially secure, you will take advantage of your imaginative ideas to achieve independence. You know how to communicate your ideas to those who have the resources to promote them. You are able to apply yourself to improve your skills, and hard work is no deterrent. Success will follow from self-development, because you know your ideas have the potential to provide long-term yields. You are not afraid to knock on doors, because you know that in time your persistence will be rewarded. But mainly you need to know that you've made the only decision possible—to alert others to your talents and skills.

Cross: 1, 7, 10 Coping with your responsibilities to yourself will be delayed if you let yourself be intimidated by your family. Alienating conditions in the home will force you to assert your independence as you establish your position in a competitive society. You will grow increasingly confident as you learn to meet challenges successfully, and you will build a strong foundation for your life. It will be satisfying to know that you have risen above your early difficult circumstances and that you have demonstrated the importance of doing it in your own way.

Inconjunct: 9, 11 Some painful sacrifices are necessary if you want to fulfill your ambitions. But having to live in obscurity is more painful to you than the necessary investment in time and energy to become financially independent. You don't want to always be at the beck and call of more successful people. You know that eventually you will serve your fellow man, but you want to decide for yourself how to do it. Getting an education will expand your options. When you have the right training, you will become spiritually committed to solving the problems of others. You will feel content with yourself for this service.

Semisextile: 3, 5 Being uninformed is your greatest liability and will keep you from accomplishing as much as you can. You must be willing to apply your talents, but you have to ask yourself if you are ready to be the best in your field. Learn to listen to others, if only to realize that you are as talented and as capable as they are. You need to dramatize your creative potentials and communicate with people outside your family to be assured of your gifts. You may have to postpone making close ties with others until you can build independence without losing your identity.

Sun in Fourth, Moon in First

Because your inner and outer worlds are quite different, you may have difficulty in making a fulfilling life for yourself. Too much loyalty to family concerns may result in some alienation and guilt. Unless you insist on greater self-determination, it will be difficult later on to meet the demands of a career and your relationships. Through your friends you can learn to be more self-confident in social situations.

Avoiding public exposure would deny you the opportunity to exploit your skills and acquire self-reliance. You need to learn a skill and become so competent in it that you never have to fear the challenge of competition. Start at the bottom if necessary and reeducate yourself as opportunities come along so you will be ready when a promotion is offered.

A partner who understands how difficult it is for you to assert yourself will reassure you of your ability to succeed. You may marry early to escape from conditions at home, but if your identity is intact, there is no reason why it can't be a happy marriage.

Sun in Fourth, Moon in Second

Although you identify strongly with your family, especially your parents, you know how to use your basic resources to sustain yourself on your own. Gaining financial and emotional security is a high priority in your life. Your parents gave you the confidence that you can accomplish this, and you appreciate their efforts in your behalf. You maintain an orderly, harmonious lifestyle, which gives you a good perspective about your relationships, career goals and personal interests. A career that allows you to serve the public would appeal to you. Your sensitivity and concern are ideally suited to helping others with their problems.

Your partner expects a lot from you, which won't be difficult to provide if you know it is appreciated. Your mate will probably urge you to excel in your career, believing in your potential for taking on more and more responsibility. The time you have to spend away from home may cause problems with your children, but this should be resolved eventually. Make certain there is always room to expand in your career, because once you get started, you won't be content until you reach your maximum.

Sun in Fourth, Moon in Third

Your early environment had a profound influence on your later development, because your parents were unwilling to let you be independent. You should live apart from your family so you can establish your own identity and extend yourself in realizing your ambitions. To survive and gain what you need, you must become more selfish in your motivation. With your highly developed imagination, you can win success if you learn how to apply yourself without feeling guilty about those who claim that you owe them a continuing responsibility. Your sentimental feelings for those who are close to you can mean that you make important decisions based on feeling rather than on the evidence; you should adopt a more realistic attitude.

There are many fields in which you can express yourself and be gainfully employed. Though you may have to start humbly, you can attain your goals if you have a program and a timetable on which to plot your progress. A career in such fields as real estate, property management, communications and allied interests would give you the means to express yourself with meaningful satisfaction.

It is highly possible that you will marry early, but it would be better to wait until your career was more focused.

Sun in Fourth, Moon in Fourth

If you are an isolationist, it is probably because your early conditioning caused you to withdraw under pressure and avoid dealing with conflicts. If this was the case, you will have to work harder to handle the problems you now must face in maturity. You should define your goals and objectives as soon as you can and not waste precious time feeling sorry for yourself when you can be learning a skill.

Real estate management, financial counseling, domestic services or social services would be ideal outlets for your imagination with a high probability of success. Be sure to take time to indulge in personal pleasures occasionally, if only for relief from your daily routine. As your self-confidence grows, you will extend yourself more broadly in your social environment.

As you circulate more freely in society, you will seek someone to share the rewards of your accomplishments, someone who truly appreciates your efforts and supports you in them. If your careers are similar, an even greater sharing will result.

Sun in Fourth, Moon in Fifth

Your ability to learn and find ways to use your imagination is a strong point in your favor, and your resourcefulness allows you to achieve security in your endeavors. Your parents gave you many opportunities to promote your creative talents, and they were willing to sustain you in developing them. However, you underestimate your potential, and you may hesitate to apply yourself as you should. Your romantic nature often distracts you from more important issues and keeps you from capitalizing on your gifts. Don't wait for parental approval before exploiting your talents. You often daydream, when a more decisive approach would give you the yield you want from your efforts.

Your temperament is suited for a career working with young people or children. You might also enjoy the performing or graphic arts as a medium for expressing your creativity, although you realize that this requires considerable training. You are not basically an optimist, but you will become more optimistic with each success.

You will be a good parent and partner because your youthful joviality is immediately disarming. Your children will adore you, and your partner will know you want a comfortable lifestyle with an abundance of happiness and contentment.

Sun in Fourth, Moon in Sixth

Although you have strong ties to your family and a deep sense of responsibility to them, you recognize the importance of developing skills so you can stand on your own. As you mature, you will transfer your concern to people in society who require your skills. You tend to let people make excessive demands on you in the mistaken idea that they can't succeed without you, but don't feel guilty when you can't help them.

You have a wide range of potentials for earning a comfortable living while helping to improve the quality of life for others. You might look into an institutional career in medicine or social work as a medium for your creative expression. Your progress will be slow in the beginning, but as you become familiar with the field, your responsibility will increase.

You will choose a mate who requires your indulgences, mainly because you need to be reassured that others need you. Having children will stimulate you to put your best foot forward, although you may question whether you are doing all that you should for them. You may be a late bloomer, but you have the talent to rise in your career and exert a positive influence on many people.

Sun in Fourth, Moon in Seventh

Your strong family ties will make it difficult to transfer your attention to other people in society. You cannot function well unless you are involved with people, and most of your opportunities will come from the social contacts you make. However, you aren't sure that you can live up to their expectations of you. Your first task is to be more detached from your family, putting them in the proper perspective that allows you the independence to come and go as the demands of your career and social life require. Your frame of reference must be increasingly intellectual, not emotional, to improve your ability to solve the many problems that can develop.

A career in public relations, sales or business would be appropriate for your temperament. It would be better still if your work makes it necessary to travel or live away from home. Your ability to perform will be increased if you can avoid getting too deeply involved with the people you deal with. Being emotionally committed in your duties would severely limit your effectiveness.

Postpone marrying until you are sure you aren't trying to compensate for a poor parental image in your choice of a partner, for such a situation is rarely satisfactory. Probably you will enjoy indulging your children; you have a strong mothering influence, and this may satisfy your hunger for attention.

Sun in Fourth, Moon in Eighth

Your inner and outer worlds are well coordinated, which will help you derive satisfaction in your endeavors. You care deeply for those who are close to you, and offering help when they need it comes naturally to you. Your highly developed psychic ability will serve you well as you seek to fulfill your potentials. You have a sense of social obligation, and the rewards that others derive from your efforts are significant and valuable.

Counseling, medicine, research and financial consulting are some of the fields in which you could succeed, because you would be stimulated to a high degree of proficiency and excellence. As you follow this course, there will be some intrusion on the time you want for personal indulgences, but the satisfaction you get will more than compensate for the loss of personal pleasure.

Your marriage should give you comfort and contentment so that you can apply yourself more completely to the demands of your career. But don't devote so much time to your career that your partner and children are denied the pleasure of your attention and mutual interests.

Sun in Fourth, Moon in Ninth

Your dependence on family and the security it creates makes it hard for you to stand on your own. But you are an avid learner, and an education will give you the exposure you need to make the transition from family to society. This won't be easy, but unless you detach yourself from feelings of obligation to your parents and family, your progress in the outside world will be slow. You hesitate to assert yourself, but the right training will prepare you for a career and give you self-confidence.

Any of the professions requiring service to the public would be appropriate for you, including medicine, law, counseling, travel and education. You are capable of handling that kind of responsibility, and you will derive satisfaction from your endeavors as well as comfortable earnings. This will give you the opportunity to plan for security in your later years. Once established in your career, you might turn your attention to politics or writing, which would further enrich you.

Sun in Fourth, Moon in Tenth

You are very attached to home and family, but unfortunately, you find it difficult to maintain an equal relationship with both parents. Your head tells you one thing, but your heart tells you something else, which may result in divided feelings. If you prefer one parent to the other, the resulting guilt could keep you in a quandary and make it difficult to establish your own identity. Leaving home may be necessary, for that will give you time to work out this problem and develop a more objective perspective. You may decide that being on your own is best for everyone concerned. The psychological realignment must continue, though, since this attitude will probably persist in other relationships.

A career in politics, business, sales, public relations or working with children or young people would be suited to your temperament. In the beginning, if you aren't adequately trained, you may be intimidated by those in authority, which is why you must get an education to qualify you for the growth you seek in your career.

Your biggest problem will be in your relationships, because you want someone who will share everything with you. You are uncomfortable as a loner, and you need the support of the one you love to make your achievements and your success seem meaningful.

Sun in Fourth, Moon in Eleventh

Your early conditioning allowed you to become an easy-going person who makes friends easily, though selectively. Your personable manner is endearing to those who are close to you, and even your casual acquaintances find you charming. You probably learned a lot from your father, although you may find that he expects a lot from you in return. The most pressing issue is to become increasingly independent so that you can assert yourself in your career. You will find it difficult to let go of the past and the security it represents, but if you define your goals and invest the time and energy to realize them, you should make the transition with a minimum of discomfort. In establishing the goals you want to reach, you may have to cope with continuing obligations to your parents, but don't let this delay you in focusing on your goals.

Working with young people seems ideal for you, and a career in sports, coaching or counseling might be rewarding. Managing or investing in real estate, managing sporting enterprises, and directing people in their creative development and expression are some areas in which you could succeed.

You will enjoy being married and having a family, especially if your mate is creative and talented. You need someone with a strong identity who will give you the attention you need.

Sun in Fourth, Moon in Twelfth

Your inner harmony is reflected in your serene disposition in even the most disturbing situations. This composure results from the satisfactory integration of your will and your emotions. You have the potential to succeed in most of your endeavors, though you may not choose to. There is a certain complacency in your temperament that does not allow you to pursue your ambitions aggressively enough. Your lack of ambition may annoy those who are constantly struggling to succeed, but that reaction does not disturb you. You have a calming effect on people, which could be useful if you learn to apply it. You probably underestimate your talents and, preferring to maintain a low profile, you may not realize how much society needs your contribution. If you cringe at brutality or human suffering and are distressed by injustice, you should work to help change the conditions that allow them to persist.

Social service, medicine, institutional work, the ministry or geriatrics would be areas in which you could find satisfactory expression. In your later years you will look back with contentment at your contributions to improve the quality of life for others.

Chapter Five

Fifth House

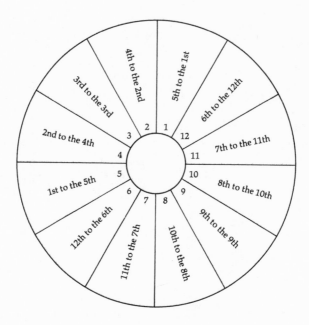

The fifth house shows your desire to express yourself in some particular way. It provides the ingredients you need for creative expression that is a visible extension of yourself. This can occur through loving someone, giving birth to a child, painting, writing, acting in a play or being completely engaged in sports. However, this department refers only to your raw talent and potential for creative self-expression. By itself, it allows you to indulge in pleasurable activity and, in a sense, to remain a child at heart. Through the affairs of this house you endeavor to become all that you potentially are and to be appreciated for your talents or gifts.

The preceding houses become incorporated in the circumstances of the fifth; your ambition to excel, which comes from the first, requires the resources of the second, the reasoning faculty of the third, the sensitivity of the fourth and the creative inspiration of the fifth to produce results. By using the fifth house properly, you can have much happiness and perhaps distinguish yourself in the world by exploiting your creative potential to the fullest in your career. A negative attitude toward the potentials of the fifth house can seriously distract you from accomplishing your objectives, if you are so fascinated with temporary pleasures that you neglect to develop your creativity. Future goals and objectives are intimately linked to the fifth house, and unless you develop your potential into usable skills, you may never gain the reward that can result from them in the eleventh house, which opposes the fifth.

Derivative House Meanings

1st to the 5th   These circumstances represent your creative potentials. You can indulge yourself or use your talents to show that you care about people.

2nd to the 4th   The creative resources of your own being are more than adequate to stabilize you in your destiny.

3rd to the 3rd   Circumstances may allow you to show how effective you are in communication, for you have the ability to dramatize your position with skill.

4th to the 2nd   If you indulge yourself or your children, you may have some problems from insufficient resources. Self-control is advised.

5th to the 1st   This is your chance to show what you can do with your creative talents. You can accomplish many things if you manage your talents with objectives in mind.

6th to the 12th   You will have to maintain a low profile only temporarily until you have learned the skills you need so you can assert yourself more publicly.

7th to the 11th   The goals you hope to reach in the future must be given a high priority so that you will achieve excellence with your talents.

8th to the 10th   Either you will indulge in temporary pleasures, or you will accept the need to sacrifice them at times to invest some effort in your career.

9th to the 9th   You have an unshakable belief in your ability to succeed, and this alone suggests that you will succeed. Love and understanding can take you far.

10th to the 8th   Investing in your creative potentials will give you a high yield. Your work with people enhances their future and sustains them now.

11th to the 7th   Unless you direct your efforts to the public, your future is limited. You should enjoy good communication with your mate or lover.

12th to the 6th   Your creative potential means little until you develop it into skills through applied effort. You abhor routine, but that is what produces competence.

1st to the 5th   Self-expression is your highest priority, and you indulge yourself whenever possible. Your charming disposition delights others, and you glow when the spotlight is focused on you.

 2nd to the 4th   You appreciate your early upbringing and the benefits you gained from close ties with your parents. You must learn to stand on your own and use your creative talents.

 3rd to the 3rd   You tend to be overly impressed with yourself and naively assume that others are also. You have a gift for dramatic self-expression and you know it, but you should be more concerned with having something to say.

 4th to the 2nd   You require lots of money in order to satisfy your desires. You must become financially secure before you can really achieve independence from those who fulfill your needs.

 5th to the 1st   Because you don't really believe that you can fail, you may neglect to develop your creative talents to ensure success. Smug satisfaction is the greatest deterrent to your success.

 6th to the 12th   You can justify your claim to fame by making some contribution to help those who are less fortunate. You tend to avoid work that does not give you public exposure. In your view, obscurity breeds contempt.

 7th to the 11th   You are impressed by the accomplishments of your peers and stimulated to match their deeds. You don't want to confront the future and accept the challenge of making it more secure.

 8th to the 10th   Achieving a position that gives you public exposure will force you to make substantial sacrifices and curtail your self-indulgent desires.

 9th to the 9th   You have visions of rising to a position of professional competence and gaining recognition for your accomplishments. Once you are established in your career, you will constantly seek to improve your position and get whatever training is required to make success possible.

 10th to the 8th   Your self-worth is determined by your effectiveness in serving the needs of others. You want the kind of career position in which people will seek your professional services. You are stimulated and encouraged by knowing that others rely on you when they need assistance.

 11th to the 7th   You want a partner who will be a loyal friend. You realize that without patronage, your future is in doubt. You want to be remembered for the important part you have played in the lives of the people you deal with.

 12th to the 6th   You need to achieve recognition before accepting a life of service. If you are willing to apply yourself even without recognition, you can earn a place of honor for your accomplishments. You could easily become fascinated with serving people who depend on your strength and creative expertise.

Trine: 1, 9 Your ability to develop your creative potentials gives you many options for self-expression. You are generally a charming person who looks at life optimistically, knowing you will reach your objectives. People who are close to you find you delightful, and you enjoy their attention. You should take advantage of your creative gifts, or the chances of achieving your ambitions will be greatly diminished. You have lots of talent, but it may be obscured by your preoccupation with pleasure, and you may not have enough time to reach your goals. You cannot afford to take that chance. It's fine to believe in your eventual success, but until you can demonstrate your effectiveness in real situations, you haven't achieved anything. The future is not a vague abstraction; it is every tomorrow of your life. Your magnetism and dramatic flair for communication are your best assets, which you should use to distinguish yourself. People like you and you like them, so you could work most effectively with the public. Once you get started, you will be filled with enthusiasm, and every success will be a catalyst for greater achievements.

Sextile: 3, 7 You know how to communicate with people, and they respond to you. You capture the public's imagination and win their confidence that you will fulfill your promises. You know how to generate enthusiasm, for which people are very grateful. Your partner will be loyal and dedicated to your causes. You may have more to choose from than most people, so your decisions may be more difficult.

Cross: 2, 8, 11 Pattern your growth after the lives of your successful associates; learn how they establish and realize their goals. You need substantial financial resources for the lifestyle you want, and you must accept responsibility for devising ways to increase your income. Even people who are less talented are able to do well financially, but you could do at least as well as they, if not better. You can easily resolve these developing anxieties about your worth by applying yourself. Before you do anything, however, you must define your goals and objectives and glow with the expectation that you will achieve them. By developing self-discipline, you can sustain yourself solely on your merits. This investment means sacrificing certain pleasures, but you will have established your priorities, which can guide you.

Inconjunct: 10, 12 You will have to give up some of your self-indulgent ways to make a personal investment that will provide long-term dividends. If you start at the bottom, you can learn how *not* to fall on your face, and if you suffer some setbacks, only a few people will know. Put your vanity on the shelf and do your best to earn the position you want. If you bring all your creative resources to the surface, you will attract the attention of important people, who can help you move up the ladder of success.

Semisextile: 4, 6 Your early conditioning has given you a good base on which to build your life. But don't think that you can coast along, letting your family take care of your needs. Your heritage should be the bottom rung of the tall ladder you will climb in fulfilling your destiny. Creative talent has no value unless you develop it. It's what you do with your creativity that determines how successful you will be. You may not enjoy hard work, but you, especially, have to accept its reality in your life. To escape from it is to escape to nowhere.

1st to the 5th Your strong response to external stimuli adds to your substantial creative imagination and provides many outlets for self-expression. You are likely to be inconstant in romantic relationships unless you feel secure with your loved one.

 2nd to the 4th Feelings of obligation to your family may keep you from forming lasting ties in a personally satisfying love relationship. Great anxiety can result if you feel torn between loyalty to your parents and the desire to gratify your own emotional needs.

 3rd to the 3rd There is a strong possibility that you can express your gifted imagination through writing. You have a good blend of feeling and the ability to express it. Finding the proper vehicle for putting your ideas to work will be a matter of great concern to you.

 4th to the 2nd You will have to use your financial resources wisely if you want to satisfy your material needs and still have sufficient funds to develop your creative gifts.

 5th to the 1st You thoroughly enjoy any opportunity to demonstrate your creative talents, for the attention you get stimulates you to improve your skill in expressing your creativity.

 6th to the 12th In order to develop your talent, you will have to accept the drudgery of hard work without recognition. You may have to be an apprentice behind the scenes to avoid the danger of rejection because of lack of training.

 7th to the 11th You may be intimidated by the success of your close friends, but this should arouse you to accept the challenge and try to match them.

 8th to the 10th Focusing on achieving important status may require some sacrifices, and your feelings of inadequacy may cause you to lose interest. Self-investment must be considered a high priority if you truly expect to gain any recognition for your talent.

 9th to the 9th Seek out the help of people who are already established, for you can benefit from their inspiration. Dedication to achieving a high degree of competence should improve your chances of attracting the attention of important people. Your gift for conversation should be an asset here.

 10th to the 8th You have an obligation to bring your talent before the general public. Public response will motivate you much more than you expect.

 11th to the 7th You will feel drawn to a partner who is sincerely interested in your future. Being loved is very important to you and will help you achieve goals that will be beneficial and bring security to both of you.

 12th to the 6th Be wary of becoming so self-indulgent that it interferes with your development. All the talent in the world is a waste if you don't apply it. You cannot afford to take time away from training if you really want to establish your worth as a truly talented person.

Trine: 1, 9 Your imagination is stimulated by learning about people who have succeeded by exploiting their talents. A romantic at heart, you daydream about having public attention for your achievements. There are many outlets for your creativity, but you must get formal training so you can meet the challenge of competition. You have many ideas for putting your imagination to use, and you may only need someone who is already established to provide inspiration. Your sensitive romantic nature makes you especially vulnerable to the distractions of personal relationships. Your major problem is to establish your priorities and then plan your life accordingly. Once secure in your profession, you will be more free to indulge personal desires. Love is very important to you, because you feel secure only when you know you are loved. You must dedicate yourself to developing and using your creative gifts.

Sextile: 3, 7 You have a flair for meeting and talking with people easily. You learn much from the people you contact every day, because you are very sensitive to external conditions. You easily accept the challenge of competition because you understand people's frailties and can establish your own position more firmly. You are romantically drawn to people who enjoy conversation and who are sympathetic with your objectives. You need to know you are loved, and you will do almost anything to show that you appreciate it. You want a partner who will support you in your efforts at self-expression, and you want to work toward goals that will be satisfying to both of you. You spend much time trying to find the proper medium for your creativity, and because you have considerable potential, you may have several choices.

Cross: 2, 8, 11 You dream about the future, when you will reach your goals, gain financial security and be satisfied with your accomplishments. But before you can achieve that goal, you must learn to balance your finances to avoid a drain on your resources. Indulging in romantic affairs or gratifying your taste for pleasure will keep you from acquiring enough money for the training you need. You should make your creative talent available to others, but this demands self-discipline. You want the public to consider you worthy before you extend yourself, because rejection is very painful to you. But proper training will make rejection unlikely. Living up to public expectations will be your greatest stimulus, motivating you to achieve even more.

Inconjunct: 10, 12 If you underestimate your creative potential, you do yourself a disservice. You must accept responsibility for developing your skills. Although obscurity may be painful, it is only temporary. Sacrifices are always necessary when you establish a goal. It doesn't mean you aren't talented, it just means you aren't ready to assume the position you want until you are properly trained. You have to make an investment of yourself so that you will be secure in the position you aspire to.

Semisextile: 4, 6 Take advantage of the assets that your parents provided and use them for your own development. The worst thing you can do is to lose interest in achieving your goals because you are used to having others take care of your needs. You might justify your inactivity by saying you are obligated to your family. It is imperative that you develop your creative potential and apply your skills so that you can be completely independent.

1st to the 5th   You are fully aware of your creative potentials and quite satisfied that with any luck you will fulfill them. You are clever in using the right words at the right time to get the effect you want. You think "young" and are generally optimistic about life.

 2nd to the 4th   Although you may not want to copy your parents' lifestyle, you know that their support has given you the ability to enjoy a carefree life. You are grateful for this.

 3rd to the 3rd   You have a remarkable capacity for devising a variety of ways to express yourself. Because you have a talent for dramatizing your ideas, you might consider writing as a suitable medium of self-expression.

 4th to the 2nd   Eventually you will have to stand on your own, but first you must grow up and accept the fact that you must earn your independence.

 5th to the 1st   You are always dreaming of having the freedom to indulge yourself, but to achieve this you will have to make an effort to capitalize on your creative assets.

 6th to the 12th   You give people the impression that nothing really bothers you, but that is not always the case. You find it painful to contemplate the possibility that you won't always be in command of the situation.

 7th to the 11th   You aspire to a career position that will net you a substantial income and, consequently, freedom from want. You are on friendly terms even with your adversaries, and you enjoy a good relationship with most of your friends.

 8th to the 10th   You may lack the staying power to persist in your chosen career simply because you fear that the necessary sacrifices are too painfully limiting to your independent nature. You hate to sacrifice pleasure for duty.

 9th to the 9th   You do believe in yourself, however, and when you decide what you want to be, you will dedicate yourself to becoming the very best. You will probably work best in direct contact with the public.

 10th to the 8th   Learning what the public wants is the key to finding the best way to apply yourself. You need constant feedback from satisfied patrons in order to know that you are making a worthwhile contribution.

 11th to the 7th   You want to know that you are important to the people you deal with and that your efforts have helped them achieve their goals. Though you may have a partner in love, you will remain in touch with close friends and associates. Your future plans include your mate, especially if he or she is willing to support your ideas.

 12th to the 6th   There might be some delay in achieving your level of greatest efficiency if you wasted valuable time in your early years trying to decide what to do and, most of all, learning to apply yourself to that commitment. Hard physical work is not consistent with your temperament.

Trine: 1, 9   Even though you are aware of your enormous creative potential, you tend to postpone doing something worthwhile with it. You are inclined to put off committing yourself, preferring to indulge in activities that serve only your own selfish interests. You tend to change the subject when someone puts you on the defensive about your lack of determination in applying yourself toward some goal. But you are sure that when the "right time" comes you will demonstrate your talent to everyone. You know that with a little luck you will prove your point. You enjoy being free, and you realize that when you make a commitment, you are bound by it. Since you often lose interest when the novelty of a project wears off, you want time to decide on your life direction. A career that brings you into close contact with the public would give you the opportunity to put your best foot forward. You express yourself so dramatically that people are impressed, which should indicate the nature of your career interests.

Sextile: 3, 7,   You know yourself better than most people know themselves, but you will feel more guilty if you fail to live up to your considerable creative and intellectual gifts. You have special talents for direct communication and writing. You can devise many ways to exploit your creative imagination in your career and personal life. Since you need to know that other people appreciate your efforts in their behalf, you may choose a profession that brings you into close contact with the public. This would give you first-hand knowledge of how effective you are in helping people, which would be enormously gratifying. You are basically a very friendly person, and it would be surprising if you became alienated from anyone, even your competitors.

Cross: 2, 8 11   Once you grow up and realize that there is a time to play and a time to work, you will find a way to stand on your own. Freedom is priceless, but you must earn it by being willing to work and contribute what you can to others. Your future financial independence rests solely on resigning yourself to this fact. There are few gifts that come without having to make some exchange in return. You have much creative potential, which you can use in worthwhile endeavors that will bring you security in your later years. Take your cue from well-meaning friends who have succeeded in reaching their goals. Once you start getting feedback from your efforts, you will have the necessary stimulus to persist. Accepting responsibility in this task is a major requirement.

Inconjunct: 10, 12   You are afraid that you will not make a lasting impression on people, but you pretend that nothing bothers you. The truth is, you want to be in control of every situation. However, there are times when you are unwilling to sacrifice your personal pleasures as a necessary investment in your career. Your carefree attitude sometimes suggests that you don't want to pay the price of fulfilling your potential. You think too much about problems that are imaginary rather than real.

Semisextile: 4, 6   Your domestic environment gave you certain advantages, although it probably delayed your maturing by contributing to your laissez-faire attitude. Be grateful that you were able to indulge yourself in your youth, but realize that achieving on your own terms means hard work now. You may have many excuses for not applying yourself, but there are probably few valid reasons.

1st to the 5th   Your naturally romantic nature inclines you to make concessions to those you love in order to stimulate warm friendly relations.

 2nd to the 4th   Your benign disposition makes you appreciate the benefits you gained from your early family life. Perhaps your parents were inclined to be more generous to you than to other family members.

 3rd to the 3rd   You are guarded in expressing yourself, because you want to avoid antagonizing anyone. You enjoy favorable relations with your brothers and sisters, and in your pursuit of harmony, you always give others the benefit of the doubt.

 4th to the 2nd   Your desire for the finer things in life makes you careless about financial resources. You find it difficult to hold on to your money when you are tempted to splurge on buying things you want rather than those you really need. You need to be more controlled.

 5th to the 1st   Because of your distaste for unpleasantness, you are overly compromising. You should develop your talent for artistic endeavor. In general you are fond of young people and children.

 6th to the 12th   You can develop your artistic talent if you are honest with yourself and admit that you have creative ability. Working behind the scenes in some worthwhile activity might be an enriching experience.

 7th to the 11th   You are overly demonstrative in expressing your fondness for your close friends, and they may take advantage of your kindness. You should be at least as attentive to your future financial security as you are to your friends.

 8th to the 10th   You need to be wary of misplaced affection that could prove costly in your career. Don't be afraid to make sacrifices to fulfill your destiny, but be realistic and don't mix business with pleasure.

 9th to the 9th   You are very fond of living the good life. This desire encourages you to cultivate relationships with people who are reasonably well established in their field.

 10th to the 8th   Your destiny could be served by helping to fulfill the needs of the public. Public relations might be a comfortable field for your benign nature. You have a talent for meeting people and making them feel at ease.

 11th to the 7th   Your idealism might cause you to postpone marriage until you find a partner whom you could enjoy in many ways, not just physically. You have a talent for meeting people and making them feel at ease.

 12th to the 6th   Because you are unwilling to see anyone's negative qualities, you are extremely vulnerable to disappointment in your love affairs. You need to question and examine closely every important contact that you make.

Trine: 1, 9 Your warm and kindly disposition attracts others. Knowing that people will seek your friendship if you seem willing to compromise, you make every effort to be on your best behavior. You know how to effectively win friends and influence people with charm and warmth. Being somewhat artistic, you try to surround yourself with the finer things in life. You have an appreciation of good music, good food and pleasurable activities, and you thoroughly enjoy them. Young people are drawn to you mainly because you are conciliatory and don't make impossible demands on them. You prefer the company of people who share your refined interests. But you must be careful not to become too wishy-washy. Have the courage to stand firm when you are right, for it's fine to be all "heart," as long as you don't lack backbone. "Make love, not war" may be your motto, but you are vulnerable to those who will take advantage of your passivity to win your submission.

Sextile: 3, 7 Generally you are on good speaking terms with all your acquaintances. You like people and enjoy the interchange of ideas. You find it hard to be angry with anyone for very long. Your interest in the people you deal with is genuine, and they understand this instinctively. People tend to be open with you about their private lives, because they feel you really care. An enthusiastic conversationalist, you bring some dramatic display into any dialogue.

Cross: 2, 8, 11 You must focus your attention more on your future goals and learn to conserve some of your assets and resources for a rainy day. You disregard common sense by indulging your desire for the many comforts that money can buy. People looking for a generous patron will find you an easy victim. You hate to ignore anyone's cry for help, even when you cannot afford it. You may win friends this way, but your financial situation could also become embarrassing, to say the least. Your primary concern should be to plan for your future financial security and independence.

Inconjunct: 10, 12 You overreact to the expectations of those who have authority over you. You resent the sacrifices that your superiors expect you to make to stay in their good graces. But you realize that you must concede to rank, and you do what is required, even though it is painful. You underestimate your creative talent, which would enrich you if it were developed. Take care not to mix business with pleasure, or you might discover that you have sacrificed an opportunity to fulfill your destiny without binding ties.

Semisextile: 4, 6 You benefited from your parents' generosity in your early years, but it may have taken away your desire to live according to your own potentials. The worst thing you could do is to live "off" someone and justify it to yourself by claiming that the person needs you. It is extremely important to develop your skills so you can sustain yourself without being obligated to anyone. Don't deceive yourself that those you love have no negative qualities. You should try to understand their failings and be willing to help resolve them if you can. You usually seek your parents' approval of anyone to whom you feel romantically attracted. Because they are not emotionally involved, it is unlikely that they will share your view, but they might give you good advice because they are detached and therefore more objective.

1st to the 5th Your behavior seems to be based on a belief in the survival of the fittest. You take enormous chances that you won't encounter someone who will resist you more strongly than you bargained for. You have a strong desire nature and won't accept no for an answer.

 2nd to the 4th You admire people with strong personalities, and you have a fondness for children. But you have a lot of growing up to do yourself. You were probably overindulged as a child, and you haven't outgrown it.

 3rd to the 3rd When you make up your mind, a team of horses couldn't change it. You are ambitious to put your ideas to work, and you know how to force an issue.

 4th to the 2nd It is important that you learn to postpone taking any action until you are sure that your plans are valid. Lack of money could take the wind out of your sails until you learn to conserve your resources.

 5th to the 1st You insist on the right to assert yourself when you get the impulse. You don't feel that you have to explain your actions to anyone, and you don't.

 6th to the 12th You avoid activities that would take you away from the mainstream where everyone else is. Your uncontrolled outbursts could put you temporarily out of commission, so conserve your energy.

 7th to the 11th You want to be first among your friends in everything you do. But the uncertainty of the future should warn you to use your energy more prudently. Plan to work more efficiently, so you are not burned out from exhaustion in your later years.

 8th to the 10th You find it difficult to sacrifice any of your desires, but some sacrifice is necessary as an investment in order to achieve the long-range goals you have set for yourself.

 9th to the 9th If you spend some time developing your mental assets, you will be abundantly rewarded. Muscles may be impressive, but brains are more enduring.

 10th to the 8th Gaining public attention turns *you* on, but unless you have a genuine contribution to make, the public may be easily turned off by your actions.

 11th to the 7th Partnerships are very important to you, but if your partners don't cooperate, you easily forget they ever existed. Your mate must accept you as you are because it is nearly impossible for you to change.

 12th to the 6th You will succeed in your endeavors because you know more about your competitors' weaknesses than they do. Direct some of your great energy to developing your talents and learning how to get optimum results with the least amount of energy. Learn to preserve your health by being more moderate and getting adequate rest between bouts of work.

Trine: 1, 9   Although you do everything enthusiastically, you sometimes lack the self-discipline required to get the most from your efforts. Your impatience makes you less efficient, but your aggressiveness is useful when the time comes for action. You have the courage and daring to take advantage of your creative potentials. When your plans go awry, you may make excuses, since it is painful to realize you've made a foolish mistake. You are well informed but often unrealistic in your impulsive outbursts. Your friendliness is endearing to others. You have a strong desire nature, and when your mind is made up, you won't take no for an answer. However, some people won't let you have your way. You can get away with doing things that others would be severely criticized for, but sometimes you take chances that you regret later. You let unpleasantness roll off your back, because you don't take yourself too seriously. Yet you insist on the right to assert yourself, and you don't feel you have to explain your actions. You would gain an even greater advantage over your adversaries if you developed your mental assets. You enjoy participating in sports, stimulating young people to take part in activities and indulging in speculative enterprises.

Sextile: 3, 7   You are creative enough to find many dramatic ways to put your ideas to work. You are really an actor, and you easily win over opponents to your point of view. The freshness of your actions wins support from competitors and associates. You are ambitious, and you know how to get important people to share your enthusiasm for your endeavors. In your personal life you want a partner who will share in your excitement as you strive for your goals, someone who will also be enthusiastic in meeting your physical demands. You want your mate to consider you the most important person in the world.

Cross: 2, 8, 11   Think about the goals you hope to reach, and remember that achieving them should be your most important priority. When you work on them, you may realize that you are not investing sufficient mental energy for the greatest returns later. You should make long-range plans for using your natural assets efficiently and using your energy to preserve your physical well-being. You tend to spend money carelessly and to get into situations that you are not adequately prepared for. High on your list of priorities must be establishing realistic values and being willing to make some contribution to others. You cannot go forth with empty hands and expect to succeed.

Inconjunct: 10, 12   It may not be easy, but you will have to forego some of your indulgences if you hope to realize substantial returns on your investments in later years. You enjoy public exposure, and your public position will be better if you take the time to develop your hidden talent. Inside, you are really a "softie" and more sympathetic than it seems toward people in need.

Semisextile: 4, 6   Your early environment may have given you the idea that your freedom is of paramount importance. Obviously you were given the opportunity to show what you could do on your own, and it is imperative that you take the time and self-discipline to cultivate your creative potentials. You may not see immediate evidence of its value, but this investment will be of inestimable value as you become stabilized in your career.

1st to the 5th Your enthusiasm is boundless, and your character is developing very rapidly. There are almost unlimited avenues for expressing your creative potential.

2nd to the 4th The opportunities provided by your early environmental conditioning has given you an excellent base for continued growth and development. Probably you are already grateful to your parents for this.

3rd to the 3rd You have a wealth of ideas to promote, and you know it. So put aside a few of your many indulgences and discipline yourself to develop your talents and ideas.

4th to the 2nd You will have a hard time keeping your financial affairs in order, because you tend to spend money as soon as you get it. Learn to save your money. Stop wasting your resources and creative talents and be more realistic about achieving freedom from financial anxiety.

5th to the 1st "Easy come, easy go" seems to be your motto. That would be fine if you were more conscious of the need to conserve your energy and to direct some of it into useful channels that would give you a better return for your efforts. But you like to pamper yourself.

6th to the 12th You are deeply concerned about the injustices you observe in society. If you focused less on your self-interests, your loving kindness could help relieve some of these problems, but you would have to work at it. One of the resources that you haven't used is your ability to help others.

7th to the 11th You know better than anyone that you must plan ahead if you want to enjoy unlimited freedom from want in your later years. Avoid buying on credit, if possible, because you tend to lose control and spend too much.

8th to the 10th You can grow and expand in your career if you are willing to make the necessary investment in time and effort. You owe it to your job and to the people who depend on you. You can't afford to settle for less.

9th to the 9th You will always want to improve your competence in your field. Because of your high ethical standards, you always follow the legal course of action in achieving your objectives. You communicate well and are easily understood.

10th to the 8th You must realize that your destiny depends largely on the contribution that you are willing to make to fulfill it. Once motivated, you will persist through thick and thin to reach your goals.

11th to the 7th You need a partner who will never stop growing and expanding, both mentally and spiritually. You are a willing listener when discussing mutual problems, and you are a friend as well as a partner.

12th to the 6th Your family is very important to you, and you want to give them the same opportunities that you received. But you will have to apply yourself and develop your creative potential. You are generous to a fault, which may cause financial problems. Your great vitality allows you to accomplish much without getting tired.

Trine: 1, 9 You have vast creative potential, but you must focus on the needs of the larger world. You know you can improve the quality of life around you, but you prefer to be a spectator rather than a participant. In spite of strong spiritual convictions, you don't give much time to others. Eventually your conscience will bother you, and you will remedy the situation. But you will continue to waste your creative resources until you find a way to reach the goals that will also serve your destiny. It is quite important to plan your affairs more carefully and avoid wasting precious time in unnecessary activities. Curb your desire to do everything at once and conserve your energy for doing one thing well. You are drawn to people in general, and you enjoy thought-provoking and lively discussions. You are well informed on many subjects and not afraid to express your opinion, even disagreeing when you feel it's called for.

Sextile: 3, 7 You have an excellent feeling for how to deal with people. You know how to communicate, and you are willing to listen to others. It is especially important to have a good understanding with your partner, who will give you ample opportunity to express your opinions and will expect you to listen as well. You will choose a mate who will work to help you realize your dreams, to your mutual benefit. Your children will take advantage of your generous nature whenever they can, and you probably won't discipline them as much as you should. You should have a warm and happy family life with good feelings abounding in your home. You want your family to know that you are always available for help when a problem arises.

Cross: 2, 8, 11 You tend to pamper yourself with material comforts and then regret it. You probably have very little sales resistance, and no matter how much you earn, you may often be financially embarrassed. You are too generous, perhaps because you unconsciously doubt that people are attracted to you, so you give them presents to compensate for that doubt. But if you learn the worth of your creative talent, that will not be necessary. You are the only one who can build substance into your life, but you will have to make an investment in time and energy, which you may not want to do. Some sacrifices are necessary if you want security in your later years. You will have to forego some pleasures in order to consolidate your resources and make plans for the future. Once you start seeing results, you will be motivated to persist through thick and thin to reach your objectives.

Inconjunct: 10, 12 Two areas of your life are particularly bothersome to you. First, you feel guilty that you aren't doing enough to serve others. This problem will be solved by making time for it in your busy schedule. There is always a need for volunteers to perform useful social services or help in public institutions. Second, you worry about the energy and time that you will have to invest toward a career. This is a more personal problem and can be solved only when you are willing to sacrifice some of your present desires to gain advantages that will have lasting value for the future.

Semisextile: 4, 6 You have a lot to be thankful for. The early influences in your life have given you a sound base to build on, and in that respect you have a head start on your contemporaries. If you work at developing your creative resources, you will be way ahead of others.

1st to the 5th You are wary of expressing your feelings until you are sure you won't be rejected. For the same reason, you are guarded in revealing your creative talents.

 2nd to the 4th Your early environment may have been somewhat austere, and you feel you were denied some advantages that others had. This may have caused some bitter feelings about your family.

 3rd to the 3rd A deep thinker, you look forward to the day when you can express yourself whenever you want, without asking permission. This preoccupation may have given you a feeling of inferiority. You tend to be an introspective loner.

 4th to the 2nd Because of your frugal nature, you will probably accumulate a substantial financial nest egg. You don't indulge yourself very much, because you are so concerned with self-preservation. You should bend a little and enjoy life more. You have a lot to offer the world, but you are restrained by worries about money.

 5th to the 1st The most important person in your life is *you*. You insist on your right to do what you want, and you don't really care if others like it. You don't feel that you are in the mainstream of social activity, and unless you are willing to join, the world will leave you alone.

 6th to the 12th If possible, you prefer to work privately and obscurely. You are far more talented than it appears, but you are happier when left to do as you want with your time and energy.

 7th to the 11th You have a starkly realistic vision of the future, and you take few chances that could risk your security in later years. You tend to choose as friends only those people who are unlikely to make demands on you.

 8th to the 10th The anxiety in your personal life makes it especially important to have security in your career. To that end you are willing to make a substantial investment of time and energy. You understand the meaning of sacrifice.

 9th to the 9th You expect others to respect your strict moral code. It isn't easy for you to start a conversation, but you can contribute meaningful ideas. You have a great respect for knowledge, knowing it can open doors that your shy nature keeps you from opening otherwise.

 10th to the 8th It may be painful, but you should capitalize on your ability to help others with their financial affairs. You know how to manage money and, though you may not be a speculator, you can rise to prominence by handling other people's resources.

 11th to the 7th When thinking of marriage, you are attracted to people who are mature and straightforward. You are not especially romantic, preferring a partner who is a dutiful friend more than a lover.

 12th to the 6th Having to work most of your life is not distasteful to you, for you are not a stranger to discipline. But you may become depressed and fail to live up to your potential. You will also be a strict disciplinarian at home.

Trine: 1, 9 You are self-centered, simply because you feel inadequate. You feel that you have to make more sacrifices than others do to get the same results. For this reason you withdraw and concentrate on your own interests, ignoring the rest of the world. You behave with propriety, guided by a fairly strong code of ethics. You don't want anyone to be suspicious of your motives, nor do you feel that you need to explain your actions. Fearing rejection, you won't express your feelings for someone until you are sure that the feeling is mutual. And you hesitate to reveal your creative talents for similar reasons. Because of these feelings of anxiety, you remain on the sidelines of social activity, where you are more secure. However, you will surely be lonely unless you are willing to participate. You respect others' rights, and you want them to respect your privacy. Although you aren't a talkative person, you enjoy discussing important matters. You seek knowledge avidly, knowing that in your career, doors are more likely to open if you are well informed.

Sextile: 3, 7 A thoughtful person, you are attracted to people who are deliberative and reasonably profound thinkers. You admire people who think for themselves, and you look forward to the day when you can speak your mind without having to ask permission. You very much want others to need you and to accept you for yourself, particularly your mate or lover. There must be respect and sincerity between you and your lover and an agreement that you will both work dutifully for your individual and mutual goals.

Cross: 2, 8, 11 A conservative person, you will probably acquire a sizable nest egg and be financially secure. The future is very important to you, and you want to be free from anxiety about material needs as you get older. You might choose to have few children or none so that you can realize your goals with as few ties and obligations as possible. You choose friends who won't make demands on your time or your bankbook. Self-preservation is a strong factor in your life and is probably the reason why you don't indulge yourself more. Life can be more enjoyable if you bend a little. Though you have a strong fear of being without the basic needs of life, that should not keep you from making your creative gifts available to the world.

Inconjunct: 10, 12 You are willing to work behind the scenes, where you can apply your skills most efficiently. With your shy disposition, you are more comfortable when working away from the glare of the public spotlight. Obviously you will make whatever sacrifices are required in order to succeed in your career. You are also prepared to invest time and money if that will help you become more stabilized in your professional position.

Semisextile: 4, 6 You must avoid becoming depressed by conditions in your work environment, for this can cause you to lose interest and become distracted from your duties. Use this opportunity to improve your skills, which will enhance your competitive position. Difficulties arising from your early conditioning are no excuse to stop trying; instead you should strive to improve on those conditions and thus break away from the anxieties that they represent. Since you are no stranger to self-discipline, this should not present an insurmountable problem.

1st to the 5th   You realize that you have unusual creative gifts, but you may put off using them until you find a vehicle that will dramatize them and you. Taking responsibility in a romantic relationship is painful to you, and you don't want to make a permanent tie.

 2nd to the 4th   You will exploit your talent when you realize that that is the only way to achieve the freedom you want from family obligations and responsibilities. Perhaps your family has urged you to make a life of your own anyway.

 3rd to the 3rd   You give much thought to developing your ideas, and you use every opportunity to demonstrate your mental skills. You can detach yourself from your early environment, knowing that you need to build your own life, with freedom to exploit your creativity.

 4th to the 2nd   The major obstacle keeping you from exercising your creative options is lack of money. You will find it painful to restrain your indulgences, but you have no other choice.

 5th to the 1st   You can capitalize on your innovative ability to bring your creative gifts to the surface so that they can enhance your position in your career. Your talent is free, but it still takes time and effort to develop it.

 6th to the 12th   You want to use your intellectual skills in ways that will attract other people's attention. But you will have to work in obscurity temporarily, which will not be pleasant. You find confinement almost unendurable.

 7th to the 11th   You admire people who are free, and you aspire to emulate them in seeking your goals and gaining financial freedom. You are able to detach yourself from old friends, for you know you will make new ones easily.

 8th to the 10th   It isn't easy to make the necessary sacrifices for investing in your career, but you know it is essential. You have little difficulty providing the services that your superiors require, and at times you may feel that you are overqualified.

 9th to the 9th   The moral guidelines you live by are more universal in concept than those specified by your social environment or by custom. You strive to increase the knowledge you have gained by getting some formal training. Probably you would be a good teacher, for you use your mental skills cleverly.

 10th to the 8th   You want to be appreciated by the people you have helped. Through service to others you will make your greatest achievements.

 11th to the 7th   You are a friend to all and rarely too busy to listen when someone needs you, especially when it concerns their future goals and aspirations. Your partner must also be a friend and give you freedom to serve others in your own way.

 12th to the 6th   You are very restless when denied the opportunity to demonstrate your talents. Conversely, when you turn down a chance to improve your skills, you really diminish the rewards you can expect. Your children may be a great burden, not allowing you to fully extend your skills.

Trine: 1, 9 You have great creative potential and a flair for finding ways to exploit your talents. Your only limitation is apathy. You can claim little credit for your talent unless you take responsibility for developing it. You are easily distracted by romantic affairs and other pleasurable activities. You don't seek out binding relationships because you feel they restrict your freedom. You might indulge your children just to get them "out of your hair," but you may regret this later, when you are faced with the effects of your insufficient discipline. You are motivated by self-interest and never miss a chance to demonstrate your abilities, especially when it might help your career. You enjoy sensationalism and will never need an agent to promote your assets. Rebellious when you want to assert yourself, you are sometimes indiscreet. Your unique code of ethics is framed in universal concepts rather than in society's guidelines. But you often moralize on other people's social behavior. You seek truth and wisdom and strive to improve on the knowledge you've acquired. Philosophical arguments give you a welcome opportunity to challenge others in mind-to-mind combat.

Sextile: 3, 7 You are more comfortable with people at the social level than in the demanding area of individual relationships. You are generally available to help people with their problems, and it gives you a good feeling to know you've helped others seek their goals. Your partner must understand your need to function on the social level. It would be ideal if you were both similarly dedicated to the needs of society. You have always known that you would have to detach yourself from your early environment in order to establish a broader base for applying your talents.

Cross: 2, 8, 11 You must exercise self-control in using your resources, or you will be forced to delay the time when you can put your talent to good use. Sacrifices are necessary if you intend to conserve your assets until you are ready to make your contribution to the world. In our present materialistic environment, we have little freedom to enjoy material benefits unless they are earned. Freedom from want can be achieved only by applying yourself to the demands of a career. The returns you receive will "buy" freedom to indulge yourself at the broad social level where your talents can be effectively used. There is no other way to do what you want to do instead of what you must do.

Inconjunct: 10, 12 Luckily, you enjoy the spotlight, for your deeds tend to attract public attention. You may have to get your training for socially beneficial service by working on the sidelines, but this will last only until you have developed your skills. Being confined is most painful to you, but that is the sacrifice you must endure in order to gain total freedom to exploit your creative energies for the rest of your life.

Semisextile: 4, 6 You are impatient when there are no opportunities for proving yourself in society and establishing a stable position with the public. It is important for you to gain your independence as early as possible, and your parents may have perceived your potential and urged you to be independent. You cannot ignore the obligation to develop your skills, or your future will be uninteresting, to say the least. Also you will shortchange both yourself and society by depriving the world of your talents.

1st to the 5th You are inspired in exploiting your creative potential imaginatively. This ability helps to compensate for disappointment in romantic relationships, which rarely measure up to your ideals.

 2nd to the 4th Your early parental training was probably inadequate to prepare you for the responsibility of developing your creative talents. You may feel guilty for the debts you think you owe your parents.

 3rd to the 3rd Many creative ideas flow through your mind, but you find it rather difficult to apply them concretely. You have trouble separating fact from fiction, but you are optimistic that eventually you will succeed.

 4th to the 2nd The anxiety of insufficient material resources will linger as long as you reject your obligations to yourself. Plan a course of action for acquiring the assets you need. You may tend to be careless with money.

 5th to the 1st Your tendency to dawdle and daydream is too much of a luxury. Fearing rejection, you may procrastinate unduly in taking advantage of your creative imagination.

 6th to the 12th Only painstaking hard work will lessen your fear that your creative expression may never attract public attention. You should think about using your talents to help people in institutions who need your compassion. You know that you must pay some debts to society, and this could be your opportunity to do so.

 7th to the 11th You are only vaguely aware of the responsibilities that you must accept before you can achieve your goals. Your friends' accomplishments tend to illuminate your failings, but this may propel you to reach for similar goals. Be wary of forming ties with people unless you are sure they will be worthwhile friends.

 8th to the 10th Make only those sacrifices that are essential in order to gain a stable position in your career. If you volunteer extra services, you may be disappointed, for they won't yield as much as you hope.

 9th to the 9th At times you are a purist, but on other occasions you display an incredible lack of moral judgment. You must be as well-informed as possible, because you tend to believe everything you hear. You have your failings, but others do also.

 10th to the 8th Generally, you can make the best contribution to society by offering your talents in service to others. People believe that you will listen to their problems sympathetically. You are probably more appreciated than you know.

 11th to the 7th You should look for a mate or lover whose professional interests are compatible with yours, someone who is as dedicated as you are to serving social needs. However, you may have to settle for a partner who only sympathizes with your goals and ambitions.

 12th to the 6th Take care not to slip into a nonproductive state of mind and fail to apply the necessary energy to developing your skills. You must believe in yourself and *know* that you can succeed.

Trine: 1, 9 If you have been disappointed in love relationships, take heart, for your creative inspiration can bring you success in many other areas. Even in love, you will learn to discriminate between those who are sincere and those who are not. In time, you will accept people as they are and not try to make them fit your ideal image. Devote more effort to developing your creative potential, for you can derive much satisfaction from your accomplishments. Resist the tendency to waste time daydreaming, when you could be using your talents for useful purposes. Your fear of being rejected will be greatly reduced if you become a true craftsman in using your skills. Getting some formal training should be a major priority if you want to win in the challenging competition of human encounter. Rather than complain about someone's unethical methods of achieving their ambitions, tend to your own affairs and criticize your own lack of persistence and dedication. Though you are a purist at times, you display poor judgment in living by your own rules instead of by society's, as others must.

Sextile: 3, 7 Your sympathetic compassion for less fortunate people is commendable. You know you have the ability to serve those who cannot serve themselves, and you would be remiss in your social obligations if you did nothing about it. It will take some time to find the best way to apply your creative ideas. You might need the advice of someone you can trust to help you choose the best career. Perhaps your partner or lover could serve in this capacity, especially if your interests are compatible.

Cross: 2, 8, 11 Your first priority should be to make an organized plan for achieving your goals. Then you must painstakingly adhere to the responsibilities that this entails. You cannot expect to get anything out of life unless you are willing to put something into it, so you must develop your skills as a commitment to your objectives. You can earn a comfortable income by putting your creative talent to work. It will require some sacrifice, but this is the most important investment you can make. It is your obligation to find out where your talents will be appreciated. Before you can help others, you must develop your own potential and establish your own worth.

Inconjunct: 10, 12 The most painful experience you can imagine is never receiving recognition for your efforts. You need feedback from those you have helped to know that your efforts have been worthwhile. But the only satisfaction you should require is knowing that the deed is important and that you are making an effort to pay off your debt to society. Institutional work could be a vehicle for creative self-expression. In any job situation, examine your duties carefully and demand that your responsibilities be spelled out exactly. You tend to volunteer unnecessarily, thereby taxing your physical capacity. If you do volunteer extra duty, don't expect any return other than the satisfaction of giving.

Semisextile: 4, 6 Your early conditioning did not prepare you for the burden of standing on your own. You may have a lingering guilt that you have somehow been disloyal to your family. This is utter nonsense, which you use to justify your refusal to develop your latent potential and acquire the independence to stand alone. If you believe in yourself, the possibilities open to you are beyond your wildest imagination, but only hard work will yield results. You will succeed when you know you can.

1st to the 5th   You have a sense of your own importance and enjoy exercising power over others. You use your creative imagination to win support for your plans, and you don't take kindly to those who resist. You are a demanding lover, and you take liberties if your partner seems fascinated by your aggressiveness.

 2nd to the 4th   You were probably more demanding than other members of your family, expecting more favors than they got and not being particularly appreciative. You can gain security by capitalizing on your talents.

 3rd to the 3rd   You know what you want and how to get it. If necessary, you will flatter people whom you want to win over. You are concerned about social problems and have many ideas for solving them.

 4th to the 2nd   It annoys you to be without money, but you have no excuse, because your creative talent will allow you to increase your resources. You expect more for your efforts than you deserve because you don't want to give up your indulgences. You should apply yourself.

 5th to the 1st   If you choose to use your creative talent imaginatively, you can earn a place of respect in the world, but you might waste your efforts in nonproductive, self-gratifying activities.

 6th to the 12th   Unless you are willing to work and fulfill your obligations to society, you run the risk of severe reversals, because you have exercised your will over others. Your ability to heal would be an asset to society.

 7th to the 11th   You are easily intimidated by your friends' achievements. But they have applied themselves and are only getting what they deserve. Your future can be as satisfying as theirs, if you accept the fact that there is more to life than indulging in pleasures.

 8th to the 10th   Sacrifice may not be easy, but it is necessary when your career is at stake. You can make a significant and enduring contribution to society, if you make a commitment to that purpose.

 9th to the 9th   You have a certain inclination for politics, in which you can succeed if you get proper training in government and law. You might also be drawn to speculative investment.

 10th to the 8th   Your interest in money matters is strong, perhaps in direct reaction to the embarrassment of your earlier years when funds were short. Your financial talents could prove very rewarding.

 11th to the 7th   You have a hypnotic effect on people that enables you to successfully challenge all adversaries. Your partner must accept you as you are and be willing to share your commitment to goals that will benefit you both. You talk compromise, but you settle only for submission. You also take this attitude toward your children, but you will defend them against any threat.

 12th to the 6th   You are a wheeler-dealer, preferring to avoid physical labor in your career. Your greatest rewards will be the result of training to be the best in your field, which may require physical effort. You will just have to accept that. Don't expect a free ride to your ambitions.

Trine: 1, 9 You exercise your will at every turn, because you have an exaggerated sense of your importance. You enjoy having power over others, and you don't meet much resistance, because you are clever in winning support by capitalizing on other people's weaknesses. You are aggressive in romantic relationships and easily offended when you are rejected, perhaps even resorting to violence. Although you want to spend all your time satisfying self-indulgent needs, you have the creative imagination to earn public respect for your contribution to social causes. You show some talent for politics, in which you could succeed with training in government and law. Other areas that might interest you are investment, insurance or medicine. You could work effectively with young people, who would admire your strength and dedication to their needs. You can teach young people to have self-confidence to make a life for themselves. It would be satisying to know that your efforts were productive.

Sextile: 3, 7 You have a gift for making your point effectively, and people usually don't realize that they've been mesmerized by your dramatic showmanship. You always find ways to satisfy your desires, and few people can resist your charm. You know what you want, and you don't beat around the bush. You will even use flattery when someone seems to resist you. Not a flighty person, you are deeply concerned about finding solutions for social problems. You do not sit idly by and tell others how to remedy the situation. You want a partner who will share your dedication to your goals. You are not really compromising, although you give that impression. You try to make others submit to your will, and that applies as well to your mate and children. You may be a disciplinarian, but you are generally fair, and you will defend your children when their well-being is threatened.

Cross: 2, 8, 11 You may not enjoy looking to the future, because you are so preoccupied with present pleasures. You must plan ahead, so that your financial affairs will be in good order. If you plan now for security in your later years, you will not have to be dependent on anyone. It is very embarrassing to you to be without sufficient funds, because you realize you have no one to blame but yourself. If you want returns and security, you will have to make a contribution for that purpose. You're a better manager with other people's money than with your own.

Inconjunct: 10, 12 You will be more of an asset to society if you accept your obligations dutifully and not mind working behind the scenes where the problems are. Your healing ability could help mitigate the unacceptable social conditions that diminish man's dignity.

Semisextile: 4, 6 Your demands are usually met, and you expect favors from others, but this has not diminished your enthusiasm for making a life of your own. You know how to use your talents productively to assure your security. Although you may be a wheeler-dealer by temperament, you know that your exaggerated self-image can't carry you through life. You know you must work at developing your skills to achieve the highest possible level of competence. This is the only way to be sure that you can successfully meet competition. The worst thing you could do is coast to your objectives by being a parasite on those who are making an honest effort.

Sun in Fifth, Moon in First

You have a positive outlook on life, and you assert yourself in exploiting your creative potentials, so you can succeed if you apply yourself with determination. Probably you have some emotional insecurity about your effectiveness and are concerned that the public won't appreciate what you do. The greatest deterrent to your success is that you would rather indulge in pleasurable activities than apply your energy in outward expression of your creative talents. You have a great capacity to enjoy life because you are basically well integrated. Of course you will have problems, but you can find ways to resolve them satisfactorily. With your dramatic sense, you can easily gain the support you need in your endeavors. You present a favorable image, and most people find you easy to know and comfortable to be with.

You are more talented than the average person, and developing those talents into skills should be the main priority of your early years. You are a late starter because of your lack of organization and self-discipline. Instead of dawdling, invest the time and energy needed to derive the maximum yield from your creative output. Once you establish a goal and are committed to reaching it, nothing can deter you from it.

Sun in Fifth, Moon in Second

Although you have some feelings of insecurity, your need to express your creative talents in a worthwhile endeavor assures your eventual success. Your early conditioning stimulated you to make the most of any situation, for which you should be grateful to your parents. With even a moderate amount of effort, you can adequately satisfy your needs and even accumulate a substantial financial reserve.

You should choose a career that allows you to utilize your creative talents in helping people manage their material resources. Working with young people would give you the satisfaction of knowing that you have helped them prepare for the future so they can achieve greater fulfillment.

Indulging in personal pleasures may be limited by lack of funds. Once you are established in your career, you can afford to enjoy yourself more freely. You will extend yourself for your partner and children, because they give you so much joy. They may be the stimulus you need to capitalize on your creative potential.

Sun in Fifth, Moon in Third

This combination shows that you are optimistic about your ability to use your creative talents with excellent results. But you may have some difficulty in getting started because of powerful parental influences. Although you are eager to take advantage of the resources your family makes available, you may not want to follow their suggestions in using them. You may feel obligated to go along with their wishes, but eventually you will resent their intrusion and insist on deciding for yourself. Be prepared for, "After all we've done for you, it's the least you could do for us."

Your thirst for knowledge assures that you will be ready when an opportunity is offered. Your sense of drama and ease of expression are suited to such fields as communications, theater, education, writing, reporting and designing. There are many careers in which you can utilize these talents in close contact with the public.

Your partner should be sympathetic with the demands of your career and allow you mobility to make the most of your talents. Yours will be a sharing experience with your partner and children.

Sun in Fifth, Moon in Fourth

Developing and implementing your creative talents may be delayed because of family limitations. You tend to underestimate your potentials, not giving them the attention that will turn them into useful skills. Preoccupation with family obligations may cause you to shelve your personal interests in deference to those of your parents. You should find a way to let go of those ties without feeling guilty.

Your rich imagination and creativity need a medium of expression in a permanent career. Your sources of inspiration are almost unlimited and can satisfy your need to be fulfilled in your identity and gain recognition for your creative efforts. You may not stray very far from your early environment, but that is all right if you function independently. Your accomplishments may take longer than other people's, so do not be disappointed if your maximum output occurs later in life.

Getting involved in early romantic relationships may be your way of establishing a life of your own, but problems in relationships may distract you from giving your career the attention it deserves. Though you need someone to depend on you, you also need to have freedom to satisfy your continuing personal and professional development.

Sun in Fifth, Moon in Fifth

Your desire to use your creative talents and be recognized for your accomplishments indicates that you will succeed in most of your endeavors. You work independently, not relying on feedback from others to assure you that you're on the right track. You generally do whatever gives you fulfillment when you express yourself in some creative activity. This could cause some problems in finding a job because you might raise objections, especially if the work doesn't allow you to apply your creative talents in your own way. Probably you were overindulged in your early years, and you assume that everyone will give you your accustomed privileges, but you will find that you must prove yourself and earn those privileges.

You will enjoy a position that brings you before the public, and you should have little difficulty handling any of the problems that may occur. People are genuinely fond of you, and you have a talent for getting their support. You should look for a career with unlimited growth potential; routine occupations would deny you the chance to make full use of your creativity. Knowing you are loved brings out the best in you.

Sun in Fifth, Moon in Sixth

This combination offers endless opportunities for developing and applying your creative potentials. Your learning ability ensures that you will find gainful employment throughout your life, and your ability to adapt to changing demands means that you will gain considerable proficiency in a broad range of skills. Slow but persistent progress early in your career will prepare you to step into more responsible positions in realizing your ambitions. You are constantly looking for ways to improve your skills, and you are never content with mediocrity in yourself or in those around you, although you never demand more of others than you would of yourself. Your parents led you to believe that you could accomplish any task if you put your mind to it.

You may do many kinds of work in your developing years until you have defined the specific goals you want to achieve. As you become more focused, working with young people, research and development, medicine, therapy or recreational endeavors may appeal to your tastes and talents. Don't be afraid to speak up when you feel you are ready to take on greater responsibility.

Sun in Fifth, Moon in Seventh

You have a deep need for personal relationships, and you express yourself easily in creative activities, which gives you many opportunities to make contact with others. You may be uncomfortable at first, but you will become increasingly relaxed with all types of people. It is through such contacts that your opportunities for promoting your talents will come. It may not be easy to detach yourself from your family, but unless you do, your progress in establishing a life for yourself will be delayed. If your parents don't approve of your friends, it may cause some discord between you.

You are ideally suited for a career that brings you into close contact with individuals or the general public. People respond warmly to you, and you impress them with the sincerity of your concern. A career in the creative arts, personal improvement programs, counseling or sales would offer you many rewarding experiences and a comfortable income.

Marrying too soon could cause problems unless you are secure in your career. Once you are established, though, a partner would be a distinct asset and would assure your continued progress and happiness.

Sun in Fifth, Moon in Eighth

You have excellent prospects for finding a suitable medium in which to express your creative talents, but this may be difficult if you are distracted by other people's needs. Because you are so in tune with people's needs and are capable in helping them solve their problems, you generally find that this is expected of you. That is fine, when you keep it in proper perspective, but when they make unreasonable demands, you should put a stop to it. Your early conditioning may have led you to believe that everyone would indulge you as your parents did, which will result in some disappointment unless you are aware of the difference between family and detached of social encounters.

Some kind of service enterprise would suit your temperament and provide reasonably high earnings. Insurance, investments, financial consulting, family counseling, working with young people or sales are some of the fields that would allow you to express yourself.

Once you get over the romantic escapades of youth, you will settle down with someone who will give you strength and courage to face any obstacles in your continuing rise to fulfill all your ambitions.

Sun in Fifth, Moon in Ninth

This combination shows that with even a modest amount of effort you have the potential for achieving most of your goals. Your eagerness to learn will give you the means to utilize your creative skills in many worthwhile endeavors. You have the foresight to apply yourself where you will derive the greatest benefit for yourself and those you serve. You are basically well integrated and can succeed where others fail, but your success may be delayed if you aren't willing to accept responsibility and deliberately mobilize your resources toward that objective.

You get along well with people in all walks of life, because they understand that you sincerely care about them. Your breezy manner and optimistic outlook are infectious, so that you have an uplifting effect on people. However, you are a bit naive and you should examine what your superiors expect of you before making any commitments.

You have numerous career possibilities that will allow you to show what you can do, including law, politics, child guidance, sports, travel, education, broadcasting, writing or the dramatic arts. You could rise to prominence in any of these fields.

Sun in Fifth, Moon in Tenth

Your need to express your creative talents can be served best if you focus on matters of public interest. The public sector will provide every opportunity for you to grow and develop to the fullest of your potentials and your broad range of talent can enhance your standing in the community if you offer some important service to the public, either directly or through some organizational effort. The continuing feedback from such activities will give you greater confidence in your abilities and stimulate you to maximum utilization of your creative talents. You may have to decide which has priority—personal indulgences or getting established in your career. Your progress may not be spectacular, but it will be consistent.

Whether or not you are status oriented, a marital partner will prove enormously beneficial in your career, especially as you rise to more responsible positions. You will literally thrive on increasing demands, and knowing that you are loved and appreciated for your accomplishments will improve your performance. Probably you will marry someone you meet through your career who understands the pressures you face. Your children may wish you had more time to spend with them, but eventually they will understand that satisfying their needs leaves you no alternative.

Sun in Fifth, Moon in Eleventh

The only thing that stands between you and success is doubt about your abilities. You have much creative potential, and developing it should be your most urgent priority so that you can face the future with greater confidence. You should also realize that you can do very little by yourself and that you require people who will stimulate you to utilize your creative talents. Perhaps your parents were so overindulgent that you never felt the need to assert yourself more positively. Whatever their influence, you have to develop your own identity and define the goals you want to reach, for your own sake. You may be apprehensive about the future, but you have the means to realize your ambitions and have security. Don't cling too tightly to the past, because it denies you access to the future. When friends try to impress you with your obligations to them, remember that you don't have to prove anything to anyone but yourself.

A career involving the public, especially with children, will bring out the best in you and give you the initial success you need to feel confident in your qualifications. You could succeed in politics, education, family counseling, vocational guidance or working in institutions that provide social services.

Sun in Fifth, Moon in Twelfth

Because you have much creative potential and a rich imagination, you should develop them and derive as much benefit as possible from them. You don't doubt your creativity, but you may question that it can provide a rich life with recognition for your accomplishments. You tend to underestimate your abilities, which may be why you will not invest the energy in developing the skills you need to become self-sufficient. The circumstances of your developing years were adequate and gave you every opportunity to learn these skills. However, you may lack the spirit of competition or feel that the results aren't worth all that effort, but it is competition that reveals how you act under pressure, so don't avoid it.

You are suited to a career in social service, such as institutional or prison work, or in medicine, a religious order, art, drama or education. You have an affinity with young people and children or with anyone who needs special attention and guidance. You may have an aversion to publicity, because you are more shy than you appear. There are fields that will give you the privacy you want while performing your duties.

You need the support of a marriage partner who understands your extreme sensitivity and who will help you bear up under the demanding requirements of your professional affairs. Getting away periodically from your daily routine will have a tremendously restorative effect.

Chapter Six

Sixth House

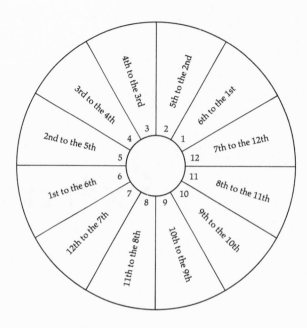

Using the potentials in the fifth house, you develop skills as the results of making a responsible effort in dealing with the circumstances of the sixth house. Psychologically, this is where you earn respect for your abilities and win a place for yourself in society. You fear that people will not approve of you unless you contribute something of value to the world, so you acquire the skills you need to accomplish your objectives. The credentials you derive here help you to become accepted in society and to perform certain tasks in earning a living.

The sixth house can be difficult, because your abilities are not always recognized while you are developing them, and you must often endure relative obscurity during this period. This feeling of inadequacy may drive you to overextend yourself in your training period, resulting in some physical problems. In your dedication to become the very best in the field you've chosen, you may neglect to get enough rest. Others may try to take advantage of you through the affairs of the sixth house; if you have a great idea, it may be appropriated by someone who earlier said it did not have merit. Through the sixth house you can learn to approve of yourself because of your ability to perform certain skills. It is not immodest to be aware of your abilities: immodesty usually is more likely in the fifth house when you make unsupported claims. Knowing that you have reached your objective by carefully applying the skills you've learned at the cost of much effort will make you happy.

Derivative House Meanings

1st to the 6th   This is where you gain skills from your creative potentials. Your earring ability originates here, as you are paid for the services you render.

2nd to the 5th   The value of your creative talents is in translating them into an ability to accomplish certain tasks.

3rd to the 4th   Your relationship with your parents conditioned you to accept responsibility for sustaining yourself as your own needs indicate.

4th to the 3rd   You want the chance to solve your problems in your own way, and you resent it when anyone suggests that you lack the ability.

5th to the 2nd   In the desire to improve your earnings, you sometimes exert yourself beyond prudent levels. You demand a high return for your efforts.

6th to the 1st   You are easily disturbed by any criticism of your abilities. You may drive yourself so that your health suffers.

7th to the 12th   Your feeling of inadequacy drives you to excel in everything you do. It pleases you when you've helped those in need.

8th to the 11th   Your dedication to your work is really an investment in your future so that you will be secure and free from want.

9th to the 10th   You hope to achieve your ambitions through development and experience, and few people at the top are as well informed as you are.

10th to the 9th   Generally scrupulous in your dealings, you can usually face public scrutiny with a clear conscience, since you adhere to ethical guidelines.

11th to the 8th   You feel that the investments you make will give you security in your later years, when you look forward to serving others.

12th to the 7th   You doubt that society will approve of you, so you make every effort to gain the skills that will bring you that approval.

1st to the 6th Your success in striving for significance depends on how well you use your creative potentials. Self-development is the key. You can be a credit to yourself by building a sound mind in a sound body.

 2nd to the 5th Knowing that you are loved gives you an incentive to capitalize on your creative talents. You will gain much personal satisfaction when you learn to use your abilities resourcefully to achieve recognition.

 3rd to the 4th You understand the need to stand on your own, and you can do so if you took advantage of your parents' teachings while you were growing up. As you go about your own business, you are concerned about your parents' welfare, and when you eventually succeed in your endeavors, you won't forget them.

 4th to the 3rd You must base your fortune on your ability to think for yourself, even though you have some anxieties about being able to make the best use of your ideas. Your brothers or sisters could help you get started, but you'd rather do it alone.

 5th to the 2nd You have a talent for making the most of your basic skills and your financial resources. You enjoy having money, but you also get much satisfaction from knowing that your creative abilities are appreciated.

 6th to the 1st Cultivate good physical habits that will assure you of sound health. At work, be cautious about doing more than your share, for your fellow workers may do less when you volunteer for extra duty. Learn to say no when others ask you to compensate for their incompetence.

 7th to the 12th You must find a way to make a meaningful contribution to society, either through personal or group activities. Your talent for improving existing social conditions is much needed. Be ready to work behind the scenes if necessary.

 8th to the 11th When you work hard, you know that you are making an important investment in your future. Friends who succeed will motivate you to plan goals that you can reach successfully.

 9th to the 10th You regard your destined role in life with reverence, and you aspire to live up to your highest expectations with moral responsibility and spiritual dedication. You work conscientiously to win others' respect for your accomplishments.

 10th to the 9th There are many ways to achieve distinction through your efforts, if you get the right education. Because you know how to bring out the best in others, you could win recognition as an educator. You will succeed in the field you choose because you believe in yourself.

 11th to the 8th In the back of your mind there is a desire to help others build a future for themselves. Using your own life as a model, you can show others how to adapt their skills to take advantage of opportunity.

 12th to the 7th Your partner is the catalyst that makes you excel in your efforts. He or she will give you support when you meet problems and appreciation when you do your job well. Your devotion inspires your partner to assist you so that you both benefit in the life you share.

Trine: 2, 10   You try to make the most of your everyday circumstances by setting up a plan for developing your creative skills. As a result, you have little difficulty finding suitable employment that allows you to increase your skills in diversified fields. You know how to use your resources efficiently and imaginatively to earn a comfortable living and have a feeling of accomplishment. Although money is important to you, the way you earn it and the skill required in your work are equally important. You believe in yourself, and you know that your dedication in carrying out your career responsibilities will one day bring you deserved recognition and satisfaction in making the most of your creative potentials.

Sextile: 4, 8   You are grateful for what you learned from your parents, and you know that their training was instrumental in preparing you for the responsibilities of making a life for yourself. Because you appreciate their efforts, you won't forget them in their later years, and you will be increasingly able to provide for them, if necessary. You look forward to a time when you can help people in general with their problems, and you hope that with your assistance they will become more self-reliant in using their resources.

Cross: 3, 9, 12   If you are willing to work behind the scenes, there is much you can do to help improve social conditions. Your understanding of how to convert people's basic resources into worthwhile tools can be of inestimable value to those who are untrained and therefore unskilled. You know how valuable your education was in making you ready for any opportunity, and you want to use your talent as an educator to give others a similar chance for success. You've learned to think for yourself and use your ideas to get ahead, although at first you were uncertain that you could do this.

Inconjunct: 1, 11   You know that it takes a lot of hard work to succeed in reaching your goals, but you consider this an investment in your future, and you are right. But it is important not to overextend yourself and neglect getting enough rest and relaxation. Don't feel obligated to lend your friends a hand unless you are sure they are making a reasonable effort to help themselves. People who have succeeded on their own will motivate you to achieve your goals as they have. At work, you should be cautious about doing more than your share and learn to say no when others ask you to compensate for their incompetence.

Semisextile: 5, 7   You work hard to provide for your family, and you hope that your children will benefit from your example by making full use of the material advantages and training you've given them. Knowing that you are loved and that your efforts are appreciated gives you much inner satisfaction and contentment. You are devoted to your partner, and in return he or she helps you in your pursuits, so you both benefit. Your mate supports you when you are down and rejoices with you in your successes, and that's a winning combination.

1st to the 6th   You are grateful for any opportunity to demonstrate how much you care about people. But in spite of this, you often complain that you don't have enough time to take care of your own needs, and you resent the fact that others expect you to do everything.

 2nd to the 5th   You must see the evidence to know the value of your creative imagination. When you have proof of your capabilities, there is no limit to what you can accomplish with your talents, and there is nothing you won't do for those you love.

 3rd to the 4th   Your early conditioning led you to believe that your role in life was to serve others. It is difficult for you to stand on your own because you lack the necessary self-confidence.

 4th to the 3rd   You are a whirlwind of ideas, and with only a little help you can use those ideas to obtain your basic necessities. You *are* able to make it on your own, but you need to be convinced of that fact.

 5th to the 2nd   You translate your need for personal security into a desire for financial independence and all possible material comforts. You respond warmly to people who exhibit substantial human values, and you love them for the stability they give you.

 6th to the 1st   Your health varies according to your moods and circumstances. When you are positive and optimistic about life in general, you can accomplish a great deal. However, when your spirits are low, you suffer all kinds of discomforts because of nervous tension, which raises havoc with your digestive system.

 7th to the 12th   You have deep sympathy for the problems of those whose economic circumstances make them social outcasts. It bothers you to realize that you can't possibly help them all, but if you think about it, you can do a great deal through social programs and institutions.

 8th to the 11th   You concede that probably you will have to work long and hard to gain the security you want in later life. You are often distracted from this objective when friends prevail upon your compassionate nature and ask favors that you can't refuse.

 9th to the 10th   You probably believe that it is necessary to work as an apprentice to earn the career position you want. But it would be easier to work at getting an education, and it would save you a great deal of time.

 10th to the 9th   You are humble in expecting to receive only the rewards you have earned. In general, you refuse to bend your moral and ethical standards to take advantage of opportunities when they are offered.

 11th to the 8th   You hope you are not being naive when you offer to help others, assuming that you will later be repaid for your efforts when you least expect it.

 12th to the 7th   Be careful not to become a doormat to your partner's desires. Any relationship requires compromises, but this can deteriorate into abuse of the privilege. Don't try to restrain your mate from becoming more self-reliant, and don't try to compensate for his or her unwarranted lethargy.

Trine: 2, 10 You are generous and warmhearted toward people in general, but especially toward those you love. Because you feel insecure about your ability to be self-sustaining, you try to compensate by accumulating material comforts. For the same reason, you want to be financially independent. You are usually involved with people who are glad to give you opportunities to show how much you care for them. But sometimes you resent it when they expect too much from you, for you know they are imposing on you. You are attracted to people who seem stable and whose actions indicate that they have the high human values that you admire. You may neglect to get an education on the assumption that you can learn everything you need through experience. This may be true, but it will make the road to success in your career more hazardous and time-consuming.

Sextile: 4, 8 You take pride in serving the needs of those around you, and your early conditioning gave you the belief that efforts on behalf of others are never wasted. You have some difficulty in serving your own needs, however, because you lack self-confidence. Because of your low self-esteem, you relegate yourself to obscure positions or those that bring limited recognition for your accomplishments.

Cross: 3, 9, 12 In view of this situation, wouldn't it be a good idea to seek work in an institution or with some social program? Your sincere concern for people in trouble or in a precarious social predicament would be an excellent basis for making a worthwhile contribution to improve their circumstances. You don't usually seek the limelight of public recognition, but you accept it humbly if it comes, knowing that you did what anyone else would have done in the situation. If you implement your many good ideas, you should be able to earn a comfortable income. You can succeed as well as others, but you won't, unless you are convinced of your abilities.

Inconjunct: 1, 11 You owe it to yourself to improve your self-image. You make more concessions to others than necessary because you feel obliged to serve them as they indicate you should. Remember that you also have obligations to yourself, and you will need security later on when you are no longer gainfully employed. Don't allow friends to distract you from this goal, because you will come to resent them for it. Another consideration is your health, which varies according to your moods. You feel fine when your spirits are high, but when you are depressed you may have all kinds of irritating ailments, such as digestive problems or nervous-tension headaches.

Semisextile: 5, 7 There are many worthy uses for your creative imagination if you recognize that you must develop your potentials. You have no difficulty using your skills to benefit your children, so why not boost your spirits by using your talents when your own career interests are at stake? You usually compensate for it when your mate slips into lethargy, but you must make it clear that each of you has to share the burdens in your relationship. Unless you let your partner become self-reliant, the marriage will suffer from lack of mutual respect. Indulge your mate because you want to, not because you've become a doormat and it's expected of you.

1st to the 6th You focus your thoughts on finding the best way to utilize your creative resources to derive the most benefit. You seek the kind of job that requires problem-solving as well as physical effort.

 2nd to the 5th You are especially gratified when your creative talents are appreciated and when you can apply them as you think best. You know your children will benefit greatly if you show them how to take advantage of the resources you work so hard to provide.

 3rd to the 4th You are grateful that your parents' teachings helped you solve the problem of finding suitable self-expression through your job. They also taught you to think for yourself and to accept the responsibility of using your ideas to gain the security you want.

 4th to the 3rd Not wanting to appear incompetent, you often neglect to ask others for help in making decisions. Consequently you learn the hard way, from your mistakes. You are never satisfied with anything less than perfection in your endeavors, and it bothers you greatly when you fail because you expected too much from your efforts.

 5th to the 2nd You will succeed in earning a comfortable living by using your skills creatively and imaginatively. It is reassuring to know that you can always find enjoyable ways to satisfy your needs.

 6th to the 1st Learn to relax and take time to unwind from the demands of your occupation. You owe it to yourself to develop good living habits and to get enough exercise to keep your body in top condition at all times.

 7th to the 12th It disturbs you when your efforts go unnoticed. If you understand how important you are to others when you help those who lack your skills, perhaps you will gain more satisfaction.

 8th to the 11th The time you spend in developing your skills is a worthwhile investment in your future security. You must realize that the only way you can achieve your goals is by making careful plans and applying yourself.

 9th to the 10th You are dedicated to your career, and you perform your duties with the required professionalism. Your superiors admire you and respect your ability to accept responsibility, and they trust you to always give your best performance.

 10th to the 9th With even a limited education, you can accomplish more than others who have more formal training. You know how to make the most of your creative potential without resorting to deception.

 11th to the 8th Your talents allow you to serve people's needs. It is commendable that your efforts have made their future security possible. You know that they will happily do favors for you in return if necessary.

 12th to the 7th You cannot turn your back on people who indicate that they need your skills. They know you understand their problems and can help them if you want to. You are too cautious about taking advantage of opportunities to demonstrate your talents. When you avoid competition because you are afraid of it, you give up a chance to prove yourself in challenging situations. You know your competitors' weaknesses, so you have little to fear.

Trine: 2, 10 You are a resourceful thinker, and you enjoy solving problems. A major issue is to find out how to apply your skills for the most benefit. You know that until you have developed your creative potentials, you don't really have any skills. Therefore you learn as much as possible to improve your chances for getting a suitable job. You believe in self-development, and you try to excel in using every talent to increase your options when opportunities come up. You put a value on your skills and rarely do any work unless you are paid according to the quality of your service. Money may not be everything to you, but it does provide a tool for judging your performance. You are willing to work to get what you want, because you don't expect others to give you anything or do you any favors. Dedicated to your career, you perform your duties with professional attention. Your superiors generally approve of your accomplishments and admire your devotion to duty.

Sextile: 4, 8 The environment in which you were raised allowed you to find a suitable outlet for your creative talents. You are grateful for the lessons taught by your parents and their urging you to think for yourself. You serve your own interests best when you serve the needs of others, for solving their problems or showing them how to deal with a situation brings out the best in you. People are more appreciative of your help than you realize and they would be happy to do favors in return when you need them.

Cross: 3, 9, 12 Finding a way to make your skills available through fulfilling some social obligation should be an important priority. You will experience great joy by making a worthwhile contribution to society, even if you act anonymously. Finding a way to do this isn't difficult if you ask people who are in the position to know. Don't be afraid to admit it when you are ignorant about some matter. Even if your formal education is limited, you can accomplish more than many who are better educated, because you know how to make the most of your creative potential.

Inconjunct: 1, 11 Stop worrying about problems that never happen. When external crises develop, learn to use them as opportunities to demonstrate your superior skill in coping. Don't do anything without a plan designed to reward you later in life, when security is so important. Take time to relax and unwind from the demands of your vocational interests. Clean living habits and physical exercise will pay dividends in a prosperous and productive way of life.

Semisextile: 5, 7 Your diligence and determination to succeed give you greater self-assurance and confidence with those you love. In a sense, these qualities are your love offering, and you hope to attract a lover or mate who admires you for them. You hope that your children will learn by your example and take advantage of the benefits you provide to make their own life. Be cautious about starting relationships with people who don't seem to want to help themselves. You could be expected to compensate for that person's incompetence by taking on his or her obligations. Still, you don't have to fear competition; instead, look at it as an opportunity to prove yourself in difficult situations. Because you know your competitors' weaknesses, you have little to fear from them.

1st to the 6th   You make whatever concessions are necessary to create greater harmony in your daily affairs. When you disagree with others, you give them the benefit of the doubt and sometimes even take the blame for their errors.

 2nd to the 5th   You apply yourself in developing your skills, knowing that this will improve your image with others, especially those whom you are romantically attracted to. You enjoy working for your family and children, and you want them to have all possible comforts.

 3rd to the 4th   Your favorable relationship with your parents gave you the self-reliance to deal with responsibility. The harmony of your parents' home made a lasting impression, and you hope to raise your family in a similar environment.

 4th to the 3rd   Sometimes when your opinion is challenged, you should take a firm stand. You give the impression that you feel you're unimportant, so people tend to take advantage of you.

 5th to the 2nd   You long for all life's comforts and luxuries, and you will exploit every available resource to gain them. With a little ingenuity, you can choose a career that will give you a substantial return for your efforts.

 6th to the 1st   In your conciliatory way, you sometimes allow others to take advantage of you. Fellow employees may do this, unless you refuse to tolerate such abuse.

 7th to the 12th   Anyone with a hard-luck story wins your compassion and assistance. Wouldn't it be better to choose a vocation in which you work with people who have problems? You would be doing what you enjoy and getting paid for it too.

 8th to the 11th   You seem to seek out the kinds of friends who always need something from you. It's fine to be helpful, but think about your own current and future needs and save some of your energy and resources to acquire a nest egg of your own.

 9th to the 10th   Your superiors are fond of you and appreciate your efforts in their behalf. You are a straight-shooter in that you don't want any special consideration on the job unless you know you deserve it.

 10th to the 9th   You are attracted to occupations that bring you into contact with persons who are polished and refined. You know how to deal effectively with people at the social level, and you enjoy it.

 11th to the 8th   Being appreciated by those you serve means a great deal to you. You hope these people will reciprocate when you need a favor in the future, but even if they wouldn't, you would serve them anyway. Being taken for granted by your partner hurts you deeply. You are likely to select a mate who depends on you and allows you to compensate for his or her defects.

 12th to the 7th   If your partner has character flaws, you will extend yourself in his or her behalf. You may resent this unless your mate makes some effort to become more self-reliant.

Trine: 2, 10 A naturally compromising person in your daily affairs, you strive for harmonious relations with everyone. You are willing to make concessions if that seems to be the only way to avoid conflict with others. Even though you know that someone else is wrong, you sometimes unwittingly take the blame for them. In spite of this, you have a productive and useful life, seeking all the comforts and luxuries you want through hard work and effective use of your resources. You will choose a vocation that gives you the greatest possible return for your efforts. Money means a lot to you, and you apply yourself with some ingenuity to get as much as you need for a comfortable lifestyle. Your superiors appreciate your efforts in their behalf, knowing they can trust you to put in an honest day's work for what you are paid. You don't expect any special considerations unless you know you deserve them. You take more abuse than necessary from your contemporaries and sometimes "hate" yourself for letting people use you as a doormat. You tend to indulge in food that is overly rich.

Sextile: 4, 8 You continue to have a good relationship with your parents, who gave you the self-confidence to make your own way without depending on their support. You were impressed by the domestic harmony you enjoyed while growing up and hope to raise your own family in a similarly fine environment. You need to be appreciated by those you serve, including your partner, who may take you for granted. You will attract as a mate someone who has certain deficiencies that you must compensate for. As long as you are assured that your partner is grateful for your unselfish devotion, you are happy.

Cross: 3, 9, 12 It would probably be a good idea to choose a vocation that brings you in close contact with people who have more than their share of problems. Your understanding and compassion go a long way in giving them relief from their anxieties. Get the necessary formal training to deal competently with the variety of problems you're sure to encounter. You work best in an environment of refinement, manners and good taste. Guard against people who try to intimidate you when your opinion differs from theirs and take a firm stand when you know you are right.

Inconjunct: 1, 11 With your conciliatory manner and your desire for good relations with everyone, you give people the impression that they can take advantage of you. This is especially true with fellow workers, who may abuse you with excessive demands. But they can't do this unless you allow it. While it is admirable to help others, you must think about your own future needs as well.

Semisextile: 5, 7 You want everything for your children and loved ones, so you have worked hard to develop your skills. This has helped to improve your image with others and made them appreciate your efforts in their behalf. Be more discriminating in forming ties with people whom you know little about, or you could regret it later. Drop those friends who expect you to continually make concessions. Fair is fair, and you should not allow anyone to make demands on you unless you know they are willing to meet you halfway in other matters.

1st to the 6th   You put a lot of effort into your work because you expect increased benefits from your accomplishments. But you sometimes overextend yourself, which depletes your energy.

 2nd to the 5th   If you act decisively in developing your creative potentials, you will improve your earning ability and learn that your skills, when properly utilized, are valuable assets. You are eager to give your children all the advantages of your efforts.

 3rd to the 4th   You know that you have to apply yourself diligently to achieve security for yourself and your family. Your parents taught you this, and you are grateful to them for encouraging you to accept responsibility.

 4th to the 3rd   It isn't always easy for you to put your ideas to work, because you sometimes doubt that they will succeed. Your only alternative is to promote your ideas at every opportunity. More often than not, your suggestions will be accepted.

 5th to the 2nd   Your resourcefulness in capitalizing on your basic skills allows you to earn a comfortable income. You don't hesitate to take a chance when there are material benefits to be gained. You enjoy having people admire your seemingly inspired actions.

 6th to the 1st   Wanting respect for your accomplishments, you often go to extremes in trying to prove yourself to others, which saps your vitality.

 7th to the 12th   It may bother you to work without recognition, but you will have to accept this situation until you are more confident about your abilities. Those who have benefited from your services will remember you and be grateful for it.

 8th to the 11th   The energy you put into your endeavors assures you of a substantial return later in life, when security will be more important than it is now. Invest as much effort in securing your own future as you do in helping your friends when they ask favors of you.

 9th to the 10th   Once you understand that achieving depends on being competent, you might consider getting more training through formal education. Satisfying your ambitions honestly is important to you.

 10th to the 9th   You know you will succeed in winning public respect for your accomplishments because you consider it a moral responsibility to do your best to serve the public interest.

 11th to the 8th   You know you will always be required to extend yourself to serve the public's needs. People will remember with gratitude that you have worked to improve their circumstances. Your partner must work with you to build a future that is secure from want. You strive to make your physical relationship satisfying and fulfilling.

 12th to the 7th   You feel that your mate has failings, for which you try to compensate when you can. Knowing you are needed by your partner gives your morale a boost and strengthens the bond between you.

Trine: 2, 10 Your willingness to really apply yourself in your chosen field of activity helps assure your success. You work hard to develop your creative potentials, for you believe that your skills will be appreciated. You are able to effectively capitalize on your basic resources to increase your earnings. You have confidence in the value of your creative abilities, so you don't hesitate to take a chance when you know there are material benefits to be gained. But you can significantly reduce the risks you take by getting a formal education. Being better informed increases your options and gives you more leverage in dealing with competitors on your terms rather than theirs. It is especially satisfying to know that you can succeed honestly and gain the respect you deserve for a job well done.

Sextile: 4, 8 You are grateful for your early parental conditioning, which taught you to be self-reliant in making your own way in life. You've accepted the responsibility for your actions, and you understand that you must apply yourself with determination in order to succeed. With this belief, you respond to people's needs and give them the services they require, for which they will pay you well. This is how your future security will be achieved. Your partner gives you the cooperation you need, which makes the effort worthwhile.

Cross: 3, 9, 12 Until you have greater self-confidence in your ability to succeed, you may have to work without getting recognition from those you hope to impress. But if you are patient, recognition will come as your capabilities grow and you take on more responsibilities. You don't have to accept obscurity if you are geared to take advantage of your creative resources. Most of the people you deal with know how competent you are to assist them with their needs, and they appreciate your efforts in their behalf. Your skills are especially valuable in helping those who can't help themselves. As your talents are recognized, your services will be increasingly in demand. People know that they can trust you to do your very best and that you take responsibility for your actions. The sincerity and dedication you bring to your career endears you to everyone, and they know they can depend on you.

Inconjunct: 1, 11 Take care not to make a nuisance of yourself by trying to do tasks for others that they can do for themselves. It's fine to be helpful, but some people resent the inference that they can't succeed without you. Find people who have real deficiencies and let them ask for your help. You can get yourself into a lot of trouble by taking on more work than you should, which may lower your physical vitality. You only have to prove yourself to you. You will win your partner's respect and admiration for your accomplishments when you compensate for his or her inadequacies. The bond between you will be strengthened when you know your mate considers you indispensable.

Semisextile: 5, 7 Always strive to improve your skills, for this will assure your future security, increase your self-worth and improve your image. You hope to win the affection of your loved one by showing that you expend a great deal of energy to earn a comfortable living and that you are sufficiently motivated to get ahead. You hope that your children will take advantage of the benefits you've provided and that they will succeed in achieving their goals. If they appreciate your efforts, you will feel amply rewarded.

169

1st to the 6th   You work exhaustively to acquire the professional skills that will increase your chances for success in your field. You hope that with determined effort you will achieve your goals.

 2nd to the 5th   Your ability to visualize the results of self-development inspires you to work enthusiastically toward that objective. You want your children to take advantage of the benefits you provide, and you will feel fulfilled if they appreciate your efforts.

 3rd to the 4th   Your parents taught you to take advantage of every opportunity to further your growth and development. Your optimism grew out of their belief that you could succeed if you wanted to.

 4th to the 3rd   Doubting the value of your ideas, you may not promote them fully. You must be willing to test your beliefs. If they succeed, you gain and if they don't, you can go on to something else without wasting any more time.

 5th to the 2nd   When you make gains by exploiting your creative resources, you literally glow. You want so much to be regarded as a successful person, and this adds to your image and self-worth.

 6th to the 1st   You need to exercise greater self-control about the amount of work you do. You can preserve your physical well-being only if you limit your efforts to a few well-chosen activities that don't tax your vitality.

 7th to the 12th   Direct some of your skills to a field of activity that provides social benefits. Your broad understanding of people's needs allows you to be of tremendous help in solving social problems.

 8th to the 11th   You must find a career that will allow you to grow into a position of greater responsibility. Otherwise you will lose interest. If you know there is a future for you in that field, you will really invest the time and energy required and live up to everyone's expectations.

 9th to the 10th   You believe in "an honest day's work for an honest day's pay." But in fact, you usually do more than your share because you consider it a moral obligation to do your best at all times. With your ambition to succeed, a formal education will carry you far.

 10th to the 9th   You might consider education itself as a suitable profession. Whatever field you choose, you will always try to serve your patrons with understanding and professional competence.

 11th to the 8th   You hope to be of service to others when they need it most, and you hope they appreciate your sincerity in doing so. You attract people who have significant deficiencies, which you are glad to make up for. Your mate will probably make heavy demands on you as a price for sustaining the relationship.

 12th to the 7th   At first you considered yourself less proficient than your competitors, and you had to extend yourself to win their approval. But you are underselling yourself; you are far more competent than you realize and certainly equal to any challenge you may encounter.

Trine: 2, 10 You have a strong desire to have all of life's comforts, and you accept the necessity of working to get them. You know you will succeed, because you have the necessary potentials, and you are willing to develop them to serve your purposes. This isn't easy, however, and circumstances sometimes force you to take on an extra job to meet expenses. You accept this situation with resignation, since you believe in an honest day's pay for an honest day's work. Not that you won't accept gifts, but you don't depend on them. You feel it's your duty to do everything that's expected of you, so you often do more than your share. You could improve this picture by getting a higher education, which will allow you to earn more while working less, with more free time for yourself.

Sextile: 4, 8 With your parents' help you learned to take advantage of opportunities and to grow and develop from the experience. You believe in yourself, just as your parents did, and you have no doubts that you will succeed. Looking ahead, you want to do what you can for those who seek your services. Others appreciate it when you help them, and they are further impressed by your dedication and sincerity. Because you had to work for what you have, you understand what it means to be in need.

Cross: 3, 9, 12 Although you believe in yourself, you have some doubts that your ideas are as good as others say they are, and you often fail to promote them as fully as you should. Consider it this way; if you try them and they succeed, all's well. If they don't, at least you won't have to waste any more time with them. You could help solve important social problems if you respond to society's needs. Your understanding and natural desire to be helpful could be effective tools to help those in need. It is quite likely that the career you choose will require you to serve the public.

Inconjunct: 1, 11 You owe it to yourself to take good care of yourself. Avoid depleting your vitality by taking on too many responsibilities, and discipline yourself to get enough rest and relaxation. You owe it to others to use your skills and talents to help solve their problems. When you know that there is a future for you in the field you've chosen, you will understand that spending any amount of time and energy will be a wise investment in your future. You never let anyone down who has come to depend on you, and they appreciate your obvious commitment to serving their best interests.

Semisextile: 5, 7 If you fail to respond by helping those who need your professional skills, you will seriously undermine your chances of winning recognition, and you would affront those who cannot help themselves. The excuse that you don't feel you are capable is unacceptable, because deep inside you know you are. This is your opportunity to prove yourself by using the creative talents you've developed. You wouldn't think of turning your back on your mate in similar circumstances, which proves that you can do something about these problems. You tend to compare yourself unfavorably with competitors and to undersell yourself. To fail others is to fail yourself.

1st to the 6th You are serious, thoughtful and resourceful in everything you do, especially in your daily career routine. You feel that anything worth doing is worth doing well, and you are impatient with those who don't live up to that ideal.

 2nd to the 5th You are determined to exploit your creative potentials to the fullest to derive as many benefits as possible from them. You plan very carefully to ensure that your children have every necessity, and you teach them to be self-reliant and secure in their ability to succeed.

 3rd to the 4th As you grew up, you learned to be self-sufficient and to accept full responsibility for your decisions. You develop your ideas thoroughly, for you know they are the base for your ambitions.

 4th to the 3rd It isn't always easy to interest others in your plans, because you are cautious and reserved about promoting them. People aren't usually fired with enthusiasm by your ideas, because you make it clear that getting results will require a lot of hard work.

 5th to the 2nd You are preoccupied with getting as much as possible from your available resources. You rarely take chances with risky ventures, for you know how difficult it is to recover losses. Few people are as competent as you are in handling finances, which is an asset.

 6th to the 1st You are afraid that you won't succeed unless you spend every minute on the job, but by working so hard, you risk depleting your physical reserves. When you know your limits, you can use your time more efficiently and preserve your energy. But then you might become overly concerned about your health.

 7th to the 12th Your need to achieve results from your belief that you are partly responsible for the problems that afflict society. You feel that your efforts can help improve social conditions, even if what you do seems to have little bearing on them.

 8th to the 11th You know you must plan for the future to gain the security that will give you greater independence. This belief mobilizes you to invest your resources for that purpose.

 9th to the 10th You realize that you must be highly skilled in your work to meet the demands of your career. You aren't afraid of competition, because you have no doubt that you will succeed—you've planned it that way.

 10th to the 9th To be truly qualified to deal with the public, you feel that you must learn by experience as well as through education. You want people to know that you are concerned about them and that you are honored when they turn to you for help.

 11th to the 8th The appreciation of those you serve gives you a warm feeling of satisfaction. You hope you have showed them how to face the future with greater optimism and self-confidence. If they remember you for your efforts, you will feel it was a worthwhile investment.

 12th to the 7th You are probably contacted most often by people with problems. Even your partner depends heavily on your resourcefulness to compensate for his or her failings. Your life partner must be willing to share your highs and lows. You are turned off by people who lack depth and perception.

Trine: 2, 10 You are very concerned about getting everything you can from your efforts. Therefore you want the training that will allow you to fully exploit your creative talents so that they can be useful tools for reaching your objectives. Knowing how much hard work is required to accumulate a nest egg, you refuse to indulge in risky ventures. You aren't afraid of competition in your field, because your training gave you the self-confidence to meet any challenge successfully. You are thoughtful and serious in everything you do, and you rarely act on impulse. You try to operate as efficiently as possible to derive the most gains while expending the least amount of energy. Few people are as competent as you at managing financial resources. You are competent in everything you do, for you feel that if it is worth doing at all, it is worth doing well. You are probably in constant demand by people who need your services. You expect a lot for what you do, but you know you are worth it.

Sextile: 4, 8 Being appreciated for what you do is like a ray of sunshine that warms you inside and out. Your skills did not just happen; as you grew up, you accepted the responsibility for developing them, and you are grateful to your parents for urging you to be self-reliant and make your own way. You know how to solve problems, because you think about the circumstances that created them in the first place. You want others to benefit from your guidance and advice so that they can face the future with security and optimism.

Cross: 3, 9, 12 While you believe in the importance of education, you feel that you can do your best work only if you have considerable experience as well. In your opinion, practical experience is what truly qualifies anyone to serve the public's needs. You hope to be able to help relieve many of society's problems, because you feel responsible for them to some extent. It isn't easy for you to get people interested in your ideas, because you are so cautious and reserved in promoting them.

Inconjunct: 1, 11 Generally you take on more responsibilities than you need to or should, but this will deplete your physical resources and isn't really necessary. Eventually you will know your limitations and realize that with efficient planning you can accomplish everything with a minimum of effort. But then you may go to the other extreme and become overly preoccupied with your health. In that case, your health may suffer because you worry about it so much. In either case, moderation is the keyword. Freedom from want in your later years can be a reality if you invest now for that purpose. Developing great skill in your field serves the same objective.

Semisextile: 5, 7 You probably do more for your children than they will ever admit, because they also remember the discipline you demanded. You always include them in your plans, and they should be thankful that you have taught them responsibility and self-reliance so that they can make their way in life according to their individual abilities. You hope they will pattern their lives after yours and be willing to work with you, but you don't demand it. Your partner leans heavily on you for support, which you accept because it bolsters your self-image. You expect your mate to share your highs and lows and to appreciate your accomplishments.

1st to the 6th Although you may be restricted by the demanding obligations of your daily routine, you manage to use your innovative ability to make your work interesting. You are clever at devising new and better ways to make your job more exciting.

 2nd to the 5th Fulfilling your obligations to your family may be irritating if it keeps you from indulging your personal interests. Still, your children consider you exciting, and they admire your many talents. Your romantic partners stay interested because they never know what to expect from you.

 3rd to the 4th You probably grew up thinking that you could do whatever you wanted, because your parents generally approved of anything you did. You were given the opportunity to grow according to your own identity, but you lacked the discipline to do so.

 4th to the 3rd You can build your life around your many exciting ideas if you develop and promote them for that purpose. In your impatience to get things done quickly, you fail to realize that you aren't always willing to accept responsibility for your actions.

 5th to the 2nd You get a high yield from even modest resources because you know how to dramatize their importance when properly used. You have a high opinion of your worth, and you expect that others do too.

 6th to the 1st You will grow only when you admit your failings and realize that it is no dishonor to start at the bottom. From there you can only go up. Be patient and learn to accept responsibility.

 7th to the 12th Your ingenuity could be valuable in helping to find ways to solve important social problems. While you might not like working in an obscure position, the knowledge you gain from the experience would help you achieve success and recognition.

 8th to the 11th You tend to live for every moment, and you hate making plans for the future, because that limits your possibilities, which you despise. Yet you always find time to do favors for your friends, and you don't consider it an intrusion on your freedom.

 9th to the 10th You may not enjoy the arduous task of getting an education, and you certainly hate to give up that free time for self-indulgence, but you know that without an education you are limited.

 10th to the 9th You have high aspirations and a vision of yourself in a position of trust and authority. This goal will convince you to get the formal training you need; you know that otherwise your aspirations are little more than fantasies.

 11th to the 8th You will become increasingly dissatisfied with yourself unless you get involved in activities that prove how valuable you are to others. By applying your talents, you can be an invaluable help to those who need your skill and competence.

 12th to the 7th You might be inclined to indulge yourself more than your partner can tolerate. You tend to have one set of rules that your partner must accept and one for yourself, giving you every opportunity to do as you want. But you couldn't respect a partner who would accept this arrangement, and that will jeopardize the relationship.

Trine: 2, 10 The demanding obligations of your daily work routine may be frustrating, but you have a talent for thinking of innovations that can make your job more interesting. Your suggestions for improving work procedures may attract attention from the people who will benefit from them. You have a good opinion of yourself because you know you can earn a good income by using your resources with creative imagination. It is inconceivable that others are not aware of your skills. You may not be a practical person, but your intuitive problem-solving ability defies all the rules. While you consider it important to get an education, you will find it painful to lose your precious freedom while getting it. On the other hand, you know that if you don't get an education, you are limited, perhaps permanently, in your ability to earn an adequate living.

Sextile: 4, 8 Your belief that you can do whatever you want no doubt resulted from your upbringing, because your parents gave you too much freedom. You had the opportunity to grow according to your own identity, for which you should be grateful, but insufficient discipline made it difficult for you to accept responsibility. As time goes on, you will become increasingly dissatisfied with yourself unless you get involved in meaningful activities that prove the value of your talents. There are many possible uses for your ingenuity and intuitive problem-solving ability, which will go to waste unless you use them where they are most needed.

Cross: 3, 9, 12 Your ideas are your most important asset, but you must develop them before you can promote them to your advantage. This is the basis for your problems as well as for their solution. You dislike responsibility, and unless this changes, you won't be able to get people interested in your ideas. You could do so much to help improve social conditions that oppress others. In this area you would gain immediate recognition for your efforts and also get the experience you need to succeed in the field you choose. If you want to function in a position of trust and authority, you must have a formal education, or your aspirations are little more than dreams.

Inconjunct: 1, 11 You owe it to yourself to accept the fact that you must start at the bottom. Learn your craft well, so you can grow into the demands of a more responsible position. Plan ahead so you don't have to submit to other people's control, and learn to have enough self-discipline to persist in a program that will assure you of independence later. Learn the art of being patient about getting results when you act.

Semisextile: 5, 7 You permit yourself greater indulgences and more permissive behavior than you would tolerate from anyone else. Also, you have established one set of rules for yourself and another for your partner. Unless you modify this position, you risk losing your mate's respect, and you will jeopardize your relationship. You have great plans for your children and want them to rise to their fullest potentials. They find you exciting and admire your talents.

1st to the 6th You look for ways to show your concern for people, especially those who have problems. It is satisfying to know that your actions have helped to improve others' general well-being, and when they appreciate your efforts, you are inspired to continue.

 2nd to the 5th You underestimate the value of your creative potentials. With a little imagination and willingness to work at developing your talents, you can earn a comfortable income. This will also improve your self-image.

 3rd to the 4th You may have been misled into assuming that your goals should be limited to serving the needs of others. The fact is, you have the ability to gain a high position in your chosen field, once you have the self-confidence to think for yourself and stand on your own.

 4th to the 3rd You might not be ready to accept the responsibility for exploiting your ideas as the foundation for your future. But your doubts about yourself are the only impediment to success.

 5th to the 2nd As soon as you get the feedback that will convince you of your abilities, you will make your most significant contribution to society and to yourself. You will enjoy financial rewards while at the same time helping those who require your services.

 6th to the 1st Be alert to the possibility that others will try to take advantage of you. Define your goals and establish their order of importance, then take whatever action is required to achieve one goal at a time. Don't be too hard on yourself when you suffer setbacks—the experience will teach you how and why they happen.

 7th to the 12th Your most persistent adversary is *you*. If you are gainfully employed and making some contribution to society, you don't have to apologize to anyone, least of all to yourself.

 8th to the 11th Be sure to plan now for the time when you will retire. Invest some energy in planning for the future so that lack of financial security doesn't become a painful reality.

 9th to the 10th You feel you have a moral responsibility to serve the public as best you can. To live up to this personal commitment, you must get as much formal education or training as possible so you can better understand how to live up to the public's expectations and be personally fulfilled also.

 10th to the 9th You generally put yourself at the mercy of the public's wishes, so it may be a struggle to convince people that you are sincerely concerned about them. But if you are properly trained, that should not be difficult.

 11th to the 8th You should be motivated to serve your patrons' needs. You can inspire them to face their problems with courage and optimism, knowing that they will eventually succeed. On a more personal level, you don't believe you can measure up to your partner's desires.

 12th to the 7th You detect people's weaknesses easily, but in your willingness to help them get through their difficulties, you may be unprepared to protect yourself from their abuse. This may also apply to your mate, who knows you will certainly be there in a crisis. Learn to discriminate.

Trine: 2, 10 You are deeply concerned about people and their problems. You feel you could help others improve their circumstances, but you aren't sure of the best way to do this. With your creative resources and a little imagination, you can provide a social service that will achieve positive results for people in need. When your efforts are appreciated, you will be inspired to accomplish even more for others and for yourself. You might consider a career in social service. Because you consider it your moral responsibilty to be helpful whenever you can, you should get the best possible formal education so you can give your best. Not only will you understand the problems, you will also have the skills to do something about them.

Sextile: 4, 8 You should understand that even though you have special skills for serving others well, you don't have to offer yourself as a sacrifice. You have the qualifications to achieve an important position and get the recognition you deserve for your accomplishments. It would be desirable to decide for yourself how and where you will apply your talents so that you can selectively help those who need it most. If you are willing to make a substantial investment in your future by developing your creative potential to the fullest, your later years will be free from insecurity and anxiety.

Cross: 3, 9, 12 You may be too self-critical and have too many doubts about your ability to put your ideas to work. You aren't responsible for solving all of mankind's problems yourself, but you should take the initiative in doing whatever you can to help. Don't assume that your ideas won't work until you have the opportunity to try them. You owe that much to yourself and to society. Any contribution will demonstrate that you are sincerely concerned.

Inconjunct: 1, 11 It is unwise to attempt a great many tasks without planning. If you get involved in too many activities and allow people to make unfair demands on you, your health may suffer to some extent. You must be discriminating in everything you do to eliminate whatever is nonessential or has low priority. Reversals or setbacks are all right, if the experience teaches you to avoid repeating that mistake. Look ahead to the future and make the necessary investments to assure yourself of reasonable financial security in your later years. Don't assume that you will take care of that problem when the time comes, because it's always later than you think.

Semisextile: 5, 7 Creative imagination and inspiration mean nothing unless you know how to use them to accomplish your objectives. If your work does not give you an opportunity to develop your creative potentials, then you must do it on your own. Your children may give you the impetus you need to exploit your talents, which will benefit them as well. There can be financial rewards if you use your talents to solve your own and other people's problems. Your ability to detect human weakness qualifies you to help those in need. Your mate knows this and may depend on you whenever crises develop. Learn to protect yourself from people who abuse you by constantly asking favors, knowing you hate to refuse. In your romantic alliances, you sometimes fail to distinguish between those who love you for yourself and those who merely want to take advantage of your desire to serve them. You will be disappointed in love if you don't know the difference between a sincere person and an opportunist.

1st to the 6th   You will be happiest in a career that requires you to solve difficult problems. Research and development in psychology, medicine or industry would allow you to benefit society and to know the joy of making a meaningful contribution.

2nd to the 5th   Because you want your family to enjoy every possible comfort, you make a great effort to provide for them by utilizing all of your creative talents. You feel it's worth it for those you truly love.

3rd to the 4th   Your parents taught you to take advantage of their training to make your own way and build a future for yourself. You know how important it is to become self-sufficient and independent.

4th to the 3rd   Though you were encouraged to think for yourself and choose your own career, you may have neglected to fully capitalize on your ideas and your ability to solve problems. Once you develop your talents, you will have many opportunities to grow.

5th to the 2nd   Your desire for financial independence may stimulate you to make the most of your creative talents. If you choose a career you really enjoy, there is no limit to the material rewards you can earn.

6th to the 1st   Exercise some restraint while pursuing your goals. When you go to extremes, you use more energy than necessary, and you also endanger your health. Moderation at all times is advised.

7th to the 12th   You feel you must extend yourself in your work, because otherwise your competitors might gain an advantage over you. You are unnecessarily worried about not always doing your best, and you feel you must make extra sacrifices to prove your ability.

8th to the 11th   It is better to make sacrifices for yourself than for others, unless they really deserve your help. Knowing that your skills satisfy an important social need makes you feel good and gives you security for the future.

9th to the 10th   It would be ideal to find spiritual satisfaction through your career, knowing that your work helps others and gives you a feeling of personal accomplishment. You hope the public appreciates your efforts.

10th to the 9th   Once you get involved in your career, you will realize that you have a moral responsibility to serve the public. A well-rounded education will help you understand people and their expectations.

11th to the 8th   There is a future for you in service to others. In return, you expect them to make concessions to your needs. It is rewarding to know that you have showed people how to become self-reliant and secure through their own efforts.

12th to the 7th   You will do almost anything for the one you love, but you resent it when your partner asks you to compensate for his or her failings. You would prefer to have your mate's support in achieving goals that will benefit you both. You take advantage of your adversaries' weaknesses in your dealings.

Trine: 2, 10 You enjoy the challenge of solving difficult problems. For this reason, a career in research and development in such fields as psychology, medicine or industry would be suitable. You have a talent for improving the techniques usually used in these fields so they can serve their objectives better. It would be advisable to get a job in an area that you find stimulating and that fires you with enthusiasm for making the most of your creative potentials. In this way you will make a worthwhile contribution and derive a comfortable income. If the public appreciates your efforts, you feel you have accomplished something meaningful that is also spiritually satisfying.

Sextile: 4, 8 Your early training made you self-reliant and willing to explore all possible ways to satisfactorily gain your independence. You accepted the responsibility of relying on others only when there was no other alternative and only until you could become self-sufficient. You don't like to depend on anyone else, and you usually know how to avoid it by taking advantage of your own resources. You feel that once you develop your skills you can help others, because you understand that many people are simply unable to take care of their own needs. It is comforting to know that your skills will always be in demand, which assures you of some security for the future.

Cross: 3, 9, 12 You must learn to accept the responsibility for your actions, for your parents won't always be there to bail you out of difficult situations. When you aren't sure of the best way to put your ideas to work, ask questions. Your parents encouraged you to make your own way and to capitalize freely on your creative resources. Develop your talents so you have the necessary tools for the work that lies ahead. This will also help you overcome your apprehension about competition in your career. A good education will give you even greater self-confidence as you meet the increasing demands of your chosen field.

Inconjunct: 1, 11 Try not to push yourself too hard to achieve your objectives. In your determination to succeed, you tend to go to extremes and expend more energy than you should, which could endanger your health. With a little prudent planning, you can succeed without taking unnecessary risks. Don't automatically extend yourself in making sacrifices for others unless the need is urgent and they truly deserve your help. Set aside some portion of your income as an investment in your future security. Your partner will concur in this matter and give you all the support you need to make certain you both can enjoy the benefits of your combined efforts.

Semisextile: 5, 7 There is little you won't do for those you love, but you resent the fact that your partner or business associate assumes that you will always compensate for them in a crisis. Because you understand your adversaries' weaknesses, you can easily manipulate them, which can be helpful in your long-range plans. It does not necessarily follow that you will use their failings for personal gain, but you have a distinct advantage over them just the same. Only your sense of moral responsibility to others can guide you in handling this problem. You have no difficulty winning necessary support for the programs you initiate. You want your family to have every comfort you can provide. When your efforts are truly appreciated by those you love, you are amply rewarded.

Sun in Sixth, Moon in First

You are a creature of habit who is content to do things as you always have but you may be living in the past. You feel insecure, so you develop an emotional barrier to protect you from others, who, you are convinced, are trying to take advantage of you. This may not be the case at all, but there is no way that anyone can change your mind. Perhaps in your early years you were let down or disappointed by your parents, so you became distrustful of people in general. The best way to protect yourself is to develop your skills to the highest degree of proficiency so you can successfully cope with any challenge. You can't afford to be intimidated by those who are more qualified.

You will probably enjoy being self-employed or having a job that allows you self-determination. With persistent effort you should become a most valuable employee, if you work for others, or qualified to name the price you want for your services, if you work for yourself.

You will probably attract someone who needs you more than you need him or her. This reassures you that you are in demand and gives you the feeling of belonging that is so important to you. Your children make your life seem worthwhile.

Sun in Sixth, Moon in Second

Because you are so willing to apply yourself in developing your basic resources, you will derive the greatest possible gains from your efforts. You have a talent for increasing the value of your assets. Your value judgment is well developed, so you waste little time and effort in nonproductive enterprises. Your ability to succeed probably comes from your parents, who taught you to assert yourself within the framework of reasonable discipline and responsibility. They supported you in your struggle to make your own way. You are generally willing to change old habits for better ones, so you are rarely locked into an attitude that might interfere with your continuing progress. Your inner and outer worlds are sufficiently integrated so that your ambition doesn't run into any serious conflicts with your temperament. Because of that, success will be easier to achieve, and you should gain it fairly early in life.

You may have some problems in relationships; you may attract a partner who expects a lot from you so that you have to really extend yourself to satisfy those expectations. Your children are the real catalysts in your life, stimulating you to higher levels of performance in providing for them. Reserve enough time for yourself so you can unwind and enjoy some of the benefits you deserve.

Sun in Sixth, Moon in Third

Although you have the ability to convert creative potential into worthwhile skills, you have some problem deciding where you should focus your attention. There is so much you want to do that it is difficult to establish priorities. Also, you may have to make concessions to your family, who may pressure you to follow their suggestions. This situation will be relieved as you get older, but by that time, you will be so conditioned to feel guilty about doing things your own way that their influence will persist. You may have programmed yourself to do what you thought your parents expected of you, but that may be completely different from their real feelings. Your communication is better with your father than with your mother. You can discuss your goals and get his opinion about the best way to reach them. You may disagree with his advice, but you can be sure he is confident of your ability to succeed.

You might choose a career in journalism, education, medicine, any of the crafts, at which you could become a true expert, public relations or social services. No matter what field you choose, you should consolidate your efforts to avoid scattering your energies. You should have no difficulty finding ways to earn a comfortable living.

Sun in Sixth, Moon in Fourth

Your circumstances allow you to succeed in your endeavors and attain your long-range goals. It may be hard to loosen your family ties, but as your competence grows this should become easier. It is essential to cut those ties so that you can be free to take advantage of opportunities. There is nothing wrong with remembering the past unless it denies you the freedom to participate in today's responsibilities and tomorrow's plans. You have to feel right about making decisions without parental approval, based on what you hope to achieve. Your highly subjective view makes you feel guilty when you take any action that you think your parents might disapprove of. You are focused on the real, tangible world where you can derive everything you need to succeed. With your gifted imagination, you can be whatever you want, if you persist.

There are many fields in which you could succeed, including social services or crafts such as masonry, carpentry, plumbing or electricity. You might even develop your own company and offer these services. Self-employment is ideal for you because it allows the growth potential you need. A partner and family who depend on you will stimulate you to derive the most from your considerable potentials.

Sun in Sixth, Moon in Fifth

You can derive excellent results by converting your creative potential into useful skills. Your early conditioning taught you the importance of developing these potentials, and you knew that your ability to succeed depended on them. In spite of these advantages, you often question your ability to deal with competitors who seem more qualified. Because of this, you make it a point to avoid challenges unless you are sure you will succeed. You seek perfection in everything you do, which indicates that you will reach your goals. You have a flair for arousing people's interest and convincing them that you will live up to their expectations.

You could express your creative talents and enjoy reasonably high earnings by working with young people or children, or through a career in education, counseling, research and development or any occupation that requires exceptional skill.

You need to know that you are indispensable to the one you love and that you have full support in your plans for the future. Your children also inspire you to extend yourself in your career so that you can satisfy their needs; their appreciation fills you with warmth and contentment. Don't let friends impose on you with constant requests for favors, unless you know you can depend on them to reciprocate.

Sun in Sixth, Moon in Sixth

The road to success in your achievements requires you to focus your efforts in the world of physical reality, which is where your interests lie. You know that when you apply yourself, there is nothing you can't accomplish. You work vigorously to develop your creative potential so that you are the best in your field and can easily confront the challenges put before you. In a sense, you are a loner, preferring to go your own way with the self-assurance that you will succeed without any outside help. You will have many chances to work at your skills, since you attract people who expect you to help them with their problems. You might as well capitalize on this by choosing a service career. You will undoubtedly become highly proficient in your field so that you can demand and get a high return for your efforts. You may have to rely on others to provide opportunities, but you will make the most of them.

Marrying too early may upset your program for reaching your goals. Your partner may make excessive demands on your time when you are just getting started in your career, or the pressure of your children's needs may be too much responsibility to take on until you are better situated in your career. Allow some time to get away from your daily routine so that you can unwind and be rejuvenated.

Sun in Sixth, Moon in Seventh

Your ability to succeed is the result of having such diverse interests that you can always turn to something else if your current project fails. You never get locked into a situation that denies you the opportunity to turn to other career options. You are quick to discern what the public expects, and you are generally able to provide it. You are eager to take advantage of any situation that needs your skills, and you know how to get the kind of publicity that generates a demand for your services. You aren't particularly effective in purely social situations, because you have some reservations about your ability to indulge in social chatter. But when your professional skills are involved, you manage well because you are familiar with the subject.

You tend to give everyone the benefit of the doubt, which means that you may indulge them unnecessarily. You should be wary of people who always turn to you for help with their problems. If you let them take advantage of you, it's probably because you want to prove how competent you are, but you don't need that kind of approval.

Any field in which you provide services would be appropriate for you, including medicine, research and development, construction, radiology, physical therapy, nutrition or family counseling.

Sun in Sixth, Moon in Eighth

Your fulfillment is intimately linked with the public as well as with the people you are close to. You depend on others for opportunities to use the skills you've learned, and when people are satisfied with your accomplishments you know that you are effective. Although you are reasonably aware of your capabilities, this kind of feedback gives you greater self-confidence. Without the response from those you serve, you find it difficult to make progress in your career. You attract people who have problems because you have the talent and skills to offer them solutions. Because of this, you should always be able to earn a comfortable living and reach the goals you have set. Your superiors are content with your performance, since you always give them what they require and sometimes more than they expect.

With your keen abilities, you could succeed in social service programs or in some area of medicine, such as surgery, pathology, obstetrics or diet and nutrition. You might also find satisfaction in construction and associated services, which would provide a good income in a field where there is need for your competence.

Sun in Sixth, Moon in Ninth

The need to be fulfilled in your identity requires that you make full use of your creative potentials. You are basically qualified for the goals you set, but you can accelerate your progress if you recognize your limitations and get additional training. You are inquisitive and have a good ability to learn, so you would derive a high yield for your efforts by adding to your skills. You can rise to the highest level of credibility and proficiency with such a program and establish an unassailable reputation before the public. You may not desire the limited privacy of public recognition, but you owe it to yourself and those you serve to do the very best that you can. You might gain recognition as an educator, lawyer, researcher, journalist, writer or counselor.

You may not be an innovator, but no one can accomplish more with a minimum of effort. You tend to underestimate your abilities, but repeated success will eventually convince you and make you more self-confident. Giving others the benefit of the doubt and compensating for their inadequacy will make more work for you than necessary. Keep your ideas to yourself until you've had a chance to promote them and derive personal gain from them.

Sun in Sixth, Moon in Tenth

Your desire to gain satisfaction in your achievements is balanced with a desire to help others seek fulfillment in their desires. You are reasonably centered in doing what you must to gain and hold the position you want, and you know how to use your creative talents to assure continued growth in your career. You have the ability to assess what the public needs and requires of you and the expertise to promote yourself so that you are often the one chosen for the task. Making the most of your potential comes easily for you, and you have an unmistakable glow when you know you did the right thing. In spite of this, you may not derive the full benefit of this combination because it is so natural to you; some circumstance in your life must exert pressure on you.

You could succeed by being self-employed, so that your earnings depend on your self-determination and ingenuity. You could provide almost any high-priced services that people require. The public would get what it paid for, because you know you have to live with yourself if the job doesn't meet your high standards. Let the world benefit from your talents while you gain fulfillment and profit as well.

Sun in Sixth, Moon in Eleventh

The habits you have developed are not easy to change; you feel that there is no need to change as long as you are moderately successful doing things as you always have. However, unless you are willing to adapt to changing circumstances, your ability to succeed is limited. Don't be afraid to look ahead and see what's coming, so that when conditions change, you can adapt your methods so that you are still in demand. You are qualified to do the research and development that must take place before changes are accepted. If you help make the changes, you will be ready when they occur.

Working with young people may give you much inner satisfaction, for you can help them learn to stand on their own. Providing a service that improves the quality of life for large numbers of people is also consistent with your temperament. Industry has many uses for your skills, and any business would be helped by your insights about how to meet the public's expectations.

A close love relationship will give you the impetus to assert yourself more in your career. You will devote yourself to a partner who appreciates you and supports you in your endeavors. Having children will also bring out the best in you.

Sun in Sixth, Moon in Twelfth

Uncertainty and apprehension are a way of life for you, but you can change that by becoming more involved with those around you in your career and your personal affairs. You tend to measure your success or failure by the standard of other people, which is a complete waste of time and self-defeating. You want so much to be assured of your own validity that you depend on those around you for approval. You can convert this negative position into an asset by choosing a career of service to the public. You are largely dependent on others for opportunities to prove how resourceful you are in using your creative talents. You are qualfied to take on a great variety of jobs, so your earning potential is comparatively high. If you don't let people exploit you, you will succeed in the field you choose and have time for personal indulgences.

Your life will be immeasurably improved if your mate is sympathetic to your goals. If you both are involved in the same profession, your rise to prominence will have a more dynamic focus. Having children too soon may involve sacrifices, thus curtailing or delaying getting established in your career.

Chapter Seven

Seventh House

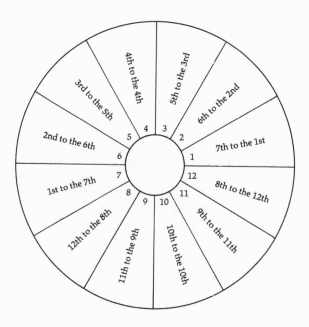

As you project and assert yourself, you are sure to encounter others who are similarly involved. The seventh house is where you run into people who offer the first real resistance you have to face. The most important challenge and the greatest test of your abilities will come from people with whom you have no previous association and therefore no precedent to guide you in dealing with them. Initial contacts with others are made through the seventh house. If you are in business, this includes your customers, patrons, clients or patients, as well as competitors, adversaries, associates and colleagues.

When you are an adult, this house represents your partner in any strong partnership in which there are shared objectives. The seventh represents the unity of marriage and the love that binds you, but it also indicates divorce when the conditions of marriage can no longer be maintained. It is the place of peace, but also of war when the climate deteriorates from consent to dissent. You may face the most demanding situations here, which you can deal with only through mature understanding and willingness to make concessions. In the struggle to exercise your privileges and to demonstrate your abilities, you will meet others who are striving to do the same, and in the contest that generally follows you can find out if you are adequately trained. Though painful, this is an opportunity to learn where you are failing and what to do about it. This is how you receive opportunities to develop so you can meet competition in the future. The seventh house is the proving ground of your abilities, showing how you will eventually perfect your craft.

Derivative House Meanings

1st to the 7th   This represents the circumstances through which you can prove yourself and gain social acceptance. It is also your mate and how you react to crisis and opportunity.

2nd to the 6th   Your ability to succeed in competition is determined by how effective you are in using your skills to meet challenges.

3rd to the 5th   You win people's appreciation for your efforts in their behalf, because you show that you are sincerely concerned about them.

4th to the 4th   You can function freely in your relationships if you've established your own roots and are reasonably independent.

5th to the 3rd   Because you are willing to share what you know with others, you can expect their support in exploiting your ideas.

6th to the 2nd   If you cultivate the right social contacts and demonstrate how valuable your skills are to them, you can improve your earning ability.

7th to the 1st   You must rely heavily on others for the opportunities you need to prove yourself. Success in competition denotes growth through self-discipline.

8th to the 12th   Although it is painful, at times you must accept relative obscurity as a necessary sacrifice in earning a place for yourself in the world.

9th to the 11th   The key to your goals is in understanding that you must consider how others will be affected before you take any action that is clearly self-serving or that excludes them.

10th to the 10th   You should understand that as you succeed in achieving status and recognition, your obligations to those around you will increase.

11th to the 9th   By establishing sound ethical guidelines, you can face the future with greater confidence that you've improved the quality of life for others.

12th to the 8th   Be careful that you aren't motivated solely by what you can gain from those around you. Giving is part of the burden you share with others.

1st to the 7th Your striving for significance means that you must depend on others for opportunities. You will derive the greatest benefit from working closely with people over whom you have some authority. You may choose a partner whose ego drive matches yours.

 2nd to the 6th You will make a better impression on the people you deal with socially and professionally if you can demonstrate your credentials. It is important to become competent in your field. If you are indifferent to competition, your achievements will be insignificant.

 3rd to the 5th Although you may be on good social terms with everyone you meet, it is your ability to understand their problems that encourages them to request your professional skills. Your way with words instantly attracts people's attention.

 4th to the 4th Your ability to form successful personal relationships depends on whether you have detached yourself from family obligations. Because your early domestic ties were so strong, it is essential that you become more detached, even at the risk of seeming disloyal.

 5th to the 3rd You have a gift for conversation and the necessary flair for effective delivery, so it would be a loss to the world not to take advantage of this creative talent. You seem to have some acting ability.

 6th to the 2nd You must meet people on mutually agreeable terms and take advantage of every opportunity to earn a reasonable income. You will probably earn your living by working with people.

 7th to the 1st You make more compromises than you should because you assume that others will make similar concessions to you. This is ill-advised. Unconsciously you are saying that you are less competent than others and therefore have to give in to them.

 8th to the 12th You feel you must concede to people, because sacrifice seems the only way to win their approval. But when you do this, you are avoiding the responsibility for asserting yourself because you fear disapproval or rejection.

 9th to the 11th If your goals are clearly defined, all you need to realize them is to get an education. You certainly know that without training, your objectives and future goals are greatly limited.

 10th to the 10th The career you choose will require public exposure. Public criticism may seem painful, but you must realize that you will also win public approval for your achievements. Weigh both factors before making up your mind—you'll probably decide to go ahead.

 11th to the 9th Your future depends on getting an education and training. You have a moral and spiritual responsibility to serve the best interests of the public. Capitalize on your ability to communicate with people.

 12th to the 8th You underestimate your ability to make an important contribution to society. You are extremely sensitive to human frailty and know how to solve the problems it causes. You might marry for financial gain or simply because you don't like living alone, which are not the best reasons. It would be better to marry because you felt you had met your ideal mate.

Trine: 3, 11 You must depend largely on others for opportunities to exploit your creative talents. Through the people you meet and deal with, you will achieve recognition for your accomplishments. Once you get the approval that you need to be reassured of your capabilities, you can use your authority to achieve your goals and objectives. You need to gain public support for the programs you initiate, so you must find a way to win converts among your competitors. You are easily intimidated by people who question your motives, and you resent having to explain your actions to anyone. Still, if you try to be understanding of others' motivations, you will have every chance to justify your position on issues and your reasons for acting as you must. Your sweeping command of language will be an asset when you are challenged, for few can resist the persuasiveness of your delivery. With a formal education, you can win over the most unyielding adversaries. You need to be fully informed at all times so that you don't have to take second place to anyone.

Sextile: 5, 9 You have a way of convincing people that you are important to them and to their dreams for the future. Your flair for communicating dramatically what people need to know about your skills is formidable, to say the least. No press agent or public relations person could match your ability to promote yourself. You feel that the public needs and wants your product, and your effective salesmanship wins you their patronage. Public relations and sales are two areas in which you could excel. You truly believe in yourself and your ability to serve the public with dedication.

Cross: 1, 4, 10 Your most persistent opponent is yourself. Even the slightest doubt about your ability to win in competition can be devastating to your self-image. You unconsciously create situations and foes that stimulate you to prove that you could win in spite of the odds against it. When you were young you might have had some difficulty in accepting this responsibility, because your training caused you to doubt your ability to compete successfully. With experience, this attitude will change. You will grow more self-confident and learn to roll with the public criticism that is often leveled at people in authority. On the other hand, the public admires and respects those who distinguish themselves by their achievements.

Inconjunct: 2, 12 You should accept the fact that you will earn your living mainly from the services you offer the public. Don't consider this demeaning, for services include a wide variety of products or skills. Instead, consider it an opportunity to exploit your talents and derive much satisfaction and fulfillment in doing so. You don't have to make huge sacrifices to win public recoginition for your efforts. Stop comparing your position to other people's, and be grateful for the privilege of utilizing your skills in ways that bring you the greatest benefits.

Semisextile: 6, 8 The public needs your skills much more than you know. Once you realize this, you will be inspired in finding ways to give people what they want and earn a comfortable living at the same time. As long as your partner doesn't threaten your self-image, the relationship will go along well. Don't choose someone who needs you to compensate for his or her deficiencies. You cannot afford to be less qualified than your opponents in any endeavor, or you risk being relegated to insignificance.

1st to the 7th Your need for companionship means that you must make many concessions to others. You generally wait for the other person to make the first move because you fear rejection or lack of interest.

2nd to the 6th You're well thought of by your fellow workers, who find you warm and considerate when they need your help. Take credit for your ability to do many things well, which may be a reason why suitors find you desirable.

3rd to the 5th When you like people, you don't hesitate to tell them so, and they eagerly respond to your honesty. But at other times, in your desire for communication you are less objective, so your flattery is often misdirected. You simply want people to like you.

4th to the 4th Your close family ties may interfere with your ability to form personal relationships. Parental conditioning has probably made you overly cautious about asserting yourself when you meet people. It isn't easy, but if you want any freedom, you must gradually detach yourself from the home.

5th to the 3rd Your ability to function socially will improve as you learn to express yourself more freely. Being a good listener is fine, but it doesn't tell people that you have many useful and creative ideas.

6th to the 2nd You will become interested in occupations that bring you before the public. Your sensitive understanding of human problems can be an asset if you decide to earn a living through public service. Be cautious, however, and don't allow people to use you as a doormat.

7th to the 1st Resist the urge to marry the first likely prospect. Your early training may have led you to believe that it is better to marry anyone than to remain single. With that attitude, you could end up being single again. A strong mothering urge is always in the background of your consciousness.

8th to the 12th In view of these factors, you would find it easy to accept any sacrifice in order to have a permanent relationship. If that is the case, eventually you would regret your involvement.

9th to the 11th You imagine that, once married, you will realize all your dreams and expectations. You forget that there will still be occasional nightmares, which can be disappointing. But if you have a sincere understanding of your situation, the future is bright.

10th to the 10th Try to get an education so you can face life's hazards more objectively. You can win recognition for your ability to deal with the public if you have the proper training and are sincerely concerned to help them solve their problems.

11th to the 9th True understanding between you and your partner is essential if your relationship is to last. There must be a spiritual bond in addition to the romantic alliance, or you will become increasingly uncomfortable in it.

12th to the 8th It is important for your partner to demonstrate that he or she needs you. You will do anything to make life comfortable and fulfilling for the one you love. But you will feel secure in the relationship only if your partner just cannot do without you.

Trine: 3, 11   You have a deep need for meaningful contacts with people at the personal level. You often make concessions to allow these relationships to develop, and you maintain a low profile to avoid being rejected. You sometimes feel that people are just not interested in you, which isn't true, of course, but it would be hard to convince you otherwise. Your initial discomfort about being with others in a social environment will change as you learn to express yourself more freely. Being a good listener will give way to actively participating in conversation, which will show that you have many creative ideas to share. You might suffer some disappointment in marriage if you imagine that it will provide the key to all of your dreams and expectations. Certainly this is possible, if you and your mate have a sincere desire to understand each other and can make allowances for each other's imperfections.

Sextile: 5, 9   You will face life and its abrasions more easily if you have a formal education. Because you are so sensitive to the highs and lows of your daily affairs, you must learn to be more objective about life. Finding a suitable career may be a problem, but you should consider an occupation that brings you into close contact with the public. Your compassion for people's problems and your willingness to offer assistance qualifies you for this type of work. You like people, and you don't hesitate to tell them so when they win your approval. You hope they feel the same way about you, because you are so anxious to have people like you.

Cross: 1, 4, 10   Your greatest liability is that you are too closely tied to your family, so it is difficult for you to meet people objectively in social situations. In your desire for personal contacts, you might marry early to escape the painful prospect of remaining in your parents' limited environment. A strong mothering urge is always at work in the background of your consciousness, so that you want to take care of others, but that is not the most desirable motive for marriage. You must gradually detach yourself from the home you grew up in and take your place in society, where you will have greater freedom to choose your destiny without being challenged. You might use your understanding and desire for personal contact in a career that allows you to help people solve their problems.

Inconjunct: 2, 12   While it is admirable to help those who deserve it, you must always be on guard against people who would abuse the privilege and use you as a doormat. Don't get too deeply involved in the affairs of those you serve. The burden might be more painful than you could endure and even affect your health. If you must make sacrifices, do so for the person you share your life with as an investment in a more secure future.

Semisextile: 6, 8   You are very talented and can do many things that others can't do. This certainly wins the attention of possible suitors, who know you will do your share to make a partnership work. If your mate appreciates everything you do and the effort you put into the relationship, you can truly be on a "high." You need someone who just cannot do without you, so that you feel important and necessary.

1st to the 7th You are mentally stimulated by social contacts with others. Social activities give you many opportunities for forming close alliances in endeavors that allow you to exploit your ideas.

 2nd to the 6th You are eager to demonstrate your skills so that the public will request your services. Your talent for promoting your abilities and products makes you an effective salesperson.

 3rd to the 5th People are almost always very interested in what you have to say, whether individuals or the general public. Your sparkling conversation attracts romantic partners.

 4th to the 4th Any difficulties you have in forming relationships probably result from your parents' suggestions that you could make a better selection. This can go on and on. You must assert your independence by picking your own mate.

 5th to the 3rd It will be easier to exploit your creative ideas if you get cooperation and support from a trusted adviser. You generally know how to communicate, but you may need some help in making decisions.

 6th to the 2nd Working with the public and offering services that are in constant demand will allow you to earn a comfortable living. It will also provide the feedback that assures you of your competence.

 7th to the 1st Compromise is an essential part of your everyday life, although you may feel intimidated by the circumstances that make it necessary. People need you as much as you need them, because you are able to appraise their problems objectively and find solutions.

 8th to the 12th You underestimate your ability to render the kind of service that produces results. You fulfill your social obligations by doing for others what they cannot do for themselves, which could be a spiritual motivation.

 9th to the 11th People like you because you seem to understand their needs. You help them exploit their creative talents by convincing them that they have potentials to develop. They are inspired by your belief in them. You will realize your goals through the social contacts you make.

 10th to the 10th People are the key to fulfilling your destiny. If you accept this responsibility, your efforts in their behalf will be recognized. Don't be intimidated by what your father expects of you or by comparisons with others' accomplishments. Be true to yourself.

 11th to the 9th You will have a permanent place in the lives of everyone you contact because you listen willingly to people's ideas. Everyone is enriched when you explore the goals that are possible with their ideas. In turn, they will help you when you need a favor.

 12th to the 8th Don't be envious of others because you assume that they are more resourceful than you, for that may not be so at all. Your partner will be more and more appreciative of your continuing efforts to enrich and sustain your relationship. You will do almost anything for the one you love, and the resulting happiness is all the thanks you need.

Trine: 3, 11   Your need for communication brings you into close personal contact with the public, and you know that your opportunities for development will come from this sector. To make the right decisions about your career and personal relationships, you need the help and advice of a trusted associate. You are indeed qualified to help people with their problems because you understand their needs. Once you've convinced them of their potential, you can help them exploit their creative talents. The resulting exchange of ideas is mutually beneficial, for your greatest opportunities will come through such contacts. You might choose a career in which you are a catalyst for people who are unaware of their talents. You may consider becoming a vocational adviser, even though you sometimes need advice yourself. In all probability, you will meet your future partner through this field.

Sextile: 5, 9   You are a fascinating conversationalist, and people are generally attentive when you speak. Your sparkling presentation arouses interest in the subject at hand. You also listen willingly to people with problems and are equally attentive to their ideas. They appreciate your efforts to help them derive lasting benefits from their ideas. You can usually count on them to help you gladly when you need help, for they remember how instrumental you were in helping them plan their future goals.

Cross: 1, 4, 10   Your most urgent priority is learning to be more self-sufficient and have enough confidence to make personal decisions. You are too easily intimidated by competition, so that you don't assert yourself enough. You should compromise only as much as your career requires. You are at a crossroads, and there is tension between your early conditioning and your aspirations. Making the right decisions for yourself, in spite of your parents' opinions, will be a critical factor in determining your destiny. To fulfill your personal desires, you must either concur with parental suggestions or risk alienation. Your task is to help people establish a foundation on which they can successfully build their ambitions.

Inconjunct: 2, 12   You need to be reassured that you can help people cope with their problems. If you persist, your earnings will grow as your experience expands. In your desire for increased earnings, you might make the mistake of expanding your operations and becoming excessively fatigued. While it is important to grow, you shouldn't exceed safe limits. Don't worry that you aren't doing all you can to fulfill your obligations to those you serve. The chances are, you have the highest motivation, which produces many rewards for others and spiritual enrichment for yourself.

Semisextile: 6, 8   The worst thing you can do is deny others the benefit of your ideas and your ability to solve problems. It would also be a mistake to focus your actions mainly on financial benefits with little attention to doing something worthwhile. This also applies to choosing a marriage partner. The best motive is love rather than financial gain, but the choice is yours to make. Marrying for love would give you the best of both worlds, for if you are happy in your personal relationship you will put your best efforts into succeeding in your career, which will benefit both of you. With your wealth of ideas, there are unlimited ways in which you can apply your skills to achieve your goals and gain the security you need.

1st to the 7th Your conciliatory manner endears you to those with whom you are in close personel contact. You always seem to make concessions, especially when a situation develops that could cause disharmony between you and others.

 2nd to the 6th You know how to win the public's approval by your tactful presentation of yourself and your credentials. Your skills can be an asset as you seek to make an impression on others.

 3rd to the 5th You are effective in saying the right thing at the right time to get the best possible reaction from people, who are impressed by your refinement and savoir-faire. You have little difficulty getting people interested in your creative abilities.

 4th to the 4th Early parental conditioning may have made you apprehensive about your ability to form personal contacts with people outside of your home environment. You may have to demand the right to make friends without your parents' approval, which could cause some bitterness in your relationship with them.

 5th to the 3rd You have a talent for communicating with people in a close social environment. These contacts can give you the opportunity to develop and exploit your ideas with creative imagination.

 6th to the 2nd You derive many benefits by cooperating with people because you know that through them you will always have a job. If the pay is reasonable, you may even work with people you don't particularly like, so you can afford all the comforts you enjoy.

 7th to the 1st While it may sometimes irritate you to do so, you make compromises because you know that eventually you will get your way. You will learn to be more self-sufficient as you become more experienced in dealing with people.

 8th to the 12th Initially it may seem demeaning, but you should offer to do favors for people who are less fortunate. You should be proud of this chance to make a social contribution that is much appreciated.

 9th to the 11th You make the necessary adjustments to get an education, for you know it will be easier to achieve your goals if you are well informed. You have the vision to know that without training, your dreams for the future can't be realized.

 10th to the 10th Your willingness to do what your family thinks best may delay fulfillment of your destiny. The public sector is most suitable for your talents and, as you grow in competence, so will your recognition and reputation.

 11th to the 9th Your services will always be in demand, because you have a talent for understanding what people want and giving it to them. You would make a good public speaker, for you can win an audience easily.

 12th to the 8th You may be attracted to people who are financially independent. This is not a good basis for a permanent relationship, unless there is genuine love as well. You might justify your materialistic attitude by saying that you are always the one who makes concessions, and this evens the score.

Trine: 3, 11   Your willingness to compromise and give others the benefit of the doubt wins you many admirers who are impressed by your desire to maintain harmony. Obviously, your pleasing personality enhances both your personal and business relationships. Your talent for making people comfortable would be an asset in your career. You know how to bring out the best qualities in people, and they in turn will provide opportunities you need to fully exploit your creative talents. Getting an education will make you more polished and refined and give you every advantage for realizing your dreams. These are glowing qualities, but some less appealing factors should be mentioned, such as your well-contrived use of passive resistance to gain your objectives. People who lose in competition with you seldom know what hit them. You know how to attract other people's talents when you need them and are resourceful in capitalizing on them when it serves your purposes.

Sextile: 5, 9   You know how to get the best reaction from those you want to impress by effectively saying the right thing at the right time. You generally get the support you want because you present your case with dramatic flair, and your creative ideas stimulate others. You give people what they want, tactfully implying that you thoroughly understand their reasons for wanting it. Since you have no trouble winning people to your way of thinking, you would be a good public speaker.

Cross: 1, 4, 10   There are times when making compromises is irritating and makes you resent those who expect it. When you are angry enough, you take the initiative and demand that others must yield occasionally. While growing up, you had to contend with your parents' demands, and now asserting yourself causes some anxiety. You want to do what's best for everyone, but you know that this is nearly impossible. It is essential that you become more independent of your family and learn to be more self-reliant, even if it means making mistakes or losing their support. Your destiny requires that you come before the public, which will be difficult if you refuse to think of it as your greatest priority. Personal relationships may not develop if you must submit your prospective partner to your parents for approval.

Inconjunct: 2, 12   Your principal income will come from working with the public. If you've taken the time to develop your skills, you will be well paid for your services. At times you may think you're not doing as much as you should, so you will volunteer to make it up through extra work, which requires more energy. But be careful, because you may become overtired. You may insist on overextending yourself, so you can increase your earnings and afford all the physical comforts you want.

Semisextile: 6, 8   Although you don't like the idea of physical labor, it is necessary to work at developing your creative skills so that you have something to offer the buying public. Being well trained is the key to winning public approval for your efforts. If you focus your attention primarily on people in comfortable financial circumstances, your motives will be questioned. There must be a meaningful exchange between you and others for you to feel good about your accomplishments. You bring a lot of warmth and social savoir-faire to your relationships, and your partner will doubtless be pleased that you are a credit to him or her.

1st to the 7th   You are naturally argumentative and easily provoked by anyone who disagrees with you. It is difficult for you to meet others halfway because you consider any resistance as a threat.

 2nd to the 6th   The best way to meet competition is to have well-developed skills, because it is useless to compete with anyone unless you are reasonably sure you can win. Properly utilized talent is what determines whether you will win public approval for your accomplishments. With your energy and a little imagination, you can succeed in any confrontation.

 3rd to the 5th   When you are trying to convince people of your talents, you drive a hard bargain. Talking about what you can do may fascinate people, but it is action that counts in the final analysis.

 4th to the 4th   Your parents may try to intimidate you by insisting that they should come first in anything you do. You will probably leave home early in life so you can make your own way independently. Your actions may be restricted if you feel guilty about this decision.

 5th to the 3rd   With a little self-control, you can be very effective in winning people's support for your ideas. You know how to dramatize them to arouse people's genuine interest in you and your ambitions.

 6th to the 2nd   You will encounter much competition in trying to get a job, but with your aggressive nature, you will not be deterred from your objective. Working closely with the public will be easy if you develop greater self-discipline and learn to make concessions at the right time.

 7th to the 1st   Doubting your ability to win over competitors, you are forced to extend yourself more than they do. This might cause you to overreact and be more aggressive than necessary. In this way you might use so much energy that you lose interest.

 8th to the 12th   You don't really mind doing things for people, but you want to be appreciated for it. It is difficult for you to work behind the scenes, where no one notices your efforts. Eventually you may derive satisfaction from what you do rather than from the notice you get.

 9th to the 11th   You know that your chances for achieving your goals will be much improved if you get an education. You have many exciting dreams about what you want out of life, and you have the inspiration to achieve them.

 10th to the 10th   Your aggressive nature can be an asset in your profession if it is balanced by compromise and common sense. If you can't control your temper, you may get only a lot of bad publicity.

 11th to the 9th   It is important that you take moral responsibility for achieving your goals ethically. Otherwise you risk losing everything you've gained. Be discriminating when your friends offer ideas that seem suspect, and be guided by your own sense of right and wrong.

 12th to the 8th   Your strong physical drive makes it hard for you to endure rejection by those you love. You always suspect that you are being used to satisfy their desires and that you can be discarded at any time. You want your partner to depend on you and appreciate your efforts.

Trine: 3, 11 An argumentative person, you must try not to get angry when people disagree with you. If you can be objective, you will understand that no one is trying to threaten you, they are simply presenting an alternate point of view. This could be an opportunity to expand your knowledge and get the benefit of someone else's experience, so don't cut it off before you have a chance to evaluate the situation. People are impressed by your aggressiveness, but they are intimidated when you act impulsively without justification. You will get support for your programs if you learn to discipline yourself, because people won't take a chance with you unless you seem more self-controlled. You arouse people's interest by dramatizing your plans. Above all, get an education so that you can learn how to promote your ambitious plans without incurring the resentment of your intended supporters.

Sextile: 5, 9 You devote a lot of time to thinking about the best way to realize your dreams. You should use an equal amount of energy to carry out your ideas, because talk is useless without action. Be wary of shady suggestions from friends, because it is imperative that you always operate within the limits of your conscience, guided by your sense of right and wrong. Freedom is so precious to you that it would be senseless to risk losing it through careless disregard for ethical behavior.

Cross: 1, 4, 10 In spite of appearances, you doubt your ability to successfully meet competition. You overreact to threats and use tactics that are more aggressive than necessary to win, or else you become quarrelsome when you suffer defeat. This probably results from the conditioning you received while you were growing up. Perhaps you weren't allowed to express yourself freely, or you were severely punished when you did. In that case, leaving home while you were young was the best action to take, although you felt somewhat guilty about it. You may be alienated from your parents, so you will have to rely on your own resources to make a life for yourself. A career that allows you to have authority over others will relieve some of your tension, but it has to be handled intelligently to be truly productive. With common sense and objectivity, you will acquire status for your accomplishments.

Inconjunct: 2, 12 You thrive on competition as a chance to demonstrate your superior ability. Your aggressive nature will pay dividends when you have the opportunity to make money. Nothing will deter you from your goal of financial independence, and this vision sometimes drives you to excess. It may be useless to tell you to relax and get away from the pressure of your work now and then, but it needs saying. When people appreciate your help, it pleases you more than if they simply pay for it.

Semisextile: 6, 8 Your "all or nothing" attitude demands that your partner be completely dedicated to your needs and ambitions. You find it painful to be rejected by anyone, especially the one you love. You don't demand complete submission, but you must be the most important person to your lover. This gives you fewer people to choose from. For those who qualify, you will do anything to preserve your relationship. In your career, you must develop your skills to the utmost to increase your chances of winning in competition. You have the energy and imagination to use your skills to obtain any reasonable goal and win the public's respect.

1st to the 7th   You are on good terms with everyone and generous in helping those who require your assistance. Through your social and business relationships you find many opportunities for personal growth and development. You are especially generous to the one you love.

 2nd to the 6th   You go to great lengths to establish your credentials before the public, and generally you live up to their expectations. Your abilities are greatly appreciated by many people, who pay well for your services.

 3rd to the 5th   You help people gain more self-confidence by showing them how to capitalize on their resources. You inspire their confidence by speaking with understanding and authority.

 4th to the 4th   Your early domestic environment may have frustrated your need to grow through social contacts. You had to impress on your family that your search for greater fulfillment required you to be more independent, but you may have felt guilty about it.

 5th to the 3rd   You must constantly call upon your wealth of ideas so they will benefit you and others. You know how to present your ideas to interested persons who have the financial resources to promote them.

 6th to the 2nd   You never run out of ideas for earning a living. Almost everyone you meet serves as a vehicle for utilizing your knowledge and skill. This is a two-way situation, for in the long run they will gain too.

 7th to the 1st   You are often overly impressed with your competitors' qualifications, so you are less forceful than you should be in asserting yourself and your talents. If someone you love and respect has a strong belief in your abilities, you will listen to him or her.

 8th to the 12th   You would like to use your talents to help those who are unable to help themselves. You have a strong compulsion to make your services available at the social level of human need as your contribution to the welfare of society.

 9th to the 11th   You have grandiose dreams of a perfect society where everyone achieves their objectives and lives in perfect harmony. To achieve these ideals and realize your goals, you must get an education. You are realistic enough to know that you cannot expect to perform miracles.

 10th to the 10th   The public will recognize your accomplishments and give you the respect you deserve for helping society. You will always be close to the public in your endeavors, because it is the best area for exploiting your talents.

 11th to the 9th   Because of your capacity to listen to and understand others' concerns, you will always be sought after. People consider you a friend to whom they can turn for help in solving their problems. And you can inspire them to seek their own future fulfillment.

 12th to the 8th   Many of those you serve may take you for granted, knowing you are always available when they need you. Your mate supports you in your endeavors and knows by your deeds that you care.

Trine: 3, 11 You are generally easygoing and compromising, so you have little difficulty forming meaningful relationships. You are understanding when people have problems, and you try to be helpful whenever possible. Most of your opportunities come from people you've befriended in the past who simply want to show their appreciation. You can take advantage of these opportunities to grow and develop while improving your social and business ambitions. Your generosity toward those who are close to you indicates that your self-image is reasonably secure and won't be easily challenged by competitors. You are sure you will realize your expansive dreams for the future if you exploit your creative talents and let people know what skills you have. Interested persons won't hesitate to provide you with the necessary resources required to put your ideas to work. You believe in others as much as you believe in yourself and, though you know it is unrealistic to anticipate a perfect society, you persist in that dream. You feel that if society is well enough informed, utopia can be achieved sometime in the future.

Sextile: 5, 9 Your greatest asset is your capacity to listen to the diverse opinions of people in all walks in life. You show them how to capitalize on their own resources and achieve their goals, which improves their self-confidence. They respect you for your understanding and your worthwhile suggestions. You are a friend to many, who are thus inspired to solve their own problems and find their own fulfillment.

Cross: 1, 4, 10 You are overly impressed by your competitors' qualifications, so you are not as forceful as you should be in asserting yourself. Not wanting to offend anyone, you sometimes allow less qualified persons to gain control over situations that you handle better. You are deeply influenced by the one you love, especially if he or she is confident of your ability to succeed. It is indeed fortunate that the public can turn to you for your services. People appreciate your dedication to service. You may be compensating for an early environment that frustrated your desire to grow in understanding through social contact. It was important for you to gain an independent position that allowed you to expand your horizons among the people with whom you feel a spiritual commitment. You may have felt guilty about severing your restrictive family ties, but this should diminish as your opportunities expand and you realize you have made the right decision.

Inconjunct: 2, 12 Although you will never run out of ways to earn a living, there is some danger that you will overextend yourself physically. Having to do so much for so many people can deplete your energy, unless you realize that others must also share the burden. You tend to think that you won't have enough time to get everything done. Enlist others in your efforts to help those in need. Certainly you will do more than your share in fulfilling your social obligations.

Semisextile: 6, 8 Your greatest adversary is greed. If this ugly desire becomes uppermost in your thinking, all your good deeds could be in danger when your true motives are revealed. But generosity also comes with this planetary position, and your deeds could serve as a testimonial to your spiritual commitment to society. You have to take the moral and ethical responsibility for everything you do.

1st to the 7th   You are reserved and cautious about starting a personal relationship until you can learn something about the other person. You seem to attract people who make demands on you and restrict your freedom.

 2nd to the 6th   You are apprehensive about being accepted by others, because you don't think you can live up to their expectations. If you have developed your creative potentials, you can easily fit into any social environment, because you've established your worth to society.

 3rd to the 5th   You may have some difficulty in promoting yourself and the services you can provide because of your inability to express yourself freely. Fearing ridicule, you are hesitant to project yourself before the public.

 4th to the 4th   Strong family ties make it painful for you to detach yourself from obligations to your parents. It will not be easy, but you must become more independent so you can take advantage of any opportunities that arise from social contacts.

 5th to the 3rd   Surely you must know that you are as competent as those whose accomplishments you admire, and you must take the initiative in accepting any challenge that will help prove it.

 6th to the 2nd   You must work to develop patronage for the services you offer. You will earn a comfortable income and improve your ability to aim for even greater goals and ambitions. Don't do more than you've agreed to do, and set aside some time for rest and relaxation.

 7th to the 1st   You can learn something from everyone you contact. Instead of trying to match their performances, which you've probably overestimated, you should develop your talents to the utmost, so that you can accept any challenge and know you will succeed.

 8th to the 12th   Because of your low self-image, you assume that you are obligated to serve everyone. With proper training to improve your sense of self-worth, you could be motivated to make your contribution to society by serving others. You will derive much spiritual satisfaction from your accomplishments.

 9th to the 11th   You know that it will be easier to realize your goals and objectives if you get sufficient professional training. If you manage your resources efficiently to deal with opportunity, your dreams will be fulfilled.

 10th to the 10th   Don't even bother trying to live up to your father's expectations unless they coincide with yours. You are all you've got, and you have to make the best of it. You are very important to those you serve in your career, which is where you should focus your efforts.

 11th to the 9th   Be ethical in all your affairs so that later in life you will know that you've achieved your goals honestly. You don't want any untidiness to contaminate the results of all your determination and hard work. Take advantage of your friends' offers that will allow you to grow throughout your career.

 12th to the 8th   To succeed, you need a partner who shares your dedication and persistence. With that support and the love you share, no goal is impossible to achieve.

Trine: 3, 11 You are cautious and reserved about meeting people, and you don't form relationships with others until you've had time to evaluate their credentials. Your apprehensiveness comes from feeling that they will somehow try to make restricting demands on you. Your negative attitude makes it essential that you get an education to improve your chances in competition, where your credentials are certain to be challenged. While you admire and respect people who are sure of themselves, you fail to take the initiative when you are given an opportunity to demonstrate your skills. You must learn to react more positively in such situations, if only to prove to yourself that you can succeed in competition. Once you realize that you have the ability to win, you will learn to manage your creative resources so that you can achieve your goals.

Sextile: 5, 9 While you may not like promoting yourself before the public, you will have to if you want people to buy your skills. Fear of ridicule is an unacceptable reason for withholding your talents from those who need them most. When you finally get over this hangup, you must establish a program to achieve your career goals ethically. It is important to keep your ambitions uncontaminated so you will know that everything you have was gained through honest hard work.

Cross: 1, 4, 10 Become as proficient as possible in your chosen work so that you aren't unnecessarily intimidated by challenging competition. Learn about your adversaries' credentials and get whatever additional training is required so that you can meet them on equal terms. You can learn something from every person you meet, socially and professionally, so take advantage of it. Your early environment had some limitations, which may have made it difficult to assert yourself as you should. Once detached from obligations to your family, you will benefit from external social contacts.

Inconjunct: 2, 12 You may have to work hard to get patronage for your services, but that can provide you with an adequate and comfortable living. Success feeds on itself, and there is no limit to the goals you can achieve. Until you are confidently established in your career, do only what is required of you in any situation, and set aside some time for rest and relaxation. You have the impression that you are somehow indebted to everyone and that they can demand payment at will. Find out exactly what you must do, such as taking responsibility for your actions, providing the best possible product or service and managing your affairs according to high ethical standards.

Semisextile: 6, 8 Find someone who shares your ambitions and can give you needed moral and emotional support when there are difficulties. There is no limit to what you can accomplish with someone you love, for you find shared experiences more enriching and fulfilling. Don't worry that people won't accept you, or you may fail to live up to their expectations. If you are properly trained and accept full responsibility for your actions, you will gain acceptance in your own social environment and win the admiration of your contemporaries as well.

1st to the 7th You seek contact with progressive people whose lives are exciting. You admire those who demand the freedom to be themselves and who have the courage to fulfill their chosen destinies. To emulate them, you seek a partner who wants a relationship of mutual growth and development.

 2nd to the 6th If you use your skills with ingenuity, you should be accepted easily by groups and individuals. It is comparatively easy for you to arouse and maintain the public's fascination because you know how to work for their best interests.

 3rd to the 5th You are eager to form relationships with persons to whom you can express your ideas freely. You know how to enlist their support for your plans because you never force your ideas on them.

 4th to the 4th You had to establish early in life that you would not submit to any control or restraint by your parents. You wanted them to understand that you had to be free to rise or fall on your own.

 5th to the 3rd You generally know how to promote yourself effectively so that you are welcome in any social environment. Until you are established and secure in your abilities, you need to make the right contacts that will open doors for you.

 6th to the 2nd The need to be concerned about the material facts of life is somewhat annoying to you. This is why you try to associate with persons who give you opportunities to demonstrate your talents.

 7th to the 1st You assume that most people are more free than you, and you say so openly. This is your way of defending your lack of success in competition, which really results from low self-confidence. You would feel intimidated by a successful partner.

 8th to the 12th You can improve your self-image by accepting the challenge of competition. This should be your investment in helping the public, from whom your greatest opportunities for self-development and success will come.

 9th to the 11th Be progressive in your thinking and try not to belittle yourself for past failures. If you look ahead, you will realize that with a little planning you can achieve your goals, but your dream must be a vivid one.

 10th to the 10th Working with the public is your key to success and fulfillment, but it involves many responsibilities. The demands of your career may limit your freedom, but through your accomplishments you will eventually gain the public's respect and greater freedom.

 11th to the 9th You cannot hope to achieve any significant goals unless you get a proper education. No one can enjoy freedom unless they earn it. With your talent for innovation, your goals are almost unlimited.

 12th to the 8th You will surely succeed if your commitment to life is based on providing the best service to those who need it most. But if you try to get as much as possible from others, your victory will be bittersweet. Discuss this with your partner, who will be honest and direct with you. He or she will be your most ardent supporter and will help you succeed.

Trine: 3, 11   In your desire to enjoy life without limitations, you seek progressive people who lead exciting lives. You apply the same philosophy in searching for a partner with whom you can have room to grow and develop. You are easily accepted in any social environment, because you don't follow any hard and fast rules that make it impossible for others to welcome you. You tend to avoid responsibility, however, which could create some problems in your career. Until you are established in your own right, you may have to rely on social contacts to open doors. This might be painful, because you don't like being obligated to others. You need to plan your moves carefully and realize that success is the product of a well-thought-out program with specific objectives.

Sextile: 5, 9   Though you think you know what's best for your children, giving them unlimited freedom may cause more harm than you know. Luckily you have good communication with them, so they may not criticize you for your lack of discipline. You know how to make contacts with important persons who can help you exploit your creative ideas. They will support you in your endeavors because you are careful not to force yourself on them. Get an education and learn how others accept full responsibility for their actions. You may then realize that you have freedom only if you earn it. With your talent for innovation, your goals are nearly limitless when you apply yourself.

Cross: 1, 4, 10   You are uncomfortable when forced to adhere to rules laid down by someone else, which was even more difficult while you were growing up, when your parents tried to control you. A rebel at heart, you needed to let them know that you had to make your own way and fail, if necessary, on your own terms. You aren't as self-confident as you appear, and working with the public will show you how much experience you need to succeed. Time is in your favor if you learn to forego some of your personal indulgences when your career demands require it.

Inconjunct: 2, 12   It may be annoying, but you must deal with the financial facts of life if you want to earn a decent income. Learn to capitalize on your social contacts and use these opportunities to demonstrate your talents. You will eventually succeed on your own and gain the freedom to be more selective about whom you are obligated to. You do owe something to your public, from whom you are willing to accept certain rewards for the services you render. Don't forget those who do favors for you. Helping them can be a wise investment in your future, when you may need them again.

Semisextile: 6, 8   You are ingenious in finding ways to gain acceptance by the general public for your contributions, which may not be spectacular compared to others'. But you fascinate people with your special brand of charm, which disarms them without their knowing it. You easily arouse people's interest in your programs, which you say are in their best interests, and for the most part you succeed. Examine your motives in all your actions. If your purpose is to get as much as possible at others' expense, your victory will be bittersweet; but if you sincerely work for their best interests, you will deserve and win their appreciation. Your partner is your most ardent supporter and will honestly appraise your accomplishments.

1st to the 7th   The relationships you seek are characterized by idealism, illusion and romantic fantasy and possibly by deception and disappointment. You should not form any attachment without an unbiased and objective opinion from someone you trust.

2nd to the 6th   You must be careful about demonstrating your creative talents so that your competitors won't use them for their personal gain. Get a binding contract before you agree to provide any service.

3rd to the 5th   Your imagination works overtime developing ways to exploit your creative talents. But you discuss your ideas too freely with others, which encourages plagiarism. Be sure of your lover's affections before making a commitment. Don't assume that it is love just because you desire it.

4th to the 4th   A disappointing childhood may have conditioned you to escape into marriage, which is hardly the best reason for such a demanding relationship. You might choose someone who is as insecure as you, out of sentimental pity.

5th to the 3rd   You want desperately to have people understand you, and you are attracted to anyone who will listen to your romantic fantasies. You dream of finding the right person to help you exploit your creative ideas.

6th to the 2nd   Be discreet about telling anyone about your earnings. Deception by those you trust can be costly, and the money will be difficult to recover.

7th to the 1st   You are a prime target for people who would take advantage of your talents. You should distrust everyone until you know they can be trusted. Serving is one thing, but being exploited is another.

8th to the 12th   You assume that everyone is superior to you and that you owe them your service. There is a degree of masochism with this position, which may cause you to rationalize the fact that others take advantage of you.

9th to the 11th   You must get as much education as possible to ensure that others can't exploit you for their own gain. Prepare a plan of action with firm goals, and do not deviate from it.

10th to the 10th   Don't be intimidated by people who tell you how to succeed. You may want to serve society, and that would bring you the recognition you deserve. You lose interest when you run into severe competition, but you must persist with the confidence that you will succeed.

11th to the 9th   You need sincere friends who truly understand and support you. Cultivate friendships with persons who are already established in their careers and ask for their advice.

12th to the 8th   You can perform many worthwhile services for people, but try not to be so obligated to others that you have no time for yourself. You should be professionally established before marrying; you need the experience and sophistication that go with success before choosing a partner.

Trine: 3, 11 You should assume that your relationships are not what they seem. Your ideal may be based on romantic fantasy, making disappointment very likely when you see the situation in the harsh light of reality. When you are attracted to someone, ask a trusted friend for an unbiased opinion. On the other hand, you may look for someone who is desperate for you to serve his or her needs. In that case you will find a parasite who clings to you until you feel strangled. Be extremely cautious about forming any binding relationships. You need to get as much education as you can afford to help ensure that others can't exploit you for their benefit. Don't do anything without a plan, and don't deviate from it. Define your goals and make sure that you adhere rigidly to your program for achieving them.

Sextile: 5, 9 Don't make any romantic commitments until the one you love leaves no doubt about his or her intentions. You should control your compulsion to share your creative ideas with anyone who will listen, because you attract the kind of people who think nothing of appropriating your ideas and capitalizing on them for personal gain. When making plans, be sure to get the advice of sincere friends whom you can trust to support you.

Cross: 1, 4, 10 Don't allow others to use your talents and ideas unless you have evidence that they can be trusted. The same applies to finding a mate. Disappointing relations in your home while you were growing up may have given you the idea that you would be better off married. Obviously this is not a good basis for a marriage, and the chances are you would choose someone as insecure as you. If sentimental pity is also involved, the tie will be precarious at best. Wait until you are established in your career before taking on a permanent mate. An early marriage indicates emotional immaturity and insecurity. You will improve your self-image by becoming successful in your career. Working in the public sector is suitable, though you may lose interest if the competition is too severe. If you are dedicated to helping those who require compassionate understanding of their problems, you will persist. Remember that success, as you measure it, is judged by a private assessment of your services.

Inconjunct: 2, 12 Don't confide your plans and ideas to anyone at work, and never discuss your earnings. There is no sense in asking for trouble when it can be avoided. You assume that everyone else is either more talented or superior in some other way, although you can't define just how. Stop indulging in this kind of fantasy; you're taking it out of yourself. You are obligated to serve only those who can benefit from your skills and talents.

Semisextile: 6, 8 Few people can provide such worthwhile services, only you don't realize it. You have a talent for attracting the seediest characters, who always have their hands extended for whatever gifts you will bestow on them. You can avoid this kind of self-entrapment if you realize that you also owe yourself certain favors and privileges. Learn to say no when you suspect that a request for help is unwarranted.

1st to the 7th Powerful forces are at work when you form a relationship, and you should examine your motives when you do. You may not realize how much energy you use to gain dominance over others, including your partner. In marriage, compromise works better than force.

 2nd to the 6th You generally know how to convince people of your skills, and you have the promotional ability to win their patronage for your services. But remember that without customers, you're out of business, so be sure to give them everything they pay for.

 3rd to the 5th You understand how to capitalize on your creative talents to derive the most benefit. While your children are young, you teach them to be self-reliant so that they will not fear competition as they make their own way in life. You impress them deeply.

 4th to the 4th You feel that you can do anything you set your mind to. The tension between you and your parents in childhood made you decide that you would never depend on anyone else for anything.

 5th to the 3rd When you are romantically attracted to someone, there are no holds barred. Never thinking that you will be rejected, you go to great lengths to win the one you love. But if you are rebuffed, you become difficult and vindictive. You promote your ideas forcefully.

 6th to the 2nd You often get involved in extreme situations with people, especially when you are utilizing your skills to earn a living. You thrive on competition, and even if beaten, you never give up.

 7th to the 1st The struggle for power never ceases within you, which is why you welcome competition with strong adversaries. You hope to emerge victorious in the struggle for survival of the fittest. Could it be that you aren't so certain you will succeed in this game?

 8th to the 12th Properly utilized, your talents can be enormously beneficial to those who lack the talent or opportunity to improve their social predicament. If you consent to serve the greatest needs of society, you will surely be filled with satisfaction and inner contentment.

 9th to the 11th You understand that unless you have a specific vision of the future and the goals you hope to achieve, all your energy may be wasted. You don't doubt for a minute that you will achieve your goals.

 10th to the 10th The public image you create is precariously poised, depending on your willingness to accept full responsibility for your actions. The public can certainly use your talents and your political leverage to correct prevailing injustices, if you are properly motivated.

 11th to the 9th You have a deep understanding of people's thought processes and motivations. This gives you an opportunity to win appreciation for the services you render, which will make their future more secure.

 12th to the 8th You alone can decide whether to exploit other people's finances for personal gain or to help them unselfishly. You will learn how much others depend on your help. Your mate supports you in your goals but may be intimidated by some of your methods.

Trine: 3, 11 You must examine your motivation in forming relationships, because your drive to gain control over others can be dangerous. The desire to gain dominance and win unquestioned support from the public is a severe test of your spiritual courage or your obsession with power. You can do many wonderful things to serve society by promoting changes in the existing laws that will create a more equitable environment for everyone. In your personal affairs, there are no holds barred when someone attracts you romantically, and you go to great lengths to secure that individual for yourself. When rejected, you can be cruel and vindictive. You have the vision and energy to achieve goals that others would find nearly impossible. But then they don't have your ability to get the necessary support to successfully carry out your plans.

Sextile: 5, 9 You teach your children to be as self-reliant as you are so they will be ready to accept the responsibilities that lie ahead in seeking to fulfill their own identities. You almost mesmerize them to accept fate as a challenge that they will surely win. Because you understand people's thought processes and motivations, you can provide them with the services that will help them achieve security for the future.

Cross: 1, 4, 10 Even if there was tension between you and your parents while you were growing up, you succeeded in putting it in proper perspective, and now you regard it as an opportunity to make your own way. You don't want to be obligated to anyone, so you bypass those who try to get in the way of your desires. You cannot fail to gain the public's attention, no matter how you choose to exploit your creative potentials. The difference between fame and notoriety is a fine line of intent and motivation. You can do much to correct the injustices that prevail in the public sector by using the leverage of persuasion to change laws or attitudes. Only you can decide if you will respond to this enormous responsibility and use your influence positively and spiritually.

Inconjunct: 2, 12 You are no stranger to extreme situations with other people. You thrive on competition, knowing that you will emerge victorious in the end. You will face any danger to gain your objectives, and even when you are occasionally beaten you are never really defeated. If you use your talents properly, you can help those who lack the talent or opportunity to help themselves. The public will be eternally grateful if you choose to work in their behalf, and the inner contentment and satisfaction you will derive are inestimable.

Semisextile: 6, 8 You always have to decide whether to serve others or to serve yourself at their expense. Although your mate may support your goals, he or she may be intimidated by your methods, for you often feel that the end justifies the means. You owe a lot to the public, without whom you would be out of business, which pinpoints the delicate balance on which your fate rests. The impunity that you justify for yourself is impermanent at best.

Sun in Seventh, Moon in First

You usually depend on other people for circumstances in which you can satisfactorily express yourself. You don't have too much choice about these circumstances, but you can choose how you will deal with them. If you are resourceful, you can succeed in handling any situation and make the most of it. Still, you react strongly to the effects that you feel other people have on your affairs. You want so much to be accepted into the mainstream of society, and you probably are, but you question that this acceptance is sincere. This pattern may be the result of your parents' influence, which has caused you to have difficulty in forming relationships of your own.

Your best development will occur in a career that requires you to be personally involved with the public, such as public relations, family counseling, legal service or social service programs. A professional environment will enable you to extend your creative talents and obtain the maximum yield from them.

A marriage partner is essential to provide support in your endeavors, which may compensate for the trying conditions of your childhood. A partner and children will show you that you are indeed capable of reaching your goals and your family's. The shared enthusiasm will add to your happiness.

Sun in Seventh, Moon in Second

Achieving significance in your life endeavors requires focusing on the affairs of others, either personally or professionally. It is necessary for you to concern yourself with the public's requirements. It should be quite apparent that you have every resource you need to satisfy this kind of responsibility, but you may be apprehensive about the value of applying your efforts this way. Your feelings of insecurity may cause you to avoid making a commitment, because you don't want to risk losing what you have already gained. You feel that others can help themselves as you have, and you resent it when others want you to always be available to them. But if you get the right training, you may find that serving people has its own rewards, especially if you offer professional services.

Investment counseling, insurance, retirement programs or family counseling are some areas in which you could find ample opportunities to succeed and have the chance to fully express your creative talents.

Your partner should be willing to share the lean years with you until you get established and reach the goals you defined earlier. It is important that you define them so that you will be properly motivated for that objective.

Sun in Seventh, Moon in Third

Your ability to succeed is enhanced by the ease with which you get involved with people. You enjoy being in the mainstream of human activity, and you have a talent for getting people to support you in your enterprises. You are generally eager to reciprocate when others need your help, which will benefit you in your long-range goals. You know how to use opportunities that come through others to derive the greatest yield, sometimes exceeding the rewards enjoyed by those who made the opportunities available. People seek your advice on important matters because you have such good insight, so a career requiring this kind of talent would be a good choice.

A career that allows you self-determination would give you a say about your growth and progress in your field. A routine job is not for you, because it would deny you the full development of your rich creative potential. Journalism, writing, broadcasting, any of the various communication media, law, politics or government service are appropriate for your talent and temperament.

Probably you will form a permanent relationship fairly early in life. If your partner is equally fascinated with change and progress, you should be very happy. Because you rarely look back, your future rewards are limited only by the commitment you are willing to make to them.

Sun in Seventh, Moon in Fourth

The main thrust of your life is in accepting society's demands for the services you can provide. By doing what you can in this regard, you will also be able to work and satisfy your own requirements. It may take some time before you can feel comfortable in this effort, because the conditioning of your formative years made you doubt your usefulness to those outside the immediate family. Acting without parental approval is hard for you, and you offer many defenses to justify the endless delays in getting established in a career that gives you personal satisfaction. When you finally take a stand in your own behalf, it may be because you are in a situation that forces you to prove yourself. Establishing your independence from your family is your most urgent priority, but that does not mean you have to be disloyal.

Working closely with the public should give you every chance to demonstrate what you can accomplish, which will make the transition from family to society that much easier. Real estate sales and management, public service enterprises, public relations or a small business are some ways in which you can apply yourself successfully and enjoy comfortable earnings too. You should consider marriage only after your career is reasonably well underway, because the added pressure of dealing with family life may be a bit heavy for you. Try not to bring your professional problems home.

Sun in Seventh, Moon in Fifth

It doesn't really matter that your opportunities generally come from others, because you have the ability to know whether they offer you a medium for expressing your creative talents. You also know how much people rely on you to show them how to better express themselves. Your parents helped you realize that you have a rich imagination and the creative potential to be successful in your endeavors. You are a

209

good conversationalist and a good listener, so you are warmly received by people in your personal and professional affairs. Your flair for dramatics enhances the impression you make and helps you win support when taking decisive action. It may not be apparent to them, but you are a stimulant to those around you, and their appreciation proves how effective you are. You are basically talented in dealing with people, but an education will give you the refinement and poise to feel comfortable in any position of responsibility. People in powerful positions will be impressed with your potential, and you must be ready when they make offers to you.

If you try to maintain moderation in everything you do, you should have many rewards and the appreciation of those who love you.

Sun in Seventh, Moon in Sixth

This combination shows that you may not assert yourself as you should in meeting challenges and may therefore not realize how capable you can be. You underestimate your qualifications for winning over competitors and overemphasize others' qualifications. You probably spend more time in contemplation than in taking decisive action. Your early training may have taught you to be nonaggressive and to endure a lesser yield from your efforts than you deserve. You owe it to yourself to be more assertive and demand that people allow you greater self-determination. While it is true that your role may be to serve others, you must take the initiative in deciding what you will do to satisfy that obligation. Since you depend on others for the circumstances that will enable you to extend yourself in your career, you might consider a profession that serves society's needs.

Don't allow yourself to get caught in the web of daily routine, where each day is exactly like the last with little hope that tomorrow will be any different. Different is not necessarily better, but it may be if it stimulates you to develop additional skills so that you are continually growing and developing to your maximum. A single important success will reassure you of your competence and effectiveness. Once you are confident in your career and have evidence that you are on your way, you can feel free to consider a permanent relationship.

Sun in Seventh, Moon in Seventh

The urge to acquire dignity and become significant in your social environment commands much of your attention. You have a strong, almost desperate, desire to be successful among your contemporaries, if only to prove to yourself that you are as competent as they are. Most of your opportunities result from contacts with friends, associates and fellow workers, and you resent it when your attempts to create the conditions you want don't work out as planned.

Although you fervently want the privilege of determining your fate in every way, you realize that to have that luxury you must depend on circumstances and opportunities provided by others, which is somewhat contradictory. It is important for you to adjust to this situation and proceed from there, or you will be fighting an uphill battle all the way. The kind of relationship you had with your parents will determine whether you will resign yourself to the unalterable situations you face or become bitter and resentful. If you establish your goals and develop your creative talents, this combination will give you the strength, courage and determination to succeed.

Public relations, management, counseling, law and social service are some areas where you can find suitable expression. Your partner must understand how vulnerable you are and realize that co-existing careers in which you sustain each other will make for an enduring relationship.

Sun in Seventh, Moon in Eighth

Your emotional poise allows you to win over adversaries. You are in tune with what they have to offer, and when you confront them, you give the impression that you are less qualified then they. You are unflappable in a crisis because you are totally aware of what you must do to handle the situation. You learn something about human nature from everyone, which will give you the edge in the struggle to succeed. Realizing that you must make the most of circumstances provided by others, you never let an opportunity slip by without making some effort to capitalize on it. People quickly learn to trust your judgment, since you are usually effective. You can calm the most excited person in your own persuasive way.

You have remarkable insight into people's problems and you know how to provide the kind of help they require. Marital counseling, law, medicine, financial counseling, retirement programs or vocational guidance are some fields in which you would excel.

Your sensitive nature requires a partner who is sympathetic to your desire to serve the public. You understand the difference between your responsibilities to the relationship and those to your public, so it is unlikely that any important conflict will arise. You have much to offer in making your marriage a happy one.

Sun in Seventh, Moon in Ninth

Your success is the result of your willingness to learn all you can about a wide variety of subjects, so that you are usually ready to take on new responsibilities. Since you know that you have to depend largely on circumstantial opportunities, you make sure that you can respond positively and do whatever is necessary to establish your credentials before the public. A good listener, you pick up valuable information in your social and professional contacts to enhance your career position, but you willingly share what you know with your associates. You see your actions reflected in the people you are close to, and their response guides your efforts at self-improvement. Your nature is harmonious, and you put people at ease by letting them discuss what's on their minds. Your sincere concern endears you to others. This combination does not favor an easy relationship with your parents, but this can work out favorably if you insist on your own independence.

Writing, law, education, politics or medicine would be suitable to your talents and temperament. In any of these fields the public would learn to respect your proficiency and effectiveness.

You know how to enjoy life, and you refuse to get so cornered by professional responsibilities that you haven't the time and energy for personal pleasures. You may marry someone who is also a professional, and the two of you may consolidate your career efforts in a combined enterprise. In any case, career responsibilities will probably not intrude and cause problems in your personal relationship.

Sun in Seventh, Moon in Tenth

In your desire to gain status and recognition for your accomplishments, you attract people who are difficult to please. You may wonder if success is worth the unpleasantness you have to endure. Nevertheless, you are ideally suited to working in the public sector, and you should learn how to insulate yourself from the negative influences of other people. Putting up with undesirable conditions is not new to you, because of your difficult relationship with your parents in your early years. This may have been the critical factor that propelled you to live on your own and become better organized so you could succeed in your own right, whether or not you got help from your parents. Don't worry about living up to their expectations; you must live up to your potentials only. Try not to compare your achievements with other people's. Making decisions may be difficult for you, which is a good reason to become well informed and get a good education.

Once you are trained, you can find satisfaction in working with the public in fields such as government service, law, consumer services, public relations or in industrial organizations that offer growth potential.

Marrying early is not advisable, since you would probably just be trying to escape from family conditions. You should get your career underway first, then turn your attention to finding the right mate.

Sun in Seventh, Moon in Eleventh

Although your efforts have to be focused on opportunities provided by others, you have the talent for promoting them to your advantage. People genuinely like you and are generally eager to see you succeed in what you do. They know you won't force yourself on them and that you will help them when they need it. Because you don't threaten them, people open up to you, confident that you won't violate their trust. This congenial situation brings out their better qualities, and they feel more positive about what they can do because of your influence. In the beginning, however, you may have had some misgivings about your ability to succeed in handling people, because of parental conditioning that made you doubt that you could be influential. You may have had to struggle to establish your identity, but you will come through poised to seek your goals.

You don't want to get caught up in the usual rat race, preferring to live and let live, free from the penalties people pay to satisfy their greed. Yours is a flowing life adventure that allows you to taste of the richest experience in human relationships. You are always successful in what you do because your measure of success is to do what is right for the moment, staying flexible about what tomorrow may offer. You should enjoy a harmonious marriage, because you don't make unfair demands of your partner, and you are secure in your identity.

Sun in Seventh, Moon in Twelfth

You give the impression that you are in complete command of your situation, but actually you are quite unsure of your ability to succeed when faced with a challenge. You tend to give others more credit than they deserve, underplaying your own abilities to avoid competition whenever you can. The fact that you underestimate your potentials should make it apparent that you need an education and training. Your creative potential merely needs to be developed so you can gain skills and compare yourself favorably with others. Only self-discipline and hard work will teach you the skills you need to succeed. Even a moderate amount of favorable feedback will dispel any anxieties you may have about your abilities. From that moment on, there will be little to impede your continuing progress.

With self-determination, you can avoid putting up with people who abuse your generosity. You should help only those who genuinely need it.

You will probably attract a partner who is in constant need of attention and who expects you to yield to his or her demands. If you insist that a potential partner establish his or her credentials to you first, you will choose the right one.

Chapter Eight

Eighth House

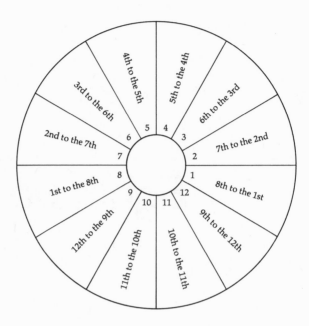

It is unfortunate that mention of the eighth house or of Scorpio, its associated sign, is often greeted with raised eyebrows, because physiologically they refer to reproduction. Sensuality does not really originate in this house, but sexuality does, and sex is as valid and important as any other human experience. People differ from other creatures in that sexual activity is not necessarily linked to procreation. Because of this and because of negative religious training about sex, there may be some problems associated with sex in relationships.

Another factor to be examined in this house is how you fit into the social environment that you are drawn to. The eighth house offers you the opportunity to earn a place in society by contributing to others' needs. In a very personal frame of reference, it is through the investments you make in yourself (second house) that you later reap the rewards you deserve for the sacrifices you've made. The eighth house relates to your indebtedness, such as a mortgage, insurance, investments, retirement programs and other such matters. It shows how you are obligated to your partner or associate, just as your second house shows how your partner is obligated to you. When these responsibilities are agreed to by both of you, the eighth and second houses become joint resources resulting from combined investments, and neither of you experiences loss.

As you assert yourself before the world, you will be expected to meet the challenge of competition. It is through your eighth house that others judge your performance to decide whether you have offered something of value. This is a giving house, and when there is a distortion in principle here, you take rather than give. Then there are sure to be serious problems in your relationships with your associates and colleagues and in your marriage. No house confirms issues more positively or negatively than the eighth house. It is life or death, sacrifice or indulgence, wealth or poverty, courage or cowardice, give or take. Through the affairs of the eighth house or the house with Scorpio on its cusp, you will make the most significant commitment of your life. Often it takes a crisis to finally motivate you and involve you with others in some special way so that your life becomes truly meaningful and productive.

Derivative House Meanings

1st to the 8th   The sacrifices you make to achieve self-development allow you to make a worthwhile contribution to others as well.

2nd to the 7th   You understand how valuable you can be to those around you by helping them become more self-sufficient as a result of your efforts.

3rd to the 6th   You are fully aware of how competent you are, and you know that your skills can benefit those who are unable to function without your help.

4th to the 5th   You want the freedom to use your creative talents to demonstrate that you are genuinely concerned that others gain the stability they require.

5th to the 4th   Your early conditioning prepared you to accept full responsibility for helping others exploit their own potentials.

6th to the 3rd   Developing and implementing your ideas serves those who need them, and the process of exchange improves your earning ability.

7th to the 2nd   These conditions help you decide whether you are primarily concerned with satisfying your needs or with satisfying others' needs.

8th to the 1st   Through the pressure you encounter here you will resolve to make a truly satisfying commitment in your life endeavors.

9th to the 12th   You have the insight to understand how to cope with and change the social problems you face in your environment.

10th to the 11th   You can achieve recognition in your career by making sure that your efforts yield benefits for those who are influenced by you.

11th to the 10th   Once you are secure in your career with the rewards it brings, you may turn your attention to less personal but equally important social interests.

12th to the 9th   You have the option of deciding whether to predicate your pursuits on sound ethical practices or whether to base them purely on personal gain.

1st to the 8th Self-analysis will show you that sacrificing selfish, personal desires can motivate you to fulfill your destiny. You should invest your creative talents in helping others fulfill theirs.

 2nd to the 7th You stimulate others to capitalize on their own resources and thus win their gratitude for your efforts. You do what you can for others because you feel you owe it to them. Your partner may expect more from you than is fair, but you think of your contribution as an investment that will enrich you both.

 3rd to the 6th You understand people's needs and are sensitive to their failings. People usually sense that they can tell you their problems and that you will do what you can to help them find solutions.

 4th to the 5th Your desire to exploit your creative talents may be frustrated in the beginning, but eventually you will find the freedom to assert yourself, when you learn to be fully responsible for your actions.

 5th to the 4th By taking advantage of the opportunities provided by your parents, you can succeed in fulfilling your obligations to them and to yourself. Your creative abilities will develop fully if you establish your own roots.

 6th to the 3rd You have always known that the public would buy your services when you had time to develop your ideas and make them work. You effectively communicate to people that you can handle their needs, and they are impressed when you live up to your promises.

 7th to the 2nd Your earning ability is tied to fulfilling the needs of the public. Your fascination with some people's financial advantages challenges you to charge as much as possible for the services that you provide.

 8th to the 1st Your deep concern for people prompts you to commit your life to satisfying their needs. This allows you to make the most significant investment of your talents, which will give you the most rewarding and enduring benefits. You may be tempted, however, to take more than you give, especially if you can't control your desires.

 9th to the 12th You must always keep your moral and ethical standards in positive focus. It would be so easy to assume that the ignorant deserve to be "taken" by anyone who is better informed. Remember that you have a social obligation to the public and that you could be held legally responsible for any deception you practice.

 10th to the 11th Friends may offer you needed opportunities for success in your career. Working with other people is suitable for your temperament, and your colleagues will probably be better off because of your efforts in their behalf.

 11th to the 10th It is important to choose a career that gives you room for future growth and development. If your profession doesn't allow you to achieve financial independence through worthwhile service to society, it may not be a wise choice.

 12th to the 9th Neglecting your moral responsibilities can destroy everything you've gained. Don't assume that people won't know the difference, because they will, although they may not react immediately.

Trine: 4, 12   Fulfilling your destiny requires participating in public affairs and serving the needs of others, even though it means making sacrifices. If you turn your strong desire nature to providing dependable public services, you will be amply rewarded for your efforts. A career in medicine, psychology, research, crime detection, insurance or financial guidance might be suitable, and you can earn a comfortable living in these areas if you accept the responsibilities. Your parents will encourage and support you until you are established in your career. Examine your moral and ethical standards, for nothing erodes your gains so quickly as taking liberties with legal guidelines. Misrepresenting your ability to perform the services that your career requires will undermine your credibility. When you agree to provide a service for someone, you are in that person's debt until the service is rendered.

Sextile: 6, 10   Your position is unique because you are so sensitive to people's failings and needs. You also understand that you have a deep responsibility to others, because they tell you their problems, knowing that you can help them, and of course you can. Make certain that your profession allows room to grow and to expand the services you give to those who need them. As you grow and develop, your earnings will increase and bring you financial independence.

Cross: 2, 5, 11   Romantic affairs and self-indulgent activities may divert you from getting established in your career. On the other hand, your desire for pleasure and freedom to enjoy yourself with your loved one and children may be so intense that you will make the necessary sacrifices in your early years. Such a sacrifice would indicate that you are willing to accept the challenges of responsibility. Contact with well-to-do people may motivate you to rise to the highest degree of competence in your field. If you give the best service, you can charge accordingly. Your friends may provide opportunities during your training period, but they may demand favors when you reach your goal. Money is very important to you, but you enjoy knowing that you are making a worthwhile contribution to the people who depend on your services.

Inconjunct: 1, 3   An effective salesperson, you easily convince people of the value of your services. They are impressed by your ability to carry out your promises, and they learn to depend on you. Be wary when you are asked to give away your talents, as often happens in a social gathering when people assume that it's all right to ask favors of you. You may have to steer the conversation elsewhere or suggest that they contact you in a different setting. In your desire to serve others, you sometimes do more than you should, which doesn't allow them to solve their own problems. You should serve in an advisory capacity and help people when they truly need you, but you should not take on their responsibilities. Be alert to the danger of becoming so greedy that you accept jobs that you aren't qualified for, simply because of the money you can make.

Semisextile: 7, 9   You demonstrate your best qualities when you stimulate people to capitalize on their own resources. This gives you an opportunity to repay any debts you feel you owe society for the benefits you've gained in serving the public. This applies to your partner, who values your talents and supports you in your endeavors. Your mate must share your desires. If you maintain high ethical standards, you can't lose.

1st to the 8th   Because you are extremely sensitive, you are vulnerable to the demands of people who may prey on your weakness. You feel a strong obligation to do what you can for others because you are so intimately aware of their needs, and you are willing to make sacrifices.

 2nd to the 7th   You know more about people psychically than they know about themselves. This ability can give you many opportunities to enrich people's lives through your efforts.

 3rd to the 6th   It can be painful to know so much about people, for it suggests that you have an obligation to utilize your creative ideas to help solve their problems. You work hard to develop your skills, because you know you can make a good living by applying them in your chosen field.

 4th to the 5th   You underestimate your creative potentials, which you must develop so you will have freedom to choose an independent base on which to build continuing fulfillment. Responsibilities to family and loved ones may temporarily divert you from your goal.

 5th to the 4th   You may have been conditioned to repress your creative imagination, preferring to indulge your parents in their desires. You might look for a way to use your talents at home.

 6th to the 3rd   You have to make a conscious effort to develop your creative imagination so that it is an asset in earning a living. Don't allow others to take advantage of your ideas and then exclude you from the benefits.

 7th to the 2nd   You do more for others than you do for yourself, including your partner, who may try to tell you that this is your obligation. You will eventually learn how resourceful you are from the people who benefit by your efforts.

 8th to the 1st   Sacrifice seems like a way of life. Although you have deep emotional needs, you tend to give more than you receive. Set aside some time for indulging yourself, and don't be shy about letting others make sacrifices for you occasionally.

 9th to the 12th   You have a deep, spiritual devotion to people who are somehow disadvantaged. Try to get the training you need so that you can serve them better, which is your social obligation.

 10th to the 11th   You are somewhat apprehensive about the future and about successfully reaching your goals. You must be involved in the affairs of society at large to feel that you have made any lasting contribution to solving its problems.

 11th to the 10th   Focus your attention on gaining a foothold in your career, for through your achievements you will gain the satisfaction and financial security that are so important for your later years.

 12th to the 9th   You will do your very best if you get the training you need to amplify your natural gifts. Compassion and sympathy for others are fine, but you can accomplish more for them when you have the necessary knowledge and training. You can either make the commitment to serve others, or you can indulge yourself by ignoring your spiritual responsibility to them.

Trine: 4, 12 Because you may not have been conditioned to fully exploit your creative imagination, you will have to make a greater effort to derive any benefit from your deep sensitivity and compassionate concern for others. When you finally decide to assert yourself in serving the needs of others, you may find that they will try to take advantage of you. People tend to make more demands on you because you are so vulnerable to their suggestions. Your psychic ability alerts you to people's problems, and you feel a responsibility to help them. You are a soft touch to anyone with a real problem, which you see as an opportunity to provide devotion and understanding.

Sextile: 6, 10 Knowing so much about people can be painful, because you feel obligated to help them solve their problems. If that is the case, take advantage of it by acquiring the necessary training so that you can earn a living with this talent. Try to establish your priorities so that you are not the last to benefit from your talents. Once secure in your profession, you will have the opportunity to expand your services and earn an even higher income.

Cross: 2, 5, 11 You do more for others than you do for yourself. You won't receive the services you require unless you ask for them, but you would rather not do that because it embarrasses you. If you develop your creative talents, you will be more free to choose the field of activity that will give you the fulfillment you want. Don't let your feelings of responsibility to family and loved ones prevent you from fulfilling your needs. By paying more attention to your own need to grow and develop, you eliminate the danger of insecurity in your later years. You must devote as much time to satisfying your own needs as you devote to others, or you will become bitter because you have accomplished little of lasting value for yourself.

Inconjunct: 1, 3 Be careful that people don't try to take advantage of your ideas for their own benefit, even to excluding you from any reward. You have an obligation to work at developing your creative imagination so that it will be one of your most important skills. Your earnings will reflect your talent in meeting the demands of your career. Don't be afraid to let others do favors for you. You will probably enjoy the attention you get, even though it may embarrass you. Sacrificing for others is commendable, but it can defeat you by leaving you with little time to indulge yourself.

Semisextile: 7, 9 You consider it an advantage that you are psychically tuned to people's real needs, which allows you to perform services for them that others cannot. You want to enrich people's lives by doing what you can for them, and you are happy when you know you've been effective. It would be a great help to get an education that would give you the credentials you need for the work you do. This would enable you to do much more with your natural talents. You may decide to accomplish your goals in one of two ways. You may dedicate yourself in a deep spiritual response to the needs of the public, or you may indulge yourself and ignore others in their moment of need, letting them find their comfort and services elsewhere. The former, more positive, direction is likely to prevail and is probably the one you will take.

1st to the 8th You are interested in examining all kinds of subjects, the deeper and more profound the better. You analyze everything and everyone that catches your attention, including yourself, because you are intensely curious to know how and why people are motivated.

 2nd to the 7th You generally understand what people want in their dealings with you. They seek your opinion because you know more about their needs than they do, and they value your judgment.

 3rd to the 6th Not content to be proficient in your skills, you look for new ways to apply your talents. You freely communicate to people that you are willing to help them with their problems.

 4th to the 5th Your ability to serve the public may be restricted by family obligations. You feel that to win the one you love you have to demonstrate your ability to achieve your goals by capitalizing on your creative potential. You want to show that you can stand on your own.

 5th to the 4th Your strong family ties are an asset. Probably your parents gave you every opportunity to develop according to your own creative needs. It is important that you accept full responsibility for exploiting your creative talents as the foundation for your achievements.

 6th to the 3rd Being curious is not enough. You must work at finding the answers to your numerous questions about yourself and the people around you, and you must find the best way to fulfill your obligations to them and yourself.

 7th to the 2nd Sometimes you are intimidated by other people's material assets and personal skills. You may question whether you have similar advantages. Working with other people's resources might be a suitable career.

 8th to the 1st You must analyze yourself to help determine what motivates you best. You will have to make some personal sacrifices to attract the patronage you want for your services.

 9th to the 12th Your fascination with the unknown leads you into little-understood areas of inquiry. An education will help remove the mystique of such subjects and give you the information required to fulfill your social obligations.

 10th to the 11th You like to reflect on what your friends are achieving in their careers, and you may use this knowledge to help find an area in which you can perform the kinds of services that will help you achieve your goals.

 11th to the 10th Look for a field of endeavor that has growth potential and that can give you the opportunity to work with other people's needs or problems. Your ability to solve problems assures you an enriching life experience that will also provide the future security you want.

 12th to the 9th Keep a watchful eye on your ethics and moral standards to make sure you don't unwittingly erode your position before the public. You have a deep spiritual obligation to the people you serve, and you cannot afford to disappoint them. Your spiritual responsibility to others distinguishes you in your commitment to them.

Trine: 4, 12   Your highly developed reasoning ability probably resulted from your deep desire to know as much as possible. You constantly search for answers to all your questions about life and about people's motivations. Your persistent inquiry reveals more answers than are found by most people. Your exceptional skill in investigating the unknown qualifies you for such fields as detection, research, financial counseling or psychology. Your early environment allowed you to develop your creative potentials and know that you could capitalize on them later. A higher education will enhance your abilities and give you the necessary skills to achieve your goals. It is to your advantage to continue your studies, no matter how successful you are, for it will expand your influence and increase your value to those you serve professionally.

Sextile: 6, 10   You let people know that you understand their problems and that you have the skills to help them. You expect to be well paid for your services, because you know you are worth it. You look for opportunities to demonstrate your talents, and you are gratified when your efforts yield results. With your ability to help people with their problems, you should seek a career that uses this skill. Look for a field with growth potential, because you need freedom to expand as the demands for your skills increase. Your earnings should provide all the security you need for your later years.

Cross: 2, 5, 11   Your career may be delayed because of family obligations. Your enjoyment of self-indulgent pleasures may also curtail the gains you could be making in your field, if you aren't investing the time and energy necessary to become professionally competent. You must establish some priorities in your professional and personal affairs. You feel you must prove yourself to the one you love and show that you have a firm foundation on which to build your ambitions. You may wonder if you are as competent as the next person, but don't be misled by other people's resources and skills—it's what you do with them that is important, and your ability to solve problems is a good place to start. See how your friends are achieving their objectives. Then, with good planning, you can accomplish everything you set out to do, and more.

Inconjunct: 1, 3   It will be rather difficult to find the best way to put your ideas to work. There are no shortcuts; only by persistently developing and promoting your ideas will you get the results you want. This means that if you want people to know what you can do, you must become so proficient that everyone will beat a path to your door for your services. Once you find answers to your own problems, you may then decide that you can help others with theirs. If you want to win patronage for your services, you must make some sacrifices, as every public servant must learn. If you are truly committed to your life's work, this won't be too difficult.

Semisextile: 7, 9   Trust your partner's suggestions concerning your career objectives. You probably recognize how valuable your mate is to you, and you want to live up to his or her expectations. Don't be afraid to change your mind when the evidence indicates that you should, for it is a sign that you are still growing. Maintain the highest ethical standards in everything you do. When you tell people only what they want to hear, you are not living up to your moral responsibility to them. You cannot afford to disappoint those who have come to rely on your expert judgment.

1st to the 8th   You have a compelling need to get involved with persons who share your strong desire for warm, sociable relationships. You are usually on your very best behavior, which you consider a good investment to win someone who attracts you.

 2nd to the 7th   You make many concessions when you want attention from someone you desire for a close relationship, and you let that person's needs take precedence over yours.

 3rd to the 6th   You understand that everyone has some weaknesses or flaws, which you can usually overlook if their positive traits are more outstanding. Generally you are willing to help others with their problems.

 4th to the 5th   Because you want complete freedom to explore ways to get greater pleasure in your relationships, you imply that you are more concerned about your partner's needs and pleasures. You may have some anxiety about your ability to satisfactorily indulge your partner or other members of your family.

 5th to the 4th   You were probably taught that it is proper to do favors for others, and you feel that giving is rewarded because it improves your social contacts.

 6th to the 3rd   Your success in reaching people and forming good relationships results from your willingness to make concessions. You are an effective salesperson, especially when you are promoting yourself.

 7th to the 2nd   You want so much to measure up to other people's expectations that you tend to overestimate their material advantages as well as their human characteristics. Then you are intimidated because you want the same things for yourself.

 8th to the 1st   Your actions toward others are motivated by one of two desires. Either you are driven by envy to gain some control of others' resources, or you are interested in people for purely romantic reasons and want to do what you can to make them happy.

 9th to the 12th   You need to understand your fears and anxieties so you can put them in proper perspective. This will allow you to understand others better and realize that you are not alone in your fantasies. You want to help others and not offend them, which is admirable.

 10th to the 11th   You would derive the most benefits from a career that requires you to deal with people and their needs. You have a talent for helping people achieve greater harmony in their lives and face the future with greater optimism about reaching their objectives.

 11th to the 10th   If you are successful in your career, you will enjoy your later years, knowing you've made an important contribution to others. You will undoubtedly be long remembered by those you've helped or influenced.

 12th to the 9th   You may not care about others' needs or want to know how they think, which only signifies that you are determined to get as much as you can from them to satisfy your own desires. On the other hand, you may be motivated by a strong spiritual commitment to serve others, in which case your results will be much greater than the sacrifices you have made for them.

Trine: 4, 12 You are attracted to warm and sociable persons who are as eager as you are for a meaningful relationship. You have a compelling need to satisfy your strong physical desires, but you are usually on your best behavior, hoping to attract the kind of person who will indulge you in your desires. You are greatly influenced by physically attractive persons who have the same needs as you but who also have qualities you admire. You enjoy doing favors for people, because you know that this increases the likelihood of making the right kinds of social contacts. At first you tend to underestimate your ability to satisfy people's expectations, because you make unfair comparisons between your qualifications and theirs. When you realize that everyone has fears and anxieties, you will be more comfortable with yourself. You don't want to offend others, which is admirable, but it doesn't allow others to know that you also bring something of value to a relationship.

Sextile: 6, 10 You are willing to make concessions to others and to tolerate their negative qualities because you truly want to understand them and their problems. You tend to regard their positive traits as sufficient compensation for their less desirable qualities. The people you help will remember you, and later in life you should derive some satisfaction from the knowledge that your efforts were appreciated.

Cross: 2, 5, 11 You must make many adjustments before you can satisfactorily indulge your personal desires. Obligations to your loved ones must take precedence over personal pleasures. You also have an obligation to fully exploit your creative talents to fulfill the demands of your career. This will improve your image before others and let them know that you share some of their material and personal advantages and that you aren't intimidated by them. Choose a career that requires you to deal with people's problems, because that is probably where you are most effective.

Inconjunct: 1, 3 You are generally successful in dealing with people, because you make the concessions that allow for a continuing relationship. They enjoy talking with you, and they know that your interest in them is sincere. You definitely need people to be a sounding board for your intellectual development and to verify that your actions in their behalf have yielded satisfactory results. You must figure out exactly why you are interested in people and what your motives are for becoming involved with them. There are two possible reasons. On one hand, you may be driven by envy to gain control over their resources, but on the other hand, you may be sincerely concerned for their well-being and want to do what you can to make them happy. You may be tempted by both motives and vacillate between them before making a commitment.

Semisextile: 7, 9 Make certain that you understand every implication of the preceding paragraph. Ideally, your actions will be directed by a strong spiritual desire to make sacrifices in helping those who lack your deep perception in handling problems. While it may often be desirable to make concessions to others, you must not allow them to gain complete control over you so that you cannot fulfill your own destiny.

1st to the 8th   You have a strong desire nature, which you often express in extreme ways. When the object of your desire is not immediately available, you patiently bide your time until it is, and then you don't accept rejection gracefully.

 2nd to the 7th   You assume that your partner is fascinated by your forceful nature, which may be so, but probably your desire to please and to provide all of life's necessities is more attractive.

 3rd to the 6th   Because you are aggressive in promoting your skills, your services are almost always in demand. You understand that to win people's attention, you must let them know that you can serve them better than your competitors can.

 4th to the 5th   The greatest deterrent to success is that you overindulge in personal pleasures and don't spend enough time on more urgent priorities. If you invest more time and energy in your career, you will have the necessary resources to satisfy your need for pleasure.

 5th to the 4th   You want to find ways to become self-sufficient so you can enjoy the privileges of being self-employed. Your early conditioning gave you a driving ambition to extend yourself and to make whatever investment is required to achieve self-sufficiency.

 6th to the 3rd   It isn't what you say you can do ,but what your actions demonstrate that will prove the effectiveness of your services to your patrons. When you work at promoting your ideas, you encourage people to notice your skills.

 7th to the 2nd   You must work constantly to prove that your skills provide greater value than other people's skills. Once you succeed in proving that this is so, you will gain the patronage you need to enjoy a comfortable living.

 8th to the 1st   Your success in everything you do, in your career as well as in relationships, depends on your willingness to make a commitment and to put some effort into getting what you want.

 9th to the 12th   Understanding your social obligations and your ability to help those who are unable to help themselves will make you realize that your efforts are important and appreciated by others.

 10th to the 11th   Working with the general public is probably the best way to utilize your talents. This will allow you to reach more people in your career and will help assure you of the recognition you deserve for your accomplishments.

 11th to the 10th   Look for a career with a future so that the investment you make will yield enduring possibilities for growth and expansion of your services. Knowing that you've made an important contribution in serving people's needs will enrich your later years with contentment.

 12th to the 9th   Examine your motives carefully to determine exactly why you feel compelled to take the career direction you've chosen. You must be directed by only the noblest reasons, including the desire to help satisfy pressing human needs. Be wary of the temptation to relax your ethics while pursuing your objectives; giving in could result in massive losses in earnings and prestige.

Trine: 4, 12   You are demanding in your relationships, and you feel bitter if rejected. You may bide your time when your wishes are not granted immediately, as long as you know that eventually you will get what you want. You want to become self-sufficient, because you dislike being obligated to anyone, which limits your plans and ambitions. You aren't afraid to work hard to get what you want out of life, and you know that any investment of time and energy will be rewarded when you start getting results from your efforts. You are important to those for whom you provide necessary services, and you consider this part of your social obligation. When your efforts are appreciated, you are stimulated to take more responsibility and to make even greater achievements.

Sextile: 6, 10   Probably you will choose a career that gives you an opportunity to grow and develop, because you are reasonably sure of yourself and of what you can accomplish with your talents. You believe you can demonstrate greater competence in your chosen field, so you don't hesitate to promote your skills whenever possible. People are convinced that you can serve them better than your competitors, so they turn to you and demand your services.

Cross: 2, 5, 11   If maintaining a high income is your main motivation, your success may be limited and you may suffer some setbacks. It would be better to develop your skills to the highest level of competence and know that you give the best value for what you earn. This will gain you the patronage you need and assure you of consistently high earnings. Working with the public will allow you to serve a large number of people and be recognized for your efforts. The main stumbling block to success in your career will come from your inability to resist indulging in personal pleasures. You must determine your priorities and accept the need to make some sacrifices as an investment in your career and the status you hope to achieve in realizing your ambitions. Family obligations may temporarily frustrate your desires, or romantic entanglements may distract you from your main objectives. You will have to develop self-control and learn to manage your personal affairs more prudently.

Inconjunct: 1, 3   Your wealth of ideas means little unless you act on them or cultivate them so they can be of some value to you. The best way to get people to notice your competence is to work at promoting your ideas and skills. Such an investment of time and energy is essential if you are to derive the most from your potentials. You owe it to yourself and to the public to make your skills available. Dedicating at least some of your talents to serve important needs of the public will enrich your later years with contentment in the knowledge that you were willing to get involved.

Semisextile: 7, 9   Your partner probably admires your driving ambition to succeed and to do whatever is required to sustain the relationship for the benefit of you both. What you accomplish is important, but even more significant is how you do it and the moral responsibility you take for your actions. If you are motivated by a desire to help people in need, then there is no problem. But if you take liberties with what is considered ethical behavior, then you will have to expect major losses in earnings and prestige. This is a decision you have to make, and the outcome is yours to determine.

1st to the 8th Growing in consciousness depends largely on being willing to get involved in the affairs of others. If you use your talent for understanding people by advising them how to handle their problems, you will make a major investment in your continuing development.

 2nd to the 7th Because of your compassion for those in need, you may be overly generous toward them, thereby diminishing your financial reserves. Keep an eye on your financial balance so you don't overextend yourself.

 3rd to the 6th You feel it is your moral obligation to make your services available to anyone who seems to need them. You know how capable you are, but that doesn't mean that you should help people who can help themselves.

 4th to the 5th You find it particularly difficult not to indulge yourself in personal pleasures at will. The only result of this will be a significant reduction in your energy so that there is little left for more worthwhile enterprises.

 5th to the 4th You tend to have a do-nothing attitude about making an important investment in your future goals. You sometimes feel that the world owes you a living and that you don't have to apply yourself if you don't want to.

 6th to the 3rd Although your ideas are rich and varied, they still need to be developed if they are to be useful to you in earning a living. If you don't want to be personally involved in developing your ideas, you should at least communicate that fact to those who can and will develop them.

 7th to the 2nd It is sometimes difficult for you to determine what has the greater priority—your needs or other people's. Giving material gifts is not the best way to win people's approval. Instead, your willingness to help others when they need it will earn their appreciation.

 8th to the 1st You are interested in what motivates people in their dealings with you. More important, however, is what motivates you. If you are sincerely concerned about people's welfare and are urged by a spiritual desire to help them, then all is well.

 9th to the 12th You know what it is to have nothing, and you know the heart-warming feeling when someone gives you much-needed help. Your gratitude stimulates you to do what you can to help relieve others' burdens. You feel it is your moral and spiritual obligation.

 10th to the 11th You are willing to extend yourself in planning for your future goals. You know that unless you plan ahead and make certain sacrifices, all your career efforts will amount to little in the way of future gains.

 11th to the 10th Since you have helped others in their needs, you hope you can depend on them for favors when you need them. Through your career you may make your greatest contribution to the public.

 12th to the 9th Be careful that in managing your affairs you don't lose sight of your ethical standards. If you keep your morals and standards above reproach, you won't have to worry that your accomplishments will collapse like a house of cards.

Trine: 4, 12 You know that your continuing growth and development depend largely on being willing to involve yourself in the affairs of those around you, so you are drawn to people less fortunate than you. With your talent for understanding their problems, you want to help them any way you can, which you consider a long-range investment in your future. You don't usually plan very far ahead, preferring to limit your plans to more immediate concerns. You don't mind receiving gifts; in fact, you accept them as though they were your due. You sympathize with those who have to do without many of life's essentials, and you make certain that you will never be forced to accept such a situation for yourself. Helping someone who truly requires it gives you a good feeling and stimulates your sense of moral and spiritual responsibility to others, so that you will extend yourself even more in the future.

Sextile: 6, 10 You have an overwhelming desire to be of service to others, because you are intimately aware of the problems that may be troubling them, and your compassion cries out to extend a helping hand. At times, though, you should think about the probable outcome of your assistance, for you may be interfering when people should help themselves. However, your overall influence is beneficial, and when you need favors later you can certainly count on the people you've helped in the past. You especially want to know that you've made an important contribution to society, so you seek a career that involves the public.

Cross: 2, 5, 11 The most significant issue in your life is to determine your priorities. Your first impulse is to be involved in other people's affairs, but you are also deeply concerned about your own needs, and this conflict will cause some inner struggle. When you are in doubt, your best choice is to help others when they cannot do for themselves. Trying to "buy" people with gifts will only lead to resentment in the long run. Your preoccupation with personal indulgences can seriously detract from more pressing career considerations. This may entail making sacrifices, but there is hardly any other way to be sure that you will have the future gains and security you need for your later years.

Inconjunct: 1, 3 Knowing what motivates people in their dealings with you gives you an advantage over them. Hopefully, you will endeavor to use this knowledge to help them as well as yourself. You can be a benefactor or an exploiter, and this decision rests solely with you. Your good intentions and sense of propriety will probably prevail because you have a deep sense of moral responsibility concerning the public. To fulfill this, you may have to apply yourself to developing your ideas so that you will achieve everything you want for yourself and others. Your physical desires and strong sexual drive may be a problem that you will have to get under control and put in proper perspective within the framework of your whole life.

Semisextile: 7, 9 Reflect carefully about your motives for dealing with people, singly or in groups, to determine the degree of your ethical and moral responsibility toward them. If your integrity is high, you won't have to worry that your achievements will someday fall apart. While your desire to help others is commendable, take care that you don't undermine your own financial stability in the process.

1st to the 8th You try to avoid being obligated to others, although your circumstances indicate that you cannot really escape it. You compare your resources with those of others as though you think your self-worth should be determined only by your personal and material assets.

 2nd to the 7th You work hard to earn the respect and admiration of your partner, for you think that he or she will accept you only if you provide all of life's necessities. You accept this requirement, but you don't generally extend yourself beyond the essentials if you can avoid it.

 3rd to the 6th Knowing how capable you are, you put a high premium on your services, and you don't mind letting people know that they must pay dearly for your services. You will probably earn their respect, but you might not win their friendship.

 4th to the 5th You are conservative in your romantic exploits, because of what it might cost you otherwise. If you have a family, you will discipline your children so that they will be a credit to you.

 5th to the 4th The demands of personal security have forced you to concede the necessity of working with and for others to get opportunities to become financially independent. You extend yourself through hard work, knowing that you will be better off in the end.

 6th to the 3rd You communicate best through your efforts on the job, and you cultivate the best public relations by working hard for those who request your services.

 7th to the 2nd Your greatest challenge comes from comparing what you get for your services with what others receive for theirs. You are easily intimidated when others demonstrate their excellence, but it also stimulates you to excel.

 8th to the 1st You are an effective organizer, and you know how to mobilize your skills to produce the best product for those who pay you. You envy your contemporaries and feel that you must extend yourself beyond them to prove your worth. To do this, you often go without personal pleasures.

 9th to the 12th You secretly fear that you won't really measure up to people's expectations. The fact is, you generally prove yourself beyond anyone's expectations. You want so much to know that you are making an important contribution to improve conditions for others.

 10th to the 11th Only a career with a future interests you. You are best suited to working with the public, which will allow you to expand your range of influence as your skills improve.

 11th to the 10th You are willing to invest heavily of your time and energy if you know that is the only way to reach your objectives. You are methodical and efficient in achieving your goals, and you don't mind turning to friends for help when your plans are jeopardized.

 12th to the 9th You are particularly resentful of "slick" operators, whose moves you try to anticipate in dealing with them. This subconscious fear makes you try to stay within ethical guidelines in your actions, for you feel safer when working within the limits of legality.

Trine: 4, 12   In the struggle to gain control over your life circumstances, you are forced to be obligated to and dependent upon others, although it bothers you. When you compare your accomplishments and resources with those of your contemporaries, your self-image suffers needlessly. Gaining personal security is so important that it has forced you to work with others as the one way to become more financially independent. Secretly, though, you aren't always sure that you measure up to the public's expectations, so you extend yourself to remove that doubt. You would be better off working for yourself in your own business, which would eliminate that problem. You are better equipped to deal with the public's needs than you realize, as should be proved by what you get for your services.

Sextile: 6, 10   After repeatedly hearing how competent you are from those who appreciate your skills, you will finally realize that they are right. Perhaps then you will place a higher premium on your talents, thus letting the public know that you will do what they require but that your services are costly. They also know that they will get all or more than they expect. Once established in your occupation, you invest heavily in time and energy to achieve your goals and objectives. You learn to mobilize your skills and resources efficiently to derive the most benefit with the least effort. Luckily, when you need favors, you can always turn to those whom you have helped in the past.

Cross: 2, 5, 11   You might neglect developing the kind of human values that are so essential in your career, especially since you will probably deal with the general public. Don't put all your values in material considerations, because if you do, many people cannot relate to you on a personal level. While you have greater sexual self-discipline than most people, the reason you are conservative in indulging your appetite is because of the cost involved. The chances are you will prefer having a small family that you can manage without being under enormous demands. You are willing to do without some of life's pleasures and direct your efforts toward your career. Because you are easily intimidated by your competitors' high performance, you strive to increase your skills and improve your position in relation to them. You want a career that allows you to grow and expand so you can increase your earnings and public status.

Inconjunct: 1, 3   Your wealth of valuable ideas amounts to little unless you work at developing them so they can be utilized in the marketplace. This means that you will have to invest a lot of time and energy to increase your value to the buying public or, if you work for someone else, to achieve greater recognition from your superiors. With your organizational ability, you should be able to mobilize your resources so effectively that you won't have to be concerned about how to earn a living.

Semisextile: 7, 9   Look around for people whose needs or situations require your skills to improve them. You are definitely tied to working with and for the general public. Your partner admires and respects your efforts, although you may think you can be accepted only to the extent that you provide every possible material benefit. Keep a sharp eye out for clever individuals who try to con you into schemes that aren't within the bounds of legality. You are sufficiently afraid of the consequences that you are unlikely to resort to lax moral behavior or questionable ethical standards.

1st to the 8th   You reserve the right to express yourself as freely as you choose. It goes against your grain when anyone suggests that you should adhere to a particular code of behavior concerning your physical interests. There may be some difficulty in finding a partner who feels the same way.

2nd to the 7th   Being obligated to others is especially painful since it usually requires that you sacrifice some personal freedom. However, you are ingenious in devising ways to handle your responsibilities while keeping the opportunity to indulge yourself when you want.

3rd to the 6th   You are gifted in your ability to help people solve their problems, because you intimately understand them and their situations. You also realize that you can expect nothing from others unless you are willing to extend yourself in their behalf.

4th to the 5th   Although having a family curtails your freedom to come and go as you like, you can accept this restraint because you know that they will become as independent and self-sufficient as you allow them to. You are happiest when fully exploiting your creative talents.

5th to the 4th   Your parents were instrumental in giving you opportunities to develop your individuality without restrictions. Probably you will enjoy a favorable relationship with both your parents as long as they live.

6th to the 3rd   You certainly have a versatile mind, which only needs to be applied to reward you in your career. Learning the virtue of self-discipline can return a substantial yield.

7th to the 2nd   Your indifference to money and financial security can result in many anxious moments. You tend to do favors for people, when actually they should pay you for your services. Pay strict attention to your finances, for you tend to overextend yourself.

8th to the 1st   You don't understand that not everyone is motivated just as you are; you have to expect to be rejected sometimes when you want others to indulge you. It will be a long time before society becomes as "free" as you are.

9th to the 12th   The key to understanding the thinking and motivation of the rest of the world is to understand yourself first. You must know that you march to a different drummer, so you must learn to listen so you can occasionally fall in step with others.

10th to the 11th   Unless you can accommodate other people's needs, you may never feel that you've made any contribution to society. After you've fulfilled the demands of your career, you should make plans to get involved in fulfilling social needs.

11th to the 10th   Choose a career that allows you self-determination and some freedom, for otherwise you will feel ineffectual. A career in which you work with large numbers of people whose future depends on you will be that much better.

12th to the 9th   You cannot afford to disregard the norms of acceptable social behavior or the established legal code of ethics, or you could risk censure. As a result, your dreams might be dashed to bits, and after all, you look eagerly to the future with those dreams.

Trine: 4, 12   Your parents allowed you to express yourself in your own way, so you assume that everyone will allow you that privilege. You will probably continue to enjoy a favorable relationship with your parents. However, you may sometimes have difficulty with people who resent your lack of inhibition. Once you understand that not everyone feels as liberated as you do, you can learn to cope with people who have to accept their frustrations. People are impressed with your ability to assert yourself, and they admire the way you defy any of society's rules that interfere with your desires. You can do a great deal to help people become more free of their inhibitions and hang-ups; you can teach them how to create a future of their own choosing, rather than be confined by the past, which only restricts them.

Sextile: 6, 10   You probably know more about the people you deal with than they do. You know their most guarded secrets, and you can show them how to accept themselves. The work you do should allow you to become involved with the public, and your efforts should help improve their general well-being. At times people are embarrassed by your habit of focusing on their most sensitive psychological inhibitions, for there are few secrets that anyone can keep from you for long. You would do well to choose a career of service to the public. You would attract substantial patronage for your efforts to help people help themselves. Being self-employed would allow you self-determination to adapt as needed as your influence becomes more extensive.

Cross: 2, 5, 11   It is important to develop your personal values with the same ardor you exhibit in pursuing a life without restraints. Self-discipline and a sense of financial responsibility will assure you of greater freedom to indulge in those matters that attract your attention most strongly. Doing favors for people all the time suggests that you have some doubts about your worth. Try to resolve this situation as early as possible, so you can get on with making your most significant contribution to society through your understanding and ability to help people with their problems. You tend to overextend yourself in making purchases, which will further delay the time when you can improve the circumstances of those who are directly affected by you.

Inconjunct: 1, 3   You must get training and education to help you achieve a high degree of proficiency in understanding people's problems. This is one of your most significant abilities, and it is your responsibility to use it where it will produce the best results. Whether you apply this talent for yourself or for others, you cannot fail to benefit from it. Because you have an obligation to serve others, you may rebel at the thought of limiting your self-indulgence because someone else depends on you. With your help, others can enjoy greater freedom.

Semisextile: 7, 9   Although you think "free," you too have some limitations, and the key to them is the public's need for your services. Your destiny requires that you extend yourself in behalf of people who do not know how to fulfill themselves. Adhere to a sound code of ethics as you become more involved with people and their affairs. In dealing with the public, even the slightest departure from moral responsibility can have disastrous results. You cannot afford to have your dreams so easily jeopardized, because your dreams for the future are very important to you.

1st to the 8th In trying to satisfy your physical desires, you are an idealist. Your fantasies spill over into the real world, and you must be extra careful not to have more liabilities than assets.

 2nd to the 7th Trusting everyone, you often fail to recover the money you lend. Be cautious about forming ties with people until they've demonstrated their credentials, and always examine the fine print before signing a contract.

 3rd to the 6th Though you may be suspicious of people's motivations in forming alliances with you, the chances are that you don't resist them very much. Make promises only if you truly intend to keep them.

 4th to the 5th If your resources are limited, it's probably because you are unable to say no to people's demands, especially to your children or even yourself, when you want something so much you can't resist buying it.

 5th to the 4th Invest in real estate only with the consent of a financial adviser. Better still, take a course in economics so that you are knowledgeable enough to be cautious about making any investment.

 6th to the 3rd You have many good ideas, but they don't mean much unless you use common sense and good judgment in applying them. Don't expect anyone to be interested in your ideas unless you've worked out some of the details and can prove how and why they will succeed.

 7th to the 2nd If you are honest with yourself about your vulnerability to deception by people who try to take advantage of you, you will be spared much heartache and disappointment. You should take responsibility for the family resources and find out exactly where your money is going.

 8th to the 1st It is devastating to find out that you've been taken by someone whom you trusted ill-advisedly. In your desire to accumulate at least as much as your contemporaries have, you may deceive yourself that you can safely take on more financial obligations.

 9th to the 12th You might channel some of your energy into fields related to social needs. You are extremely sensitive to the problems that afflict certain segments of society, and you have the talent for making an important contribution to improving those conditions.

 10th to the 11th You must choose a career with clearly defined objectives, in which there is growth potential for you. Don't shrink from asking favors of friends in important places when an opportunity comes up, for you will be able to reciprocate later.

 11th to the 10th After fulfilling the demands of your profession, you will probably find a new outlet for your talents. Occult studies might be interesting enough to command much of your attention and time. You have an affinity for such fields and would gain much from them.

 12th to the 9th Don't underestimate your chances for gaining the public's confidence in your ability to help people deal with their problems. A good teacher could help you accomplish more with your psychic talents than most people do with physical and tangible skills.

Trine: 4, 12 You are very sensitive emotionally, and you indulge in all sorts of fantasies. You may find it difficult to separate fact from fiction, so that you are intensely attracted to a casual acquaintance and ignore your obligations to those who are truly close to you. Your value judgment seems impaired at times, and occasionally your closest friends may misunderstand your motivations. You tend to become involved with people who make no contribution, perhaps overlooking your spouse's fine qualities. You should not make investments without the advice of a financial counselor. Later in life, you may be attracted to occult studies, which you should benefit from. Long after you've succeeded in your career, you will probably make a substantial contribution to society through what you have learned from studying the great philosophers and mystics. You have much to offer society.

Sextile: 6, 10 You attract people with problems, and your suspicions of their motives in dealing with you may be justified. The chances are they just want help with their problems and are drawn to you because you seem to thoroughly understand their situation. But you must learn to be discriminating about whom you help, or you will be literally buried in their troubles. You owe it to society to be available when help is needed, and you might find such a career appealing.

Cross: 2, 5, 11 The major stumbling block to your success is your lack of restraint when tempted by physical pleasures or the desire to have all the comforts you want. You should choose a career that allows room to grow and expand as your skills improve; otherwise you will lose interest. Don't be afraid to ask friends for help when an opportunity comes up. You can always return the favor later. Although usually both partners should share the management of joint resources, it would be better for you to take that responsibility. If you find out exactly where your money is spent, you will become more self-disciplined about such matters. Be cautious about lending money simply because someone gives you a hard-luck story. You attract people who think nothing of borrowing money with no intention of repaying it.

Inconjunct: 1, 3 You have an active imagination and many good ideas, but unless you invest some time and energy in developing those ideas, they might as well not exist. You may have some difficulty getting people to show any interest in your plans unless you've worked out the details and can show why they are worth getting excited about. Keep a close watch on your financial reserves and resist the temptation to overspend on items that you can easily do without. This placement often precipitates dire financial predicaments, usually because you just can't resist making purchases.

Semisextile: 7, 9 You are more trusting than you should be and are therefore more disappointed when people don't measure up to your expectations. Let people prove their value to you before making any commitments to them. Part of your social responsibility is to help people acquire substance other than the purely physical or material and to appreciate qualities such as compassion, sacrifice and integrity. People seek your counsel because you unwittingly create the impression that you care about them and their problems. Don't make it more difficult to fulfill your destiny by being uninformed and failing to make an important commitment to the world.

1st to the 8th You are in touch with the pulse of social evolution. You can play an important role in determining the quality of society by your personal commitment to the highest and most spiritual behavior.

 2nd to the 7th Others will seek your guidance as they strive for a life filled with worthwhile human values. In a more mundane context, you seek the company of people with strong characters who are not slaves to materialism. Your partner must share your life focus.

 3rd to the 6th You are physically sensitive to the social chaos that results from public indifference. But you can arouse enthusiasm for a positive effort to stimulate better social conditions. You feel you have a job to do, even though you may not be aware of what specific role you can play.

 4th to the 5th You are not accustomed to having your desires frustrated, and you become very impatient when your lover is noncommital about your relationship. You inspire your children to assert their own identities.

 5th to the 4th Your parents gave you the training you needed to achieve yor objectives by utilizing your creative potentials. You know that in the long run you will stand strong on your own merits.

 6th to the 3rd You have strong opinions about social conditions that need to be changed, but if you want to derive any benefit from your ideas, you must accept the burden of developing and implementing them at the social level.

 7th to the 2nd You consider your values important only to the larger purpose of helping people improve their circumstances. Don't be afraid to invest heavily in your ability to rise above petty issues and reveal the enormous power of the values you have acquired.

 8th to the 1st You might go about your business with hardly a thought of making any greater commitment to life than that of succeeding in your personal goals. Someday, however, you will feel compelled to make a greater commitment that will make an impression on society.

 9th to the 12th Your sensitivity to unacceptable social conditions may force you to make some sacrifices to ensure the elimination of those conditions. Many legal resources are available to help you force the public to reexamine the social values involved.

 10th to the 11th Even though you may be preoccupied with attaining mundane objectives, you will sense a subtle inner urge to eventually become involved in endeavors that will increase the public's awareness of its pressing needs. In that way you will make a permanent impression on society.

 11th to the 10th Seek a field of professional activity that allows you to make a worthwhile contribution to the future and to humanity. Enlisting the help of friends in your programs will give you the necessary energy.

 12th to the 9th The work that lies ahead for you may not yet be clearly defined, but with persistent effort and study you will understand the process. Learn to resist any pressure to take liberties with the law; otherwise your dedication to humanity will be distorted.

Trine: 4, 12   Because you are in tune with the continuing process of evolution in your social environment, you are in the enviable position of helping to determine the content and quality of society. Your psychic awareness of the most pressing human needs forces you to be responsible for making a contribution to improve social conditions. You have the advantage of great creative potential with which to accomplish this objective. Your parents allowed you to utilize your creative talents in any way that would give you the most satisfaction and fulfillment. As you grow, you will learn to exploit those potentials and stand strong and secure on your own merits. When you join with others who are similarly inclined, you will find that you have more power at your disposal than you realize, and the combined effort and energy can help you achieve the important goals required for a better integrated social environment. You may have more ideas than you realize for changing prevailing social values.

Sextile: 6, 10   You understand people intimately, and you have the strength to help them deal with their problems without getting caught up in the situation. You can inject the enthusiasm that people need to become more self-sufficient through their own efforts. Although you may not yet fully realize now you can contribute to society's needs, in time you will define your medium. This will happen slowly and imperceptibly, until suddenly one day you're involved! You seek a career that gives you an opportunity to work with people in the broadest terms, so that your influence will be extensive and far-reaching. You will probably form close ties with persons who are similarly inclined, and even greater benefits will result from combining your energies.

Cross: 2, 5, 11   You may run into frustration early in your career because a partner expects you to make great sacrifices to acquire possessions. While your children are young, they also will cramp your style because you will have to concede to their needs. Still, you will inspire them to achieve according to their own abilities. You have a fairly strong desire nature, which often indicates enormous creative potential. At times you may think that you will never get the opportunity to be truly fulfilled in all aspects of your being. Be patient, for fulfillment will come when your more personal and mundane obligations to others diminish. Then you will turn your attention to the more subtle inner voices that suggest how much more there is to do before your destiny is fulfilled. You will be involved in helping society at large.

Inconjunct: 1, 3   Your most urgent priority is to make your vast world of ideas tangible and real through development and training. Get involved in social issues and environmental problems and use these situations as a platform for testing your ideas. As time goes on, you will get more and more involved, and eventually you will be dedicated to relieving some of the problems you observe on the personal or social level.

Semisextile: 7, 9 Make sure your ethical standards are high, and resist any pressure from special interests to take liberties with the law in any area. The vision you have of a better world is undoubtedly valid, and you should strive to see it made real. Be available when others need your courage and focus to help them achieve direction in their lives. You generally attract people who have their own inner strength. Ideally, the focus of your partner's life should blend with your own stated purposes.

Sun in Eighth, Moon in First

An important feature of your life is getting involved in circumstances relating to others' needs, either publicly or privately. It is critical to your continuing development that you help others become self-sufficient. In a sense, you owe that kind of effort to society, because you are so intimately aware of what is needed. But you also have to cope with your own feeling of insufficiency, and it will take considerable effort to satisfy the demands others make on you while fulfilling your own needs. Until you feel secure, you will focus primarily on your own interests. But as you mature and realize that doing for others can be fascinating and rewarding, you will give them the attention they need. You can succeed in a career in serving the public and enjoy a comfortable income without anxiety about material security.

If your efforts are appreciated, it means that you've developed worthwhile skills and are making a valuable contribution to the world. Your self-doubts about your abilities will fade as you grow increasingly successful in meeting the challenge of competition. Medicine, financial and investment counseling, insurance and retirement programs are some of the many careers that are suitable for you.

Sun in Eighth, Moon in Second

Fulfilling your identity with all of its potentials will be easier if you make your skills available to those in need of them. This doesn't mean that you can't accept payment for what you do, but simply that getting paid should not be an exclusive condition for those services. At first you may find it difficult to get a balanced perspective on giving and receiving, but experience will tell you when you achieve the right balance. It's not easy for you to let go, perhaps because you don't want anyone to have control over you. And yet your continuing development requires that you focus your attention on gaining future security. Investing your skills in a worthwhile contribution to society is the best way to gain the highest yield from them. But fear of losing what you already have may prevent you from making this kind of commitment. In that case, you can expect very little growth in the assets you now have. This combination is precisely defined by the expression, "Nothing ventured, nothing gained." Don't let your preoccupation with earnings dominate your life, or you may lose the support of those you love, and it may take a long time to regain it.

Investment or financial counseling, retirement programs, medicine and psychology or psychiatry are some of the vocations in which you could succeed, both professionally and financially.

Sun in Eighth, Moon in Third

Your desire to make the most of your basic resources increases your chances of success. This combination indicates that you are very well qualified to make a worthwhile contribution to society through your services. Without training, you may find it difficult at times to discriminate between reality and fantasy. You can't afford to risk using undocumented and therefore fragile information. You have a gifted imagination, but you need the discipline of a training program to be reasonably effective when you apply it. Developing your creative talents may involve sacrifices, but this investment will pay off by giving you the skills with which to pursue your goals and objectives and by allowing you to help others reach their goals.

Communications, writing, reporting, education or sales are some fields in which you could succeed. You also have a flair for investing people's resources in profitable enterprises, which you might consider. If you control your spending habits, you will avoid the anxiety or lack of energy that may result from financial insecurity.

Sun in Eighth, Moon in Fourth

Your early conditioning helped your personality development and allowed you to succeed and be fulfilled. Because of your harmonious temperament, you can cope with frustration while establishing your position in the world. You know how to adapt to changes with favorable results, but you may not be as aggressive as you should be. This combination indicates that you often let matters wither away because you fail to act decisively, perhaps because you feel that a better situation may develop. Unless you develop a plan for gaining the goals you want and are willing to persist in that effort, they won't materialize. You may be overly influenced by your parents' expectations, but you can make your own decisions. Real estate, financial investment, physical therapy or medicine are some of the possible outlets for your creative talents.

With your understanding and compassion for people, you will probably attract a partner who needs your support, both personally and professionally, to achieve a harmonious relationship. But you may feel that your mate doesn't give you the support you need in your goals.

Sun in Eighth, Moon in Fifth

Deriving the most benefit from your fine creative talents depends on your willingness to satisfy the needs of others. Your early conditioning may have taught you that you don't have to get involved with others or extend a helping hand if you don't want to. With this attitude, the road to success in your career and in relationships will be paved with frustration and conflict. With your creative potential, you can make a valuable contribution to society, and you must accept the responsibility for making it available. A vast world of opportunity will open up when you become aware of this.

Because a comfortable lifestyle is important to you, the best way to get what you want and improve the quality of life for others is through a career that involves public service. The difference between success and failure is the ability to integrate your feelings and will so that emotional distress does not interfere with your ability to perform well in your career. Once you relax your defense mechanisms and realize that everyone has failings, you increase the chance of having satisfactory relationships. Usually a permanent relationship is the best way for two people in love to fulfill their needs for each other, and that doesn't necessarily mean that one is using the other, except in mutual interest.

Sun in Eighth, Moon in Sixth

Your desire for a fulfilling life is in harmony with the emotional satisfaction you derive by being helpful. You have compassion for people's problems, and you assert yourself in ways that serve their needs. Your success comes from your ability to understand people. Your upbringing taught you how to effectively provide the services that people need. Also, this medium of self-expression gives you the opportunity to gain a high degree of skill. With greater competence, your earnings will increase and you can establish your professional credibility. You may not want a position with high visibility, but it is satisfying to know that you are respected by those in authority for the excellence you demonstrate in your tasks. However, in your desire to help people with problems, you also attract those who make no effort to help themselves.

Medicine, physical therapy, psychological counseling, vocational guidance, ecological enterprises, nutrition and family planning are some of the many fields available to you. It would be better if you postponed a permanent relationship until you are better established in your career. Be wary of accepting a submissive role with your partner.

Sun in Eighth, Moon in Seventh

Because of emotional anxiety and fear of inadequacy, you may not take advantage of opportunities for meaningful social activity. Your deep sensitivity enables you to make a worthwhile contribution to society through your career, because you are so keenly aware of the causes of social problems. You are insatiably curious about getting to the root of important social issues, and you can detect the seemingly insignificant details that result in social frustration, so you should certainly seek a career that involves this responsibility. The legal and political ramifications of such a course make it important to have a broad education, especially in the social and behavioral sciences.

With the right training, you can withstand the abrasive situations you may face and succeed in spite of them. Your career should bring you into close contact with people, for you need them as much as they need you; through them you will reach the fulfillment of your potentials. If you can, get out on your own and build a foundation of personal security so you can extend yourself more positively in pursuing your goals. The legal profession, government service, public relations, social programs and sales are some of the many careers you could choose from. A partner who combines his or her efforts with yours would be ideal, but in any case, your mate's support for what you are trying to accomplish would go a long way to make your marriage succeed.

Sun in Eighth, Moon in Eighth

Whether you enjoy success or endure failure is a direct result of making or rejecting a commitment to others. You resent it when anyone tries to pressure you into making decisions, especially concerning matters that are none of their business. Decision-making is an important issue in your life, and you will deliberate long and hard before deciding on the career you should follow and whether or not you can accept being responsible to the public for the services or products you offer. You want the freedom to express your creative talent so that you derive personal satisfaction, but unless this also benefits others, people will avoid you. You can't insulate yourself from people, because they know you have the qualifications to help them with their problems. Like a magnet, you attract people, with and without problems.

Medicine and medical research, financial counseling, insurance, crime detection, psychoanalysis, physical therapy and chemical engineering are some of the many ways to exploit your creative talents. Be certain that your contract spells out exactly what is expected of you, and be wary of people who suggest that you should freely offer your services without some reward.

Sun in Eighth, Moon in Ninth

Your search for a fulfilling career and meaningful relationships will be rewarded if you are properly trained to use your creative skills in the most effective way. Very likely you want a career in which you provide high quality service to the public, to whom you want to dedicate your life efforts. You are deeply motivated to help improve the quality of life for those who seek your assistance, and you can. This inner urge will drive you to develop a high degree of skill to satisfy your responsibilities to the public. You know that the world judges you by your performance, and it would be painful if you offered anything less than the best of your capabilities. People generally credit you with more knowledge than you actually have, but you learn quickly and respond to their demands. Your distaste for hard work can be overcome as you grow increasingly competent in handling problems. People usually reveal their personal affairs to you, which helps you give them the assistance they need.

Among the many fields in which you could succeed are medicine, psychology, marital counseling, vocational guidance, family planning, financial investment, education, writing and politics. All of these would bring you into close contact with the public, where you can help people become more self-sufficient.

Sun in Eighth, Moon in Tenth

You should be able to find the best way to capitalize on your creative talents, because you are so sensitive to the effect of social problems on individuals and groups. This awareness arouses you to choose a career in which you can offer your skills to help solve some of those problems. You are a channel through which people can become increasingly aware of their ability to succeed when they take advantage of their resources. Showing people how they can be self-sufficient is an important feature of your career responsibilities. Your family may insist that your personal desires must not violate your loyalty to them, but don't let that deter you from achieving the goals you have defined for yourself. Put your family obligations in perspective.

The careers you can follow, all of which involve close contact with the public, include medicine, research and development, investment counseling, human services, sales, insurance, union management and banking, especially as a loan officer.

If your partner understands your career responsibilities and the sacrifices that may be required, you will enjoy a happy marriage and be able to provide adequately for your family. If your mate is demanding, your career effectiveness may be seriously reduced.

Sun in Eighth, Moon in Eleventh

If you are delayed in getting your career underway, it is probably because you can't decide which field will give you the greatest return for your efforts. You are deeply preoccupied with finding a job that will give you security in your later years, rather than one that permits you to exploit your creative talents as fully as possible. Perhaps you should back up a little and reexamine your motivations. You may discover that your creative potential can satisfy certain needs of the larger society. This planetary combination offers you many opportunities for applying your skills where they are most urgently needed. When you focus on providing a service that makes demands on your creative talents, security for the future is a natural by-product.

Communications, government service, politics, social service, vocational guidance and teaching are some of the ways to use your talents and make a worthwhile contribution to society. Nothing is as satisfying as knowing that you have helped make the world a better place for everyone. If you and your partner complement each other, you both will be supported in reaching your goals.

Sun in Eighth, Moon in Twelfth

You must get a good education, so you can make a worthwhile contribution to society, which is what you wish to do. You readily get involved in the problems of your environment, so you are probably quite aware of what is needed to solve them. You may not take that action personally, but you will at least alert the proper authorities and arouse public support. You may underestimate your own ability to take command in such an effort, and yet you know that many people need help. In the beginning you might focus your attention on individuals who need assistance and learn from them how capable you are. Lack of self-confidence keeps you from taking on large-scale programs, but that will change as success reassures you of your competence.

A career in institutional work, as in medicine, correctional facilities, homes for the mentally or physically handicapped or the elderly would be suitable for you. Education and social programs also offer many opportunities for self-expression and success.

Defer marriage until you are reasonably well situated in your career. Your partner may require a lot of your attention, or you may have to compensate for your partner's problems in getting professionally established.

Chapter Nine

Ninth House

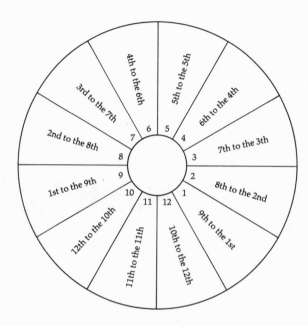

As you tap into the circumstances of your ninth house, you find more opportunities to gain self-confidence. This is the sector of higher education, which allows you to grow in awareness of the world within and of the world that extends to the ends of the universe. The dazzling concept of infinity belongs as much to the world within as to the outer world. In more ordinary terms, the ninth house offers you the chance to improve on the basic skills you have acquired through the sixth house and thus achieve a high degree of professionalism in your endeavors. It allows you to have high expectations of realizing your dreams of the future. This house also prepares you to accept full responsibility for your actions by establishing a personal code of ethics based on your knowledge of right and wrong.

This house brings you into intimate contact with those around you, for it pertains to their concept of you. Conversations with others occur through the interaction of the third and the ninth houses. Your ninth is their third, and your third is their ninth, which suggests the need for mutual understanding of each other's views. This house offers you to grow in knowledge, awareness, confidence and devotion to maintaining the ethical standards you've established in your struggle to fulfill your destiny. You will not find wisdom here, but you will find the means to become wise as you extend yourself in the world of situations and relationships. This house propels you into the world of the unknown, so that you are constantly searching for answers, and you will develop a philosophy that sustains you in your pursuits. The enigma of this house is that every answer reveals further questions, enticing you to extend yourself in an ever-widening arc. This is how you grow and learn to make the most of your creative potentials. With every success comes greater awareness and self-confidence, so that your beliefs and convictions are never shaken. This is a fire house, where enthusiasm is high and fervor is intense.

Derivative House Meanings

1st to the 9th   As your knowledge increases, so does your confidence in applying your skills in responsible tasks, which can establish your reputation before the public.

2nd to the 8th   Your awareness of what people require and expect of you gives you enormous power over them, and you can be held accountable for your actions.

3rd to the 7th   You have the understanding that people need in your dealings with them, and they may turn to you for guidance in their affairs.

4th to the 6th   These circumstances allow you to refine your skills so that you can build a secure position for yourself and gain the independence you want.

5th to the 5th   The people you love inspire you to develop your creative talents to a high degree of proficiency. You demonstrate your skills with dramatic flair.

6th to the 4th   Your early conditioning may have forced you to really apply yourself to gain the knowledge you have, which forms the base for your endeavors.

7th to the 3rd   No amount of knowledge relieves you of the responsibility for broadening the field of interest in which you may gain recognition.

8th to the 2nd   With understanding comes the commitment to apply your resources and values where they will be universally beneficial.

9th to the 1st   The ability to succeed is largely a result of never doubting that you will. Your infectious self-confidence influences others.

10th to the 12th   Social problems can be solved when you include them in your personal objectives. You must involve yourself in such problems at some time in life.

11th to the 11th   After you've achieved your worldly goals, you will apply yourself to helping others achieve their goals through your efforts.

12th to the 10th   You should regard your reputation before the public as a sacred trust and as a building block on which to build your spiritual credits.

1st to the 9th   You will achieve personal fulfillment by exploiting your higher mental faculties with creative imagination and inspiration. You have confidence that your ideas will make an indelible impression on others.

 2nd to the 8th   Your knowledge sustains those who need intellectual nourishment. You realize that unless you are willing to devote some part of your life to helping people become more self-reliant, your growth will be limited.

 3rd to the 7th   You understand people's problems, and they look to you for the insight they need in finding solutions. You will try to find a mate who shares your enthusiasm for the goals you hope to realize.

 4th to the 6th   You want to be free to use your creative abilities in activities that are far removed from the usual boring routine. You want to be self-employed if possible, but even if you are employed by others, you should have self-determination in your job.

 5th to the 5th   Your creative spirits are supercharged when you get a chance to apply your talents freely to achieve the objective you want. You give your children the same privileges.

 6th to the 4th   It is to your credit that you can look eagerly to achieving your goals, for you probably had little help from your parents. In fact, burdensome obligations at home may have delayed the time when you could begin to fulfill personal objectives.

 7th to the 3rd   Your most urgent priority should be to ask questions. You should never assume that you are well enough informed about any subject, for your continuing progress depends on sustained interest and enthusiasm.

 8th to the 2nd   You have substantial resources, and if you are motivated to use them as your major investment, you will never be disappointed in the returns. You will probably have to pay for your own education.

 9th to the 1st   You believe in your ability to succeed, and you are willing to take certain risks to prove yourself. Once involved in a pursuit that offers you an opportunity to grow, you will dedicate yourself to achieving its objectives.

 10th to the 12th   Because you are aware of the enormous problems in society, you are obligated to do what you can to help solve them. You find it stimulating to know that people in need will turn to you because of your expertise.

11th to the 11th   You know that you can realize your goals only if you are properly educated. You can anticipate what your objectives will require you to do, and you get the education you need to make certain you won't fail. Friends will help you achieve your goals.

 12th to the 10th   Don't imagine that you can achieve recognition without some sacrifices. You may have to work in obscurity at first, but eventually you should become reasonably secure.

Trine: 1, 5 Because you believe in yourself, you will probably succeed in your endeavors. Not one to avoid any opportunity to demonstrate your talents, you eagerly rise to every occasion that offers a chance to prove yourself. At times you are willing to take risks because you are so confident. Once involved in a project, you grow increasingly enthusiastic and sure that it will succeed, but your patience may wear thin if there are delays beyond your control. You want to know that your efforts have influenced others, and when they appreciate what you are trying to accomplish, you are even more inspired. Your children are especially aware of your ability to inspire others, and they hope to do the same and live up to your expectations. You offer your children every opportunity to exploit their potentials, and you let them make mistakes, knowing it is the only way that they will take full responsibility for their actions.

Sextile: 7, 11 You know you must have training to achieve your goals, so you strive to get the formal education that will enhance your natural talent for creative self-expression. You get involved only in enterprises in which you can visualize success. You know how to cultivate the right contacts through friends and associates to help achieve your plans. You prefer a professional career that will bring you into close contact with people, for you understand their problems. They look to you for insight to find solutions to their difficulties. The partner you choose will be most helpful in your affairs and will share your enthusiasm for the goals you seek.

Cross: 3, 6, 12 You will go far if you don't assume that you know everything there is to know. Your sustained interest in acquiring knowledge will assure you a permanent place in the public eye and eliminate the necessity of having to work at routine tasks. Many occupations would be too boring and tedious for you, since you need considerable mobility and freedom to express yourself. You should be self-employed if possible, or at least have a career that allows you some self-determination. You can serve people by helping them understand their predicaments and thus arrive at solutions. You have much to contribute to society, and you will not live up to your greatest potentials unless this objective is part of your career.

Inconjunct: 4, 2 Your accomplishments may have little relation to your parents' lifestyle, for they may not have helped you get established. The chances are you had to work hard to prepare a base on which to build your own life. It is also possible that family obligations delayed the time when you could utilize your talents for personal objectives. Any sacrifices you made to get an education were worth it, for that is the best investment you could make in the security you want for your later years.

Semisextile: 8, 10 Your major obligation is to help people whose lack of education or skills has denied them some of the privileges you enjoy. You can derive much satisfaction from knowing that you've been instrumental in improving the quality of their lives. Your own growth is intimately tied to your ability to handle this responsibility. You might have to accept some obscurity during your developmental years until you are competent enough to fulfill the public's expectations in the career you've chosen.

1st to the 9th   You have an immense thirst for knowledge, and because you are so well informed, you feel that you will succeed. Your ability to absorb diverse kinds of information may qualify you for many different professional positions.

 2nd to the 8th   Your ability to respond to other people's needs is especially beneficial because you know how to stimulate them to take advantage of their own resources. You have an unusual talent for teaching.

 3rd to the 7th   You are a good listener and can deal with people effectively, because you show you genuinely care about them. This kind of communication must exist between you and your partner in order for the relationship to succeed.

 4th to the 6th   You prefer a profession in which you can work with the general public. Purely physical work would not allow you to utilize all of your skills to the fullest.

 5th to the 5th   Working with children would be particularly consistent with your talent for making others feel that you understand them. Children realize that you want them to have the opportunity to exploit their potentials.

 6th to the 4th   You may have found it difficult to satisfy your family obligations and still devote enough time and energy to getting an education. Making your own way in life should be your most urgent priority, in spite of limitations imposed by others.

 7th to the 3rd   Because you are so well informed, people seek you out to help them solve their problems or simply to provide information. Never assume that you already know everything you need to know.

 8th to the 2nd   Your ability to accumulate the material necessities of life depends largely on whether you are willing to invest in a higher education. You might consider a career in financial management or investment.

 9th to the 1st   You will become more self-confident as you grow in knowledge and understanding. People lean heavily on you for support, but you believe that most of them can succeed on their own terms, just as you have.

 10th to the 12th   Working with the public will give you the best opportunity to achieve your goals and feel comfortable with your achievements. Fulfilling the demands of a career involving the public will earn you their respect and appreciation.

 11th to the 11th   Your imagination works overtime dreaming up new goals and objectives to turn your attention to. You never feel that you have exhausted the available opportunities.

 12th to the 10th   You owe it to the people you serve in your career to maintain a high standard of ethical behavior. Your superiors may ask you to take liberties with the law, but remember that your personal reputation can seriously affect your position in the world.

Trine: 1, 5 In your desire to make the most of your potentials, you utilize every opportunity to increase your knowledge and skills. You know that success depends on having the proper training when a job opening is available. Your intellectual interests are unlimited, so you can adapt to many kinds of opportunities and handle them adequately. Because you absorb new information readily, your development on the job usually proceeds well. To enhance your career position you will probably consider taking extra educational courses. Mainly you are attracted to persons who, like you, are not content merely with a basic education and who show much promise in their continuing development. Working with children would be especially meaningful, for you can impart the enthusiasm that children and young people need to exploit their potentials. You generally give people the benefit of the doubt and allow them to demonstrate that they can succeed.

Sextile: 7, 11 A good listener, you get along well with people if they have something substantial to say. You are easily annoyed with trivia, for you consider it a waste of time. You make a generous contribution to every conversation, because you are so well informed on many subjects. Your keen imagination is blended with creative inspiration, and you constantly think up new goals and objectives for yourself. You are drawn to friends who have similar interests and who are equally enthusiastic in pursuing their aspirations.

Cross: 3, 6, 12 Solving your own day-by-day problems and helping others with theirs will add much meaning to your life. You always want to be an active participant, and you abhor people who lack the backbone to get involved in the important issues of their environment. Your career should bring you into close contact with the public. Never assume that you know everything there is to know about people, because dealing with the public effectively requires you to be at least one step ahead of their demands. Purely physical work is not for you because it would not allow you to extend yourself to the fullest of your potentials.

Inconjunct: 4, 2 You will be much happier if you learn to be self-sufficient. It may be quite difficult for you to achieve independence from your family, for they may try to make you defer your own needs and fulfill your obligations to them. But you must establish that your own destiny requires you to be more detached. Getting an education may require some personal sacrifice, but the results are certainly worth it. A career in education, travel, politics or financial management would be especially well suited to your temperament.

Semisextile: 8, 10 Maintaining a high standard of ethics in your job and in your dealings with the public is very important. Otherwise you risk severe chastisement, which could undermine your career. Your superiors may ask you to take liberties with what is legally acceptable in your career, but you must refuse. You don't need that kind of harassment, and you can surely succeed without it. With your resources, you can always offer your professional services to people who need them. Your career could be in family counseling as well as in counseling groups or individuals about their financial affairs.

1st to the 9th   Your interests are mainly intellectual, and your skills are largely in the development of ideas. You feel a responsibility to communicate your knowledge skillfully to anyone who needs and wants the information.

2nd to the 8th   You know that you must apply yourself to get the necessary training to fulfill the commitment you've made to your goals. The sacrifices that are required will add meaning and value to the knowledge you seek.

3rd to the 7th   You know how to interpret what people say they want and need from you. You ask the right questions to learn about their interests and desires, and you can help them be more objective so they can solve their own problems. You want a mate who communicates openly.

4th to the 6th   To avoid having to do just physical labor, you look for a field in which you can exercise your mental faculties. The chances are that you will grow into a staff or management position on the job.

5th to the 5th   You enjoy travel, with its unexpected situations and developments. You want to share your experiences with your children, and you are deeply pleased when they indicate they want to follow in your footsteps. You know how to convert potential into reality.

6th to the 4th   You may seek an education in order to improve conditions at home, which are probably not up to your expectations. It may not have been easy to convince your parents that they should help pay for your education.

7th to the 3rd   It irritates you when you don't know the answer to a question. This emphasizes how important it is to ask yourself if you should be better informed in any area. Avoid displaying your intellect in an arrogant or pompous way.

8th to the 2nd   Your financial situation will improve if you make a commitment with the knowledge you've gained. Improved earning ability may have been your real reason for getting a higher education, but it also builds character.

9th to the 1st   You know that if you learn to understand yourself, you will probably understand others better too, which will enhance your chances of succeeding with the public. You are confident that you can get whatever you want, and you probably will.

10th to the 12th   You are unusually vulnerable to the danger of fellow workers conspiring against you on the job. You must be constantly alert to this problem and completely informed to keep it from happening.

11th to the 11th   Your wide circle of friends and associates will be an asset as you move forward in your career. Be sure to redefine your goals as earlier ones are realized. You probably look forward to the independence that comes with a comfortable income.

12th to the 10th   Periodically examine your behavior and standards of ethics in your career to keep them at the highest level. It's so easy to let these matters slide until deep problems develop, seemingly without warning.

Trine: 1, 5 The circumstances of your life allow you to develop your mental faculties extensively and give you the privilege of utilizing your creative potentials to best advantage. You are eager to share your knowledge with those who want information, and you are skillful in your presentation. You look for ways to dramatize your own creative potentials, as well as your children's. They look up to you for inspiration as they seek to fulfill all your expectations of their creative talents. If they choose to follow in your footsteps, you will be deeply satisfied. In your professional pursuits, you know that if you understand yourself, you will probably have a better understanding of the people you deal with. You may occasionally wonder whether you will gain your objectives, but with your naturally self-confident nature, you are very likely to succeed.

Sextile: 7, 11 You get along well with people because you understand them, and you know how to interpret what they need from you. You can help them see their difficulties with objective clarity, for which they are generally appreciative. Your wide circle of friends and associates is an asset in your career. It is important to define new goals periodically, as the old ones are realized. Your ability to earn a comfortable income in your career will help you achieve the independence you seek. Your partner will be a distinct asset, as long as communication flows freely between you. You want a mate who understands your goals and who shares your enthusiasm in reaching them.

Cross: 3, 6, 12 You don't pursue physical work if you can avoid it, preferring to utilize your ability to solve problems and resolve crises in your daily responsibilities. Conditions beyond your control may force you to accept duties you don't particularly like, but the chances are that when you demonstrate your special talents, you will be offered a job at the management level, for which you are better suited. While it bothers you when you don't know the answer to a question, it merely shows that you must learn more in some areas. Be especially alert to the danger of being undermined in your job by fellow workers, although this can occur only if you are not well informed. You understand people's failings and liabilities, and you should seek a career that is related to helping solve these problems.

Inconjunct: 4, 2 Your education is the base on which you can build the material security you want. Getting an education may not have been easy if your parents did not support your desire for it, and you probably had to extend yourself to get it. While being able to make more money may have been your principal reason for getting formal training, the resulting character development and polish are also important. But all your education will amount to very little if you aren't willing to use it to help people who require your skills. This will advance your position before the public.

Semisextile: 8, 10 You probably worked very hard to gain the knowledge that you have, so it is all the more urgent to apply it wisely. You should make sure your ethical standards are always at the highest level in your dealings with people. Lack of sufficient self-discipline in this area can erode the results of all the hard work you've invested to achieve your ambitions.

1st to the 9th   You go to great lengths to gain acceptance in a social environment that will improve your social standing. You may even indulge in social politics if it will enhance your position.

 2nd to the 8th   You usually know what people expect from you, and you are willing to go along with them, knowing that your investment will prove beneficial in the long run.

 3rd to the 7th   An excellent tactician, you let everyone believe that you share their views. You endear yourself to others by indicating that you are attracted to people of quality. Your partner admires your poise and skill in handling people, which helps you both.

 4th to the 6th   You are not particularly fond of menial tasks, so you would prefer a career that allows you to grow and develop according to your particular abilities. You are willing to work hard to gain the approval of your fellow professionals.

 5th to the 5th   You willingly adapt as needed to fully exploit your creative potentials. You cultivate a similar enthusiasm in your children so that they will fulfill their own identities. You don't hesitate to tell people you like that you find them very attractive.

 6th to the 4th   You will achieve your important goals mostly because you are so determined. Your early training may not have helped in this regard, but you will apply yourself to achieve your objectives. Family obligations may have delayed the time when you could do this.

 7th to the 3rd   You have an affinity for solving problems that require sophisticated solutions. But your rise to public prominence will be easier if you understand how much you need to know to win people's respect.

 8th to the 2nd   Always the entrepreneur, you continually seek out important people who can introduce you to a wider circle of social contacts. You regard this as a worthwhile investment in spite of the personal sacrifices involved.

 9th to the 1st   It annoys you to concede to people when they are wrong, yet you fear you will alienate them if you don't. As soon as you are firmly established in your career or social position, you will go back to being honest with yourself and others.

 10th to the 12th   "Seedy" elements in society hold little interest for you, but these are precisely the people who most need your ability to intercede for them with persons in high places.

 11th to the 11th   You always have a goal, because you never feel that you've acquired all the comforts life has to offer. You capitalize on your friends when necessary, but you are willing to reciprocate when they need favors.

 12th to the 10th   You must plan your moves carefully to avoid undermining those who have helped you achieve your objectives. Because you probably chose a public career, you must remember your obligations to those who are affected by your actions.

Trine: 1, 5   Being accepted in the social mainstream is most important to you. Though it annoys you to concede to others when you know they're wrong, you feel that it is politically advisable and that doing otherwise might jeopardize your chances of being accepted. Once you are established, however, you won't make such concessions because you consider it unbecoming. You prefer honesty, and you are perfectly willing to tell people you like them if they seem pleasant and attractive. You enjoy your children as they enjoy you, and you know how to cultivate their desire to live up to their own creative potentials. You try to be understanding of your partner's needs, and you are always willing to discuss any problems that come up. If the lines of communicaton are kept open at all times, you feel that most difficulties can be resolved. You know how to adapt to any circumstances that allow you to fully exploit your creative potentials.

Sextile: 7, 11   People are attracted to you because you know how to make them feel important. Even with people you've just met, you tactfully let them believe that you share their views and that you find them pleasing because you have "always been attracted to people who have a keen sense of values." Your mate finds you delightful because of your poise and skill in dealing with people, even those who are socially undesirable. Never satisfied with your accomplishments, you constantly set new goals to reach. Though you accept favors from friends, you usually reciprocate when they need help from you.

Cross: 3, 6, 12   You find repetitive jobs tedious and boring. You are drawn to occupations in which there is a minimum of routine and you are free to deal with the public. You also want opportunities to grow and to demonstrate your competence as your skills increase and you are ready for greater responsibility. You are somewhat turned off by people who lack polish and sophistication, but it is through them that you can show what you can accomplish in your career. Your position might allow you to intercede with those in high places who can help people in need. You will grow as long as you realize that you need to know a great deal to earn the respect of those whom you serve in your profession.

Inconjunct: 4, 2   You should pursue your goals with the same determination you showed when your early conditioning taught you that nothing in life is free. Fulfill your family obligations first, and then you can devote yourself to exploiting your creative potentials in your career. Any sacrifice you made to gain a formal education was the most worthwhile investment of your life.

Semisextile: 8, 10   The worst thing you could do is to imagine that others' needs are less important than yours. If you let yourself think that they only want to get something out of you, you will miss a great opportunity to achieve your goals, because others will doubt that you deserve to achieve them. On the other hand, conceding to the needs of others enriches you more than it does them. After all, aren't they giving you the chance to prove yourself? Plan your moves carefully so that you don't unknowingly undermine those who helped you when you were starting out.

1st to the 9th Your eagerness to be noticed by important people in your profession is nearly boundless. You assert yourself forcibly to demonstrate that you won't be intimidated by even the most determined competitors.

 2nd to the 8th When you are physically attracted to someone, you are not easily put off, and you might even use your professional position to advantage in such matters. You let people know that you have the professional services they need, which you put a high premium on.

 3rd to the 7th In a confrontation, you generally get both the first and last word. Your mate will have to adapt to this trait, which suggests that you aren't as sure of your abilities as you seem.

 4th to the 6th You don't like being told how to work or how to stay healthy. You insist on your right to do what you want, and you defiantly resist anyone who says you can't. But slowing down would certainly improve you well-being.

 5th to the 5th Your children delight you because they bring out your ever-present youthful vigor and enthusiasm. You probably fancy yourself quite the romantic lover, and you generally try to live up to your partner's expectations.

 6th to the 4th You may have had to put off your dreams for the future because of obligations at home. Your parents may not have indulged you, but still you yearned to prove that you could accomplish your goals even without their help.

 7th to the 3rd You must learn to listen to others and postpone decisions until you are thoroughly informed. You tend to jump the gun, when it would be better to go slow, which wastes precious time and energy. Learn to plan for your goals.

 8th to the 2nd Because you hate to appear broke, you may take on more responsibilities than you can handle. A good education is the most worthwhile investment you can make. Don't borrow unless all else fails, because being obligated to others takes the starch out of you.

 9th to the 1st You will probably succeed most of the time because you assert yourself optimistically. You aren't afraid to take risks, but be wary of speculation. With your self-confidence and proper training, you can be the best in your field.

 10th to the 12th Taking liberties with the law or relaxing your moral code could mean disaster. You should direct some of your energy to programs relating to society at large. You will probably be recognized for your social service efforts.

 11th to the 11th You feel that it is perfectly all right to cultivate friends whom you can ask for favors, since you are willing to return the favors whenever they need them. You always have a goal.

 12th to the 10th Remember that you're important only as long as people need your services. There are always some hazards associated with success, and one is the problem of eliminating or ignoring those who are at the top. Accepting your obligations to the public is the price of recognition.

Trine: 1, 5 You are eager to prove yourself to even the most determined challenger. When you focus on an objective, your enthusiasm is nearly boundless, which almost always gains the attention of the important people you are trying to impress. You will certainly succeed in your endeavors because you believe in your ability. At times your actions seem inspired with imagination. Not afraid of risks, you take on tasks that others would avoid, but you should be careful of speculative and hazardous risks. You should have a good relationship with your children, for they are delighted with you and your daring temperament. You indulge them and tell exaggerated stories of your adventures. You certainly encourage them to promote their own potentials, giving them opportunities to develop. You try to live up to your partner's expectations as a romantic lover, and you will probably always be a lover to your spouse.

Sextile: 7, 11 Although you always seem to get the first and last word in a discussion, you aren't all that sure of yourself, and you use this intimidating method to put others on the defensive. If you take time to become thoroughly informed about matters that others find interesting, you will add to your long list of friends. Your partner must learn to live with your insistence on having the last word. You know how to take advantage of people's offers of help when you need it, and you generally reciprocate. You pursue your many goals with creative enthusiasm.

Cross: 3, 6, 12 Because you dislike taking orders from anyone, you would do well to be self-employed. You really should be on your own, so that your mistakes are yours alone to correct and only you know you made them. You should learn to listen when others have something important to say. Postpone taking action until you have all the facts at your disposal. There is no harm in asking for advice, and it may prove beneficial in the long run. If you keep your moral and ethical standards high, you will never feel the apprehension or guilt that can make life uncomfortable. You should strive to work in behalf of socially disadvantaged people, for you could be a champion who represents them in their predicaments.

Inconjunct: 4, 2 It wasn't easy to gain the independence to do what you wanted. Family responsibilities may have forced you to be patient about your own desires, but you still yearned to prove that you could achieve on your own. The only way to make sure that this will happen is to get an education and training. This is the best investment you could make, with a yield that will continue for years. Don't borrow unless there is no other alternative, and stay within reasonable limits. You don't like being obligated to others, so why take on this kind of embarrassment deliberately?

Semisextile: 8, 10 When you are attracted to someone, you are not easily put off. You might even use your professional position to advantage in your romantic affairs, though that would hardly seem necessary. In your career, you should promote yourself so that people will use your services. But don't forget that you are important only as long as people need what you have to offer, which carries a great deal of responsibility. Don't ignore the people who helped you get started, and remember them when you fulfill your goals. Your position has built-in risks, in that you must fulfill your obligations to those who have given you the recognition you wanted.

1st to the 9th   Your ability to understand people and their problems offers many opportunities for professional success. Your growth is assured, because you will commit yourself to serving the public.

 2nd to the 8th   Your career will involve working with large sums of money. You could do very well in money management, insurance, stock brokerage, law, education, medicine or personal counseling. People believe that you will always live up to their trust.

 3rd to the 7th   A good listener, you know that this often helps people who need someone to talk to about their problems. You insist that you and your partner must always feel free to discuss your problems. Like you, your mate is an intellectual.

 4th to the 6th   Probably you were impatient to grow up because you were anxious to prove that you could succeed if given the opportunity. You dislike working at ordinary jobs that don't make sufficient demands on your talent.

 5th to the 5th   You want the very best for your children, as well as for your lover. You enjoy giving presents to show how much you care, and sometimes you are extravagant in this regard.

 6th to the 4th   The need to stay close to home while you were growing up may have been painful, especially if you had family obligations. You may have done quite well if you were being groomed for a family business, but you would probably prefer to strike out on your own.

 7th to the 3rd   It is important not to assume that you know everything there is to know. You are uninformed about many matters that could simplify the task of seeking your goals. In your dealings with others, you dislike having anyone question your motives.

 8th to the 2nd   To achieve the many goals you have in mind, you will have to make some kind of investment. If financial return is your only motive, you are denying yourself the truly significant achievements you could accomplish.

 9th to the 1st   You have sufficient self-confidence to succeed in endeavors where others would fail. Don't assume that you can ignore the rules of the game and trust to luck, for that would be a mistake.

 10th to the 12th   You can make the best use of your talents by applying them for some social purpose. Your skills are urgently needed by those people in society who are most lacking in resources.

 11th to the 11th   You will continue to develop as long as your objectives are related to those of society. You can help improve the quality of life for many people by sharing your skills with those who want to improve their station in life.

 12th to the 10th   As you pursue your objectives, don't ignore the chains of command. You can easily be victimized by people whom you have disregarded in achieving your ambitions. Gaining recognition for your accomplishments gives you a heavy responsibility to those who have made it possible.

Trine: 1, 5   With your ability to realize your many dreams for the future, your growth potential is almost unlimited. You are a good learner, and there is no end to the ways you can achieve fulfillment. Your understanding of people and their problems gives you the opportunity you need to accomplish your objectives. You are drawn to a career that clearly involves you with the public, and you consider it part of your destiny to serve their needs. You are quite confident that you will succeed, even when others have failed in the same circumstances. As long as you observe the established rules of society in your dealings, you won't have to trust to luck for success. Because you want the very best for your children and your loved one, you indulge them occasionally with extravagant gifts.

Sextile: 7, 11   You understand that people are often helped in their difficulties simply by discussing their problems. You are that kind of willing listener, which your partner appreciates. Like you, your mate is probably an intellectual. Your growth is assured if you choose to work on behalf of people who lack your advantages. Your efforts can substantially improve the quality of their lives.

Cross: 3, 6, 12   You were impatient as you grew up, because you didn't want to wait to prove what you could achieve with your great creative potential. You especially dislike having to work at tasks that are not sufficiently demanding. As long as you don't assume that you already know everything you need to know, you will probably accomplish your objectives early in life. Stay well informed, and you won't ever have to suffer the embarrassment of not knowing the answers that everyone expects you to know. You can make the best use of your talents by helping those people in society who lack the personal resources and talent to handle their own affairs or deal with their problems.

Inconjunct: 4, 2   If family obligations forced you to put off working to achieve your own goals, you probably consented to it, even if it caused you some anxiety and frustration. But if that obligation concerned a family business that your parents wanted you to take over, you probably did very well. More likely, however, you wanted to prove yourself by striking out on your own. You should realize that you need a formal education in order to make the best investment of your life. The only problem here is whether you are motivated by the financial returns or by the useful service you can provide to society. You are shortchanging yourself if you are looking only for financial benefits.

Semisextile: 8, 10   You can be a great help to those who need your skills if you consider this your contribution to society and devote yourself to the task. If you feel that other people's resources are yours to use as you want, you probably won't contribute to anything or anyone except yourself. Your destiny requires that you become part of the real world where you can make an enduring tangible impression and where your reputation will grow as your level of influence increases.

1st to the 9th   Although you are keenly aware of the difference between right and wrong, you consider it essential to test public opinion before taking any action that would reflect on your credentials.

 2nd to the 8th   You demonstrate your talents by helping people with problems. You know how to cope with their needs, and you can offer them the chance to make better use of their resources. If necessary, you will pay for your physical pleasures.

 3rd to the 7th People respect your knowledge and ability to understand their problems. You want people to turn to you when they are in need. Your partner must respect your need to be alone with your thoughts occasionally.

 4th to the 6th   You want to be self-employed, although you are willing to work for others at first to get experience. Your continuing career development depends on how competently you respond to people's demands for your skills.

 5th to the 5th   You realize that the best way to take full advantage of your creative potentials is to get a formal education, and you want your children to do the same. You are selective in choosing a lover, and you offer a mature, secure love relationship that will benefit both of you.

 6th to the 4th   You probably got the education you wanted through self-determination. In school, you may have had to work to support yourself if your parents did not help you. This conditioning gave you more training than you realize.

 7th to the 3rd   It is painful not to know the answers to questions that people ask you. This should only intensify your determination to be informed at all times. Probably your brothers and sisters seek you out when they need advice.

 8th to the 2nd   You realize how important it is to sacrifice some of your self-indulgent desires to improve your future security. The investment you make now will reward you later in life by ensuring security and comfortable circumstances.

 9th to the 1st   You are a professional, whether or not you fall into that stereotyped classification. You are guided by firm standards in your dealings, and the public relies on your ethical behavior in handling their affairs.

 10th to the 12th   You are best suited to working with social problems. It would be advantageous to follow a career that has the objective of relieving these problems. Your strength can uplift those who lack the resources to solve their problems alone.

 11th to the 11th   You must plan carefully for whatever you hope to achieve, not assuming that everything will work out all right in the end. Don't be afraid to ask friends for help when you need it, for you can return the favor later.

 12th to the 10th   Adhere strictly to the rules of the game, for your superiors will certainly notice any unacceptable tactics you use to achieve your ambitions. You have the talent to get to the top without questionable practices. Your reputation is at stake.

Trine: 1, 5   Your intellect is profound, but you still consider it necessary to test public opinion before taking any action that might reflect on your credibility. You realize that the best way to take full advantage of your creative potentials is to get a formal education. You hope your children will do the same and will go on to fulfill their own identities. In choosing an associate, friend or lover, you are selective, preferring someone who is mature and willing to make a substantial contribution to the relationship so that it will endure. You are guided by a high sense of ethics and moral behavior, for which the public has learned to respect you. People know that you can be trusted to handle their affairs or provide them with services.

Sextile: 7, 11   Because you may not be particularly verbal, your partner must respect your need to be alone with your thoughts now and then. You often solve your problems in quiet contemplation, away from the many distractions of a busy world. People admire you for your knowledge and for your integrity in dealing with their problems, and you hope you will always maintain their confidence. You must plan ahead for the goals you want to reach and not assume that everything will work out all right in the end. Your friends are probably willing to help you when you need it, but you will have to ask. You can always return the favor later when they need help.

Cross: 3, 6, 12   Always assume that there is much you don't know, and when you lack information, have the determination to find it out. This will allow you to be self-employed, which will give you greater self-determination concerning your destiny. You will continue to grow as long as you respond to the public's demands for your skills. The public sector may offer the best opportunity to prove yourself and win the recognition you deserve for your accomplishments. Weak and disadvantaged people would very likely turn to you for support and guidance, because your strength uplifts those who can't solve their problems alone.

Inconjunct: 4, 2   You may have gotten an education through your own efforts, if you did not get help from your parents. But even if you had to support yourself, you feel that it was worth it, and it was. Education is the best possible investment, for its rewards will continue to pour in throughout your life and provide the comfortable circumstances you deserve. You aren't afraid of hard work when you know it will result in future security.

Semisextile: 8, 10   Make certain that you adhere to the rules of the game and avoid using tactics that would be embarrassing if they were made public. It would be tragic to lose everything after making such a tremendous effort to achieve your ambitions. You have the talent and skill to get to the top without resorting to questionable practices. Your reputation is too much to risk for any temporary gain. People with problems depend on you, because they know you can cope with their difficulties and show them how to make better use of their resources. If you think they don't need you, you are deluding yourself, perhaps to avoid accepting them as your responsibility.

1st to the 9th   Your need for freedom is so strong that you use every possible opportunity to achieve it. You know that the key to freedom is knowledge, and that getting an education will make it possible to achieve your goals.

2nd to the 8th   Realizing that you are always eager to share what you know, the public seeks your help in solving problems. They know that you can show them how to better achieve the means for survival.

3rd to the 7th   Few people can successfully deceive you, because you are intuitively alert to dishonesty and insincerity. You will do almost anything for those who are honest with you. Your mate is probably as highly developed as you and shares your destiny.

4th to the 6th   You are very innovative in your career, and you demand the freedom to exercise your skills ingeniously to solve the problems you face. Being restricted on a job diminishes your enthusiasm.

5th to the 5th   You demonstrate that you can accomplish a great deal with your varied creative potentials if you are permitted to develop them as you want. You hope your children will follow your example and exploit their talents according to their own needs.

6th to the 4th   Your parents should have instilled in you a respect for education and taught you that you could achieve many objectives that were beyond them. But you may have had to devise a way to get an education while still satisfying family obligations.

7th to the 3rd   Being well informed is so important to you that you learn as much as you can about many subjects. Because of this, you always make a worthwhile contribution to a discussion, often amazing people with your wealth of information.

8th to the 2nd   The investment you've made in learning as much as possible has greatly enhanced your ability to earn a comfortable income. You understand the importance of financial security in giving you freedom to succeed in new and greater objectives.

9th to the 1st   You don't doubt that you can accomplish nearly anything you want. Your faith is limitless, and your devotion to any task is so complete that you can "move mountains."

10th to the 12th   Living up to your vast potential requires that you apply yourself to the enormous responsibility of dealing with society's needs. No one is more aware than you of the limitations imposed on certain groups in society, and you can do a great deal to help these people.

11th to the 11th   No matter how successful you become and how many goals you achieve, you will continue to search for new ones. You are especially concerned with making a contribution that will improve the quality of life for those around you.

12th to the 10th   If you limit yourself to achieving personal goals and ambitions, you will deny yourself the full benefit of your vast potential. Don't give in to anyone who suggests that you use your skills in an irresponsible way to achieve certain objectives. The risk is too great, even for personal reasons.

Trine: 1, 5 Freedom is so important to you that nothing will stand in the way of getting the education you need to achieve your goals. In your view, anyone who is uninformed is likely to become trapped in a life situation or career that limits their personal privileges or their ability to assert individuality. You want the opportunity to develop your creative potentials and prove what you can do with them. You demand the same for your children, and you offer yourself as an example of what someone can accomplish through individual fulfillment. You give them the chance to exploit their identities to the fullest. Your innovative talents make you a creative lover as well, and your partner is probably quite content with your skill in lovemaking. You have enormous faith that you will succeed in anything you attempt, and your devotion to your responsibilities makes it possible for you to "move mountains."

Sextile: 7, 11 You have a good understanding of people and their problems, and it is rare when anyone deceives you successfully. You know intuitively when someone is not telling the truth or is insincere. You are generous in helping those who truly need your assistance, and you willingly share your knowledge to help them solve their own problems. You never lose sight of the future and the goals you still plan to achieve. You want to know that your efforts have helped improve the quality of life for as many people in society as possible.

Cross: 3, 6, 12 It is essential that you always be available to those who need your knowledge and skills. Though you are well informed, you still have to apply yourself to acquire new information. No one knows everything, not even you, and your growth depends on your continued search for more knowledge so that you can better use your skills. You need the kind of career environment in which you can use your talents fully and not be restricted so that your enthusiasm wanes. You could distinguish yourself in many fields, but whatever you decide, you should make some contribution to benefit the most needy members of society. Because you are in tune with society's problems, your efforts can help reduce or eliminate many of them.

Inconjunct: 4, 2 Though you may have yielded to family responsibilities, you were innovative enough to find a way to pursue your education at the same time. This probably required that you make many sacrifices, but you realized that you could not afford to pass up the chance to invest in your future security. This also taught you how to plan for the future, for you know that increased earnings will give you freedom to succeed in newer and more satisfying objectives.

Semisextile: 8, 10 The right to pursue your own objectives does not allow you to ignore those who have come to depend on you for help and guidance when they need it most. For the most part, you recognize that you play an important part in their lives, so you are usually available. Don't deny yourself the full benefit of your creative resources by aligning yourself with people who want you to lower your ethical standards while working in their behalf. You don't need the apprehension of fearing that someone will learn about your lack of integrity and cause you to lose much that you have gained.

1st to the 9th   Your social and spiritual obligations are largely the product of early conditioning, when you felt that your teachers knew more than you did about life. You will be very disappointed when you learn that much of what you believed was an illusion.

 2nd to the 8th   The problems of the real world require that you help relieve people's burdens. You may resist doing this if you feel that people are only trying to take advantage of you.

 3rd to the 7th   When people tell you their experiences, you tend to embroider them with your own ideas. This can cause you to make false assumptions about what people have said, which can result in disappointing love relationships.

 4th to the 6th   It is essential to get as much formal education as possible so you can avoid getting locked into a job situation that seems to be going nowhere. Guilt feelings about your assumed inadequacies can lead to health problems.

 5th to the 5th   Your creative imagination is second to none, but you need to develop it. By playing down your creative gifts, you derive less benefit from them. You may get vicarious satisfaction from your children's self-expression, which you encourage. You're a romantic.

 6th to the 4th   You may have to postpone carrying out your life plans until your family obligations are satisfied. This could take some time, for you always imagine that they still need you. Plan now, and refuse to be deterred from your goals.

 7th to the 3rd   Don't be afraid to ask questions of people who have proven credentials. Being misinformed is no better than being uninformed, and it will delay the time when you can begin to assert yourself to reach your goals.

 8th to the 2nd   It is important to invest in sound training that will give you the necessary skills for earning a comfortable income. Don't think that you can aim for a financially rewarding career unless you are qualified in temperament and abilities.

 9th to the 1st   Though you may be inclined to do the right thing and stay within the bounds of acceptable practices, you should be alert to deception by those who would use you to satisfy their own ends.

 10th to the 12th   You can accomplish many worthwhile goals in service to your community, but you need not stop there. You should gain some recognition for your efforts in behalf of people who need your devotion and sympathetic understanding.

 11th to the 11th   Realizing your goals always seems to be in the distant future, because there is always an immediate task before you. When you reach one goal, another emerges, which means that your excellent services are always in demand.

 12th to the 10th   You must clearly define what you want out of life and not allow others to intrude on your destiny by conceding to theirs. Never doubt that you can and will realize your ambitions. And you won't have to resort to deceit to achieve them.

Trine: 1, 5   Your exceptional creative imagination is sometimes inspired. Making the best use of this gift requires training and development so that you will be aware of its value. In this area you tend to underestimate yourself; you need the feedback that will come from using your imagination and getting people's reactions to it. At some period in your life you experienced disappointment because you discovered that much of what you were taught as a child was based on tradition and not supported by the evidence now before you. You may still be deceived in some instances, as when people take advantage of your willingness to give them the benefit of the doubt. They may try to use you to satisfy their own personal objectives, not caring whether they endanger your goals.

Sextile: 7, 11   Your ability to serve the needs of others means that your services are always in demand. This may make you feel that your future is undefined, but really it means that you have a never-ending role to play in contributing to the general needs of society. Learn to accept what people tell you about their experiences and avoid mentally embroidering their conversation with what you want to hear. You can enjoy good relations with the public and your loved one by accepting them honestly in spite of their failings.

Cross: 3, 6, 12   Once you know that you cannot afford to be uninformed, you will develop well and grow successfully in your career. Throughout your life you should work at dispelling the errors instilled in your childhood, and this should give you the urge to pursue a higher education. You can avoid getting caught in a job situation that is going nowhere by getting as much formal education as possible so you won't feel guilty about your lack of knowledge. Concentrate your attention on people who have the greatest needs. Your efforts in their behalf will not go unnoticed, and helping them when they can't help themselves will enrich you with much inner satisfaction.

Inconjunct: 4, 2   Make it a point to deal with family obligations as soon as possible so that you can then devote your time and money to developing your own goals. You might find it difficult to pull away from your family because you assume they still need you, but remember, you need you also. Investing in an education will bring rewards beyond your imagination. Just be careful not to choose a career on the basis of financial returns, unless you know that your basic temperament and abilities qualify you for it.

Semisextile: 8, 10   There is so much you can do for people, both individually and in groups, that you should have no trouble deciding how to apply yourself in a career. Once you know that you are in demand because of your compassion and understanding of people's problems, you may decide to enter a profession in which serving people is the primary objective. It is so easy for you to allow others to intrude in your life and make demands that serve only their ends. Try to define what you want to accomplish with your life and concede to others only when you are certain that they truly need your assistance. As to your own goals, never doubt for a minute that you can and *will* realize your objectives. If you question that, you are giving in to your own negative delusions. If you doubt this, ask for advice from someone you trust and whose opinion you respect. You'll find they will concur with what is said here.

1st to the 9th   The broad field of the occult is deeply interesting to you, and your reading covers philosophy, religion, metaphysics and psychology. You are easily disturbed by social problems and by the political processes that fail to solve them.

 2nd to the 8th   People seek your guidance because you are able to sense the source of their problems. You feel that if you had the opportunity, you could offer much help to those who need it.

 3rd to the 7th   When people speak, you listen attentively to find out what motivates them. Often you are rewarded with keen insight into their problems, even if they haven't said that anything was wrong. You seek a partner who shares your perception and deep concern for people.

 4th to the 6th   You are troubled when you see so much that needs to be done for people who are unhappy or disturbed, but you feel that you lack the training to do anything about it. Your life work must include some important service to society.

 5th to the 5th   Instead of complaining about the quality of life around you, do something about it. You have the creative resources to accomplish this task, but you must be willing to develop the right skills. Eventually you will pursue this course because you truly care.

 6th to the 4th   Your early conditioning may not have given you the financial resources or the opportunities that you wanted. You had to pursue them on your own with determination to succeed.

 7th to the 3rd   It may be difficult, but you must revise your opinion on important issues when new evidence comes in. This refining process will continue throughout your life, and you will ask the questions that provide the right answers.

 8th to the 2nd   Preparing for a life of worthwhile service to others will involve much sacrifice, but you will eventually enjoy a reasonably comfortable lifestyle. You know that your efforts will not be wasted.

 9th to the 1st   Because you have to live with yourself, you must find a way to make a substantial contribution to society. With your devotion to serving people's needs, you will feel spiritually enriched if you can have a positive influence on others.

 10th to the 12th   Observing or learning about human suffering affects you deeply, but you can do something about it. In fact, your destiny will be truly satisfied only if you exert pressure in the right places to help improve social conditions.

 11th to the 11th   You may never retire, for you know you can accomplish much in your later years. You feel the time will be wasted if you don't remain productive. Friends will surely help you if you need it, and they know they can turn to you as well.

12th to the 10th   If you are obsessed with gaining public attention, you should examine your motives carefully. People will pick up that kind of vibration, and they may hold you in disdain for it. Focus on doing the best you can, with or without publicity. What really counts is your accomplishments.

Trine: 1, 5   You are tuned in to current social and political problems and disturbed by the failure of those who are largely responsible for dealing with them. Your reading includes philosophy, religion, metaphysics and psychology. You feel that government officials must have a more comprehensive understanding of the great social problems that cut across the barriers of race, creed and national origin. By developing your own skills, you could make a substantial contribution through political or social activity. You obviously care enough to make this effort, but you need training to accomplish your objectives. Finding a suitable career should come first on your list of priorities. Serving the public's needs would exert a positive influence where it's most needed and would give you a feeling of spiritual enrichment as well.

Sextile: 7, 11   People often seek your counsel, because you listen attentively to their problems, and they know you can offer them valuable advice. You generally hear more than is being said, as if you were reading between the lines of their conversation. This gives you keen insight into people's problems and an understanding of what motivates them. Your partner must share your interest in social issues and should be similarly concerned about finding solutions to them. It is not likely that you will ever retire, because you consider it a waste of time when you can still accomplish so much. Though you may not require it, you can always turn to your friends for help.

Cross: 3, 6, 12   Be prepared to revise your past opinions as you gain new information. This will assure that your views are always current and will allow you to withstand those who try to intimidate or gain control over you. If you are troubled by conditions that you observe in your environment, the only answer is to learn whatever skills are required to do something about them. You can be instrumental in guiding people to greater freedom by helping them find solutions to their problems. You should incorporate this objective into the duties of your career. You are deeply sensitive to human suffering, whether the cause is physical, social, political or economic, and you can do much to relieve these anxieties.

Inconjunct: 4, 2   Don't depend on getting a lot of help from your family in your endeavors. They may be sympathetic to your aims, but they may not provide you with the financial resources you need to get the education and training for achieving your goals. Resolve to go after what you want with determination that you will succeed. There may be sacrifices in preparing for the life you want, but the rewards will more than compensate for what you have to do without in the meantime.

Semisextile: 8, 10   In general, people trust implicitly in your judgment because you give the impression that you are intimately concerned about them, and you are. They derive many benefits when they capitalize on your suggestions about using their resources more effectively to achieve their goals. Pay some attention to your motivation, though, for if you are primarily interested in winning public attention, your achievements might boomerang. People pick up that kind of vibration and may resent you for using them to satisfy your personal desires. If publicity comes with accomplishment, fine. But even if it doesn't, do the very best you can.

Sun in Ninth, Moon in First

The road to success for you is to develop a wide range of skills from your creative potential. With good training, this process will be greatly simplified and more usefully applied. If you define your goals and have a plan for reaching them, you will not fail. Your emotions are in harmony with your ability to take decisive action in your affairs, which will allow you to enjoy considerable success. But when you are deeply involved in romantic ties, you tend to lose control, because you have feelings of inadequacy. Probably you reacted negatively to some of your parents' conditioning, so that you felt it was difficult to enjoy truly satisfying relationships. You have some anxiety about not measuring up to a suitor's expectations, so you avoid making commitments to people you are attracted to. On the other hand, you might nourish a romantic alliance and then find that you aren't ready yet for a permanent relationship.

Until you are more mature emotionally, you should direct your attention to career interests. You will certainly succeed in your career because you are so knowledgeable and can effectively deal with responsibility. Some careers you could follow are in law, politics, government service and in private business that brings you into close contact with the public. Don't follow your parents' career suggestions unless you feel it will give you personal satisfaction.

Sun in Ninth, Moon in Second

You will always be able to distinguish yourself as long as you can prove that your accomplishments are valuable. You tend to overextend yourself and then stop short when you reflect on the losses you might suffer by taking unrealistic chances. There is a constant struggle between your desire to assert yourself, confident that success will naturally follow, and your apprehensions about personal or material security. In time, you will learn to put this situation into perspective and take action only when the circumstances offer a reasonably high probability of success. When your Sun in the ninth urges you to throw caution to the winds, let your feelings guide you with common sense. By deferring your decision in important matters until you've had time to examine them thoroughly, you will avoid a lot of unnecessary grief. Your valuable insight is often sought by people in high places. There are many choices available to you in selecting a career, including law, politics, business administration, education, government service and journalism.

Your mate should understand that you must choose your priorities carefully so that you can devote enough time and energy to career development while still fulfilling the demands of a marriage. In that case you should enjoy success and happiness in both areas of responsibility.

Sun in Ninth, Moon in Third

Your faith in your ability to succeed is a strong point in your favor, but it does not completely override your anxiety about being ready when an opportunity is presented.

Consequently, you strive to improve your qualifications by finding additional ways to use your creative ideas. To do this, you might form associations with people who are already involved in fields that interest you, so that you have access to the means for promoting your ideas in the future. You may also have to cope with powerful parental conditioning that made you feel apprehensive about winning approval from people in important positions. Certainly your parents want you to succeed, but is that for you or is it to satisfy their own feelings of insufficiency? This combination often has this effect, which may condition you to seek an outlet for your creative potential that meets with your parents' approval. Your rise to prominence is intimately linked with the affairs of others, but because of that you can easily fall victim to people who would use you to enhance their goals.

Some fields in which you can find a satisfactory career are communications, writing, the news media, education and law. Any of these would bring you into close contact with the public, where your creative talents can thrive.

Your partner should be someone who is similarly motivated to excel in his or her career and who is sympathetic to the struggle you face in achieving excellence in yours.

Sun in Ninth, Moon in Fourth

Strong parental conditioning may have delayed you in setting a course and becoming established in your own identity. Strong family ties may cause you to alter your initial plans until you can feel comfortable taking on responsibilities that are strictly your own. You need to put in perspective the obligations you have to others and those you owe yourself. Gradually you should relinquish your grip on the security provided by your family and make your own way, whatever the outcome. With some education you will realize that you have plenty of talent and creative ability to succeed on your own; your progress will accelerate until you are in complete command of your destiny. Your task is to make the transition from feeling insufficient to knowing that you can exploit your creative potentials to derive whatever you want out of life.

Some career fields that might interest you are medicine, law, politics, consumer services, family planning, education or creative writing. Any of these would give you opportunities to extend yourself in using your creative talents. People need someone who is genuinely interested in their problems, and no one is better qualified than you to render assistance.

You will be a good parent, because you realize how vitally important it is to offer children every chance to mature in their own way so they become self-sufficient adults.

Sun in Ninth, Moon in Fifth

This combination indicates that you will enjoy excellent results in enterprises that allow you to exploit your imagination and creative potentials. Your early conditioning cultivated the firm belief that you could succeed in anything you attempted if you tried.

The problem is that you don't always feel inclined to make the effort, so that you may miss some opportunities. You may feel that nothing is so urgent that it cannot be done later or that there will always be other opportunities to demonstrate your capabilities. This self-indulgent attitude means that there may be delays before you can attain the position for which you are qualified, and reaching your goals will take longer than usual for someone with your creative advantages. You may be one of those who must fail before they can succeed. But a little application will give you the credentials to get established in a career.

The career you select should allow room to grow to your maximum development and give you opportunities to demonstrate your creative talents. Working closely with people, individually or in groups, is particularly suited to your temperament. You have a talent for dealing with people and for stimulating them to excel in their abilities. You will have little trouble getting the support you need in your objectives.

People are probably impressed by the total companionship you have with your marriage partner. You may spoil your children by overindulging them, as you always do with those you love.

Sun in Ninth, Moon in Sixth

All your dreams and desires of what you hope to accomplish are meaningless unless you are resigned to the necessity of working to achieve them. Before you can be recognized for your achievements, you must learn how to perform whatever tasks are involved with a high degree of skill. You should not be one of those who are content to be average in what they do, and the only way to distinguish yourself is to reach a higher level of competence. Your learning ability and memory are better than average, so all you need is the determination to acquire the skills you need to qualify for responsible positions. You have keen insight about people's problems, and once you are trained to deal with them, you should enjoy comfortable earnings. But until you can offer the professional services that people need, stay clear of friends and associates who want you to help them with their problems. It may be flattering to your ego to indulge them, but eventually they will abuse the privilege.

You are suited to a wide variety of service professions, including law, medicine, social service, vocational guidance, unions, research and development, engineering, physical therapy and teaching aids. Your family, especially your children, will serve as the best stimulant to the success you will achieve.

Sun in Ninth, Moon in Seventh

This combination indicates greater success in your career than in personal relationships, simply because you are more focused in that direction. You are stimulated by challenges, and nothing annoys you more than a competitor who tries to intimidate you into conceding defeat without a confrontation. Your striving for significance is ideally matched with the inner poise of your feeling nature, which allows you to assert yourself in stressful situations while staying calm and composed. This ability gives you an advantage over your adversaries, and it is highly likely that you will enjoy success early in your career, especially if you offer some kind of service to the public. This is where you are most effective and where you can enjoy comfortable earnings. Your early conditioning and your emotional apprehension about handling people who become too familiar will eventually pass.

Medicine, law, government service, politics, public relations, marital counseling, family planning, writing and sales are some of the fields in which you could be successful. They offer ample opportunity for growth and substantial earnings.

Proceed cautiously about getting involved in a marriage relationship until you are professionally established. You may want to marry just to compensate for the early family ties that you miss, making it difficult to be on your own.

Sun in Ninth, Moon in Eighth

Because you are adventurous and believe that you can succeed, you probably will. It pleases you to know that you are effective and that people admire your "never say die" attitude. What the public does not know is how much you have to mask your feelings to give that impression. You are constantly apprehensive that your plans may not succeed. Your early conditioning should have prepared you to accept occasional reversals or failures; you know that learning how and why you failed in a particular instance makes you better equipped to handle a similiar situation the next time. This planetary combination gives you opportunities to make the most of external circumstances to gain success and security from your efforts. You have a talent for getting people to be open with you and perhaps reveal information that will be useful in the long run. The energy you expend in helping people with their problems or providing products or services is the best investment you can make in gaining security for your later years. It is important that you not be motivated only by what you can get for your efforts, that you are sincerely concerned for the people who require your services.

Law, medicine, especially surgery, research and development, financial counseling, mining, oil, geology, land development or crime detection are some fields in which you could be happy and enjoy financial success. Failing to develop your creative talents would severely limit you, so a good education is certainly necessary.

Sun in Ninth, Moon in Ninth

You have an unusually strong drive to achieve significance because your faith in your ability to succeed is never diminished. You approach opportunity with positive anticipation, so that you get the results you want even in ordinary circumstances. Your early conditioning may have made you feel overly obligated to your family. Even now, you may have trouble living up to your parents' expectations, but when you think about it, you will realize that you don't really have to. Parents can guide you when you need some suggestions, but in the end you have to proceed in the way that seems right for you. You may have to discipline yourself to stay on course because you are so easily distracted by other interests. You tend to avoid tedious work because your attention span is limited; you prefer work that allows you mobility and self-determination. That is fine, if you develop self-discipline and a high degree of competence.

You should choose a career that gives you opportunities to exploit and implement your fine creative potential, perhaps in medicine, politics, government service, education, investment counseling, journalism, writing or spiritual counseling.

Your mate should have a similar career discipline or at least understand the commitment you have made. Your relationship with your children will be bound with much love.

Sun in Ninth, Moon in Tenth

Your emotional identification with your parents is a powerful force in your life that may cause some delay in becoming established independently. Coping with your feelings of divided loyalty to each of your parents may have been difficult. Probably you lean toward the dominant parent, which could cause some guilt feelings. Let this situation be, for you will look back one day and realize how inconsequential it was in terms of the destiny you must fulfill. You need a champion to look up to, someone whom you will pattern yourself after. The important thing is not to lose sight of your own identity. You don't have to win your parent's support for your career or lifestyle.

You may have to give a lot before you realize any rewards for your efforts, but then you should enjoy very substantial earnings, because you handle responsibilities so well. You may prefer a career that allows you some privacy and yet provides a useful product or service to the public. Ideally you should become qualified for management enterprises, at which you will excel. Government service, social programs, political interests, land development and real estate management are some of the outlets through which you can find meaningful expression.

Sun in Ninth, Moon in Eleventh

There is some discrepancy between your desire for a fulfilling life experience and your emotional anxiety about letting go of the past. Your equilibrium may be unnecessarily disturbed if you dwell on past conditions that cannot be altered. It is better to remember what you learned from your experience and use this information to improve future conditions. Your situation is ideal for allowing every opportunity to succeed in a way that will make you comfortable, secure and fulfilled. You may feel guilty about asserting yourself as your identity demands because your feelings of obligation to your family are so strong, but you don't really have any other alternative. This is your life, and you must live it as fully as your creative potentials allow. The chances are that your parents want you to be more assertive and self-reliant so that you can enjoy a life that is rewarding to you. An education will give you the stimulus to be more self-sufficient about acting in your own behalf.

You may find it difficult to deal with people in authority when you first take your place in the career you choose, but this will fade as your abilities improve and are recognized. Your problems may be largely emotional, and you will eventually learn to insulate yourself from abuses. Avoid getting locked into a career with limited mobility; you should seek self-determination so you will have the authority to implement your plans. Ideally you and your partner should be in a similar career.

Sun in Ninth, Moon in Twelfth

Although you may be more qualified than others in similar circumstances, you always feel that you aren't and therefore are not ready to take on responsibility. The truth is, you are probably overqualified for the demands of most responsible positions. You are somewhat afraid of making a fool of yourself or of being caught without the necessary credentials. What this amounts to is a powerful defense mechanism to avoid confronting a challenge. If you feel you aren't qualified, you should get the education or training that you need. You can do so much for those who lack the resources to help themselves, so you should choose a career with that in mind. Your heart goes out to people who are caught in difficult social situations, and you can accomplish more, even with modest resources, than most people would think possible.

You might consider serving the public through a career in medicine, law, psychology, vocational guidance, nutrition, self-help programs, social service, correction or institutions for the mentally or physically handicapped. The important thing to remember is to find a way to implement your creative imagination and make a substantial contribution to improving society.

Chapter Ten

Tenth House

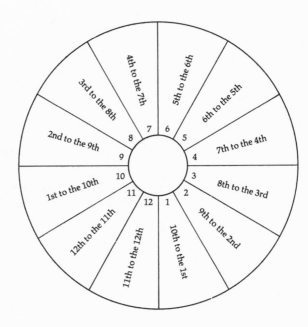

The circumstances of the tenth house and Capricorn, its zodiacal counterpart, have an affinity with their ruler, Saturn. This house represents your chance to prove yourself before the world so that you gain recognition for your achievements. More important, however, is that your achievements make you feel worthy. This is really the end of the line as far as the visible results of your efforts are concerned, for this house represents how well you've mobilized your resources and talents to achieve the public standing you want.

Among the influences you face in the tenth house is that of your father or your more dominant parent. He is generally the impetus you need to strive to excel in your own identity. Through the situations you meet in your developing career you will learn to function on your own, but you will have to face people who try to impress you with their authority. If you are properly trained and qualified to accept responsibility, you should not experience any insurmountable difficulty. Much depends on how well you have built the foundation for your life's endeavors through the affairs of the fourth house, which opposes the tenth. If you have established your own substantial roots, there is no reason why you cannot distinguish yourself in your achievements. The interaction between the matters represented by the fourth and the tenth houses is critical, for unless you can detach yourself from the obligations you owe your parents and transfer your attention to your obligations to yourself, your attempts to gain fulfillment in your own direction will be seriously threatened. This has nothing to do with loyalty, but merely with gaining a true perspective on your own destiny.

Derivative House Meanings

1st to the 10th   This represents the circumstances through which you can achieve fulfillment of your destiny and receive recognition for utilizing your potentials.

2nd to the 9th   The self-discipline you develop to get an education will reward you with the effective resources that allow you to demonstrate your value to the public.

3rd to the 8th   Understanding the needs of those around you enables you to apply yourself in satisfying their interests.

4th to the 7th   Your efforts in behalf of those you deal with give them the opportunity to gain a more stable foundation in their lives.

5th to the 6th   These are the conditions that promise success when you use your skills effectively to gain the attention you need in your pursuits.

6th to the 5th   Applying yourself to the task of implementing your creative talents will bring you the recognition you need for your accomplishments.

7th to the 4th   Your early conditioning may have programmed you for success, and you will succeed if you have established a secure foundation that is unmistakably your own, not your parents'.

8th to the 3rd   A meaningful investment in developing your own ideas and plans will undoubtedly reward you with significant achievements.

9th to the 2nd   Developing your basic resources realistically to a high level of proficiency will improve their value and enhance your status-seeking.

10th to the 1st   Any position you achieve is the result of asserting yourself and effectively mobilizing your resources to satisfy your ambitions.

11th to the 12th   With thoughtful attention, you can make an important contribution to society's needs while still achieving the goals you anticipated for yourself.

12th to the 11th   Your apprehensions about the future can be dispelled if you plan ahead to gain the security you need for your later years.

1st to the 10th   Your strong desire for recognition impels you to seek a career in which you can pursue your objectives in your own way. You will find satisfaction in a responsible position in which others must rely on your good judgment and expertise.

 2nd to the 9th   Your achievements depend on successfully integrating what you've learned to satisfy the demands of your career. You continually seek new information because you know it's the only way to maintain control.

 3rd to the 8th   Knowing what people need, individually or in groups, gives you a distinct advantage over others. With your training, you can provide the services that they require, and they will feel enriched because of your efforts.

 4th to the 7th   It is very important to you to have control over your competitors and the respect of your associates. But you must remain sensitive to their needs also. You want a partner who fully supports you in your goals and gives you strength to persist in them.

 5th to the 6th   Your work is creatively inspired, and you can reach objectives that most people would shy away from. Your enterprise and ability allow you to make the best use of even the most ordinary skills.

 6th to the 5th   You have many plans for your children, and you hope they take advantage of the training you've provided to achieve on their own. Preoccupation with your career may make a dent in your romantic life and be disturbing to your lover.

 7th to the 4th   Try to spend enough time with your loved ones to avoid the danger of becoming a stranger to them. The pressure of trying to live up to your parents' expectations may be difficult.

 8th to the 3rd   Your most difficult task is to admit that you may be wrong and to realize that you must make compromises to win the support of those around you. You shouldn't be afraid to capitalize on your ideas by investing in them.

 9th to the 2nd   You understand how to use money effectively in your continuing development. You know the value of talent, and you are willing to pay well to get help from those who have the talent to assist your endeavors.

 10th to the 1st   In fulfilling your goals and objectives, you must expect some loss of freedom and privacy. Your ability to promote yourself is your best asset, and you let others know that you are ambitious.

 11th to the 12th   You should not form any secret alliances unless you are fully informed about the people involved. Try to define exactly what you hope to achieve and periodically reexamine your goals. You are helpful to many who may never know the source.

 12th to the 11th   If you tell your friends what you want and show that you are willing to help them, they will remain your friends for a long time. Deceiving them will cause immeasurable harm. You will derive much satisfaction from improving social conditions around you, and your security in later years will be assured.

Trine: 2, 6 To realize your ambitions, you utilize every opportunity that arises. You are determined to gain recognition, but in your own way. Having a position that requires responsible leadership will help you feel important, because others will depend on your skill and good judgment in fulfilling their needs. Your enterprising ability enables you to achieve many objectives with ordinary creative talents. For the most part, you truly like your work, and you energize others who are involved in your goals. You understand the value of money and can use it effectively to buy the talents you need. You avoid being obligated to others, because you want to keep control of your own destiny.

Sextile: 8, 12 You generally know what people want, and you offer yourself as the person most qualified to provide it. You aren't afraid to promote yourself, and you are convincing enough to win people's confidence. You realize that you must plan ahead so that you will be prepared when an opportunity comes along. Don't form secret alliances with so-called friends who may be using you to satisfy their own objectives. Being well informed at all times should prevent this. Try to be specific about what you hope to achieve in life, and don't be misled by well-meaning friends. You can accomplish almost anything if you are willing to sacrifice some immediate pleasures. And you will gain the resources you need for security in your later years.

Cross: 1, 4, 7 Your domestic relationships may be strained if you become so obsessed with satisfying personal goals that you neglect to spend time with your family. You could be trying to live up to your parents' expectations, who may have unwittingly programed you that way. Your need to assert yourself and win over your competitors could alienate you from your loved ones. You must expect some loss of personal freedom and privacy when you are in the public spotlight, so be prepared to live with it. One of your best assets is knowing how to promote yourself, which will bring you many gains. You probably want a partner who supports you in your objectives. Your mate's sympathetic understanding of your needs will give you additional strength.

Inconjunct: 3, 5 Probably your children have a high priority in your life and will serve as the catalyst to your success. You hope they will benefit from your experience, and you give them training so that they can achieve according to their individual needs. Your preoccupation with a career may not leave enough time or energy to fulfill your responsibilities to your loved one. Admitting you are wrong takes courage, but it also gives you the opportunity to correct your errors. Your many valuable ideas need development, but you will gain a great deal if you decide to invest in them.

Semisextile: 9, 11 If you assume you can do whatever you want without acquiring the necessary skills, you are deluding yourself, as you are if you feel you can work outside the law or ethical guidelines. Because you are better informed than most people, you can be held more accountable for your actions. Don't assume that everything will work out favorably in the end unless you have planned carefully to make it so. If you treat your friends kindly, they will help you when you need it. You should derive much satisfaction from working to improve social conditions. The chances are good that you will also gain the security you need for retirement.

1st to the 10th You are most responsive to public opinion and distressed if it is unfavorable. You would enjoy a career that involves working with the public, for you feel a strong obligation to help other people.

 2nd to the 9th You may sometimes feel that you aren't adequately prepared to fulfill the demands of your profession, but probably your fears are unfounded. You are more capable than you know at utilizing the lessons you've learned.

 3rd to the 8th Your sensitivity to people's needs makes you qualified to deal with their problems. Your sympathetic concern means that you can serve people very well if you choose to.

 4th to the 7th You may complain about all the work that others expect of you, but you wouldn't change it if you could. You worry because your career intrudes on your marriage and other relationships. You hope your partner understands your need to be involved in a career.

 5th to the 6th You react instinctively to the needs of people in distress and immediately get the wheels turning to give them the help they require. Knowing that you can apply your skills effectively makes you very happy.

 6th to the 5th Although it may be difficult, you will manage to satisfy your responsibilities to your children and still have a career that satisfies your desire to achieve recognition for your services.

 7th to the 4th Your dilemma is to cope with the demands of your career and still satisfy your family's needs. It's possible that you will feel guilty about not doing everything you should in both areas. Perhaps you were taught that your most urgent priority should be your family.

 8th to the 3rd Don't neglect to consider how important you are to yourself. You have an obligation to develop your ideas in whatever way will help you achieve your goals. Serving others is fine, as long as you don't sacrifice your own personal needs.

 9th to the 2nd Your deep sense of devotion to others comes from your early religious training. It is important to you to know that others consider you indispensable. Your efforts bring you much spiritual fulfillment.

 10th to the 1st It may be difficult, but you must not lose your own identity through helping others. But you must also realize that others' needs have a high priority and that your personal desires may have to come second.

 11th to the 12th Throughout your life, you may dream of not having to concern yourself with anyone else. And you wonder whether you will ever retire, since there is always someone who needs your help, and you hate to refuse.

 12th to the 11th Reserve some time and space for yourself, and don't let others crowd you with demands. That is the only way to guarantee that you will have enough time to indulge yourself without feeling guilty about it.

Trine: 2, 6 You have a strong need to be involved with the public in your career, but you are easily distressed when people react unfavorably to your efforts. You sincerely want to be helpful, so don't worry if others criticize your methods. That happens to anyone who works with the public, so don't feel you are being singled out in this regard. When you see human suffering, you react instinctively to get the wheels turning right away to provide whatever help is needed. It makes you happy to know that you have provided a valuable service when it was needed most. Since you are devoted to the demands of your career, it should be spiritually uplifting to know that many people consider you indispensable.

Sextile: 8, 12 No one understands people as well as you do, and your sympathetic concern makes you qualified to help them with their problems. Because of this faculty, people seek your advice, for they know you will do everything you can for them. All your life you will have to cope with this kind of situation. You may dream of the day when you can think only of yourself, but probably there will always be someone who needs your help, and you won't have the heart to refuse. For your own protection, however, it is imperative that you insulate yourself somewhat to avoid the crisis of becoming so overburdened that you lose contact with reality. You have to learn to allow yourself time and energy to use in the way you want; you need to reserve space for yourself. You should not feel guilty when you say no to people who always expect you to agree to help them—it's a matter of personal survival.

Cross: 1, 4, 7 You face the dilemma of trying to accommodate the demands of your career with your family's needs. You are bothered by the fact that your career sometimes intrudes on your close relationships and causes distress to your partner. If your partner is understanding, this situation should not cause too much tension between you. It is important not to lose your own identity while helping others. While it is good that you consider other people's needs as most urgent, it may mean that your own priorities will have to come second. But don't feel guilty for not doing all you can under the circumstances.

Inconjunct: 3, 5 With your skill in management, you will find a way to satisfy your responsibilities to your children and family and still remain active in the career that you have chosen, which is commendable. But don't forget that you are important, too, and that you have an obligation to develop your ideas so they will serve your goals and ambitions. You shouldn't sacrifice your objectives simply because others feel they deserve your attention.

Semisextile: 9, 11 You are probably more qualified than you know, and you will receive deserved recognition for your accomplishments. Because of your natural feelings of inadequacy, you will always try harder than others to live up to the public's expectations. You have a vast storehouse of valuable information that will help you when you need it most and expect it least. Don't forget to put aside time and space for yourself and don't let people talk you into indulging them. You deserve some time to indulge yourself without feeling guilty about it.

1st to the 10th   You dwell on achieving sufficient status in your career so that you will know you have lived up to your potentials adequately. You know how to deal with the demands of your superiors.

 2nd to the 9th   Realizing that your superiors may have weaknesses, you use your training and skills to compensate for what they lack, and thus you earn their respect. You know that the knowledge you have gained justifies your actions.

 3rd to the 8th   You make a point of asking people about their needs and opinions, and they appreciate that kind of attention. You are generally willing to help people with their problems.

 4th to the 7th   Your partner is probably the source of your inspiration for continually progressing to higher levels in your career. Although you do need this urging, you also have to feel that you are free to exploit your potentials in your own way.

 5th to the 6th   Your ability to solve problems is your greatest asset, and a career involving public service would be to your advantage. You enjoy your work and the attention you get for doing a job well.

 6th to the 5th   Your career gives you added opportunities to exploit your creative potentials more fully. You urge your children to capitalize on the advantages you have given them to achieve success.

 7th to the 4th   Your parents prepared you well for the competition you must face in fulfilling your role in society. You know that you must establish a solid foundation before pursuing your own personal goals, which may be different from what your family wants you to do.

 8th to the 3rd   You realize that the sacrifices you make today in developing your ideas are the best possible investment in your future. You have a sixth sense about what you should do to achieve your goals.

 9th to the 2nd   You have a deep respect for the value of money, but you also understand that you must maintain sound ethical standards in dealing with the public. Otherwise, something would be missing from your material gains.

 10th to the 1st   Although you realize that everyone must answer to someone else, you feel that the most crucial measure of success is whether you are living up to your own potentials. Gaining recognition depends entirely on your forcefulness in asserting yourself in spite of hazards.

 11th to the 12th   Always on your mind is the fear that you might not live up to the public's expectations. You hope you can be of service to people who can't help themselves. You usually remember each person who has helped you in the past, and you reciprocate when possible.

 12th to the 11th   You are deeply concerned about fulfilling your ambitions and achieving financial security for your retirement. That is why you want a career with growth potential, so that you can make as many gains as possible.

Trine: 2, 6 You are very concerned with making the most of your creative potentials to achieve status before the public. You will probably choose a career that involves serving the public, for your ability to solve your own and other people's problems is your greatest asset. Because you enjoy your work, you extend yourself and obtain better results than others do in the same capacity. It's no secret that you enjoy the attention you get when you do a good job. People trust your judgment because you demonstrate high ethical standards in your dealings, and they know you won't deliberately let them down. You have a deep respect for the value of money, but you also understand the importance of basic human values in winning the public's admiration and respect. You know that you must maintain an untarnished public image, or else your progress and your material gains won't have much meaning in the long run.

Sextile: 8, 12 Your success is based partly on the fact that you aren't afraid to ask people how you can serve their needs. You are a good listener, and they love you for giving them such attention. Because you show that you are able and willing to help them with their problems, they are happy to pay what you ask for your services. You are concerned about living up to the public's expectations, and you want to always be helpful to people who are unable to help themselves. You are not above accepting favors from friends to get established, but you must remember to reciprocate when they need help in the future.

Cross: 1, 4, 7 Because of your parents' training, you understand that it is important to succeed on your own according to your own potentials. If your parents chose a career for you, you certainly resisted. You want to know that you have successfully met the challenge of your career by using your talents effectively. If you occasionally fail, you have only yourself to blame. You aren't afraid of competition because you know that it will sharpen your abilities. Your partner stimulates you to look for new opportunities and makes you realize that you must be aggressive in going after the position you want. Your progress is assured as long as your work makes new demands on your skill. You know that you can expect little from life unless you assert yourself forcefully.

Inconjunct: 3, 5 You are reasonably efficient in capitalizing on your creative potentials, and you hope that your children will take their example from you and succeed according to their own needs. Any sacrifices you make will repay you many times over later on. You know that making sacrifices is an investment that you can't afford to neglect, as your future security will attest. You are rich in ideas concerning your career, and you usually know the right time to promote them.

Semisextile: 9, 11 The worst thing you could do is lose faith in your ability to realize your goals and objectives. At the same time, don't forget those who have helped you in the past. A job without growth potential would greatly dampen your enthusiasm. Take advantage of every opportunity to demonstrate your competence, even if by doing so you reveal your superiors' inadequacies. They will respect your ability to compensate for the areas in which they are weak. You owe it to yourself and to the public to prove the value of your training by providing useful services.

1st to the 10th   You want very much to be in the public eye, and you know how to take advantage of any situation to improve your public image. You are ambitious without making an issue of it. You get what you want without making anyone angry.

 2nd to the 9th   To make sure of getting the best possible results as you pursue your goals, you use your training and polish to gain the attention of important people. Your superiors believe that you can fulfill their expectations, and they have confidence in you.

 3rd to the 8th   Not wanting to alienate anyone who could be useful to you later, you agree with the opinions of those around you. You know how to make people feel good by conceding to their needs.

 4th to the 7th   You worry about whether you can successfully meet the challenges of competition. But you find out a lot about your adversaries without their knowing it. Your partner may question your methods, but he or she can't deny your effectiveness.

 5th to the 6th   You know how to get along with your fellow workers by giving them the benefit of the doubt in a confrontation. You adapt easily to the circumstances of your job, and you never complain about uncomfortable conditions.

 6th to the 5th   Your love relationships sometimes get in the way of achieving your goals, and you find it difficult to decide which has priority. You want the very best for your children, and you are proud that your achievements allow you to give them the best.

 7th to the 4th   Domestic life does not appeal to you, so you devote most of your time to your career. But you will adjust to family life later when you've made a mark in your career. Having to concede to your parents' wishes caused you some anxiety.

 8th to the 3rd   You tend to keep your opinions to yourself because you don't want to alienate people by disagreeing with them. You look forward to the day when you can achieve your goals by utilizing your ideas as you choose.

 9th to the 2nd   You enjoy the comforts that money can provide, so you want to have a good income. You try to maintain high ethical standards, for you know that otherwise you will sustain severe losses. You don't like to work with people who take liberties with the law.

 10th to the 1st   You know how to put your best foot forward with finesse. You have adjusted to the fact that if you are reticent in your job, someone else will get the promotion.

 11th to the 12th   You look forward to the day when you will have security and can anticipate retirement. But instead of retiring, you will probably take up a new avocation. You enjoy being in the mainstream of human activity.

 12th to the 11th   You plan carefully so that you always have something to do, and you will probably be very active in retirement. Being useful is so important to you that you will always find ways to keep busy and gain fulfillment.

Trine: 2, 6   You know how to use your good qualities to achieve the best results. Not wanting to incur anyone's displeasure, you make any necessary concessions to gain the public's attention and still satisfy your ambitions. When a dispute threatens, you generally maintain harmony by giving the other person the benefit of the doubt. Although you may be unhappy with conditions on the job, you adapt to them without complaining so that no one suspects you are displeased. You love to have the comforts that money can buy, which is why you want to be successful in your career. You won't resort to underhanded methods to get what you want out of life, knowing how easy it would be to lose everything you have gained. You take pride in your ethical behavior. When you know that others are taking liberties with the law, you are upset, for you know you are powerless to do anything about it.

Sextile: 8, 12   People enjoy being around you because you know how to make them feel comfortable. You don't make demands, and they can express their opinions freely with you. Not that you don't have opinions of your own, but you feel that you can achieve your ultimate purposes best by cultivating as many friendly relationships as possible. You look ahead to the day when you will no longer have to be occupied with your career and can turn your attention to pleasurable avocational pursuits.

Cross: 1, 4, 7   You don't find domestic life particularly appealing, although you may be a good parent just the same. You can usually find a way to fulfill the demands of family life while devoting most of your energy to your career. You need to prove that you can be successful in your career, even though it is not what your parents would have chosen for you. It is easy for you to put your best foot forward with finesse. You understand that if you are reticent, someone else will get the promotion.

Inconjunct: 3, 5   You find it difficult to decide whether your love relationships or your career should have priority. Each of these areas seems to constantly intrude on the other. You may be concerned about your ability to satisfy your family's needs and give them every advantage and opportunity to become successful. You similarly use every chance you get to demonstrate your abilities and further exploit your creative potentials. But you don't mind waiting for the appropriate moment to set forth your ideas in planning for your future. You know how to keep your opinions to yourself when it will enhance your position before the world and in your career.

Semisextile: 9, 11   The most negative thing you can do is to doubt your ability to do what you want with your future or believe that you are any less qualified than others. If you develop a feeling of responsibility for those who are influenced by you and realize how much they depend on you, you will be increasingly aware that you are needed. You know how to capitalize on your training to get attention from people in important positions. Your superiors have confidence in you and are impressed with your growth potential.

1st to the 10th   You play the hazardous game of challenging every opponent who seems to stand in the way of your ambitions. Much of your daring results from the stimulating influence of your parents.

 2nd to the 9th   You know that those who shrink from demonstrating their skills are ignored, while opportunities are given to adventurous individuals who aren't afraid to act on the knowledge and skills they have acquired.

 3rd to the 8th   You are quick to give people the services they require, and being first helps assure you of their patronage. Satisfying your sexual needs occupies much of your attention, and you are very annoyed when a lover rejects you.

 4th to the 7th   You want to attain a position of status and power so that you can develop your skills without restraint. You want a partner who shares your plans for the future and supports you in your climb to the top.

 5th to the 6th   You have learned many skills because you enjoy finding new uses for your creativity. Although you may not be more talented than the people you work with, you are more innovative.

 6th to the 5th   You will encounter some tension if you try to achieve your career goals and satisfy your romantic interests at the same time. You work hard to succeed so you can give your family every advantage. You hope your children will follow your example and succeed according to their own needs.

 7th to the 4th   More than most people, you feel the burden of your parents' expectation that you will fulfill their ambitions for you. You resent their intrusion in your private affairs, and you insist on your right to follow your own destiny.

 8th to the 3rd   You know how to dramatize your ideas to attract the attention of important people. You invest a lot of energy in promoting your career plans, and the intensity of your motivation never seems to waver or diminish.

 9th to the 2nd   You are fully aware of your impact on those around you, and you let everyone know that you are a person of substance. You take pride in your abilities, and you know when your efforts are no longer producing the results you want.

 10th to the 1st   At first you may have some doubts about asserting yourself as strongly as you do, but in time you will learn to be more restrained and avoid difficult situations.

 11th to the 12th   You look forward to getting out of the rat-race and turning your attention to social issues. You cultivate friends in unlikely places, but in the long run they will help you. You want to feel you've been helpful to those in need.

 12th to the 11th   When you do something, be sure that you have an objective in mind and aren't simply blowing off steam. If you don't focus your energy, it will be wasted. Don't forget to return favors to friends who have helped you.

Trine: 2, 6 The public admires your courage and your ability to react forcefully under pressure. You don't appear to have any anxieties about challenging opponents in your struggle to reach your career goals. Your early conditioning stimulated you to assert yourself even under adverse conditions, for you know that this is the only way you can prove yourself. Although not necessarily more talented than your fellow workers, you have the gift of using your talents in the most effective way. You enjoy meeting adversaries as an opportunity to demonstrate your abilities. Others are impressed because you seem to have the good judgment and substance that they lack. You work to your limits but rarely beyond. You take much pride in your achievements, and each success stimulates you to go on to more.

Sextile: 8, 12 You know instinctively what people require of you, which gives you an advantage over your competition. There is no lack of customers for the product or service you offer because you are usually the first one to provide it. Your many associates and friends are helpful when you need it, and you understand that some day you may be asked to help them in return. You look forward to the time when you will be free from the demands of your career and can turn your attention to social issues. You like to feel that you've helped people in need become more self-sufficient. You have a strong sexual drive, and it upsets you when your advances are rejected.

Cross: 1, 4, 7 You want to be free to pursue your own course in life without having to answer to anyone for your actions. You seek a partner who shares your ambitions and supports you in your objectives. The demands of your career may cause some difficulty in your marriage unless you try to integrate your personal and professional life better. It may be difficult to resolve any conflicts between you and your partner, because your early conditioning taught you to resist any interference in your plans for your future and your career. Your early attempts to pursue your ambitions aggressively could result in serious problems with superiors until you learn to be more restrained. You must learn that compromise will usually bring you the same results without incurring the displeasure of your superiors or fellow workers. You can't afford to become alienated from those who hold the key to your goals.

Inconjunct: 3, 5 You must find a way to keep your personal life and your career separate, or serious difficulties will develop. You are so anxious to get the best for your family that you may go to extremes in your ambitions, but this is likely to result in losses. You hope your children learn from your example and achieve their own goals for their own reasons. Your ability to attract attention comes from your skill in dramatizing your ideas and plans for the future. You are willing to invest a lot of energy in your career, and as long as you get results, this intensity will not diminish.

Semisextile: 9, 11 You pride yourself on being able to make the most effective use of your formal education, and you rarely hesitate to demonstrate your skills. You know that reticent people are usually passed over in favor of those who show a driving ambition to succeed. But you must have a focus, or much of the energy you expend will be wasted. You might not be sure you have what it takes to reach your goals, but your doubts will fade as your experience grows and you see the results of your efforts.

1st to the 10th You have high expectations that you will be able to grow into a responsible position of authority. Your self-confidence tends to assure that you will achieve your goals.

 2nd to the 9th You are willing to extend yourself to show how much your education has helped you reach your objectives. Probably you geared your training to a specific purpose, and you intend to gain recognition for your achievements.

 3rd to the 8th You are motivated by a very strong desire to satisfy the public's needs, so you want to have the necessary skills. A true professional, you understand your patrons' needs and you help solve their problems with compassion.

 4th to the 7th You find it difficult to live up to your public's expectations, for their demands sometimes seem excessive. You hope your partner understands the pressure that you work under and will give you the support you need.

 5th to the 6th You truly enjoy your work, which gives you every opportunity to grow to the limits of your potential. You may be a bit careless about overextending yourself in your career, so you may become exhausted.

 6th to the 5th You are probably a super parent who overindulges your children in the mistaken belief that you will endear yourself to them. You should let them develop self-discipline so they can achieve their goals through their own efforts.

 7th to the 4th If you are overconfident, it's probably because your parents let you believe that you could achieve your goals without self-discipline. You will know that this is true if you continually fall short of your objectives.

 8th to the 3rd You have a wealth of ideas that only need to be promoted to be useful. You want to invest in your ideas because you know they will bring you excellent returns for a long time.

 9th to the 2nd You understand the value of money, and you will have as much as you need if you put your resources to work. You are wise enough to get advice about investing for the future, and you pride yourself on achieving your goals ethically.

 10th to the 1st Any nagging doubts about your ability to succeed should be resolved as soon as possible. Your major problem is getting involved in matters that are beyond your ability to handle. Prudence should be your watchword.

 11th to the 12th You probably have your heart set on early retirement so you can take up the activities you had to postpone during your career. You should plan for this by achieving the security you need to be independent.

 12th to the 11th You always think that your goals are just around the next corner, which may be true, but the chances are you have already accomplished more than most people in similar circumstances. Don't forget your benefactors and learn to be content with each achievement.

Trine: 2, 6   Your high degree of self-confidence gives you an advantage in achieving your goals. You have little doubt that you can grow into more important positions if the opportunity comes along. Because you usually enjoy your work, you are more involved in developing all your creative talents to become successful. But sometimes you overextend yourself and get fatigued. You should learn to exercise some restraint. Knowing the value of money as you do gives you a further advantage over your competitors because you can make better use of your basic resources to become financially secure. You stay well informed, and you get the right advice before making any investments. It is satisfying to know that you have achieved your objectives without resorting to unethical practices. The chances are good that you can successfully manage a varied program of financial investment if you seek proper counsel.

Sextile: 8, 12   You show quiet enthusiasm in your work, and the people you serve are impressed with your compassion and understanding in helping them find solutions to their problems. If you plan ahead for the day when you can indulge in your favorite pastime, you should be able to achieve the necessary financial security. For you, retirement is not likely to mean total inactivity, for you have so much to offer beyond your career. You can be a source of inspiration to younger people who will follow your example by capitalizing on their own creative potentials.

Cross: 1, 4, 7   Living up to the public's expectations may be difficult sometimes, because you encourage people to make excessive demands on you. Your partner must understand this predicament and be supportive when the pressure seems unbearable. Often you take on more work than you should and feel unable to live up to the goals you've established. This probably results from the fact that your parents taught you that you could not fail, regardless of what you tried to do.

Inconjunct: 3, 5   You have complete confidence that with your creative talents you can accomplish almost any goal imaginable. What you need most is the self-discipline to develop and promote those talents so that they are useful skills. Success in your career depends on this, and there is no substitute for hard work to achieve that objective. You must realize that if you invest some of your ideas in the marketplace, they will yield substantial returns for the rest of your life. Don't overindulge your children in the belief that they will be forever grateful. You could be denying them the opportunity to achieve on their merits by learning self-discipline.

Semisextile: 9, 11   You understand the value of your education and training, and you are willing to extend yourself to gain the recognition you feel you deserve. The proof of any education is in what you can accomplish when you enter the real world of competition. You probably planned your career carefully to waste as little time as necessary in gaining the public status you wanted. You hope the public regards you as a true professional and appreciates your accomplishments. Don't forget the people who helped you get started. You will always think that your goals are just around the next corner, which is good, for it stimulates you to sharpen your skills.

1st to the 10th   You plan ahead for every eventuality, knowing that circumstances will not necessarily fall into place as you want. You are ambitious, and your performance usually proves that you won't let anything distract you from your goals.

 2nd to the 9th   Although you always seem to be in control, you are secretly apprehensive about achieving all of your goals. This fear probably isn't justified, because you know how to plan carefully to get exactly what you want.

 3rd to the 8th   You understand what the public wants because you have carefully evaluated what product or service is most needed, and you try to provide it. You have strong physical desires, but you don't allow them to get in the way of achieving your goals.

 4th to the 7th   You prefer to work on your own, but you will consider a partnership if that will serve your goals better. You don't generally allow your marriage to interfere in your professional life, but you enjoy the cooperation of an understanding mate.

 5th to the 6th   You would rather be a specialist than a jack-of-all-trades. Because you want to be the very best in what you do, you may have to specialize. The public is confident that you will always give them full value.

 6th to the 5th   You are a firm disciplinarian, and your children will certainly feel the pressure of your desire that they mature with a strong sense of responsibility.

 7th to the 4th   Probably you grew up in austere circumstances. This increased your determination to acquire as many comforts as possible, even if you have to take a second job. Your parents' love may not have been as warm as you would have liked.

 8th to the 3rd   You are determined to promote all your ideas to your own advantage. You are willing to do without some of life's pleasures temporarily in order to guarantee your future security.

 9th to the 2nd   You have a deep respect for material possessions as a symbol of your accomplishments as well as an extension of yourself. You prefer to abide by the rules because of the losses that could result if you don't. You rarely make promises you can't keep, so people respect and admire your reliability.

 10th to the 1st   You aren't always sure you can carry out all your plans, because you doubt your ability to live up to the enormous responsibility of success. You achieve through painstaking effort.

 11th to the 12th   Financial independence is very important to you. You want to have security so you can enjoy retirement in relaxed comfort. You abhor the idea that you might have to live out your final years in an institution because of lack of resources.

 12th to the 11th   Your natural fear of the future makes you determined to achieve complete security. You plan to have a nest egg at all times, and you will repay those who have helped you achieve your goals.

Trine: 2, 6 You are serious about your professional affairs, and you realize that circumstances will not always fall into place as you want. Therefore, you plan ahead to get what you want from your efforts. You are ambitious, as your accomplishments prove. Essentially you are a specialist, and you pride yourself in being the very best in your field. The public has confidence in you, because you rarely make promises you can't keep. People know from experience that you always live up to your contract. You are preoccupied with money and material possessions, largely because you consider them an extension of yourself and tangible proof of your worth. You usually abide by the rules in your dealings because you know how painful it would be to lose what you've worked so hard to gain.

Sextile: 8, 12 You understand what the public needs, and you offer them the very best services possible. This makes it highly probable that you will achieve future security and freedom from want. You are not a fly-by-night operator, so you have to be concerned about continuing patronage. Your physical desires are quite strong, but you manage to keep your private and professional lives separate. You know how easy it would be to become so involved in an affair that your career would suffer from lack of attention.

Cross: 1, 4, 7 Basically you prefer to go it alone in your career, although you would consider a partnership if that would make it easier to achieve your objectives. Your determination to succeed probably resulted from the circumstances of your childhood. You wanted to be certain that you could rise above the material and emotional austerity you experienced while growing up. You are always cautious about taking on responsibility unless you are absolutely sure you can live up to it. By paying close attention to every detail, mobilizing your resources and managing efficiently, you will certainly succeed.

Inconjunct: 3, 5 A firm disciplinarian, you won't let your children indulge themselves without taking on some responsibility. You feel you worked hard to give them the advantages you lacked, and it would be a tragic waste of human resources if they did not derive substantial benefits from them. But you insist that they apply themselves as you have. You strive to implement every idea that shows promise in the marketplace. You always try to put aside something for a rainy day when your earning ability may be less. You feel that you must plan and invest now for the security you want for your later years.

Semisextile: 9, 11 Your ability to act on what you know is your greatest asset and proves that getting an education was a good investment. Because you are trained, you don't have to resort to questionable practices to achieve your goals. And you wouldn't feel comfortable doing so, knowing that at any moment you could lose everything because of some legal indiscretion. You look to the future with apprehension that you won't have the security you need. This keeps you on your toes and forces you to make the extra effort that sets you apart from others. Be sure to repay any kindness you received from others when you needed help.

1st to the 10th   You have high expectations that you will achieve your ambitions and gain recognition for a job well done. You pride yourself on being an individual, but it bothers you that your freedom is often curtailed by career demands.

 2nd to the 9th   Your innovative ability allows you to make the most of your training and education, and you are very effective at turning the most ordinary circumstances to an advantage.

 3rd to the 8th   You know how important it is to plan for the future, and you can usually find a way to make the kind of investment that will assure you some financial independence in your later years.

 4th to the 7th   Although you are bothered by obligations to others, you are ingenious enough to fulfill them and still enjoy considerable personal freedom. Your partner must give you room to capitalize on your talents, which will benefit both of you.

 5th to the 6th   At times you seem almost inspired in your ability to solve day-to-day career problems. With your creative talent, you can easily handle the most difficult job situations.

 6th to the 5th   You believe there is no limit to what you can do if you put your mind to it. You work at developing your creative skills so as to attract attention from the right people. Your children are inspired by your accomplishments.

 7th to the 4th   You found it difficult to fulfill your parents' expectations unless they happened to coincide with your own plans. To get around your obligations to your family, you had to become self-reliant as well as self-supporting.

 8th to the 3rd   You never stop looking for ways to implement your ideas, and you take whatever risks are necessary to prove that they work. Probably you are successful in your career because you offer better ways to get results.

 9th to the 2nd   You realize that to stay in demand, you must continue to improve your skills. You are generally straightforward in using your resources and are annoyed when anyone suggests otherwise.

 10th to the 1st   Even though you have a strong desire to achieve your ambitions, you also must be willing to apply yourself and work hard. There are many lessons to learn and no free rides.

 11th to the 12th   It would be good to direct some of your energy to solving the social problems that urgently need your expertise. In so doing, you will improve your chances of future security, and you will enjoy knowing that you've helped improve the quality of life for others.

 12th to the 11th   It is important to repay any favors received from friends and associates earlier in your career. Don't assume that tenure is guaranteed in your job. You must work constantly to maintain your position, for there is always someone waiting to take over if you falter or relax in your efforts.

Trine: 2, 6 You have high expectations, so you take advantage of every opportunity to demonstrate your talents and skills. You don't doubt that you will achieve your goals and ambitions, but you are troubled when the demands of your career limit your freedom to come and go as you please. Still, having your efforts recognized more than compensates for the inconvenience. You know that it isn't easy to keep your position unless you continually strive to provide better services. You pride yourself on being able to succeed without having to resort to questionable practices or unethical behavior. With your creative inspiration, you are usually able to solve most of your problems, so you are more likely to be considered for promotion than those who are less innovative. Probably you enjoy your work, and you add vitality to even the most ordinary job situation.

Sextile: 8, 12 You listen carefully when people tell you what they need, and you let them know that you can provide the service they want. Your efforts are usually helpful, so you will always have customers for your skills. You consider this part of your program for investing in your own future, when you want to be truly independent. You want to know that you've made an important contribution to society and helped solve many of its problems.

Cross: 1, 4, 7 Your early conditioning and family obligations may have limited your ability to take full advantage of your intuitive skills. Even while you were young, you knew you could not follow your parents' programs or expectations unless they let you be yourself. You had to learn to be self-reliant so you could seek your destiny in your own way. You know how to handle your responsibilities so that your freedom is not too severely curtailed. Your partner must allow you enough freedom so you can make full use of your creative resources, which will benefit both of you. Strong desire won't give you what you want unless you are willing to work hard and accept full responsibility for the results. When you learn this lesson, it will be much easier to realize your goals.

Inconjunct: 3, 5 Because you believe in your ability to get what you want out of life, you don't give in to problems. You develop your creative resources to the fullest so that you can offer them when seeking attention from important people. You know how to improve on traditional methods, and the results you get enhance your position. Your children are aware of your success and will follow your example to assert themselves according to their own needs.

Semisextile: 9, 11 You probably got more out of your education than most people do, for it triggered a desire to keep on improving your skills to gain attention. You know how to accomplish a great deal under ordinary circumstances, which gives you a great advantage over your competitors. In your long climb to succeed, you must not forget those who have helped you in the past. Don't assume that your present position is the end of the line. There is always something more that you can accomplish, and you should plan your future with progress in mind at all times. You cannot afford to relax, thinking you have tenure and don't need to work as hard as you did, for there is always someone looking for a chance to replace you.

1st to the 10th   Using your skills to help improve social conditions is an important part of your destiny. You may do this either with individuals or with groups. Whatever you do should require using your creative imagination to the fullest. You may be disappointed in your earlier efforts, but eventually you will succeed.

 2nd to the 9th   You want to know that you are using your knowledge to best advantage. You don't feel adequately prepared for the many responsibilities that will come when you fulfill your ambitions. Because of this, you may put off bringing your skills before the public.

 3rd to the 8th   You are easily intimidated by people's expectations. When they imply that you are obligated to help them, you aren't prepared to challenge them. You are more intimately sensitive to their problems then you realize.

 4th to the 7th   Fear of competition only delays the time when you can meet it successfully. When you avoid a confrontation, you miss an opportunity to learn how to deal with challenges. A partner who doesn't understand you can be a severe liability.

 5th to the 6th   You make the most of your talents and probably adapt well to any job situation. You need the chance to prove that you can solve most of your personal and professional problems. You may not follow the rules strictly, but you will find the answers.

 6th to the 5th   You feel least competent when you are required to demonstrate your most creative skills. You put a low value on your creative potentials, but with a little work, they can serve you well.

 7th to the 4th   While you were growing up, your home life may have been disappointing, which made you feel less adequate than others. You may feel guilty because you believe that you have not lived up to your parents' expectations.

 8th to the 3rd   To make a life for yourself, you had to develop your ideas in any way you could find. This ensured your future security. When you are deep in thought, others may get the impression that you are only day-dreaming.

 9th to the 2nd   In financial dealings, your early religious training prevails, and you insist that everything be strictly legal at all times. You need a financial advisor to help you make investments.

 10th to the 1st   You underestimate your competence in the marketplace of open competition. You are more hesitant than most people in asserting yourself in your career, so it may take a longer time for you to achieve your goals.

 11th to the 12th   You secretly doubt that you will ever realize your ambitions. You have more friends than you realize, but you don't usually take advantage of their friendship. However, you are a friend to those in need.

 12th to the 11th   You probably work better with large groups than with individuals, because you identify with the larger social environment. Unless you plan ahead, your future will be uneventful.

Trine: 2, 6   Utilizing your creative skills to help improve social conditions should be an integral part of your destiny. Although you may be disappointed in the beginning, you will eventually learn how to be effective. It makes little difference whether you work with individuals or with groups, for you can adapt to almost any job situation; your particular medium doesn't matter too much. What is important, though, is to get involved in a field that requires you to deal with people's problems. Your techniques may be unusual, but the results will justify the method. You are cautious in your financial affairs, because you don't want to take unnecessary risks that could put a strain on your resources. Your early religious training taught you not to take liberties with acceptable practices in your dealings. You should not make any investments without getting sound financial advice.

Sextile: 8, 12   People can intimidate you fairly easily and make you believe that you owe them help with their problems. You are extremely sensitive and therefore more vulnerable to people's suggestions that you are obligated to help them. You feel that since you understand others' situations, you are more responsible to them. Secretly you doubt that you will ever achieve your goals in life. You tend to put other people's needs before your own, but this only delays satisfying your own needs. Don't be afraid to accept offers of help from friends who feel you need it. The chances are that you are a friend to those in need yourself.

Cross: 1, 4, 7   While you were growing up, conditions in your home made you feel uncertain about your ability to succeed in a competitive environment. Also you may feel that you have let your parents down by not living up to their expectations. If you avoid challenges, you won't learn how to face them in the future, and you delay the time when you will at last succeed. If you marry, it is important for your partner to understand this problem and give you enough time to achieve your objectives.

Inconjunct: 3, 5   You feel it is a burden when someone asks you to demonstrate your creative skills, because you are so sure that your talents are less than adequate. If you work at them, however, you will learn that they are more valuable than you thought. You have to be given plenty of time to get your head together and make full use of your creative ideas. When you are deep in thought, people sometimes assume that you are daydreaming.

Semisextile: 9, 11   If you doubt the value of your ideas when you apply them, you will delay responding to life's challenges. Believe in yourself and start making a life for yourself. Probably the public considers you far more competent than you do. At first you could work in a field that brings you into contact with large groups of people, which will help hide your personal inadequacies. In time, you will become more self-confident about your abilities and can choose the career you want, whether it relates to individuals or to groups.

1st to the 10th   You are deeply disturbed by unethical behavior, both in government and in the private sector. You secretly yearn for the power to alter many conditions, and you want a greater part in determining the future of society.

2nd to the 9th   You know that knowledge is power and that to achieve your goals you must learn to use your knowledge effectively. With power comes great responsibility, and you must do what you can to fulfill society's most pressing needs.

3rd to the 8th   Your success in handling broad social issues results from your uncanny ability to understand people's needs. People sense that you are concerned with their problems. You also know that money can help you accomplish more in the direction of your life commitment.

4th to the 7th   You are impatient with people who don't have the courage to stand on their own. Your partner must share your dedication to the goals you've set for yourself and support you even if your career intrudes on your relationship.

5th to the 6th   You know how to promote your creative skills when there is pressure in your career so that you always have a solution to your problems. You attract attention from important people.

6th to the 5th   You are demanding of your children because you want them to take full advantage of the benefits you have given them to make a place for themselves. You may have to put off your romantic interests until you have taken care of your career.

7th to the 4th   Because of strained conditions in your home between you and your parents, you decided to commit your life to helping others. You may be sublimating your personal dissatisfaction by carrying out your parents' wishes to improve conditions for others.

8th to the 3rd   You know what you want out of life, and you are determined to get it. You have a talent for arousing public interest in your plans, and you know how to use power to intimidate others, if necessary, to achieve your goals.

9th to the 2nd   Money is very important to your schemes, for through its influence you hope to create a better world, using force if necessary. You make the most of your basic resources to improve your financial state and gain the security you want.

10th to the 1st   With power and position come responsibility, and you know that your gains can be overcome by losses unless you live up to the public's expectations. You want tenure and you will probably get it.

11th to the 12th   You have a deep sense of obligation to the victims of political, social or economic injustice. You feel you have an important mission to help those who cannot help themselves. Your future depends upon how well you satisfy these social obligations.

12th to the 11th   If people in the past have helped you reach your objectives, then it's obvious that you will have to repay the favor. Through your efforts, you can help determine the evolution of social conditions.

Trine: 2, 6 You are disturbed by your knowledge of what's wrong with society, and you know who must be held accountable for the problems. If you had the chance, you know you could help reverse those conditions. In fact, it is part of your destiny to pursue that goal in addition to satisfying your personal ambitions. Your career will give you sufficient leverage to help determine how society will evolve. You know how to solve problems, especially those of large groups of people. You exert the right pressure to achieve your objectives, and no one is better at applying creative skills for that purpose. You naturally attract the attention of important people. By effectively using your financial resources, you can influence the right people to help create a better world. This talent assures that you will have the financial security you need so you can indulge yourself in this important pursuit.

Sextile: 8, 12 You are deeply sensitive to the problems of society and to people who are victims of political, social or economic injustice. Because you understand people's individual difficulties and problems, you are better able to cope with larger social issues. You use any tool you need to help those who cannot help themselves. Privately you feel that you are destined to serve society by fulfilling this obligation and that in the future you must be dedicated to serving others.

Cross: 1, 4, 7 Relations between you and your parents were probably strained, but you resolved to succeed in spite of that fact. You may have sublimated some of your resentment and decided to prove that you could succeed without their support. This is probably why you want to improve the quality of life for others while improving your own life. You are impatient with people who lack the courage of their convictions or who have no convictions. You are happy to help those who are willing to help themselves. Your mate must share your enthusiasm for your goals and support you, even though your career may cause problems between you at times. You realize that your gains will be overcome by losses if you aren't ready to accept all the responsibilities that go with an important position of trust.

Inconjunct: 3, 5 With knowledge comes power as well as the responsibility for upholding the highest standards in using that power. You have an opportunity to satisfy the most pressing needs of society, because of your talent for getting people interested in the programs you start for their benefit. You have the power to do whatever is necessary to have them accepted. Because you are devoted to the task, you will win the support you need to achieve your goals and help others achieve theirs. You are demanding of your children, and you expect them to take full advantage of the benefits you have provided to succeed in their own lives. The demands of your career may intrude on your romantic interests, but that is how you established your priorities.

Semisextile: 9, 11 You have the power to accomplish your objectives and to decide how abundant or austere life will be for those who are under your care. You have the great privilege and awesome responsibility of helping to determine how social conditions will evolve. Don't forget those who helped you when you needed it. One good turn deserves another, and you will have many opportunities to repay the favors you received when you needed them.

Sun in Tenth, Moon in First

This combination shows that there is little you cannot accomplish when your feelings and will to achieve are brought under control through self-discipline. The toughest roads require a superior vehicle, and you have such a vehicle, but you must understand its potential and its limitations. Dealing with frustration will give you the determination to withstand further conflicts, and conflict will stimulate you to utilize your creative potential in solving your problems. In this way you will eventually rise to prominence and have the authority to motivate others to support you in your objectives while realizing theirs. The public will be quick to approve or dismiss you, so you must prepare yourself for the abrasive situations you will encounter. It is important to establish some defense against this kind of emotionally painful abrasion, or your effectiveness will be considerably diminished. People expect a lot from you, and you are eager to reach out to them, but your early conditioning may have made you too vulnerable emotionally to withstand the difficulties.

There are many fields you can choose for your vocation, but you should be equipped to handle authority, because very likely you will eventually have a position of authority. You will rise early to a prominent position in government service, politics, industry, public relations or law.

Sun in Tenth, Moon in Second

Your ambition is stimulated when you realize that there are many available opportunities through which you can exploit your creative potentials and gain a position with greater social status. You know that this will require a lot of hard work, but you willingly accept this, determined to gain the greatest yield from your efforts, for you have decided there is no other way to achieve the material security you want. With increased resources you will feel more composed, comfortable and stable. You believe you can offer the world something of value, and your success, either now or later, reassures you that society respects and admires you for your accomplishments. Your early conditioning was important in your rise to prominence because your parents, especially your father, served as a catalyst to seek the best use of your potentials. Your mother gave you confidence because she knew how much you could accomplish if you disciplined yourself.

There are many careers you can choose from, but management is best suited to your temperament and growth potential. You might choose politics, government service, the armed forces, law, ecology, mining, financial counseling or real estate. The chances are quite good that you will make substantial progress in a very short time. Your spouse may be demanding, so don't marry until you are established in your career.

Sun in Tenth, Moon in Third

This combination can cause some subtle problems whose origins may be difficult to detect. The powerful influence of your parents has deeply infiltrated your consciousness, forcing you to qualify your opinions and views so they meet with your parents' approval. Your parents may not intend to subvert your own thinking, but the result is the same as if they planned it that way. You are conditioned to feel guilty if you don't concur with your mother's views, resulting in diminished ability to express itself. The Moon in the third house makes it absolutely necessary to get involved with persons outside the family, and getting an education away from home may be the ideal way to serve that purpose. The Sun in the tenth shows that you may have to struggle to establish your own authority after coping with your father as an authority figure. Your parents may not understand your need to have your own identity and may not give you opportunities to grow and mature in a direction that is exclusively your own. You should get out on your own as soon as possible.

You could find satisfaction in politics, journalism, government service, news service, broadcasting, design or architecture. Whatever career you choose, be certain you have enough room to grow and develop to the fullest of your potentials. There is so much you can accomplish if you have the determination to pursue it.

Sun in Tenth, Moon in Fourth

Nothing is more important to you than establishing a solid foundation on which to build a life for yourself, secure in your own identity so that you can successfully exploit your creative potentials. Your roots are deeply implanted in family affairs, which may keep you from developing according to your own identity. You may have some problems functioning as a separate entity. Gaining a greater sense of personal importance will give you a better perspective about loyalty to your family and your own independence. If you get an education and take some courses in the behavioral sciences, it will be easier to make the transition to a life of your own.

You might follow a career in industrial management, government service, land development, estate planning and development, real estate sales, ecology and natural resources, economics or family planning. Self-employment in one of these areas might be advisable.

Any problems in forming personal relationships may be attributed to your parents' insistence on approving every personal contact you made. Your shyness about asserting yourself will moderate as you gain greater self-confidence. Achieving success in your career may trigger a significant change and make you more comfortable with people. You will reach your objectives if you realize that exploiting your creative talents is the key that unlocks the door to your future.

Sun in Tenth, Moon in Fifth

Although you may be serious about matters relating to your career, you also enjoy relaxing from professional responsibilities. It may not seem evident to others, but you are a romantic at heart, and you enjoy life more than most people. You don't take yourself too seriously, and you've learned to unbend, even when the occasion doesn't require it. You make the most of circumstances to further your ambitions by using your well developed creative imagination. You should realize that unless you devote more time and energy to developing your creative talents, your professional progress may be limited. In the early stages of your career, you may have some difficulty keeping your personal indulgences in check. You will always have to discipline yourself in personal pleasures so that you can stay better focused on matters that are important to your career development. Your lifestyle may be the envy of your peers, but be wary of taking too many chances without counsel from someone who is better qualified in such matters.

You are a good manager because you know how to motivate people to help you gain your objectives. You could find satisfaction in working with young people, in theatrical enterprises, real estate investments, recreational facilities or any career that allows you self-determination.

You should be a good marriage partner because your affections are reasonably constant, and you would bring stability to the relationship and amply satisfy the needs of family life.

Sun in Tenth, Moon in Sixth

You have the ability to make even the most routine job useful in working toward the goals you hope to reach. You are ambitious, but you don't make an issue out of it; you simply go about your business, knowing that you will eventually succeed in gaining the career position that you want. You want to live up to your parents' expectations, which are similar to your own plans for what you hope to achieve. You are confident that everything will work out as planned, because you have laid a good foundation of self-discipline and organization. You should be grateful to your parents for urging you to accept responsibility so you could capitalize on your creative potentials. This initial programming will be valuable as you become more self-sustaining and gain greater independence through your own resourcefulness.

You may be overly impressed and intimidated by other people's qualifications, but if you confront them, you will realize that you are probably more competent than they are. Direct your efforts toward enhancing your career development to gain the security you want for yourself and your family. You will do well in many fields as long as you have the opportunity to apply your knowledge and creative imagination in ways that will satisfy the responsibilities that have been entrusted to you.

Sun in Tenth, Moon in Seventh

Succeeding in your career will not only bring you personal satisfaction, it will also give you status before the public and thus improve your self-image. You sometimes make concessions to people that are painful to your ego, and you feel that the best way of avoiding this problem is to gain respect and admiration for your professional achievements. A career-oriented person, you will meet many people from various walks of life through your professional affairs. Therefore you must learn how to cope with them, so that your professional development will be enhanced by the support they can give you. Some of the tension you feel with other people comes from your early conditioning about loyalty to your parents rather than to anyone outside the family. You may have grown up feeling hesitant about extending yourself to people whom you were attracted to, unless you were sure your parents would approve. To avoid the problem, you focus your energy on career interests. This situation will improve as you meet more people with similar interests.

Some careers that are appropriate for you are in business management, public relations, sales, government service, law, politics and family planning and counseling. Whatever career you choose should bring you into close contact with the public.

You may marry early to challenge the conditions at home, but the chance of a marriage succeeding on that basis is questionable. It would be better to wait until you are established and secure in your profession or business.

Sun in Tenth, Moon in Eighth

Your sensitivity to the needs of the public is combined with the ability to take responsible action, and this combination enables you to realize your ambitions. You identify with people's problems because you can recall your own struggles with similar problems. In addition to being sensitive to these conditions, you are also aware of your responsibility to those who face them now. You are resourceful enough to take advantage of this insight as the foundation of your career. Getting started is the major hurdle, because the Sun's position often indicates some tension between you and your dominant parent, even though you may enjoy considerable support from the other parent. You need to get in touch with your own identity and insist on having room to grow to the limit of your potentials. Conserving your energy is critical in meeting your professional commitments. This means you may have to say no to people who try to impose additional burdens on you.

You may attract a partner whose demands add to the pressure you already face in your career. If you choose someone who is associated with your field and understands your problems, the tension will be minimized.

Sun in Tenth, Moon in Ninth

You assimilate information easily and are knowledgeable about a wide variety of subjects, which enables you to take advantage of opportunities to achieve your ambitions. You know how to stay abreast of developments within your field so that your career position is reasonably stable. You are alert to subtle changes and adapt to them, maintaining an even flow in your affairs. You must be constantly concerned about the ethical standards that guide you in your ambitions. Examine all of your professional and social contacts with care before you get deeply involved with them, for you could lose control to forces which exert a very strong pressure. Your early conditioning made it seem urgent to not only live up to your parents' expectations, but to exceed them if possible. In general, people admire and respect you for your professionalism, and they may seek your help with their problems.

Some fields that are suitable for you are politics, government service, education, vocational guidance, business management, law, psychology and many of the human services offered by government agencies. Your career should involve considerable self-determination and offer unlimited potential for growth.

You should be able to find a partner who shares your objectives and goals. It would be ideal if your career interests were along similar lines, for if you understand each other's problems, you can help each other maintain harmony in your relationship.

Sun in Tenth, Moon in Tenth

The principal focus in your life is to find a suitable medium for using your creative talents so you can realize your professional ambitions and achieve a position of status before the public. Because of this, getting a good education is very important.

You will probably find it most comfortable to remain independent in your rise to prominence so that you can take advantage of opportunities for advancement without having to check with someone else. You have the discipline to become a self-made person, with no need to patronize people in important positions to win a place for yourself. You have the resourcefulness to win your objectives without compromising your skills or ethics. It seems unlikely that you will experience any major problem in earning a comfortable income if you maintain a sound competitive position.

You may prefer to be self-employed, but there are many other ways to exploit your creative talents satisfactorily and gain financial security. Business administration, politics, government service, public relations, public housing, architecture, the building trades and financial management are some fields that are appropriate for you.

Sun in Tenth, Moon in Eleventh

In the struggle to realize your ambitions and goals, you may occasionally be torn between the desire for stability in your career and the need to be progressive enough to withstand the pressure of competition. You need to stay well informed by getting additional training or education throughout your professional life. Through careful planning, you can realize your ambitions and enjoy the benefits for many years. You are certainly aware that change is inevitable and that you must be ready when it occurs. To be resistant to change is to run the risk of being overwhelmed by it. You are no stranger to responsibility, which is a natural result of the discipline you received during your developing years, and you should be grateful for that. You might help those who presented the greatest challenges when you were getting started, because you realize how qualified they are.

A public career is advised, as in politics, government service, education, public relations or organizations involving young people. In spite of your ability to win public support for the programs you initiate, people in powerful positions may try to subvert your efforts. By standing firm in your convictions and free of the contaminating influence of those with questionable ethical standards, your accomplishments will stand every test of criticism that can, and probably will, be leveled against them.

Sun in Tenth, Moon in Twelfth

Your highly developed creative imagination and your ability to discipline yourself in applying it should allow you to enjoy many advantages. While you are ambitious to achieve as much as your creative talents allow, you are sensitive to the many people who may have helped you along the way, and you usually demonstrate your appreciation. Your concern with helping enhance the quality of life for large numbers of people is commendable; probably you want a career with that objective in mind. You are able to arouse public feeling about social conditions that should be changed, and you urge public officials to take decisive action.

You could find much satisfaction in careers relating to politics, government service, social programs, correctional institutions and facilities for the handicapped. Urban planning, parks, museums, designing, education and social service are also fields in which you could fully utilize your creative imagination and have a rich, fulfilling life.

If you take time to relax periodically and unwind from the routine pressures of your career, your effectiveness will remain at a high level. Don't be afraid to delegate some of your authority to others so you can keep a fresh perspective and clear focus.

Chapter Eleven

Eleventh House

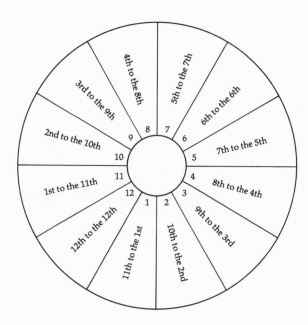

This is the house where your goals and objectives are fulfilled. In looking back at the creative potentials shown by its opposite house, the fifth, you can see the importance of those potentials in helping you reach your goals. While friends are an important part of this house, the influences found here are more significant. You must define your far-reaching plans for the future so that you can develop the skills that can best serve your ultimate purpose. This house shows what yield you can expect from the investment you made in yourself through the eighth house, which motivated you to get the training or education you needed in the ninth house. This training made it possible for you to succeed in your career, and you were rewarded for your efforts by achieving your goal of greater independence and financial security.

It is through this house that you become identified with the needs of the larger society. You might become interested in helping those around you as they seek to improve their circumstances. In your eagerness to share your good fortune, you may participate in activities that benefit large numbers of people, and this contribution will further add to your feelings of self-worth. Through the activities of the eleventh house you can gain much contentment from your accomplishments. If you are fulfilled and can share with others, you are functioning on the Uranian frequency. If you resist or resent any intrusion into your privacy, you are operating on the Saturnian frequency. The first is progressive, while the second is limiting and repressive.

Derivative House Meanings

1st to the 11th   The goals you seek and the security you hope to gain will give you the independence you want for your later years.

2nd to the 10th   Achieving your ambitions and the financial independence they provide makes you more aware of how you can benefit society at large.

3rd to the 9th   It is the plans you have for the future that make you realize how important it is to get an education and to always stay informed.

4th to the 8th   You want security in your later years, and you know that it's necessary to be cautious about investing in yourself and your assets.

5th to the 7th   When you share your good fortune, you make it possible for others to have the opportunity to apply themselves in their creative development.

6th to the 6th   There is never any freedom from the obligation to render a worthwhile service to others, and fulfilling that obligation assures your continued growth.

7th to the 5th   Your need to stay involved in important social issues shows that you care enough to make the effort. This is universal brotherhood.

8th to the 4th   The circumstances of your early years may have made it imperative to make sacrifices to achieve your goals.

9th to the 3rd   You have the opportunity to devote yourself to others and demonstrate how effective your ideas are when you apply them.

10th to the 2nd   The ultimate purpose of the resources and talents that you were granted was to use them to gain any goal you desire.

11th to the 1st   If you fail in your social obligations, you fail in yourself, and the resulting guilt feelings can haunt you for the rest of your days.

12th to the 12th   No one is more aware than you of what must be done to improve the quality of life for others. Feigning ignorance is no excuse.

1st to the 11th Your life is focused on striving to reach the goals you've established, which will provide security for your later years. You face each day eagerly, and you hope that you will always be as physically and mentally active as you are now.

 2nd to the 10th Your future success depends completely upon fully exploiting your skills before the public in your career. The benefits you derive are exactly proportional to your ability to face and deal with your responsibilities.

 3rd to the 9th You are fully aware of the importance of achieving your objectives honorably. You know how to capitalize on the knowledge you've gained so that you can be proud of your accomplishments.

 4th to the 8th It is essential to recognize the necessity of making any sacrifices that are required as you invest your talents to get a sufficient yield to provide for your later years.

 5th to the 7th If your partner supports you in your endeavors, it will be a great help in satisfying your mutual needs. The patrons for your services or products generally approve of you and your manner of dealing with them.

 6th to the 6th You will achieve the security you want only if you are willing to make the most of your talents and skills. Your deep concern about the future may affect your health if you do not allow time for indulging in personal pleasures.

 7th to the 5th You are probably preoccupied with giving your children every opportunity to reach their own goals and objectives according to their individual needs. Be careful not to alienate them by telling them what they should do with their lives.

 8th to the 4th If necessary, you will sacrifice your personal desires to ensure that your family has what they need. They certainly provide the most significant motivation for achieving the goals you've set for yourself.

 9th to the 3rd Early in life you knew what you wanted to accomplish, and now you want very much to fulfill your lifelong dreams. You know how to promote your ideas to derive the most benefit from them.

 10th to the 2nd You realize that you have something to offer the world, and you are determined to make the most of what you have. Financial independence may be one of your goals, and you stand a good chance of attaining it.

 11th to the 1st Your friends help you achieve your objectives. Even when the going gets rough, you can rely on them for support, because they aren't likely to be fair-weather friends. Whenever you reach a goal, you establish a new goal to replace it.

 12th to the 12th It is urgent that you try to enrich the quality of life for others in some way. To neglect this social obligation is to deny yourself a source of rich contentment and satisfaction. You have an excellent understanding of social problems, and you also have the talent to do something about them.

Trine: 3, 7 Your life circumstances are such that you seek opportunities to freely exploit your talents. Because you want to be free from financial burdens in the future, you willingly work at your career to get the greatest yield from your efforts. You look for opportunities to promote your ideas, for you know you can satisfy the demands of your job and have some assurance of tenure as well. Your partner must support you in your endeavors and show appreciation for your accomplishments. Reaching your goals will benefit both your partner and yourself. Your income will allow you to enjoy a comfortable lifestyle while you are employed and will assure you of security in retirement. The public you serve is generally pleased with your efforts because you know how to serve them. You are very skilled in communication, which is reflected in your success in dealing with people.

Sextile: 1, 9 You take great pride in being able to reach your objectives without having to resort to questionable practices. You are sure of what you know, and you aren't afraid to communicate that fact to your superiors. Your ability to satisfy your employer's needs and objectives makes you a valuable employee. You enjoy the friendship of your personal and professional associates, whom you can depend on for support if you need it. As you realize each goal, you immediately set yourself a new one, ever widening your sphere of influence among your colleagues and in general.

Cross: 2, 5, 8 The one factor that may frustrate your desires is being overburdened by family obligations so that you are forced to accept an inferior job that will provide an immediate return. Even with this predicament, you can still strive to reach your goals if you plan carefully. You want the best for your children so that they can better exploit their potentials according to their dreams for the future. As long as you don't try to tell them what to do with their lives, they should appreciate what you have done for them. You may have to make some sacrifices as you invest in your personal development, and you and your partner may have to curtail your spending for a time, but the eventual returns will more than offset your present discomfort. You have the necessary potential for growth and development, so you don't ever need to fear that you won't achieve financial security.

Inconjunct: 4, 6 You can guarantee your future by being willing to work at refining your skills. If you plan carefully, you won't jeopardize your health while pursuing your objectives. Be sure to set aside time for simply indulging in personal pleasures. The need to satisfy your family obligations makes you push yourself beyond safe limits, but you should avoid doing that. As long as their needs are being met and you have sufficient opportunities to expand your area of responsibility, you should feel all right about yourself.

Semisextile: 10, 12 You have all the resources you need to satisfy your material requirements and achieve fulfillment. With a reasonable amount of self-discipline you can achieve your goals. You are lucky to be so aware of the social problems around you, because you have the talent to do something about them. It can be rewarding to know that you have stimulated the people around you to improve the quality of their lives.

1st to the 11th It is a struggle for you to let go of the past so that the future can unfold. Your apprehension about the future causes you to resist change and limits your ability to take advantage of opportunities.

 2nd to the 10th While you may enjoy a certain satisfaction in your career because of the return you get for your efforts, you would be better off to extend yourself even more and capitalize on your wealth of knowledge.

 3rd to the 9th Because you fear the unknown, you usually stay with the tried and true rather than take risks. But you know your fears are unwarranted, for you've come this far without running into serious hazards. Education may help you achieve a more substantial position.

 4th to the 8th You want to be sure that you have satisfied your family's needs so that you are no longer obligated to them. Your anxieties about the future will be lessened by improving your earning abilities, which may entail some sacrifices.

 5th to the 7th You work very hard to convince your partner that you care, when it probably isn't necessary. Your partner already gives you all the support you need to expand your area of responsibility.

 6th to the 6th You may say that you can't wait to retire, but when the time comes you may resist it, for you enjoy being involved in the world around you. You don't need to worry about filling your leisure time, because you have a rich variety of outside interests.

 7th to the 5th Your family is very important to you, and you are constantly worrying about whether they have everything they need. But you should direct your efforts toward developing new skills that you can use when your family no longer requires your attention.

 8th to the 4th Early in life you were conditioned to concentrate on your family and endure the sacrifices required to help them. Once free from this obligation, you should invest in your own future, so that you will have security in retirement.

 9th to the 3rd Because you are so effective in communicating with the public, you should look for a job that requires direct involvement with people. People often tell you their problems because they know you understand them.

 10th to the 2nd You are far more resourceful and qualified than you know. Find a career that makes demands that will force you to utilize your natural talents. If you do, you will be paid well.

 11th to the 1st If you feel apprehensive about the future, you are only projecting your own feeling of inadequacy. You should establish fairly easy goals at first, so that you will feel assured that you can succeed. Then you can enlarge them.

 12th to the 12th Because of your hesitancy about the future, you must plan ahead so that you know what is coming. Your talents will be fully appreciated if you use them for social causes, and good results will be quickly evident.

Trine: 3, 7 Because you are somewhat tied to the past, you deny yourself opportunities to benefit from the future. You are likely to look for a career that will give you security in your later years, but in so doing you lose the chance to increase your security now. Your partner will certainly support you in your goals and encourage you to extend yourself in your career. Because of your effectiveness in dealing with people, you should find a responsible position that brings you into close contact with the public. People are drawn to you, because you let them know that you understand their problems.

Sextile: 1, 9 You have probably told yourself a hundred times that you needn't be so apprehensive about the unknown, but you feel that you just can't help it. However, you can help it by learning more about those matters that cause you anxiety. If you need a higher education, get it, for it will increase your value to yourself and to those around you, especially your superiors. Also you will improve your earning ability and eliminate your anxieties about future security. In the beginning, establish goals that are fairly easy to reach, and as you succeed you can increase them in proportion to your skills.

Cross: 2, 5, 8 Your family is very important to you, and you want to be sure that you have fulfilled your responsibility to them. You should start soon to become more self-sufficient so that you can start pursuing your own interests as your family's needs diminish. You are naturally resourceful and more competent than you admit to take on major tasks. You should look for a career that makes continuing demands and forces you to extend yourself to meet its requirements; otherwise you will not reach your maximum development. You don't give yourself full credit for what you can accomplish if given the opportunity, although others around you are aware of it.

Inconjunct: 4, 6 You enjoy the daily routine of business and activity, and even though you say you can't wait to retire, you probably won't when the opportunity is offered. When you do retire, you have a rich variety of interests to occupy your time. It is important to remain fairly active when your career and family obligations are reduced and you have time to indulge yourself in personal interests.

Semisextile: 10, 12 Some distressing anxieties may plague you during the early part of your life. These worries will be mainly concerned with whether you should direct your efforts in behalf of people who may never know that you've made a contribution to them or, on the other hand, whether you should guarantee your personal security by remaining focused on materially satisfying endeavors. If you stay informed, you will be less anxious about the unknown. Furthering your education will also enhance your value to yourself and your employer and give you more security for the future. You should find out how you can make some kind of contribution to society to help those who are unable to help themselves. Probably you will get greater recognition for your services later in life than while functioning in your career.

1st to the 11th You look forward to achieving your goals in the future, and you endeavor to carry out the plans that will bring you success. You also look forward to the times when you can pursue your hobbies more freely.

 2nd to the 10th You hope to derive all possible benefits from your career so that your future needs will be met. When a promotion comes up, you let your superiors know that you are qualified to take on greater responsibility.

 3rd to the 9th You stay informed because you know that makes you more valuable to your superiors and to your career. You make a good impression on people because you show that you are sincerely concerned about their problems.

 4th to the 8th It troubles you when you can't satisfy other people's needs, and you never feel comfortable unless you have been helpful. You are pleased when you can show people how to become more self-sufficient by effectively using their own resources.

 5th to the 7th Probably your partner shares your dreams for the future and supports you in every way. Your shared goals bind you together in your commitment to each other.

 6th to the 6th The course you've chosen to fulfill your goals allows you to fully utilize your skills if you make a great effort. You may retire at an early age, and if so, you will undoubtedly deserve it.

 7th to the 5th You will probably be attracted to someone who seems interested in your goals. You know that you can accomplish a great deal with your partner's support. You want to provide adequately for your children's needs.

 8th to the 4th You are concerned about establishing roots, so you work hard to secure a solid foundation. This may entail sacrifices, but you know the results will justify them. Family obligations may slow you down at first.

 9th to the 3rd Impatient to grow up, you couldn't wait to begin putting your ideas to work in a program to gain success and security for the future. You don't doubt that you will realize your goals.

 10th to the 2nd The most troublesome problem in your life is finding the necessary financial resources to launch your plans. Any financial advantage you gain now will help you achieve a more abundant life.

 11th to the 1st You don't expect others to give you anything, because you have the talent to gain your goals on your own. You prefer not to be limited by obligations to others.

 12th to the 12th Although you seem to be in complete command of your life, you worry about your ability to carry out your plans. You want to help make the world a better place to live, so you can look back without regrets.

Trine: 3, 7   You are a progressive thinker with your sights set on your future goals and objectives. You have a flair for defining your goals, and you know how to solve the problems you will face. You want to be free from the demands of your career so that you may pursue personally satisfying hobbies. Luckily, you probably chose a partner who shares your dreams and who is eager to become involved in enterprises that will enrich your life together. You have always had a strong urge to be free from financial obligations. You have always known that once you satisfied your material needs, you would embark on a more exciting course, doing all those things that you couldn't do earlier because of your responsibilities.

Sextile: 1, 9   You are valuable to your superiors because you stay informed, and you are always qualified for a higher level of responsibility. You will probably be promoted quite often during your career, and your efforts will bring you the recognition you deserve and considerable appreciation from the public. People are impressed by your genuine concern, for you show them how they can solve their problems. The public is warmly disposed toward you, and you probably have a wide circle of friends from whom you can expect favors if you need them. But you would rather not be obligated to them, preferring to use your own talents to get through any difficulties.

Cross: 2, 5, 8   You feel it is critically important to continually demonstrate your creative ability. Your loved ones enhance your potentials by indulging you in your need to prove yourself. It is to satisfy your family's needs that you work so hard to exploit your potentials. You sometimes doubt whether you can satisfy the needs of the people around you, and you aren't really comfortable unless you know you've been helpful. It is especially heartwarming to know that your efforts have helped people become more self-sufficient in handling their own resources. You suffer some anxiety when lack of money delays your plans. Being financially embarrassed is particularly painful to you, for it slows you down and dampens your usual enthusiasm.

Inconjunct: 4, 6   You focus on achieving financial independence, and you apply yourself energetically to that objective. You seem unusually competent in your work, and you deserve to retire early if that is what you want. Probably you won't truly retire, however, for you have many outside interests that give you much personal satisfaction. You are willing to make sacrifices while you are working to achieve your goals, because you know that you have to establish your own roots. Family obligations may have delayed the time when you could accomplish this.

Semisextile: 10, 12   It is important to you to make a substantial contribution to society, either in your career or as a private citizen. You've always felt some apprehension about your ability to carry out your plans as originally defined, although the public may never be aware of this secret anxiety. The chances are that you more than compensate for any subtle fears about your qualifications. You should be reassured by your superiors' approval of your effectiveness.

1st to the 11th Probably you have cultivated a desirable social environment, but that may have necessitated spending a lot to acquire the right social image. Social acceptance seems to be an important goal for you.

 2nd to the 10th You prefer a career that provides social advantages as well as a substantial return for your services. You may measure your own worth by how well you succeed before the public.

 3rd to the 9th You know how important it is to have a formal education if you want to gain the advantages that come with success, so you make the necessary adjustments that will allow you to get the training you need.

 4th to the 8th You get your cue for your goals from the people you admire, when you observe the benefits they enjoy. You will make sacrifices to acquire similar luxuries.

 5th to the 7th You fit easily into the mainstream of society, charming the people you meet and form relationships with. You know how to indulge people and make them comfortable, which endears you to them. You are an asset to your partner, who shares your dreams.

 6th to the 6th Although you don't enjoy routine physical labor, you will endure it if it helps you grow. You offer to help people who need it, but you resent having anyone impose their demands on you.

 7th to the 5th You look for a partner who is on the way up or who shows promise. You refuse to get involved in any situation that doesn't use your creative talents to the maximum. You probably spoil your children by not enforcing discipline.

 8th to the 4th No one knows much about your origins or your early environment, which you consider personal. No matter what your early environment was, you want to improve on it. Your strong family ties could have resulted in many obligations.

 9th to the 3rd Part of your life plan is to show that you have plenty of ideas for achieving an abundant lifestyle. You are good at activities that allow you to demonstrate your skills in handling people.

 10th to the 2nd You want to become financially independent so that you can enjoy all of life's comforts. You may have to adjust your plans if they depend on huge expenditures of money. You must learn to build slowly and consistently, expanding your plans as you go along.

 11th to the 1st You know exactly how to reach your goals, but you must stay within your limits so that you aren't unnecessarily disappointed. At the same time, extend yourself to your maximum. Be a friend to others, and reap their loyalty in return.

 12th to the 12th You are qualified to make an important contribution to society. Remember the people you pass on the way up, for you may meet them again on the way down. You have a deep appreciation of the finer things in life, which you will probably acquire.

Trine: 3, 7 You focus strongly on achieving a comfortable and abundant lifestyle, enriched by a rewarding career and good friends. In order to fit into the social environment you aspire to, you may have to overspend to acquire the right social image. Being accepted is very important to you. But you fit quite naturally into the mainstream of society, and because of your easygoing manner and flair for communication, you generally qualify for the groups you want to join. You know how to make people feel comfortable, which endears you to them. You enhance your partner's social position, and he or she shares your dreams for the future. When given the opportunity, you prove that you can promote your ideas to achieve the goals you've established. You are especially skilled in dealing with people in your personal and professional affairs.

Sextile: 1, 9 In your struggle to achieve your goals, it is important to recognize your limitations so that you don't waste your time and energy in unrewarding enterprises. You know what you want out of life, and you have a feel for how to go about getting it. You know that a formal education will further qualify you to accept a responsible and rewarding position. You are willing to make any necessary adjustments in your plans to get the training you need to satisfy your objectives.

Cross: 2, 5, 8 You are attracted to persons who seem destined to succeed in their endeavors, and you will probably select your partner from this group. It is important to you that you and your partner have equal opportunities to demonstrate individual talents in your respective careers. You look for situations in which you can promote your creative talents to the maximum. You may have to curtail your plans to satisfy your family's more immediate needs. In time you will find a way to achieve your long-range plans. You must be content to build slowly and consistently, expanding as your resources allow. Much of your desire for financial independence and a rewarding lifestyle comes from observing those around you who have arrived at those goals. You may get many helpful suggestions from your associates.

Inconjunct: 4, 6 You don't generally discuss your origins and early environment, for you consider those matters private and privileged. Nevertheless your early environment stimulated you to improve the quality of your life. You may have had to put up with some obligations to your family, which indicates how strong your parents' influence was. You will accept and endure routine physical tasks if they give you a chance to improve your skills. Though you are generous in helping others, you resent it when people demand that you help them.

Semisextile: 10, 12 Don't underestimate your qualifications for helping improve the quality of life for others. The people you help will remember you fondly for your efforts, and being appreciated does wonders for your self-image. You would prefer a career that gives you social status and allows you to mingle with people who have distinguished themselves by their accomplishments. Don't forget those who helped you in your struggle to achieve your goals; remember, you could meet them again on the way down. You will undoubtedly acquire the finer things in life, which you have a deep appreciation for.

1st to the 11th   You have a strong desire to achieve your goals, and you are guided by common sense. You know that careful planning will bring you the best yield for your efforts. You cultivate friends who will help you reach your goals.

 2nd to the 10th   Because you apply yourself in your career, you expect to be well rewarded for your accomplishments. You look forward to achieving financial independence so that you can enjoy a more leisurely life in your later years.

 3rd to the 9th   You have always known what you want to accomplish, and you have used every opportunity to increase your knowledge. Getting an education was important, for you knew it was the best way to realize your dreams.

 4th to the 8th   You have strong physical desires, and you do whatever is necessary to satisfy them. Professionally, you are willing to make sacrifices to serve your best interests later.

 5th to the 7th   You will work hard to find a mate who enhances your objectives, especially if they are shared. You bring out the best in people by stimulating them to get the best results when they apply their skills.

 6th to the 6th   You aren't afraid of hard work, and nothing can stop you when you apply yourself to satisfy the demands of your career. You may have some problems unless you learn to be more restrained in your physical efforts.

 7th to the 5th   You work diligently to satisfy your children's needs so that they will have the opportunity to succeed according to their own desires. Knowing you are loved helps you be more creative.

 8th to the 4th   Your parents probably made some sacrifices to enable you to reach your goals, and you are grateful to them. You will make sacrifices to fulfill your obligations to them, but you also know that you have to prepare a proper foundation for yourself.

 9th to the 3rd   You want to fulfill your dreams, and you will work enthusiastically to see them realized. You apply yourself confidently, with full assurance that your ideas can be successfully implemented.

 10th to the 2nd   You dislike financial limitations, because they keep you from doing all that you want to do. If you learn to be more disciplined in handling your resources, you will be able to satisfy your desires. Careful planning will give you great returns.

 11th to the 1st   You look forward to the time when you are no longer forced to earn a living and can have greater freedom to decide how to use your time. You want to enjoy your friends more fully and indulge yourself more freely.

 12th to the 12th   If your freedom is limited, you bitterly resent it, which brings out the worst in you. Try to be grateful for the opportunity to show what you can do under pressure. You can help people who lack your innovative ability.

Trine: 3, 7   You hope to achieve many goals, and you apply yourself to them knowledgeably and with common sense. You have plenty of energy, and you assert yourself to get what you want in your career and your personal affairs. You've cultivated friends who will gladly assist you in reaching your objectives, and you offer them help in return. Your mate shares your enthusiasm for doing whatever will benefit both of you. You know how to bring out the best in people in everyday situations, and they reward you by getting satisfactory results. You are confident that you will eventually achieve your objectives and enjoy a comfortable life. You have a zest for making your dreams materialize as you want them to.

Sextile: 1, 9   Because you want to be completely free to come and go at will, you must succeed in your career and be financially independent. With this in mind, you got the education you needed to qualify for more important and responsible positions. As you progress, you dream of having the freedom to indulge in your personal interests and enjoy your friends more fully. Financial independence is important to you, for it will allow you to enjoy privileges that are out of the question when you have to be gainfully employed.

Cross: 2, 5, 8   You demand opportunities to show what you can accomplish with your creative talents, and being challenged by competitors only stimulates you to prove your claims. You give your children every chance to succeed according to their own needs. Being appreciated and loved brings out the best in you. Your strong physical desires demand to be satisfied, but you must also consider your partner's expectations. You aren't afraid to make sacrifices in your career to help achieve your long-range objectives. Financial burdens are especially painful, for they limit what you can accomplish. You may have to resign yourself to earning a living before you can indulge your outside interests. That is why financial stability is so important, so you can relax your anxieties about independence. With some self-discipline, you can satisfy your current needs and still continue with your long-range plans.

Inconjunct: 4, 6   Your parents probably made some sacrifices so that you could pursue your own course in life more freely. You appreciate their efforts, and you don't mind making sacrifices for them now, although you realize how important it is to build a foundation for your own accomplishments. You aren't afraid of hard work, because you know it will make you that much more valuable to your superiors and to yourself. You should exercise some restraint so that you don't exceed your physical limits.

Semisextile: 10, 12   Tension really builds when you can't be as free as you feel you deserve to be, which makes you resent the people who are imposing their will on you. Because of this, you apply yourself in your career to derive the greatest return for your efforts. You want to be able to come and go at will and enjoy a more leisurely life in your later years. Helping people who lack your fortitude, daring and talent will bring you contentment, and you should be grateful for the opportunity to prove how sensitive you are to people's problems.

1st to the 11th   You have high hopes of realizing your expectations and enjoying a bountiful life. This should happen if you prepare a program to achieve that purpose.

 2nd to the 10th   You have full confidence in your ability to reach the top level of your profession if you fully exploit your creative potentials. You want the public to remember you for your accomplishments and appreciate your efforts.

 3rd to the 9th   You are never content with your knowledge or accomplishments, and you continually seek to learn more about the world, so that you can be ready to assume a more responsible position. You maintain the highest ethical standards in your affairs.

 4th to the 8th   You have a talent for dealing with people's problems, but you might not want that responsibility. Your success might come through a profession that serves the public's need.

 5th to the 7th   You are a benign influence on people, and you generally give others the benefit of the doubt. Your partner can make a valuable contribution by supporting you in your endeavors. You want a partner who is as eager to grow as you are.

 6th to the 6th   It may not be easy, but you must make some concessions in your work and accept full responsibility for your gains and losses. Allow enough time to provide the services that people need and expect from you.

 7th to the 5th   Your greatest fear is not having opportunities to demonstrate your creative talents. You must exploit your potentials in your career and in your private life. If you overindulge your children, they might not capitalize on their own talents.

 8th to the 4th   You feel so deeply obligated to your parents that you might sacrifice your own goals to satisfy their expectations. If you overextend yourself, you won't have enough time or energy to invest in yourself.

 9th to the 3rd   You have never doubted your ability to succeed in reaching your goals, although now and then you may have been distracted by family responsibilities. But you are optimistic that you will come out ahead in the end.

 10th to the 2nd   Your greatest liability is lack of restraint in spending. Don't think that you can always realize your ambitions tomorrow. You need to get organized to derive the full benefit of your resources.

 11th to the 1st   You can accomplish anything you want as long as you understand the responsibilities that go along with it. Aim for less and do what has to be done rather than simply talk about it. Your future is yours to use well or dismiss.

 12th from 12th   Your fear of losing what you have may tempt you to disregard your responsibility for helping to solve society's problems. What you can gain from social action is spiritual rewards.

Trine: 3, 7   You hope that later in life you will have the financial resources necessary for a bountiful lifestyle. If you really want to guarantee that this will happen, you must devise a program with that goal in mind. You don't doubt your ability to succeed in achieving your expectations, although you are often distracted from the necessary course of action. Still, you are optimistic that you will eventually realize your objectives. People often turn to you for guidance because you show that you are sensitive to their needs. Your benign influence will help you succeed if you decide to enter a professional service field.

Sextile: 1, 9   Your ability to grow and expand your field of influence is nearly unlimited. You have the capacity to acquire new information, which will certainly increase your value to yourself and to the world. You are always ready to assume a more responsible position, and you don't have to resort to chicanery to achieve what is expected of you. As your level of accomplishment rises, the burden of responsibility increases, so you may wonder how you will cope with it. If you are concerned about this problem, aim for less until you feel confident that you can fulfill your responsibilities.

Cross: 2, 5, 8   You question whether you will always have opportunities to fully demonstrate your creative talents. But you must keep looking for opportunities, because it is urgent that you exploit and promote your potentials so that you will attract the attention of people in important positions. Your abilities are not questioned by those who benefit from them. Be cautious about overindulging your children, for they may not make the effort to exploit their own potentials. Do your homework and learn to curb your spending habits. If you can't seem to get organized, get help from a qualified person. You can accomplish much with your resources and get a substantial yield that will assure your future security.

Inconjunct: 4, 6   You must accept full responsibility for your own losses as well as your gains in your work. Although you might not enjoy the arduous tasks required by your career, doing them will improve your competence until you are ready for a more important position. You are qualified to render services that people need, so you must find time to accommodate them. You are grateful for the benefits that your parents provided, but along with fulfilling your obligations to them, you have to establish your own roots.

Semisextile: 10, 12   You will be greatly enriched if you set aside your fears and anxieties and work to help those who cannot help themselves, thus solving some of society's problems. Not wanting to be unknown, you may refuse to work behind the scenes, but that is precisely where you will reap the greatest spiritual rewards. It would be heartwarming, of course, to have the public remember and appreciate you for your accomplishments.

1st to the 11th   Although you have set ambitious goals for yourself, you are apprehensive about being able to achieve them. Your fears are probably groundless, as you will find if you work according to a careful plan.

 2nd to the 10th   You know you are competent to handle your career responsibilities and get the greatest return for your efforts. Your parents taught you how to make the most of your resources and take advantage of opportunities to make your own way.

 3rd to the 9th   You may be politically motivated with this position, and if so, you have a good chance of attaining your goals. You can compete with even the most qualified opponents because you learned so much from your formal education.

 4th to the 8th   Your career plans probably include serving the public, for you understand their needs. You hope that someday you can prove how effective you are in serving the public's best interests. You must work hard and extend yourself to win public support.

 5th to the 7th   People generally trust you with their affairs, and you could achieve your objectives by offering them a needed product or service. Your spouse will help in your endeavors because you share similar goals, and he or she respects your abilities.

 6th to the 6th   You are determined to be the best in your field, but you should also take some time to indulge in personal pleasures to relieve the tensions that may develop. People often ask you to help them solve their problems, and you don't like to refuse.

 7th to the 5th   Knowing your partner loves you, you will extend yourself in exploiting your creative potentials. Love brings out the best in you. If your career separates you from your family, reassure them that you are working to satisfy their needs.

 8th to the 4th   Your upbringing motivated you to prove that you could achieve on your own. You are grateful for the sacrifices your parents made to provide opportunities to become your own person.

 9th to the 3rd   Your level of comprehension is high, and you learn much even from casual conversations. You are determined to promote your ideas to gain the security you want for the future.

 10th to the 2nd   You dream of a more abundant way of life, and you want to make the most of your basic resources so that you can satisfy your anxieties about the future. You want to enjoy a more leisurely life in your later years.

 11th to the 1st   With a little self-discipline and careful planning, you can achieve most of your objectives. You can depend on friends when you need them. If you want, you can probably retire early.

 12th to the 12th   You fear the unknown, so you should try to be well informed at all times. You are more qualified than you realize, and society can benefit greatly from your efforts. Being denied the freedom to do what you want is most painful for you.

Trine: 3, 7   Your goals are very important to you, and you work hard for the public support you need to achieve them. People approve of your plans, and they trust that you will satisfy their needs. They believe that you can provide the products or services they require. Your partner recognizes how important your goals are to you and shares your desire for a comfortable and secure lifestyle. You respect each other's individual needs and ambitions. Although your fears are probably groundless, you are apprehensive about reaching your goals. You are fortunate to have such a high level of comprehension so that you get something of value from every communication with your colleagues or friends. You are determined to succeed in your ambitions and to gain independence.

Sextile: 1, 9   You have the skill of a politician, but that does not necessarily mean that you will pursue a career in politics. You are notably effective in organizing your affairs and in motivating people to support your endeavors. With self-discipline and careful planning, you can realize your goals reasonably early in life, which will allow you to indulge in personally satisfying activities. You are grateful that you had the good judgment to get a formal education, which has given you an advantage over even your most qualified opponents in achieving an important position. You value your friends and appreciate the fact that they have helped when you needed it.

Cross: 2, 5, 8   It is very important to determine which of your creative potentials to develop. Developing a limited number of creative abilities is the key to deriving the most from your efforts. If you know you are loved by your mate and children, you are stimulated to make the most of your talents. Once launched in your career, you may spend considerable time away from home, so you must reassure your family that you are working to satisfy their needs. You want to make the most of your basic resources to get a substantial yield and a more abundant lifestyle with no anxieties about financial security. By providing a service to the public, you can prove how effective you can be. With your partner by your side, confident in your ability to succeed, you should enjoy a rich life with satisfying rewards.

Inconjunct: 4, 6   You might prefer a position of authority, but you can learn a lot and grow in your chosen field by working your way up the career ladder. You aren't afraid of hard work, especially when you know the public wants your skills. You are probably grateful for your parents' motivation during your early years. Their sacrifices allowed you to seek your own way in life and satisfy your own potentials.

Semisextile: 10, 12   Your fear of the unknown should stimulate you to be as well informed as possible. Then you will realize that you are far more competent than you thought at first. Success in your career will bring optimum rewards for your efforts. There are people in society who really need your skills, and they could benefit if you make an effort in their behalf. You must be aware of how much leverage you have to help people whose choices are limited, often because of unfortunate circumstances beyond their control. Surely you can understand what it must be like to feel trapped, so that escape is nearly impossible.

1st to the 11th   You have your sights firmly focused on the future, with high expectations of eventually achieving your goals. To you, freedom means realizing your objectives.

 2nd to the 10th   You find it painful to fulfill the demands of a career, but you know you will never be really independent unless you are willing to invest of yourself to find your role in life.

 3rd to the 9th   A highly intuitive person, you always know what the result will be when you begin a new project or plan of action. Your insight makes it easy to decide on the right training for the career you want. You are more often right than wrong.

 4th to the 8th   You are conscious of your obligations to society, and you know you must serve others' needs in order to fully justify your claims to success. Helping others get started in their endeavors should be rewarding.

 5th to the 7th   You will probably choose a partner who shares your need to exploit your potentials. Your permissiveness in relationships gives you the mobility you need to prove yourself before the public.

 6th to the 6th   Your ingenuity helps you solve problems in your career decisively. You feel that you must do this to be free to pursue your objectives. Bogging down in endless problems would delay your progress in your career.

 7th to the 5th   You want your children to use all of their potentials, so you do what you can to give them that privilege. When they appreciate your help, you are satisfied. You will probably have more than one career because you accomplish your objectives so quickly.

 8th to the 4th   You are grateful that your early environment stimulated you to make sacrifices to achieve on your own. The valuable lessons you learned from your parents gave you the initiative to prove yourself.

 9th to the 3rd   You demand the opportunity to promote your ideas, and you can generally support your claims about what you can accomplish. It is important to get some formal education so you can capitalize on your creative ideas. You uphold the highest virtues and deal honestly with others.

 10th to the 2nd   Your ingenuity is especially valuable in your efforts to make the best use of your resources. You aren't afraid to take some chances with your financial reserves, because you are confident of reaping benefits from them.

 11th to the 1st   In pursuing your own interests, you may ignore others. You feel that you must take advantage of opportunities when they occur. When someone questions your judgment, you simply go ahead with your plans alone. You know that only you can set the stage to get what you want out of life.

12th to the 12th   Losing your freedom to come and go at will is proably the worst thing that can happen to you. You fear the limitations imposed by society because they hamper your freedom to improve the quality of life around you.

Trine: 3, 7   Your sights are firmly focused on your goals, and you have no doubts that you will achieve them. You demand freedom to exploit your creative ideas so you can prove to yourself and the world that they are valuable assets. For the same reason you wanted a formal education that would allow you to successfully promote those ideas and benefit from them. Your partner shares your dreams and recognizes that you both need to satisfy your personal ambitions. You don't resort to questionable practices, because you know you can achieve your goals through hard work and innovation.

Sextile: 1, 9   Your intuitive insight gives you an advantage over your competition, for you usually know how your plans will come out before you start. You learned a lot more from your formal education than most people do because of your intuition. Generally you know how to solve problems quickly and decisively. When someone questions your judgment, you simply go along by yourself, certain that you will succeed.

Cross: 2, 5, 8   You aren't afraid to take on heavy responsibilities because you know that carrying them out successfully will give you great satisfaction. Always eager to demonstrate your competence, you quickly earn the public's respect and admiration for helping them with their problems. You are willing to take financial chances because you know you won't fail if you use all your basic talents and resources. Being loved by your mate and children brings out the very best in you and gives you confidence that you can cope with any obstacle. You want to give your children opportunities to prove themselves according to their own identities, and if they appreciate the advantages you have given them, you are satisfied. You will probably have several careers since you quickly fulfill the demands of any one job.

Inconjunct: 4, 6   You solve your career problems ingeniously, but you should try not to live up to impossible demands, for that will result in frustration and tension. You don't like to turn down anyone who needs help, seeing each request as an opportunity to improve your skills and take on greater burdens. You are grateful for your parents' training, so you willingly sacrifice to help them as long as you can fulfill your destiny as you choose. You have to know that you achieved independence and financial security through your own efforts.

Semisextile: 10, 12   The worst thing that could happen to you would be to lose your freedom to come and go as you want. You are disturbed that many people in your environment are in such a predicament. The fact is that you can do a great deal to relieve those conditions. You have the talent and ingenuity to provoke the leaders in your community to take legal action to change them. You would derive much satisfaction from knowing you have helped improve the quality of life for people trapped in difficult circumstances. No matter how much you desire it, you can never be truly free as long as there are social conditions you can do something to change. You must be willing to invest of yourself to fulfill the demands of your career and your chosen role; otherwise you will never really be independent.

1st to the 11th In attempting to reach your goals, you are frequently disappointed, so you must redefine them periodically. Unless you work to improve the quality of life for those around you, you may never feel content with your achievements.

 2nd to the 10th You are responsive to society's most pressing needs, which suggests a career that involves helping those who are unable to help themselves. You may be underpaid and perhaps not fully appreciated by your superiors.

 3rd to the 9th You are deeply concerned about government conditions and distressed that the leaders aren't more responsible. You are generally well informed, though you may fail to act on your knowledge. Your future demands that you get a formal education.

 4th to the 8th You must learn to make appropriate investments to ensure security later in life. You find it difficult to get free of obligations to the people around you in your personal and professional affairs.

 5th to the 7th You rely heavily on support from your partner in reaching your goals and objectives. You tend to be overindulgent with your mate because you are afraid that otherwise your love relationship will not be secure.

 6th to the 6th Make a special effort to derive the full benefit from your skills. You may have to compensate for ineffectual fellow workers who rely on you to carry the bulk of the workload.

 7th to the 5th Giving your children all the advantages you didn't have is an important component of your goals. But remember that they have to fulfill their potentials according to their own interests. You are often unrealistic in your romantic affairs and are frequently disillusioned.

 8th to the 4th You feel a strong obligation to your parents, so you may put aside working toward your own goals in order to help them. You may resent them for imposing this burden on you.

 9th to the 3rd You sometimes indulge in fanciful daydreams, creating goals that are difficult to achieve. You have a creative mind, and you could benefit greatly by developing it through formal training. Learn to focus on attainable objectives.

 10th to the 2nd You must face life realistically and discipline yourself to make the most of your basic resources. Being solvent will dispel your anxieties about the future. You hope the public understands how valuable you are to society.

 11th to the 1st Your friends love you for your thoughtfulness and concern. They can help you in your pursuits if you aren't afraid to ask for help when you need it. You should work toward your goals according to a planned program.

 12th to the 12th You underestimate your talents and tend to let others gain the advantage over you. You are qualified for a career that involves helping solve the problems of society, thereby enriching those who truly need assistance.

Trine: 3, 7 You tend to indulge in fanciful daydreams about the goals you hope to achieve, when you should examine your potentials more realistically and establish a plan for realizing your objectives. Otherwise, you may face considerable disappointment simply because you expect too much from your capabilities. If you want greater fulfillment, get involved in some professional activity that serves the public. Knowing that you've improved the lives of those who rely on you can be richly rewarding. Certainly your partner supports your desire for a more abundant life, which you will achieve through your private endeavors if not through your career. A formal education or technical training will allow you to develop your creative abilities. Then you can focus on objectives that are within your limits.

Sextile: 1, 9 You are thoughtful and considerate of your friends, and they appreciate your indulgences and will offer help when you need it. Don't be afraid to ask for help, because you can always reciprocate. You are concerned about staying within society's guidelines, so it is imperative to know where you stand in relation to the laws. Since you are disturbed by current conditions in government and appalled by the irresponsibility of its leaders, you might become active in local or national politics. To do this, you obviously require a formal education so that you are never embarrassed by being uninformed.

Cross: 2, 5, 8 You want to find a way to exploit your creative potentials and gain the satisfaction of accomplishing your objectives. Your children and partner make your goals seem worthwhile and stimulate you to work hard and gain security for them and yourself. Be careful not to dictate to your children the achievements you expect from them. It would be better for them to excel in their own areas of interest than to be mediocre in the careers you desire for them. Because you are a romantic, you've probably been disillusioned many times, and you can certainly appreciate the disappointments your children will face if they try to live according to your wishes. Set up an investment program that will bring you benefits later in life, even if that means dismissing the demands of people who feel you owe them indulgences. Self-discipline will enable you to make the most of your talents and resources. When you demonstrate your value to people, you will win public admiration and respect.

Inconjunct: 4, 6 You must always strive for excellence in your work so that you can demand a good return for your services. Be wary of fellow workers who expect you to compensate for their lack of qualifications and rely on you to carry a major portion of the workload. It is admirable to help your parents, but it limits the time and energy you need to exploit your own potentials and satisfy your own needs. If they have imposed this burden on you, you may resent it, for it will delay pursuing a life of your own.

Semisextile: 10, 12 Probably you will be underpaid for your professional services. If your career involves you directly or indirectly with the public, the increased satisfaction will compensate somewhat for your inadequate pay. You are able to deal with society's most pressing needs, although you may underestimate your ability to do this. Many institutions urgently need people with your compassion to help those they serve. Those who benefit from your skills would be greatly enriched.

1st to the 11th Many kinds of people are attracted to you, from the highly cultured to those at the lower end of the social spectrum. You are destined to deal with all kinds of people, for you understand their behavior and motivation.

 2nd to the 10th Because you are tuned in to society's most urgent needs, you must use you skills to help satisfy those needs. You go to great lengths to become skilled so that you can demand a good price for your services and gain recognition for your achievements.

 3rd to the 9th You understand much about law, politics and the ideologies that guide nations and their people. If you get a formal education, you can contribute to the evolution of society, which will make everyone's life richer.

 4th to the 8th You may become deeply motivated to serve society by working with others who are dedicated to helping people who can't sustain themselves by their own resources. On the personal level, you find it difficult to endure frustration in your physical desires.

 5th to the 7th Your partner is probably sympathetic to your long-range goals and avidly indulges in the same kind of dreams. Winning support for your endeavors isn't difficult because you know how to arouse the public by focusing on their desires.

 6th to the 6th Becoming a specialist in some skill will bring you the financial rewards you want. You may endanger your health, however, if you fail to get sufficient rest.

 7th to the 5th If you make excessive demands on your children, they may rebel. In any case, you may lose them eventually as they pursue a life of their own. Consider them as stimulants that make you fully exploit your creative potentials so you can satisfy their needs.

 8th to the 4th You will make whatever sacrifices are required to get freedom to establish your own roots. Initially, you may have made sacrifices to satisfy obligations to your parents.

 9th to the 3rd You've always known that some day you would have the opportunity to go after the goals you selected early in life. You are always eager to prove yourself to the world, and you pursue your ideals with devotion.

 10th to the 2nd You want to be financially independent so you can further your dreams. You work hard to use your resources fully. You want to be recognized in your field for your values and your good judgment in serving others.

 11th to the 1st You willingly extend yourself to reach your goals, knowing they might escape unless you remain strictly focused on them. You demand the freedom to do whatever is necessary to make a better life for others.

 12th to the 12th Be careful about the people you associate with and avoid anyone whose motivations are suspect. Stop, look and listen for evidence that will force you to change your course. If you are sufficiently alarmed by the predicament of people in need, you will find ways to solve their problems.

Trine: 3, 7 In your struggle to achieve your goals, you will attract many kinds of people, some highly cultured and some at the lower end of the social ladder. You are drawn to this diversity because you are equipped to deal with it. In fact part of your destined role in life should involve concern for society and its evolution. You can help bring about favorable evolutionary principles, which will benefit individuals and groups. You understand what motivates large masses of people, and you know how to stimulate progress where apathy prevails. Your partner should sympathize with your objectives and cooperate in your endeavors. You probably chose someone who is happy to work with you on your plans. In your eagerness to prove yourself, you grasp at every opportunity to exploit the ideas you put forth. You are devoted to seeking a better life for yourself and others.

Sextile: 1, 9 You have a keen perception of what's wrong with society and the world, and you should get a good education so that you can take action to solve society's problems. You aren't afraid of the demands of your career, because you know that the results will make the sacrifice worthwhile. You know that you must stay focused on your goals, adapting as the situation warrants. You demand freedom to do whatever is necessary to make life richer for everyone.

Cross: 2, 5, 8 Try not to make severe demands on your children. They are likely to rebel or submit temporarily, biding their time until they are independent. If you think about it, you will realize that they give you the opportunity to exploit your creative potentials and give them what they need. In looking for ways to fulfill your dreams, you may align yourself with others who are dedicated to serving the needs of people who can't make full use of their resources. Although you may not suffer greatly when your career is beset by delays and problems, in your personal life you find it difficult to endure frustration of your physical desires. Eventually you want to have financial leverage to further your goals, so you work hard to derive as great a yield from your assets as you can. When others appreciate your effectiveness in satisfying their needs, you feel truly rewarded.

Inconjunct: 4, 6 Though you may have been delayed in setting your own course because of obligations to your family, you persisted, knowing that in time this frustration would be relieved. You accept the necessity of sacrifice while building toward your goals. Becoming a specialist in some area will hasten the time when you achieve what you desire. Be sure to get adequate rest, and don't let your obsession with accomplishment endanger your health.

Semisextile: 10, 12 Carefully examine the credentials of the people you associate with, or you run the risk of losing what you have gained. You attract all kinds of people, but you should try to be selective. Society can benefit greatly from your skills if you choose to make a contribution. If you are alarmed enough at the predicament of many people, you will do what you can to improve conditions. Your skills qualify you to take on many tasks relating to social improvement, and you would be well paid for your services. Appreciation and recognition are almost certain if you work privately or professionally in this effort.

Sun in Eleventh, Moon in First

Your moods fluctuate quite a lot, varying from emotionally high to passively low. Because of this temperamental condition, you need the company of people who understand you. It is reassuring to have friends you can depend on when you occasionally need their support. You may be overly preoccupied with personal matters when you should direct your attention to external affairs. Your feelings of insecurity may have developed early in life, when doing what your parents expected meant curtailing your personal desires. This pattern may have made it more difficult to establish an independent life for yourself. Your future success depends on breaking with the past, which restrains you, and establishing what you owe yourself.

You can find a satisfactory career in fields such as communications, broadcasting, journalism, social service, public relations, education and perhaps, the ministry. Any of these professions would bring you into close contact with people who need your sympathetic understanding. Knowing you have been helpful can be enriching.

Unless you are mentally and emotionally composed, you should avoid marrying early to compensate for parental insufficiency. Your partner should realize how important it is that you have the opportunity to succeed or fail on your own terms.

Sun in Eleventh, Moon in Second

There is a basic conflict between your desire to achieve your goals and your habit of holding onto circumstances that give you security. It is extremely difficult to have both without making some concessions. Your purpose should be to gain dominion over your physical circumstances so they no longer limit your development. Emotionally, you feel it is precarious to take risks with what you have and assume that the future will take care of itself. The future won't take care of itself, of course; you must develop a program for reaching your goals and then act decisively. Your early training should have prepared you to make the best use of your resources; if you don't, time will reduce them until they are completely inadequate to sustain you.

You will probably choose a career that offers high earnings and very little danger of loss. Some suitable professions are financial counseling, medicine, law, politics, government service or education. Tenure was probably established by someone with this combination and, while it has advantages, it sometimes results in apathy.

Sun in Eleventh, Moon in Third

This combination shows that you understand the importance of keeping abreast of current events. You eagerly participate in the affairs of your environment, and this gives your life added meaning. Your progressive thinking means that you are focused on developments that will one day enrich society with greater privileges and opportunities. You rarely look to the past, but when you do you are grateful for the freedom you now enjoy. You want everyone to benefit from your experience, so you willingly share what you've learned with anyone who is interested. You are probably more free in your attitudes than most people are; you understand how easy it is to fall victim to the desire for material possessions and be dominated by the responsibility they impose. Although you may have been taught to feel responsible for your parents' welfare, that did not deter you from exploiting your creative potentials in your own behalf. You value your roots, but only as the foundation for your life.

You should choose a career that brings you into the center of human activity, where your talent for effective communication will have results. Your temperament seems well suited to a career in politics, government service, public relations, writing, education, broadcasting, news analysis or world affairs. The joys of your marriage will last throughout the years.

Sun in Eleventh, Moon in Fourth

You have to resolve some limitations before you can be comfortable in pursuing the kind of life that suits your identity. The main issue is coping with your responsibilities to family, which your parents consider your first priority. If you are a rebel, it is probably with good reason, since no one else should determine your priorities for you. Your first attempts to establish your own identity may be filled with frustration, but you must persist, or your future holds little promise. Education and training will increase your career options. It is important to develop your creative potentials into skills that will allow you to succeed in your career. Success will stimulate further development and give you some assurance of reaching your goals.

Although you are basically friendly, you may be apprehensive about forming close relationships. Much depends on your ability to loosen the emotional ties to your family and gravitate toward people you meet socially. To enhance this development, you might consider a career in public relations or some other field that requires public contact, such as family counseling, especially with children and young adults, creative writing, vocational guidance, real estate or private business endeavors.

Sun in Eleventh, Moon in Fifth

The circumstances and conditioning of your formative years made it comparatively easy for you to express yourself. You enjoy people, and they feel comfortable with you, so you can have a reasonably active social life if you want to. Because your parents offered you certain advantages that others lack, you may be rather spoiled and have neglected developing your creative potentials. It is essential to discipline yourself and work at gaining the skills you need in a career. This planetary combination creates problems in earning a living, because you tend to give personal pleasures more attention than they deserve, thereby sacrificing valuable time and energy that should be devoted to career development. But the chances are good that you will develop skills because you enjoy challenges, and you know you can't succeed competitively otherwise. Your friends and associates will support you, and they may provide some opportunities, even though you like to think you can reach your goals without any help.

You might consider careers in the creative or performing arts, working with young people or children, in recreational enterprises, professional sports, investment in land development, real estate or your own business. You should enjoy a good marriage, and your children will form the nucleus of your success. You are a romantic, and your relationship with your children will bring you much happiness throughout your life.

Sun in Eleventh, Moon in Sixth

Your principal focus should be developing skills so that you will not have to worry about security in your later years. Your parents probably taught you how necessary it is to develop your creative potentials and learn the skills that will allow you to reach your goals. You enjoy being in the mainstream of social activity, but you often attract people who want favors from you. Not wanting to appear selfish or reticent, you usually give in to them, only to feel annoyed later for not having the courage to say no. Be grateful for the opportunity to help people with their problems, because it is the best investment you can make in reaching the goals you've established. But learn how to discriminate between people who genuinely need your help and those who are using you to compensate for their unwillingness to help themselves.

There is no better way to realize your hopes for the future than to follow a career that allows you to make a worthwhile contribution to society. Social service, programs for the needy, teaching aids, vocational guidance and ecological systems management are some fields to consider. If your mate is similarly concerned and shares your enthusiasm, your relationship should be a contented one with many rewarding experiences.

Sun in Eleventh, Moon in Seventh

Probably you will reach most of your goals because you know how to take advantage of opportunities. People are impressed when you show your concern that they succeed in their objectives. You are reasonably confident that you have the talent to gain a secure position in your career, and you offer guidelines to help others promote their creative potentials to their advantage. At the same time, you may have some problems in forming satisfactory personal relationships because of parental conditioning. Their genuine concern for the company you kept when you were younger might persist into your adult years, but now it is interference.

Once you learn to judge people and situations, you should be able to handle the demands of a career. Public relations, government service, sales, law, marriage counseling and psychology are some of the fields that might appeal to you and would allow you to use your creative talents fully. You should develop enough security in your own identity to enjoy successful relationships with the people you deal with personally or professionally, and your marriage should be happy as well.

Sun in Eleventh, Moon in Eighth

Your ability to succeed in your career and in efforts before the public depends on being willing to make some sacrifices. You should focus your attention on providing services or products that will satisfy people's needs. The key to your future lies in taking advantage of the opportunities people give you to express your creative talents in their behalf while satisfying your own material needs. Through this kind of mutual service you can realize your ambitions and reach your goals. In spite of the favorable environment provided by your parents, which allowed you to enjoy success early in life, you are easily distracted by personal indulgences, which may cause delays. The frustrations that may develop in relationships are probably the result of your emotional sensitivity, which makes you vulnerable when someone rejects your attentions.

Some fields that are suitable to your temperament and creative potential are financial counseling, medical research, social security or medicare programs, crime detection and insurance. These are only suggestions, but there are many variations of these that would be equally satisfactory. With the appropriate education or training you should do well in any of these careers and enjoy the satisfaction they bring.

Sun in Eleventh, Moon in Ninth

Your ability to absorb unlimited amounts of information on a wide variety of subjects indicates that very likely you will reach your anticipated goals. You know how to apply the knowledge you've gained to succeed in your career, and getting a high return for your efforts gives you the security you want for the future. You have high expectations for the future, and this is consistent with your ability to exploit your potentials and derive the greatest gain from them. People often engage you in conversation, and your talent for communication is an important point in your favor. You awaken people to greater awareness of their own potential and stimulate them to develop according to your suggestions. Some of your success may be the result of your dominant parent's influence, especially your father, who, you feel, has some doubt about your ability and resourcefulness. Don't worry about getting his approval; you owe it to yourself to see your own dreams take form and have the satisfaction of a job well done.

Psychology, law, education, writing, foreign affairs and vocational guidance are some of the fields in which you could excel and gain public recognition for your accomplishments. The person you marry should be similarly motivated in offering urgently needed services to the public. If your careers can be combined, the rewards gained and the benefits offered for all would be sensational.

Sun in Eleventh, Moon in Tenth

Your emotional vulnerability makes it absolutely necessary to get the best possible education so you can cope with the pressure of competition in getting established professionally. Without the insulating defense that knowledge provides, you may find that abrasive, challenging situations may be overpowering. Some of your apprehension may be the result of parental conditioning that taught you to be reticent about taking on responsibilities unless you were absolutely sure you could handle them. But remember, "Nothing ventured, nothing gained," so you must find a way to be more assertive once you've defined your objectives. Freedom, which is so precious to you, can be achieved by developing the skills that will enable you to succeed in your career.

The career you choose may cause some problems in your marriage, because you may have to be away from home more than your mate and children care to endure. You must establish your priorities and be convincing when you have to be away, for you need their support to perform at your best. You might consider a career in public relations, government service, business management, sales, education or politics. The important factor is that there be growth potential in whatever career you choose.

Sun in Eleventh, Moon in Eleventh

You are proud of the fact that you are in command of your destiny and that you don't allow anyone to restrict you. This positive outlook is admirable, if you also extend yourself to achieve success in your ambitions. You have a lot going for you, not the least of which is confidence in your ability to succeed. You look back only to learn from your mistakes, so that you don't repeat them in the future. Your parents may have programmed you to assume that you should live up to their expectations, but that was difficult for you to accept when you thought seriously about it. You know that you could never follow in someone else's footsteps, even if they were your parents'. Your rebellious nature made it necessary to find a way to fulfill the demands of your own identity, even if that meant sacrificing favors from your parents.

If you have already reached this decision, you are ready to take on the responsibilities defined by the career you choose. You should consider a profession that involves you with social conditions that you are familiar with. A career in managing social programs, politics, law, youth enterprises, recreational activities, financial counseling or foreign affairs can give you the excitement and mobility you need for success.

Sun in Eleventh, Moon in Twelfth

Reaching the goals you have set depends largely on improving your self-image so that you feel you deserve them. Your creative talents can allow you to enjoy a fulfilling life if you get the right training. You shouldn't blame your parents for your problems in getting started on a career that is satisfying to you and rewarding to others, for your early environment allowed you to express your creative imagination. You may feel that you owe your parents so much that you must put a low priority on your personal interests. Unless you change that attitude, you will let precious time pass without focusing on what you owe yourself. Your intellectual awareness of social injustice provokes a compassionate response, suggesting that you might work in an enterprise that offers solutions to social problems. Once you get involved and realize how effective your contribution can be, you will have the foundation on which you can build a career that is enriching for you and for those you serve. You may encounter some painful situations, which you can learn to handle by being more objective.

You should select a career that makes sufficient demands on you and that allows you to use your creative potentials, including work in hospitals, correctional facilities, programs for people who are deaf, blind or mute, medicine, physical therapy or pastoral care, where understanding and compassion are critical.

Chapter Twelve

Twelfth House

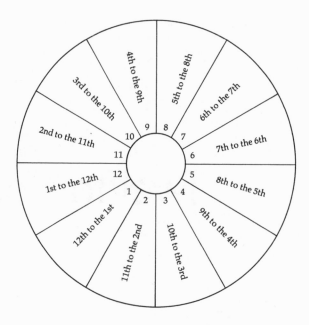

This house pertains to your social responsibilities and the contributions you make to enhance the quality of life for others. This house shows the spiritual debts carried over from previous life experiences, which may haunt you on occasion as you observe injustices in your environment or throughout the world. This house represents the gnawing feelng you have when you hear about individuals who are caught in physically painful situations or who must endure dehumanizing conditioning because of social, political, economic or religious restraints. This house stimulates you to respond with compassion or to abdicate your responsibility if you are passively disposed. These are the circumstances that activate your imagination with divine inspiration to find ways to cope with these problems. All of your unresolved problems lie here, buried under the debris of consciousness.

But the twelfth house also contains many hidden resources, which are often denied you because they are buried with the unpleasant facts about yourself that you cannot face. When you consent to help someone who cannot help himself, you are not only doing a service, you are also dealing with these repressed fears and anxieties. You may be required to do something unpleasant, perhaps quietly and without fanfare. The relief you feel in doing this comes not only for helping someone else but also for repaying an inner debt that subconsciously disturbed you. If you keep its contents bottled up and unresolved, the twelfth house can intrude on your need to assert yourself as aggressively as you should through the first house.

Derivative House Meanings

1st to the 12th   These are the circumstances that you feel insecure about, for you underestimate your ability to make an important social contribution.

2nd to the 11th   You understand how to deal with social problems, and you have the necessary resources to help those who need it the most.

3rd to the 10th   You must consider carefully whether you can accept the loss of personal privacy when you extend yourself in your ambitions.

4th to the 9th   If you fail to get the training you need, you must accept relative obscurity because you will be unprepared for responsibility.

5th to the 8th   You might choose to work quietly behind the scenes in your endeavors, and in that case low visibility might be acceptable to you.

6th to the 7th   You could decide that your best contribution to the world is the services you provide rather than the attention you get for them.

7th to the 6th   The low value you place on your abilities forces you to really apply yourself in developing additional skills so you can feel competent.

8th to the 5th   You may choose to make sacrifices so that your children will have the opportunity to achieve what they want with their lives.

9th to the 4th   You are devoted to those who cared for you while you were growing up, and you show your gratitude by maintaining them in their needs.

10th to the 3rd   You should express yourself more openly; otherwise, the world may never benefit from your imaginative ideas and creative inspiration.

11th to the 2nd   You can gain much by using your resources in some useful endeavor that will give you the security you want for your retirement.

12th to the 1st   One of your highest priorities is taking advantage of your hidden resources and knowing without a doubt that you can succeed.

1st to the 12th   You can fulfill your own needs by using your ability to serve others. Making a contribution that improves the quality of life for others will allow you to reach the limits of your potential. You may have to maintain a low profile in your achievements.

 2nd to the 11th   Everything you do is based on a plan for maximizing your output, and you expect a high yield for your efforts. Reaching your goals will bring you security in your later years and freedom from financial anxiety. You know how to use your friends' resources for the benefit of all.

 3rd to the 10th   You secretly plan how to promote your ideas for the greatest gain. You are always looking for better ways to use your creative imagination.

 4th to the 9th   Not being able to come and go as you please is painful for you, but that will motivate you to get a higher education. You prefer to work independently, but to gain that privilege, you must get as much training as possible.

 5th to the 8th   You keep your personal life out of the spotlight, for you insist on your right to privacy. You know how to successfully exploit your investments for additional profit.

 6th to the 7th   Your partner should know when to get involved in your pursuits and when to let you be by yourself. It would be ideal if your mate sympathized with your objectives and worked with you to achieve them.

 7th to the 6th   You must find ways to translate your imaginative ideas into worthwhile activity. Your career may cause some problems in personal relationships if your partner resents the time and attention you devote to it.

 8th to the 5th   It may not be easy to find the best way to capitalize on your creative talents so that they are a worthwhile investment of your time and energy. Luckily you keep your personal and professional affairs separate.

 9th to the 4th   You understand that you must establish your own roots and reach your goals entirely on your own innovative talents. But you can't do everything yourself, so you obtain the services of people who are qualified in their own fields.

 10th to the 3rd   You have thought a great deal about finding the right focus for your energies to achieve maximum results from your creative ideas. If you get to the top in your field, it will be through careful planning and meticulous work.

 11th to the 2nd   Whether or not you reach your goals depends on how much effort and ingenuity you apply in making full use of your resources. If you persist in this effort, you certainly should become financially independent.

 12th to the 1st   Your greatest drawback is in failing to recognize your potentials. When you promote yourself aggressively, you will emerge from obscurity and take your place among those who are making an important social contribution. You can either extend yourself before the public or remain behind the scenes.

Trine: 4, 8 You can achieve significance and successfully exploit your creative potentials if you use your skills for some cause that improves the quality of life for others. You may have to maintain a low profile, but that should afford you privacy to come and go freely according to the demands of your work. You need to go your own way in your career, so you can grow into increasing opportunities to demonstrate your skills. You invest your resources as necessary, and you expect a favorable return. An imaginative and creative person, you realize you can't do everything yourself, so you obtain the services you need from people who are qualified in their fields. It is important to establish your own roots to prove to yourself that you can achieve on your own. You keep your private life separate from your professional affairs, rarely allowing one to interfere with the other.

Sextile: 2, 10 Your career allows you to utilize your ideas in a program designed to satisfy your need for personal security. You need to know that you are independent and that you can extend your field of influence when the opportunity comes up. You see what goals can be achieved by capitalizing on your resources, and you have the focus and determination to pursue your objectives with consistent effort. Your ability to improve your financial condition is unlimited, and you have the imagination required to succeed where others fail. Success inspires you to even greater achievements.

Cross: 3, 6, 9 You will always be challenged to find worthwhile ways to use your skills creatively to get the results you want. You will have to be very discriminating in handling challenging situations, which may occur often in your career. This may cause some problems if your partner resents the time and attention you give to your professional interests. Getting an education will enable you to define your goals and objectives and decide on what training you need to pursue them. You have always known that you have the potential for success, and you spend much time formulating plans for making the most of your creative ideas. Success depends on paying attention to all the details of a project, so that you know the results in advance.

Inconjunct: 5, 7 You must invest in your creative potentials if you want to derive any benefits from them, and you should establish priorities in your professional and personal objectives. It's simply a matter of deciding which is more urgent. Your career may have to take precedence over personal considerations, for that requires the greatest coordination of your skills. Succeeding in the marketplace also satisfies your need for gainful employment and security. Ideally, your partner should get involved in your career, but he or she should also realize that you need some time to be alone with your thoughts. A sympathetic mate will stimulate you to greater achievements.

Semisextile: 1, 11 Failure to recognize your potentials can be a serious liability. You can succeed if you promote your skills aggressively. Obscurity in your developing years doesn't matter if you know your efforts are appreciated by those who benefit from them. You might prefer to keep a low profile so that you can have a private life away from the public eye. At the same time you will know you've made a significant contribution to improving the quality of life for other people. You can satisfy your own needs when you work to serve others.

1st to the 12th   Your overactive imagination creates fantasies from ordinary circumstances. You are extremely sensitive to environmental conditions, but many of your reactions are probably inaccurate. Still, your creative gifts are considerable.

2nd to the 11th   Your friends probably take advantage of your eagerness to help, but with your great compassion, you can render valuable service to others. You may have some doubts that you can achieve your goals.

3rd to the 10th   You spend much time pondering what to do with your life and how to establish yourself in a satisfying and worthwhile career. Try not to compare your skills with other people's, because that will intimidate you further.

4th to the 9th   It is critical that you get some formal education or training so you can prove your professional abilities. You want the same career privileges that others enjoy. A service-oriented profession would be well suited to you.

5th to the 8th   All your potential means little unless you willingly invest the time and energy to develop it into a skill that the public will pay for. However, it is easy for you to neglect this task in favor of more self-satisfying pursuits.

6th to the 7th   People will seek your help when they need direction in their affairs. You can offer services that the public requires, and they will appreciate your help in showing them how to be more successful.

7th to the 6th   Rather than assume that you cannot do something, get the training that will qualify you to succeed in it. Once you gain the credentials you need, you will probably become a specialist in some area of endeavor.

8th to the 5th   You should appreciate your imaginative talent, for it allows you to reach many goals. Decide on the area that gives you the most satisfaction and develop those skills as your major priority. Don't sacrifice all your own needs to satisfy your children's expectations.

9th to the 4th   You are very aware that you have to stand on your own, but you are easily distracted from this course because you feel obligated to go along with your parents' views about what you should do with your life.

10th to the 3rd   You are certainly well equipped mentally to set your own goals. It is simply a matter of organizing and setting forth your ideas so you can put them to good use in a position that will give you fulfillment.

11th to the 2nd   One of your goals should be to attain a reasonably independent lifestyle and substantial monetary rewards for your efforts. Security should be an important consideration when you choose a career.

12th to the 1st   You yourself are the primary reason for any conflicts you face in achieving your objectives. You tend to hide your talents for working with a wide variety of people in diverse situations to help them help themselves. You have the right to expect a reasonable return for your efforts.

Trine: 4, 8   You are well aware that you must learn to stand on your own, but your overactive imagination plays tricks and creates fantasies out of ordinary circumstances, which distracts you from this task. Certainly some of your reactions to external conditions are inaccurate, and that keeps you from developing resistance to people who try to intimidate you. You don't have to take a submissive role, as you will discover if you invest in yourself and learn the skills you need to deal successfully with challenges. The public will gladly pay for your services when you are well trained. Perhaps your feelings of obligation to your parents kept you from developing your own ideas about what you should do with your life.

Sextile: 2, 10   You should try to prepare a program to guide you in your affairs, and be sure to include a plan for increasing your financial resources. You can lessen your feelings of inadequacy by freeing yourself from anxieties about security. Take enough time to decide on a career that will give you satisfaction and make you feel that you are providing a worthwhile service. Stop comparing your skills with other people's, because that will only intimidate you further.

Cross: 3, 6, 9   You may need professional help in choosing a career that will be rewarding and give you a comfortable living. If possible, get a formal education so you can more effectively meet the challenges presented by your competitors and thus enjoy the more abundant lifestyle that they have. A service-oriented profession seems best suited to you, but that decision is yours to make. You are well qualified to be a specialist in any field in which you feel comfortable. Your feeling of inadequacy makes you overreact to the challenge of your competitors, and you will probably become more qualified than anyone else.

Inconjunct: 5, 7   By applying some discipline in developing your creative potentials, you can derive many benefits; you cannot afford to neglect this task. You must be aware that you are qualified to provide unique services to the public. Finding an appreciative patron will give you greater self-confidence. Be careful not to overindulge your children so that they expect you to sacrifice your needs to satisfy theirs.

Semisextile: 1, 11   Don't feel obligated to "friends" who try to take advantage of you. You are always willing to help those in need, but that doesn't mean you should play host to every parasite who wanders into your life. You have the rare gift of sincere compassion for people in need of help, which you might utilize by following a career that requires close contact with people. You deserve a fair return for your efforts, and you must be firm in demanding to be paid accordingly. It is a waste of time to doubt that you can achieve your goals as well as others do. All you need to do is establish goals that are within your abilities and right for you. You have all the resources you need to get everything you want out of life, and at the same time you are willing to commit yourself to serving others.

1st to the 12th   Your imagination is rich with ideas, but you may have some difficulty finding a suitable field in which to apply them. You are contemplative and serious, rarely sharing your innermost thoughts with other people.

 2nd to the 11th   You are preoccupied with reaching goals that will also satisfy your needs for financial security. You are generally thoughtful and considerate toward your friends.

 3rd to the 10th   Not content with success in only one field of endeavor, you develop skills in other areas, which you can turn to if your primary career no longer seems attractive. You accomplish your objectives without a lot of fanfare.

 4th to the 9th   You especially want to be free to come and go, to travel and circulate among others who are eager to excel. It is essential to get an education so you will have the knowledge you need to make your dreams a reality.

 5th to the 8th   Although you may not make an issue of it, you have a strong need for intimacy in relationships, which you are generally able to achieve. You enjoy making investments, and you know how to keep your business affairs private until they are satisfactorily developed.

 6th to the 7th   Your mate must be willing to support you in your dreams and work with you to see them realized. You will be happy when your career allows you to shower luxuries on your partner.

 7th to the 6th   You are bothered by trivial details in your career, and you are anxious to be on top of every situation that develops. Try to get away from your job occasionally, if only to gain a fresh perspective on your problems.

 8th to the 5th   You are willing to make sacrifices for those you love if you know they will reciprocate. You don't mind working without recognition while developing your creative talents so that you can demonstrate them to the world.

 9th to the 4th   Your early environment had a strong influence on you and was an important factor in your drive to achieve. Though you may have doubted your ability to succeed, your parents probably had more faith in you than you realized.

 10th to the 3rd   Your career should involve working with the public in some way, particularly in helping individuals or groups deal with social problems. You prefer to fulfill your responsibilities with a certain amount of privacy.

 11th to the 2nd   Your career must show promise of providing personal and financial security, or you will lose interest. Your keen insight helps you derive a substantial yield from your resources. Be wary of fair-weather friends.

 12th to the 1st   Self-analysis would help you appraise your potentials more positively. In time you will realize that you are far more qualified to succeed than you knew; don't underestimate your abilities.

Trine: 4, 8 Because of your early upbringing, you feel free to pursue your own life and establish a foundation that is comfortable for you. Your parents probably had more faith in you than you realized, and they undoubtedly brought you up so that you could succeed on your own terms. Although you are cordial to others, you reserve the right to make your own choices and achieve goals that you alone define. You are rich with ideas, but at first you may have some difficulty finding ways to apply them. You generally try not to attract attention, especially when you are attracted to someone and don't want the relationship to gain public notice. You are clever at negotiating your financial affairs quietly until you feel confident that they are sufficiently developed to be made public.

Sextile: 2, 10 Your interests are diversified, so you always have an alternative direction to follow if your current program fails or becomes uninteresting. Because you work quietly behind the scenes to develop your skills, your career is far more advanced than anyone can tell from appearances. You have the ability to apply your basic talents and resources to achieve your goals. The financial rewards of such a career will satisfy your need for security.

Cross: 3, 6, 9 Developing your skills should have a high priority, because others may not always be available to help you. A good education will teach you how to use your potentials to accomplish your objectives. You cannot afford to neglect the trivial details that you encounter in your career, even though they seem like a waste of time. Through dealing with these chores you can become independent of the people you would otherwise have to rely on. This is the only way you can be in complete control of any situation that develops in your career. Your career should involve working with the public in some way, for you are qualified to solve many kinds of social problems. Social service might be an attractive field for you, and it would give you freedom to come and go as you choose in performing your duties.

Inconjunct: 5, 7 You don't mind making some sacrifices for those you love, but you resent it if sacrifice is expected as a condition of the relationship. You should choose a partner who sympathizes with your goals and who will work with you to reach them. You would resent a partner who is unwilling to share your highs and lows, successes and failures, or someone who constantly asks you to indulge him or her. You will work without recognition until you feel qualified to establish yourself firmly in your career. You consider this a good investment in developing your creative talents.

Semisextile: 1, 11 Careful self-analysis may help you appreciate your creative potentials and understand how using them positively can help you reach your goals. You tend to underestimate your abilities and credit others with more talent, even though theirs is no more significant than your own. You are sometimes more generous and thoughtful to your friends and associates than they deserve.

1st to the 12th You are deeply sensitive to others' needs and always ready to offer assistance, but people may take advantage of your generosity. You hope that success will allow you to afford fine clothes and the other trappings of wealth.

 2nd to the 11th You are always generous to friends and hope they will reciprocate if you need help some day. You want sufficient security to retire early if you choose to, although you probably won't.

 3rd to the 10th You know you must make concessions to others while striving to succeed in your career, but in return you generally get the cooperation you need. You are temperamentally well qualified to deal with the public in your career.

 4th to the 9th It may be troublesome, but you must be thoroughly informed if you are to realize your dreams for success. Though it may delay your plans, you prefer to stay within the law instead of taking the chance of losing what you have worked so hard to gain.

 5th to the 8th You prefer a relationship in which you can satisfy your physical needs without undue pressure. But unless you know you are satisfying your partner's needs for companionship as well as his or her physical requirements, you will lose interest.

 6th to the 7th People expect you to take care of all their needs. This includes your partner, whom you tend to indulge. But don't become overburdened by other people's demands. Even your competitors are impressed by your ability to succeed.

 7th to the 6th You are especially upset by disharmony among your fellow workers, and you do whatever you can to restore order in such a situation. You really work hard to make your daily affairs run as smoothly as possible.

 8th to the 5th You willingly indulge anyone in whom you are romantically interested, in order to create a happy relationship. Similarly, you develop your creative talents so you can derive the yield you want.

 9th to the 4th You are confident that you can make your own way once you've established a solid foundation. Then you can expand according to your needs. Your parents understand your desire to conduct your affairs in your own way.

 10th to the 3rd You usually achieve your goals by successfully implementing your ideas without arousing the anxieties of those who work with you. Your ability to present your ideas convincingly is one of your strong points.

 11th to the 2nd You want a comfortable lifestyle with all the fine things that money can buy, so you quietly plan for the future. You don't forget those who helped you in your early struggles.

 12th to the 1st You hope that your efforts can enrich the people who have helped you along the way. You never assume that you have reached your maximum, and throughout your professional career, you will strive to improve.

Trine: 4, 8 You are sensitive to other people's needs and always ready to offer assistance, which means that some people will try to take advantage of your generosity. You are imaginative and confident of your ability to make a worthwhile life for yourself once you've established a solid foundation. Then all you need is the opportunity to grow and expand as your needs indicate. Luckily, your parents probably understood your need to go about your business in your own way. Once free to seek your destiny, you may turn your attention to satisfying your personal desires in a relationship. You want to be a good companion as well as a lover to your partner, but you are turned off by pressure to commit yourself in a binding alliance.

Sextile: 2, 10 Your temperament is well suited to dealing with people in your daily affairs, both in your profession and in personal relationships. You are willing to make concessions to succeed, and the people you are competing with usually cooperate. You work quietly until you feel confident that your plans for the future are working. In this way, you are more sure of reaching your goals and having the means to buy all the finer things in life. The people you've helped won't forget you, and you don't forget those who helped you when you were struggling to succeed.

Cross: 3, 6, 9 You realize how important it is to be well-informed about many subjects, and this will improve your chance of achieving lasting success. You deplore the fact that some people bend the law to reach their goals, for you know this can jeopardize the gains that have been made. You reach your goals by carefully implementing your ideas without letting your plans intimidate those around you. Your skill in getting the cooperation you need attests to your communicative ability. Also you are effective in dealing with disharmony among the people who are working with or for you, restoring order so that your daily affairs run smoothly.

Inconjunct: 5, 7 You attract people who expect favors from you, and you may feel that everyone with severe problems comes to you. The fact is, you are a comfort to others when the going gets rough, and anything you can do for them will be helpful. This can be trying, but even your competitors are impressed with your ability to solve most of your problems. You don't mind indulging someone whom you are romantically attracted to, because you know the investment may bring about a happy relationship. You invested just as much time and energy to develop your creative talents, which will enable you to derive the results you want for the future.

Semisextile: 1, 11 You want to be secure enough to retire early if you decide to, but the chances are you won't. You never assume that you have extended yourself enough, either in quantity or quality of effort, and you keep trying to reach your maximum output. You hope that others will be enriched by your accomplishments, and it is highly likely that they will be. However, it would be senseless to make yourself the victim by following a course that nourishes others while leaving you with psychological malnutrition and social starvation. That would make you useless to the world and to yourself. It's simply a matter of exercising thoughtful restraint, knowing when to share and when to insist that others make a genuine effort to help themselves.

1st to the 12th You find it difficult to accomplish your objectives, because you are never sure you are doing the right thing. You are likely to meet frustration if you neglect to consider those who could benefit from your efforts.

 2nd to the 11th Sharing your skills in activities that enrich others would make it easier to reach your goals. Working with groups would improve the quality of life for those around you and allow you to make a rewarding contribution.

 3rd to the 10th You can fulfill your life's work through action, not words. By making a courageous effort to put your ideas to work, you can achieve the position you want. That is the only way to get the recognition you feel you deserve.

 4th to the 9th Getting an education should have a high priority in your plans. Without it, you will be less effective. You must get the training you need so you are better prepared to meet the challenge of rising to your highest level of accomplishment.

 5th to the 8th Satisfying your physical desires is fine, but don't let it become your sole purpose in life. If you do, you will neglect your more important endeavors, to which you should direct much of your energy.

 6th to the 7th Channeling your energy into activities that fulfill other people's needs will relieve your anxiety about being useful to society. Your partner should work on this problem with you.

 7th to the 6th Your education must allow you to develop skills that will be useful in your career. Without skills, you cannot render any service to others or to yourself, but with training, you can work toward your goals and provide valuable services too.

 8th to the 5th Protecting the welfare of your partner and children may be the motivation you need. To fulfill your potential, all you need to do is work hard and develop your talents so that you can satisfy your most urgent obligations.

 9th to the 4th You understand that you need to establish your own roots before embarking on a gainful life endeavor. The memory of your childhood environment should guide you in this matter.

 10th to the 3rd With your many ideas, you can pursue a rewarding career and make a truly important contribution to society. Knowing you've done a good job will give you much contentment when you reflect on it in your later years.

 11th to the 2nd Among your goals is attaining financial security and independence. Achieving this will give you the freedom to come and go as you choose without having to endure the frustration of being limited in your desires.

 12th to the 1st You alone can determine your fate and circumstances. When your life seems strained by a lack of positive activity, probably your fears and feelings of inadequacy are responsible. Apathy must yield to courage in striving for more positive results.

Trine: 4, 8 Before you can take up any purposeful activity, you must have a reasonably firm foundation. Your childhood environment may have taught you the importance of having your own roots, just as your parents needed theirs so they could accomplish their objectives. When you feel secure, you should be less apprehensive about doing the right thing in striving to reach your goals. You will be more successful in your life's endeavors if you start from a reasonably stable position so that your goals are more sharply defined. If your objectives include serving others as well as satisfying your personal needs, so much the better. Occasionally you may be so preoccupied with satisfying your physical desires that you neglect giving your more significant objectives the attention they deserve.

Sextile: 2, 10 Plans and noble intentions mean nothing unless you act on them. You will be fulfilled only if you invest the time and energy to achieve your dreams with devotion and self-discipline. In addition to satisfying your needs, you will get the recognition your skills and accomplishments deserve. There is no other way you can gain financial security and independence so that you can come and go as you want.

Cross: 3, 6, 9 You may have many useful ideas, but you must carry them out deliberately if you want any rewards from them. By accepting this kind of personal responsibility, you can make a valuable contribution to society. Your progress will be greatly simplified if you get an education that will teach you how to develop your skills. With skills, you can meet the challenge of rising to your highest level of achievement. Without some formal training, you might have to resign yourself to mediocrity or relative obscurity in the world. You can do so much to help relieve social problems that it would be a significant loss to society and yourself if you neglect this task.

Inconjunct: 5, 7 Probably you will always attract people with problems who feel that you can help them. You can be highly effective in helping people learn how to help themselves, and doing this will lessen your feeling that you aren't really useful to the world. Your partner may be the first to show you how qualified you are to render assistance to others. He or she may work to help you think more positively about yourself. You have enormous potential, but you must be willing to make whatever sacrifice is required to develop and apply it. Your family may be the stimulus you need to motivate you to act. The results will prove that you are qualified for many endeavors.

Semisextile: 1, 11 You must avoid negative thinking, for that will make you more uncertain of your ability to take the right action at the right time. You can get rid of your feelings of inadequacy by getting the training you need and acting decisively. If you make a mistake, find out why and learn from it. Take advantage of any opportunity to participate in group activities, for you can be effective in improving the quality of life for others.

1st to the 12th   Your sensitivity to the needs of those around you is an indication of much potential for growth and development. You have the ability to make worthwhile contributions to help relieve many social problems.

 2nd to the 11th   You should begin focusing on your destiny by helping those who are close to you. It is extremely important to define your goals and objectives and to understand that you have the resources necessary to realize them.

 3rd to the 10th   You are reasonably aware of what will be expected as you rise in your career. You should be able to convince your superiors of your qualifications, and probably they will offer you opportunities to demonstrate your abilities.

 4th to the 9th   It is urgent that you get a good education so that you can better translate your potentials into worthwhile activity. Understanding the problems that you will have to deal with increases the likelihood of solving them successfully.

 5th to the 8th   Guard against spending too much time and energy in self-indulgent activities. You show people how to sustain themselves by using their basic resources more effectively, and you motivate them when they lack enthusiasm.

 6th to the 7th   You want a mate who understands your occasional feelings of inadequacy and supports you in your endeavors. You do everything you can to serve your partner's best interests.

 7th to the 6th   You are drawn to people who seem less adequate. Subconsciously you hope to improve your self-image by helping them do what they cannot do for themselves. For that reason you might choose a career in some area of social service.

 8th to the 5th   Your highest priority is to develop your creative potentials. The sacrifice involved will repay you many times in higher earnings and increased creativity. Developing your own talents is the best investment you can make in your children's future.

 9th to the 4th   Your parents probably have great faith in your ability to succeed, which has helped your self-confidence. By establishing your own roots as early as possible, you can extend yourself in new areas to realize your dreams.

 10th to the 3rd   You should capitalize on your gifted imagination, for you alone are responsible for making the most of your creative ideas. With resourcefulness and hard work, you will reach goals that seemed beyond your reach.

 11th to the 2nd   It is important to put aside something from your earnings on a regular basis. By doing this, you can realize your hopes for financial security in later years. The older you get, the more resourceful and effective you become.

 12th to the 1st   Through meditation, you can discover the full measure of your hidden resources. Then you will know that you are equipped to cope with most of your problems. You're richer than you think.

Trine: 4, 8 Because you are sensitive to other people's needs in your personal and professional affairs, you will probably respond and demonstrate that you can serve their best interest. This ability assures you of continued growth and development and indicates that you will reach your goals. But your contributions may be considerably lessened if you spend too much time and energy in satisfying your own desires. Those who lack your resourcefulness may turn to you to learn how to sustain themselves more effectively. If you have learned from your parents' example, you know you need to establish your own roots before you can succeed in your endeavors. Your parents' faith in you helped you realize that you are qualified to seek your own destiny. By setting your own course in life, you will be able to extend yourself to reach your objectives, which will inspire you with greater self-confidence.

Sextile: 2, 10 You are always eager to demonstrate your abilities to your superiors, who quickly feel confident of your ability. Probably you will be given many opportunities to prove that you can take on even greater responsibilities. You generally know what is expected of you, and whenever possible you try to exceed that. Knowing how important it is to be financially independent, you can see the wisdom of regularly saving something from your earnings. This will lessen your anxieties about security in the future, when your earning ability may be lessened. Plan to put something aside for a rainy day, for you could run into foul weather at some time in the future.

Cross: 3, 6, 9 People with problems are drawn to you, perhaps because they recognize that you can help them. You should seek a career in some area of personal or social service. As you succeed, your confidence will increase, thereby improving your self-image. Capitalize on your gifted imagination by getting the education you need to successfully exploit your creative ideas. When you understand the problems you face and have the training to deal with them, there is no limit to the heights you can reach. Hard work, along with your wealth of creative inspiration, will certainly lead to success and the satisfaction of reaching goals that seemed beyond your limit.

Inconjunct: 5, 7 You can meet the challenge of competition if your partner shares your dreams and supports you. Knowing that someone depends on you spurs you to excel in your endeavors. All this can happen if you invest in developing your creative potential into skills. Your children may want to pattern their lives after your example, so you should learn how to increase your creative output. You may find it difficult to satisfy your children's needs as well as your own. Reason and good judgment must prevail, but unless you can improve your output, it may be difficult to fully satisfy their needs.

Semisextile: 1, 11 You are probably not aware of all your hidden resources, which will be revealed through meditation. By reflecting on your problems, you can always come up with a solution. It is essential to define your goals and prepare a plan for mobilizing your resources so you can reach them. Serving people who are less qualified or less fortunate brings out the very best in you. Knowing that you've stimulated those around you to succeed on their own will give you great fulfillment.

1st to the 12th Anxiety and fear make it difficult for you to fulfill your objectives. You underestimate your ability to make a worthwhile contribution to the world. You enrich others more than you know, even though your accomplishments may not gain the notice they deserve.

 2nd to the 11th Your greatest asset is your ability to work quietly at tasks that greatly enhance the quality of life for others. You can establish programs to benefit society, but their true value may not be recognized immediately.

 3rd to the 10th In time you will choose a career that enables you to make a significant contribution to society. This social need will stimulate you to make your best effort to satisfy it, which will give you a feeling of accomplishment.

 4th to the 9th You fear that you are destined to remain in obscurity, but you can rise above this by getting as much education as possible. This will allow you to extend yourself in ways you never thought possible. You need training in efficient self-management and the best use of your talents.

 5th to the 8th The broad social programs you have outlined will be initiated when others recognize your effectiveness in dealing with people's problems. Their reaction to your abilities will earn you the support you'll need later.

 6th to the 7th You serve your own best interests when you follow a career that serves others. But preoccupation with your work may strain your personal relationships. Try to satisfy your partner's needs along with your career demands; otherwise your mate may be alienated.

 7th to the 6th You may occasionally be overwhelmed by the responsibilities of your daily affairs, especially in your career. If you get the right education and training, you can overcome these obstacles.

 8th to the 5th Your feeling of inadequacy motivates you to make sacrifices to give your children the resources they need. You want them to be able to distinguish themselves without having to pay the penalties you have paid.

 9th to the 4th Always grateful for your parents' training as you grew to maturity, you appreciate their confidence in you and their urging you to grow and succeed on your own terms.

 10th to the 3rd Although your ideas sometimes seem implausible, your ability to apply them with discrimination is your greatest asset. You temper reason with consideration of people's feelings, which is why your efforts will fulfill others' needs as well as your own.

 11th to the 2nd By carefully planning how to use your resources, you can reach your goals and realize the financial security you want for your later years.

 12th to the 1st You can make your dreams a reality by focusing on developing your creative potentials. You have the strength to sustain those who require your help in learning to cope with their problems.

Trine: 4, 8   Subconscious anxieties deter you from fully implementing your talents, but you justify this by consciously underestimating your ability to make a worthwhile contribution to society. Because your activities don't give you much public visibility, you assume that you haven't accomplished anything significant. You should become involved in showing people how they can sustain themselves better by using their basic resources more effectively. Their success will let you know how qualified you are to render a useful service, which will encourage you to take on more ambitious group programs. Reflect on the fact that your parents had confidence in you and urged you to grow and develop so you could succeed in your own way. You might find that you utilize your skills most fully in an institutional setting. In any case, serving the urgent needs of social groups would suit you and allow you to grow at the moderate pace you prefer.

Sextile: 2, 10   It is important to take inventory of your present abilities, the basic resources that you use right now. Learn to consolidate these assets and utilize them in a program that will yield financial rewards. Once you know what you have to work with, it will be easier to define the goals you expect to reach and make a significant contribution to the world at the same time. It is essential to know that you are improving the quality of life for those who benefit from your efforts.

Cross: 3, 6, 9   Your greatest potential asset is your ability to reason and solve problems, which you can demonstrate conclusively if you get a good education. This will allow you to prove yourself in competition and increase the range of possible jobs, making it more likely that your accomplishments will be recognized. There are few problems you can't handle, which makes you valuable to your employers and to those who use your services. A good education and the right training will allow you to control your destiny and win society's approval for your contribution.

Inconjunct: 5, 7   You should look for a career that serves the public, because that would suit your interests and help improve your self-image considerably. The time-consuming duties and pressures of your career might cause some problems in your marriage. Choose a moderate course of action so that neither your mate nor your job suffers. Your children may be the motivating force that makes you seek to excel in your profession, if only to provide them with the advantages and opportunites they need to succeed.

Semisextile: 1, 11   Although it may not be immediately apparent, your efforts will produce long-lasting benefits for those who are affected. This should be reassuring, since your activities don't always gain public attention. Luckily, you can work away from the glare of the public spotlight as long as you know that you are making a worthwhile and appreciated contribution. Your strength sustains those who are weak or less resourceful in making their dreams a reality.

1st to the 12th   Although it may be painful at times, you must accept the limitations imposed by society. Until you decide to help others learn how to have greater self-determination, your anxiety about restricted freedom will persist.

 2nd to the 11th   Your total awareness of society's problems carries a responsibility that you cannot ignore. You have the resources that can help people find their way out of the darkness of ignorance.

 3rd to the 10th   An important feature of your destiny is sharing your talents with those who need to be informed. You have the ability to arouse people to support you in your endeavors, which in time will prove beneficial to them.

 4th to the 9th   Awareness alone will not bring you success or allow you to reach your goals. A good education will enable you to translate your intuitive understanding of social problems into workable solutions.

 5th to the 8th   Knowing that someone is depending on you stimulates you to extend yourself in their behalf. You know how to arouse people to use their own resources so that they can sustain themselves without you. Having them satisfy your physical needs should not be a condition of your help.

 6th to the 7th   Because of your ingenuity in solving people's problems, you should gain a good reputation for your services. A career in social work, medicine or some other scientific field would be a suitable outlet for your talents.

 7th to the 6th   As your reputation grows, so will the number of people who request your talents. Your growth is closely tied to the need for your services. You will be required to use great skill in handling the problems people bring to you.

 8th to the 5th   You always want to indulge yourself in personal pleasures, and it will require great sacrifice to put them aside when there is an opportunity to demonstrate your skills. Those you love, especially your mate and children, can make the sacrifice seem worthwhile.

 9th to the 4th   Your parents gave you the chance to prove what you could do with your creative imagination. Their confidence in your ability is justified, and you owe it to yourself and them to develop your talents to a high degree.

 10th to the 3rd   You are always ready to use what you know to achieve your objectives, and your career will be enhanced if you have the opportunity to deal with your responsibilities in your own way. What some consider impossible becomes routine for you.

 11th to the 2nd   Freedom is precious to you, so you endure the limitations of your career because you know it is the only way to gain financial independence and the freedom to come and go as you choose.

 12th to the 1st   Your freedom depends on your willingness to encourage others to gain theirs. You cannot ignore your social responsibilities, for by fulfilling them you will feel pride in your accomplishments.

Trine: 4, 8   Your parents indulged you and gave you plenty of opportunities to prove what you could do with your creative imagination. You owe it to yourself to develop your talents so that you can make your own way successfully. At first you may have to accept the limitations that society imposes on you, but this will pass as you make your own contribution to its needs. When you see others enjoying greater freedom because of your efforts, your anxiety about restricted mobility will pass. Knowing that someone needs your skills gives you the enthusiasm to put forth your best efforts. You can motivate people to utilize their resources more effectively, but you should not expect any sexual favors as a condition of your help. You can satisfy your physical needs in a different setting.

Sextile: 2, 10   Although your freedom is very precious, you put up with the limitations of your career because you realize that after you've achieved your goals you will have a more lasting freedom, with financial security. Surely you must know that sharing your talents is part of your destiny, and the enrichment you give others will be returned when you review your life efforts later.

Cross: 3, 6, 9   Until you focus on providing a unique service, your progress will be slow. To learn the necessary skills, you must get a good education. You can't hope to succeed on your intuitive gifts alone, and formal training will help you find the best way to apply yourself. Your insight gives you an advantage over your competition and enables you to solve many problems that baffle others. You are keyed to the social problems in your immediate surroundings, and your finger is on the pulse of the major problems of the larger society. You should have little difficulty attracting patrons for your service, and as your reputation grows so will your patronage. It will be to your advantage to seek a career that allows you self-determination and opportunities to grow and develop to your maximum potential.

Inconjunct: 5, 7   A career in science, medicine or social work might be appealing to you. These fields would give you the opportunity to deal with their inherent special problems, and recognition will surely follow your achievements. However, you will have to sacrifice some of your personal pleasures to invest the time and energy in exploiting your creative potential. Your partner and children will make any sacrifice seem a worthwhile investment.

Semisextile: 1, 11   You carry a heavy burden of social responsibility, because you are so aware of society's problems, and you have the talent to help solve them. This responsibility you cannot ignore. The freedom you enjoy depends on your willingness to share your skills with those who do not have such freedom. You have the resources people need to lead them out of the darkness of their ignorance. Later you will feel very proud when you reflect on how much your efforts meant to those who benefited from them.

1st to the 12th Society's problems are deeply disturbing to you, but sometimes you feel powerless to do anything about them. This is simply indulging in defeatism and is probably a subconscious rejection of your social responsibility. If you are sensitive to the problem, you are responsible for helping to find the solution.

 2nd to the 11th Your compassionate nature allows you to focus sharply on all facets of a problem and its probable solution. You may be required to serve others before you can serve yourself. When your friends ask for help, you hate to turn them down.

 3rd to the 10th In your desire to succeed, you often accept tasks that others have rejected, assuming that this will win you the approval of important people. Don't assume anything; get it in writing.

 4th to the 9th You must get the best possible education, because you often assume that everyone else is more qualified. You must persist in your studies if you want to derive the most benefit from them. Try not to get distracted or indulge in daydreaming, because that wastes time.

 5th to the 8th The old saying, "The spirit is willing, but the flesh is weak," applies to you, and this tendency can mean much wasted energy in nonproductive but pleasurable activity. It is better to indulge others, because that will let you know how useful you can be.

 6th to the 7th Because you are "tuned" to other people, you should consider a career in human services. You have the talent and disposition to help people find a more abundant life, with more highs than lows. You are sensitive to your mate's endeavors.

 7th to the 6th Your first priority is getting training for the career you are interested in. Without it, you run the risk of having a nonproductive life and not being recognized. Even you can't face that!

 8th to the 5th Beware of wasting time in fruitless self-indulgent activity. Sacrificing personal pleasures is the best investment you can make for your own future. Perhaps your children's needs will be a reminder that you owe them your best efforts.

 9th to the 4th Your early upbringing should have taught you to become more self-reliant. It is obvious that you must make your own way and rise to excellence by using your own skills as the basis for your accomplishments.

 10th to the 3rd With your imagination and sensitive intellect, you can make a worthwhile contribution to the world. As you develop your skills, your reputation will grow and you will receive the recognition you deserve.

 11th to the 2nd It is extremely important that you make a plan for reaching your goals and adhere to it; otherwise your efforts will be wasted or at least diminished in yield.

 12th to the 1st Avoid feeling that your efforts are futile if you don't immediately see evidence of your effectiveness. Sometimes your contribution is low key, even though its value is high.

Trine: 4, 8   Although you are sensitive to the social conditions around you, you feel powerless to make a contribution to alleviating them. You know that a serious need exists, but you may subconsciously reject the idea that you can do anything about it. The fact that social conditions bother you should tell you that you can help. Your compassion for human suffering should alert you to find a way to help relieve it. Your early parental conditioning made you aware that you should become more self-reliant, but first you must establish your own foundation and be secure in your own being. Instead of moaning about the problems, admit that you might be able to find a solution, and then apply yourself to the task. By serving the needs of those around you, you will come to see that you are indeed useful and important to those you serve. It is easy to have excellent intentions, but you may lack the courage to carry them out.

Sextile: 2, 10   In your career, you often accept responsibilities that others reject. You want to make a good impression on your superiors and thereby get the opportunity to prove that you can handle even greater burdens. You are deeply aware of the enormous responsibility of a career in serving the public, and you want to live up to their expectations. To better accomplish this objective, you should adopt a plan that will allow you to derive the benefits you deserve while making a valuable contribution to society.

Cross: 3, 6, 9   Your first priority should be to get the very best education and training you can afford. This will lessen the danger of being intimidated by others who are well qualified. With self-discipline, you can gain the credentials you need to advance in your career. Try not to indulge in nonproductive activity, for you tend to wander about aimlessly, with little to show for the time. If you pass up formal training, you might have to be content with an unfulfilling life because you contributed so little to it. With training, however, your skills will gain the attention of the public, and you will be recognized for your accomplishments.

Inconjunct: 5, 7   Consider a career that deals with people's problems, such as medicine, social services, institutional work or spiritual enterprises. The field you choose should involve relieving people's suffering or improving the conditions that restrict their development. You can stimulate people to seek a more productive life with more highs than lows. You may have to make sacrifices while developing your creative potentials, but your love for those close to you may motivate you to endure these temporary limitations.

Semisextile: 1, 11   Occasionally you feel sorry for yourself, believing that your efforts are futile, but if just one person appreciates your efforts, your optimism returns, and you realize that you are necessary to the world. Your low-key manner may obscure the high quality of your effort. Though you may find it necessary to serve others first, be assured that in doing so you also serve your own needs. By involving yourself in other people's problems, you will find yourself. Don't allow others to persecute you with their demands, for when this happens, your physical health will signal that you've exceeded your limits.

1st to the 12th Very likely you will be among those who are personally affected by important social, political or economic upheavals. You should join forces with others like you to protect your rights and cope with these problems.

 2nd to the 11th With a little imagination, you can convert a liability into an asset. By dedicating yourself to activities that enrich others, you can build security for the future. Through group endeavors, you could help those who lack the resources to change their circumstances.

 3rd to the 10th You tend to be suspicious of people in powerful positions, so you demand that they keep the lines of communication open and that they be ready to reveal their objectives.

 4th to the 9th You want an education, so that you will be well informed about a variety of social issues. You question the integrity of public officials and fear the power that public servants have over you. But you should seriously examine your own integrity as well.

 5th to the 8th You eagerly share what you know, to help others become more self-sustaining and in control of their destinies. With your skill in capitalizing on other people's resources, you might choose a career in investment, finance or medical research.

 6th to the 7th You always rise to the occasion in helping those who need your skills. Look for a partner who shares your desire to help people in need. Helping solve people's problems gives you a feeling of accomplishment.

 7th to the 6th Nothing stirs you to action more than attacking a problem that others can't deal with. You can succeed consistently in this if you acquire skills that others lack. It would be too bad to miss an opportunity for lack of training or education.

 8th to the 5th Your children spur you to extend yourself to give them the advantages you may have lacked. You accept the lack of recognition during the learning process as a necessary sacrifice, and you know that the rewards will be worth it.

 9th to the 4th You know that if you settle for less, you will certainly get less. You appreciate your parents, who urged you to grow and establish your own foundation.

 10th to the 3rd You are determined to uphold your strong convictions, even when challenged by other people. You know that when you forcefully project your claim, no one can take it from you without a challenge.

 11th to the 2nd If people try to take something from you, they find that you are a force to reckon with. You can make your future productive if you capitalize on the capital or goods you now have. Your investments usually pay dividends.

 12th to the 1st Your best asset, which is not easily recognized, is your willingness to take on powerful adversaries. Examine your motives carefully, though, for you might be tempted to deny others their rights while you struggle to preserve yours. You should not have any trouble finding a method that is equitable for all.

Trine: 4, 8 You appreciate what your parents accomplished for you, and it should be apparent that you too have an obligation to help others. You have a talent for making the most of your basic resources. It is likely that you will be personally affected by important social, economic or political changes, so you should join with others who are similarly affected to correct any injustices. Always willing to help those who lack your strength of purpose, you truly glow when you know you've helped people learn to utilize their resources and enjoy a more abundant life. Your flair for capitalizing on your own and other people's resources suggests a career in finance, investment or medical research, in any of which you could excel.

Sextile: 2, 10 Naturally suspicious of those in powerful positions, you demand that they keep the lines of communication open and discuss their objectives with you. This is particularly important if you are personally affected by those goals. You can be devastating in dealing with someone who tries to take something from you, and you demand that he or she be held accountable. You know how difficult it is to accumulate the comforts of life on an ordinary salary, so you make sure that your investments are worthwhile.

Cross: 3, 6, 9 Facing problems that others can't deal with brings out the best in you, and you are usually ready when an opportunity is offered. If you have acquired the education and training you need, no problem will ever be too much of a challenge. Your education also has taught you to critically examine the behavior of public officials, for you know they have the power to determine your fate. You want the privilege of demanding that they retire from office if their actions warrant it. Your strong convictions never waver, even when challenged. Before you change your opinion, you have to be shown the evidence that you are in error.

Inconjunct: 5, 7 Your loved ones, especially your children, move you to definitive action. You endeavor to give them the advantages you lacked so they can succeed in their own life directions and establish their own identities. You don't mind the lack of recognition you face in your developing years, for you consider it part of your investment to acquire the skills you need. Once you have these skills, you use every chance to prove your effectiveness to those who need your help. You want a partner who shares your dreams and will work with you to help those who genuinely need it.

Semisextile: 1, 11 You are a most effective spokesman for the underdog, representing them as if they were your own flesh and blood. If necessary, you will establish programs to help people with inadequate resources become self-sustaining. You aren't afraid to take on the most powerful adversaries, and you generally succeed when you do. Be careful that in struggling to preserve your own rights, you don't deny others theirs. If you take some time, you can surely reach a solution that will be fair for everyone.

Sun in Twelfth, Moon in First

Your life efforts should be focused on improving the quality of life for people who are unable to help themselves. The satisfaction of making a worthwhile social contribution would certainly improve your self-image and enrich you with the feeling of having fulfilled a useful role. A deeply responsive person, you are profoundly influenced by the forces—both positive and negative—in your immediate environment. This vulnerability may have resulted from your early conditioning when you could do little without parental approval, although at times you may have been criticized for not taking the initiative. A feeling of uncertainty and apprehension may have developed from this, making it difficult for you to feel comfortable in asserting yourself.

It is urgent that you examine your creative potentials and determine which ones can be developed into the skills you need to be effective in your career. At first there may be painful moments when you compete with qualified people who try to intimidate you. Don't underestimate what you can do, and remember that any reversals or failings along the way will teach you more than you can learn in any other way.

You should seriously consider a career that brings you into close contact with people, especially if they depend on the services you offer. The limited visibility of such a calling may not appeal to you, but your accomplishments will more than compensate for this by allowing you the privilege of greater privacy in your affairs.

Sun in Twelfth, Moon in Second

This combination shows that you are reasonably well integrated in handling most circumstances, so that life is comfortable and meaningful for you. You are not bothered by the fact that your life may not be relevant to your social environment, but you should be. It isn't easy for you to extend yourself to others, because you are so preoccupied with personal security. The fact is, you should stop worrying about not having the necessities of life, for any such apprehension is probably unjustified. Unless you are willing to give when someone genuinely needs help, you can't expect others to reciprocate. Reciprocity is your best guarantee of security, and sharing with others can be a truly enriching experience. A feature of this combination is that you must be willing to satisfy your social obligations in order to live up to your enormous creative potentials. You have the opportunity to develop your creative skills and use them where the greatest good can be accomplished.

You are cautious in forming relationships, because you don't want to get caught in situations that are difficult to get out of. You expect a lot from the person you love, and you won't settle for a partner who lacks the potential to be successful.

Sun in Twelfth, Moon in Third

You want to succeed in realizing your ambitions primarily to improve your self-image, for you are filled with uncertainty and apprehension about your abilities. You try to convince yourself that you have the qualifications to reach your goals, but at the same time you find it difficult to define exactly what you want. Many people have some such anxieties, but are motivated to overcome them. Your early parental conditioning is the main cause of your unwillingness to deal with your responsibility to develop your creative talents so that you can succeed. You may have assumed that you had to have your parents' approval before taking action, so you lost interest. You must be allowed to make decisions and to fail in them if necessary, so you don't make the same mistake again. Unless you are free and independent, you will never know the joy of success. You may be surprised to learn that many of your friends and acquaintances admire you for your knowledge and your readiness to help those in need. With those qualifications alone, you can choose a career that will bring success and satisfy your need for a job. Your creative imagination and ability to communicate could form the base for a career in writing, reporting, broadcasting, psychological counseling, medical research or education, among others.

A partner who understands your hang-ups and who believes in your abilities will work wonders for your self-image, so that you will be as successful in your marriage as you are in your career.

Sun in Twelfth, Moon in Fourth

Your most urgent priority is to make the necessary investment to develop your creative potentials into the skills that will enable you to succeed in your career. Both the Sun and Moon are in the areas of your chart that require you to discipline yourself in your creative development and also invest in the education that will enable you to reach the highest level of excellence. This combination makes this process fairly easy and enormously rewarding if you begin as soon as possible. However, because of the harmony between your desire to achieve and your untroubled emotional nature, you may not have the impetus to begin this process. You have the dramatic ability to arouse people to correct social injustices. A low-key catalyst, you can accomplish a great deal without attracting a lot of attention. It's not your nature to use violence, and you get the job done just the same.

You can be effective in a career in politics on the local or national level, building construction, design, environmental enterprises, land management, natural resources, real estate or the creative arts, such as acting, dancing, painting or sculpture. A little training will reveal your enormous potential, which can be used even in its undeveloped state with success.

Sun in Twelfth, Moon in Fifth

Your problem is that you may fail to develop your creative talents and use them to satisfy your social obligations. Perhaps observing the injustices and unacceptable conditions that exist for many people will stimulate you to gain the skills to deal with these social problems. No one has greater compassion or is more sensitive to the degrading conditions in which some people live than you, and it is part of your responsibility to do something about it. Your sensitivity won't allow you to disregard these problems forever, and then you will really begin to live to the fullest of your potential for the benefit of everyone concerned. If you decide to work with young people or children as a big brother or sister, you can do wonders in helping them develop their own identities. You don't need to get involved with individual cases to be effective; you can work through agencies or in programs designed to give young people a better start in life. The end result is to produce a better social environment for everyone through improving the quality of life for the people.

A suitable partner for you is someone who feels that life would be meaningless without you and who can inspire you to reach goals you thought were impossible. It should be reassuring to know that your mate is devoted to you and supports your efforts to build a comfortable life that you will enjoy sharing with your children.

Sun in Twelfth, Moon in Sixth

You have everything you need to realize your ambitions and goals if you learn to convert your resources into workable skills. Since your learning ability is excellent, this should not present a serious problem. You know how to face reality, although at times you have difficulty deciding on what action you should take to get the most effective results, partly because you have insufficient information.

You will attract people who want you to indulge them when they ask for help, but you should avoid letting them take advantage of you. You have the temperament and qualifications for succeeding in your career, especially if you provide some service to individuals or groups. It might please you to know that when you serve others you are also serving yourself, because the chances are that you will be well paid. Before long, you will win the respect of your superiors for your ability to work for their best interests, so that you will be favored when promotions are offered. Be grateful for your privacy if you have a low profile in your career. If your career makes sufficient demands on you and you earn a comfortable living from it, you have the best of both worlds. Providing for your family should never be a problem, because you have a variety of skills that you can turn to if necessary. You will probably marry someone who expects a lot from you, so you may occasionally worry about how you will meet the demands.

Sun in Twelfth, Moon in Seventh

Making sacrifices for others takes your attention away from personal interests and denies you the energy you need to develop your own creative potentials. Without this development, there will be many delays in getting established in a career so you can realize your goals for the future. You often feel that you owe people special favors, though you can't offer any justification for this indebtedness. Perhaps you want their approval or support because you are insecure about your abilities. Whatever the reason, you have to decide to work for yourself, or you will never get the chance to fulfill your own destiny. Indulging people may be a carry-over from your early years when your parents made you feel that your greatest responsibility was to them. This feeling of obligation to others will eventually fade when you realize that people are taking advantage of you and that you have little to show for your efforts. In love relationships, too, you should avoid being the one who does all the giving.

Some careers that are suitable for you are in public relations, sales, marriage counseling, law, social service, vocational guidance or any other that will bring you into close contact with the public.

If you unwind periodically from the unsettling affairs of your daily routine, you will be a better mate and parent, and you will have a chance to enjoy your leisure time.

Sun in Twelfth, Moon in Eighth

You have incredible insight into what motivates people in their behavior, so you probably should choose a profession requiring this kind of sensitivity. Your childhood circumstances gave you the opportunity to develop without psychological problems so that as you matured, you were able to integrate the various forces within you. Your ability to succeed is strengthened by your basically harmonious nature, which enables you to handle conflict or frustration before it becomes a major crisis. You are gifted in handling people and solving their problems. You have a talent for being noncommittal even when people exert pressure, which shows that you have poise and self-control. You might have problems in relationships, because you attract people who make excessive demands and expect you to comply with them.

You are most effective when you apply your skills in a professional capacity to serve the public. The rapport you have with people makes them feel comfortable and confident that you will help them. You place a high premium on your services, because you know how valuable they are, so you should enjoy deservedly high earnings from your career. Converting your potentials into skills probably required considerable sacrifice. Some outlets for your talents are careers in financial counseling, psychological counseling, physical therapy, medicine and related fields.

Sun in Twelfth, Moon in Ninth

If you experience problems in finding a suitable outlet for your creative talents, it's probably because you lack sufficient information to make that decision. An education will give you the knowledge you need to realize your ambitions. You can't rely on faith or luck to see you through the lean years; you need skills so that you will have the self-confidence to reach the outer limits of your potentials. Otherwise, you must accept obscurity or the limited income that goes with limited qualifications.

This planetary combination shows that you have the talent and the temperament for becoming a true professional in the career you choose. People are eager to discuss their problems with you because they have confidence in your abilities. All of your hidden talents and resources will come to you when you need them, and at times you will wonder how you solved a particular problem. You like to do things the easy way if possible, for you are bored by tedious tasks.

Your mate will understand your hang-ups better than you do and may compensate when you feel overwhelmed by a difficult situation. Your partner gives you strength when you weaken, courage when you falter and encouragement when your enthusiasm wanes, and for this you should be grateful. By applying yourself to the responsibilities of your career, you will win your partner's respect.

Sun in Twelfth, Moon in Tenth

You can achieve your goal of helping to make the world a better place to live if you put aside your survival anxieties and concern yourself with social problems. You are sensitive to the predicament that many people face in finding a suitable foundation on which to build their lives. If you direct your efforts to finding a solution to this dilemma and offer yourself as a guide whom people can follow, you will achieve the fulfillment you want. This is the underlying motivation in your life, but you can accomplish this objective in many ways, either through your career or in your private life.

You may experience problems with your partner because you devote so much time and energy to career interests. You may have to make some concessions for the sake of harmony, but you will probably feel annoyed when pressing developments in your career require your personal attention. You don't want your mate to distract you, because you know that reaching your goals will be mutually beneficial and that you must stay on course.

You would be a good manager, because you are knowledgeable, sensitive and caring enough to achieve your career objectives without burdening the people under you with overbearing discipline or unreasonable expectations.

Sun in Twelfth, Moon in Eleventh

You will have to make adjustments so you can be sufficiently organized to achieve fulfillment of the goals you want. At times you are emotionally frustrated because you are aware of the debt you owe society. You should focus on what you can do to give others opportunities to promote and utilize their creative potentials. The effects you produce will be rewarding, but that doesn't necessarily mean that you will also enjoy the warmth and personal attention you need in an individual relationship. You circulate freely among the masses without noticing that you are often alone. Your ability to remain emotionally detached is what makes you so effective in dealing with the demands and expectations of the various people you have to cope with.

You should choose a career that gives you the mobility to be where you are most needed. You would succeed in enterprises that serve the public, such as politics, fund-raising, education, vocational guidance, public relations, stock investment, retirement programs and other similar fields.

Forming a relationship with someone who is as idealistic as you and who shares your enthusiasm for what you hope to accomplish would give you the inner contentment you need to make your life meaningful.

Sun in Twelfth, Moon in Twelfth

This combination is more favorable for emotional development than for achievement, because this position of the Sun frustrates creative self-expression. Your imagination is highly developed and can provide you with the solutions to most of your problems. It is important for you to find a vehicle that enables you to satisfy your social obligations and at the same time to express your creative potentials. Providing such services will make you feel fulfilled in having lived up to your own expectations.

You are a private person who only occasionally invites others into the sanctity of your personal life. You enjoy expressing yourself to the extent that your career requires it, but you are not interested in the high visibility that others find satisfying. Because of your contemplative nature, you need time away from the busy mainstream of social activity to reflect and plan for the future.

Your mate must understand how much you need support and appreciation for what you are trying to accomplish. You attract people whose demands and expectations can be burdensome, so you may have to insulate yourself from these types. Your commitment to your career suggests that you should defer marriage until you are reasonably well established and can afford the time and energy to indulge a partner.

Appendix

Thoughts on the Use of House Systems
by Michael P. Munkasey

Two important questions in astrology today are first, what are the houses? and second, which house system should an astrologer choose?

To clarify the role of the houses in the horoscope, we can compare the various chart factors to the cardinal signs. The planets are like Aries, the fire of the horoscope, supplying the impetus or energy of what is happening in the chart. The signs of the zodiac are equivalent to Cancer, or the water of the chart, providing shades of meaning and nuances that the planetary energies take on so that the potential of the chart can develop. The aspects are like Libra or the air, giving and taking, balancing and spreading the Arian energy. This leaves the houses to provide the earthy or Capricorn structure of the horoscope. But Capricorn indicates more than structure; it also indicates time. It is the foundation, which is essential so that the impetus of the planets can be measured against the background of chaos.

With this perspective, the reason for including the houses in interpretation becomes rather obvious. Anyone who has studied enough astrology can certainly delineate a chart without them; you can also delineate a chart without the signs of the zodiac, and cosmobiologists do both all the time. But it is more difficult to omit the symbolism of the two positive elements, fire and air, which represent the planets and the aspects, and derive some useful particular meaning from the symbolism of the receptive elements, water and earth. The receptive signs provide the framework for the positive, initiating signs. Without the signs and houses, there is something missing from the horoscope interpretation. The answer to the question of whether or not to use the houses depends more on the astrologer's desire for completeness than on his or her philosophy or the immediate situation.

Here is an example to show the differences that occur when the receptive elements are added to the delineation picture. If a person has Moon trine Saturn, we might say that he or she is particular about ways of bestowing protection and care, of which there is an abundance, on others. When we add in the sign and the house positions of the planets, a deeper interpretation is added to the aspect symbolism. If the Moon is in Taurus and in the third house, and Saturn is in Virgo and in the seventh house, the delineation above can be expanded to read: the structured, protective caring is given with efficiency (Virgo) and determination (Taurus) to those who are nearby (third house) and in partnership (seventh house) with the individual. The astrologer, of course, can decide which of the two delineations he or she wants to give in a particular situation.

Now that we know what the houses do, we can answer the second question: how, to choose a house system. Before choosing a system from among the twenty-five or so that are currently in use, one should first consider the two functions that a house system should fulfill if it is to be useful to the astrologer. These two functions are first, to divide space in a way that is meaningful to the astrologer and second, to provide cusps that events can be timed to. Different house systems fulfill each of these requirements equally well in different ways. The issue of whether a house system is correct or incorrect, inclusive or exclusive is immaterial as long as the system fulfills the functions of meaningful space division and cusps that events can be timed to. Even if the house system fulfills only one of these functions, and fulfills it well, it does have some merit. If it does not fulfill either function, its usefulness must be questioned.

House systems are constructed in one of two ways: either directly on the ecliptic or by projection onto one of the great circles of the heavens such as the horizon, celestial equator, prime vertical, polar axis or meridian. The ecliptic systems are constructed by adding integral multiples to one of the established points in the chart, such as the Ascendant, MC, Sun, Moon or the IC. This orientation ties the horoscope perspective more soundly into the astrologer's perspective; orientation to one of the other celestial frames of reference ties the perspective into a broader dimension of experience, an expanded perspective on what is occurring in the space around the birth or other event. The approach that the astrologer chooses depends on the perspective required for the analysis.

A case can be made for a third classification of house systems if we subdivide the projected systems into those that are easily and directly drawn and those, like Placidus and Koch, that are not so easily represented. They can be explained, but not simply, and it is not possible to draw neat, precise diagrams that represent all of their symbolic subtleties. This is not to say that these systems should not be used, but that like the outer planets that are invisible to the naked eye, they incorporate higher functioning that cannot be perceived directly.

The ecliptic systems include such popular divisions as the equal house and solar house systems, which make spatial divisions according to harmonics of these points along the ecliptic. Because the ecliptic represents the Sun's path as seen from Earth against the background of the fixed stars, it is symbolic of the Sun. Thus a house system that uses the ecliptic exclusively incorporates the solar principle—the ego or the creative self—directly into the framework of the horoscope. Unconsciously, this is the effect of any ecliptic system on the structure of the horoscope. If you want to emphasize or measure a Sun function, you should use the equal house or another ecliptic system.

Going beyond the ecliptic to one of the other circles of the celestial sphere necessarily incorporates a lunar influence into the chart, because none of the other circles can be represented directly in the horoscope as it is now conceived and drawn. Like the Moon, which transmits light or energy reflectively, projection systems of house division necessarily include some subconscious aspects of personality development in the structure and delineation of the horoscope; these aspects do not exist in a house system based on the ecliptic alone. Using the Placidus, Koch, Meridian, Regiomontanus, Campanus or any other of the twenty-odd projection systems described in contemporary astrological literature, implies unrecognized or undescribable attributes, in a consciousness sense.

When using one of the other circles besides the ecliptic, one first decides what effect one wants to produce in the horoscope. There are three great circles—the celestial equator, the horizon and the prime vertical—that can be practically used to cut harmonic divisions on the ecliptic, although the divisions do not have to be strictly harmonic intervals. The meridian and the polar axis projected out as a circle could also be used, but because of other considerations they would be disregarded because of the gross distortions they present when projected on the ecliptic. Each of these five circles also provides poles for projection of these divisions onto the ecliptic. Again, the meridian provides a pole that is not adequate for other reasons, and the polar axis is itself a pole to the celestial equator. This leaves four poles—the ecliptic, equator, prime vertical and horizon—to project three types of circles—the horizon, equator and prime vertical—onto the ecliptic. The types of division—harmonic or weighted—and their beginning points are limited only by the inventiveness of the house system originator.

Thus, to narrow down the choices, one looks to the circles involved to see what types of energy will be applied. The horizon represents the here and now, that which is at hand, surrounds us, is in our immediate environment. The equator represents what is beyond our environment, our involvement in and through the world. The prime vertical and the meridian divide the space in our immediate environment and give us an immediate and conscious framework for perception and classification. The meridian serves as our celestial timekeeper, tying us to a fixed reference point in the heavens, which relates our progress not only in the world but in life. The prime vertical separates our awakening functions from our doing functions and serves as the symbolic division between our beginnings and our endings, awakening and sleeping, that which is us and that which is other in our lives. Once you decide whether you want to emphasize the near or the far, the close or the more universal view, awakening or terminating or timing to the universe, you will know what type of house system to select.

The Campanus house system uses divisions of the prime vertical from poles of the horizon, projected onto the ecliptic. Because it is a projection system, it incorporates the lunar or unconscious aspects of the personality, stressing a mutable concept of beginnings and endings and a fixed concept of the here and now.

The more complicated Placidian system involves aspects of the cardinal points, declination of the Sun, a doing and redoing until perfection is reached. It implies more worldly placements in the sense of how it divides space (mutable) as well as how it projects into space (fixed) in a greater perspective. This system is good for emphasizing overall life goals.

The Placidian is by far the most popular and well tested of the projected house systems; more astrologers use the Placidus than use any other system. Its most valuable feature is that it fulfills so well the function of dividing space in a meaningful way; when the Placidian system puts a planet from a rectified horoscope into the eleventh house, it has been my experience that the placement is correct, and I can use eleventh-house manifestations in my delineation with assurance.

Using the Placidian system to time events to the cusps presents some difficulties, because most of the generally available Placidian tables are incompletely calculated. The tables provided by Neil Michelsen in *The American Ephemeris* (Astro Computing Services, 1976) are an exception in that they are complete and correct. This system is very popular for horary and electional astrology, because its cusps do provide meaningful timing answers.

The Koch system is another complicated system that involves the projection of the horizon (fixed quality), using the oblique ascension (daily workings, what we do immediately as opposed to long-range goals). This system is excellent for determining where you are and where you are going, your current choices.

The Meridian house system divides space using the equator, implying the mutable qualities of a more worldly view, projected by polar axis lines (the lines emanating from the polar axes and hence oriented to the equator) which again implies a worldly but fixed view. This system emphasizes the events of life or the circumstances that we have preselected. It is strongly recommended as a meaningful system for timing events to cusps.

One other feature of the projection systems is that they incorporate the geographic latitude of the location, which is not accounted for by any ecliptic-based system. Of course, geographic latitude is used in calculations for the Ascendant, so the equal house system does indirectly compensate for this lack for that point only, but all of the projection systems incorporate geographic latitude computations for each cusp.

Some of the projection systems, such as Porphyry, Koch and Placidus, also incorporate the concept of planetary hours, equal division of day and night rather than harmonic divisions (equal divisions of space only). By ancient custom, the day was divided into the same number of hours as the night. In the northern hemishpere, there are actually more daylight hours in summer than in winter, and hence the planetary hours are longer in the upper part of the horoscope when there is a longer period of daylight. The esoteric implications of this are not immediately clear.

In this brief discussion of house systems, I have attempted to cover quite a lot of ground and provide some useful guidelines without getting technical or mathematical about the differences among the various systems. There is no one answer to the question of which house system to choose, for each one has its merits and disadvantages. It is not necessary to reject a particular system just because it fails at some time of day or in some area of the world; the method you choose depends on your perspective and your purpose. I do not advocate one system over another, rather I advocate selecting the system according to the effect that one wants in the horoscope reading, which requires a thorough understanding of the basics of astrology.

How To Order Your Astral Portrait

Use the order form on the opposite page or, if you prefer, use another piece of paper. Send the following information plus $12 for each Astral Portrait to Para Research, Dept. 4, Rockport, Massachusetts 01966. The price is subject to change.

Name, Address, City, State, Zip Code

The address to which the Astral Portrait(s) should be sent.

Time of Birth

Accuracy to the minute is important. Don't rely on parent's memory. Consult hospital records or birth certificate. Midnight and noon are neither AM nor PM; AM is between midnight and noon; PM is between noon and midnight. To avoid confusion, if you are submitting a noon birthtime, please write "noon." If you are submitting a midnight birthtime, please write "midnight" and two dates: the day that was ending and the day that was beginning. For example: "June 19/20, 1947, 12:00 midnight."

Please do not convert from daylight saving time to standard time. Just send us local clock time and we will convert. Or if you cannot do this, please explain. If you do not send birthtime, we will use 12:00 noon.

Date of Birth

Month, day and year.

Place of Birth

If you were born in a small town that may not be on our maps, please give us the name of the nearest city.

Please Print Clearly

Keep a copy of the birth information you send us for comparison with the computer printout. Notify us in case of error.

Guarantee

Para Research guarantees every horoscope. If for any reason, you are dissatisfied, please return the Astral Portrait for a full refund.

Please allow two weeks for processing and delivery.